FIRESIDE

JOIN, or DIE.

The first American cartoon, at left, was published by Benjamin Franklin in his Pennsylvania Gazette May 9, 1754. The broken parts of the snake are the divided American colonies. Above, a portrait of Franklin about 1748.

AMERICAN PAST

A History of the United States from Concord to the Great Society by ROGER BUTTERFIELD

TOLD WITH THE AID OF ELEVEN HUNDRED PICTURES, REPRODUCED FROM PHOTOGRAPHS, PAINTINGS, LITHOGRAPHS, CARTOONS, ENGRAVINGS, AND DRAWINGS, SELECTED AND ARRANGED TO ILLUMINATE AND ILLUSTRATE THE POLITICS, PERSONALITIES, WARS, AND PEACEFUL PROGRESS OF THE AMERICAN PEOPLE.

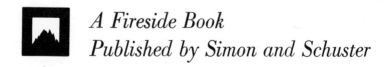 *A Fireside Book
Published by Simon and Schuster*

Foreword

IT WAS HENRY ADAMS who decided, around the turn of this century, that the one sure fact about history is that it moves faster and faster. Adams belonged to the only American family that ever produced father-and-son Presidents; he wrote a classic history of the early Republic, and he studied American politics from a privileged seat in Washington. Adams came to think of history mostly in terms of power. He plotted rising curves to show the speedup of man's power capacity through a long Mechanical Age (including the steam engine); an Electrical Age (which was new when he wrote), and a coming Ethereal Age —we would call it Atomic—which he expected would start about 1917. Adams calculated that the human intellect could lose its race to keep up with technology as early as 1921, and perhaps at the latest by 2025 A.D. "Law, in that case, would disappear," he wrote. "Morality would become police. Explosives would reach cosmic violence. Disintegration would overcome integration."

His third prediction has already come true, and is part of the subject matter of this book. Today the acceleration of history—whether we call it population explosion, nuclear-arms race or something else—is the biggest fact in American politics, because it is the biggest fact in the world. When John F. Kennedy in 1960 urged Americans to "get this country moving again," when Lyndon B. Johnson in 1965 warned Americans they would have to rebuild their country in every respect (not just in terms of architecture) in the next thirty years, these two Presidents were taking note of Henry Adams' law. A successful nation must go on succeeding, and at a faster rate than before. Or else history passes it by.

This new, bicentennial printing of *The American Past* celebrates the end of a decade of division, defeat and disgrace, and the start of a new forward trend in America's affairs. No attempt has been made to include the details of the Vietnam War or Watergate. They are abundantly available elsewhere. Perhaps the best way to explain them is to recall that two powerful and conflicting impulses have always dominated American politics—the desire to be free and to see other men free, and the desire to be stronger, richer and more influential than anyone else.

This book was conceived in the 1940s, when picture-and-word histories were not very numerous. It has had a steady sale through nearly thirty years, which suggests that it is not as ephemeral as pictorial histories tend to be. The general emphasis has been on politics, by which I mean more than party conventions and ward-heeling and Boss Tweed (although they are here, too). Politics is history in the making while the outcome is still in doubt. I have tried throughout to make the men and women, the events and issues, look and sound as they did to their contemporaries. I hope these pages will persuade present-day readers that American politics—taken as a whole—has been exciting, constructive, and "good to behold."—R.B.

All the noisy tempestuous scenes of politics witnessed in this country—all the excitement and strife, even—are GOOD *to behold.* —WALT WHITMAN

Table of Contents

FOREWORD

THE AGE OF THE FEDERALISTS   PAGE 1

The First Inauguration—Washington Becomes President, 2. "First in the Hearts of His Countrymen"—Washington's Life and Times, 4. Washington Leads the Revolution, 6. Tories and Mutineers—Political Struggles of the Revolution, 9. Shays' Rebellion—The Confederation Breaks Down, 10. The Federal Convention—Writing the Constitution, 11. The Constitution Ratified—Triumph of the Federalists, 13. The New Nation Takes Shape, 15. Washington's Cabinet—Rivalry of Jefferson and Hamilton, 16. Hamilton Wins the First Round, 18. The Rising Opposition—Jefferson and the Anti-Federalists, 20. Washington Under Attack—His Farewell Address, 23. Stout John Adams, 24. "No, No, Not a Sixpence!"—The Naval War with France, 26. The Federalist Reign of Terror—Alien and Sedition Laws, 28. Death of Washington, 30.

THE JEFFERSON REPUBLICANS   PAGE 31

Beware of Aaron Burr!—The Disputed Election of 1800, 33. Jefferson in Power, 34. The Militant Republicans, and the Midnight Judges, 37. Winning the West—The Lure of the Frontier, 38. Jefferson Buys Louisiana from Napoleon, 40. Aaron Burr Kills Hamilton, 42. But Hamilton Still Lives, and Burr is Dead and Gone, 45. "To The Shores of Tripoli"—The American Wars in Africa, 46. Isolation and Insults—Jefferson Tries to Avoid War with France and England, 48. The Charming Madisons, 50. Two Political Beasts—The Gerrymander and the Ograbme, 51. The War Hawks Take Over Congress, 52. "On to Canada" —The War of 1812, 54. The United States Takes a Beating—the White House Is Burned and "The Star-Spangled Banner" Is Born, 56. New England Talks Treason—Cartoons of the War, 59. Victory at New Orleans, 60. Peace and the Era of Good Feelings, 62. "Our Country! May She Always Be Right," 64. Sectional Politics—Webster and the North, Calhoun and the South, 66. Henry Clay, the Master Politician, 69. The Missouri Compromise—"A Firebell in the Night," 70. The Monroe-Adams Doctrine, 72. The Presidential Foot Race of 1824— J. Q. Adams in the White House, 75. Americans on the Move—The Erie Canal and the Railroads, 77. Jackson Gets His Revenge in 1828, 78. Death of Jefferson, 80.

THE JACKSON DEMOCRATS   PAGE 81

Old Hickory Takes Over, 83. "To the Victor Belongs the Spoils"—The Peggy Eaton Affair, 84. Nullification Attempted and Blocked—Jackson Says "I Will Hang John C. Calhoun!" 87. Hayne Criticizes Massachusetts, and Webster Replies to Hayne, 87-88. Jackson Kills the U. S. Bank, 90. The Reign of King Andrew, and the Men Who Fought Him, 92. Political Cross-Currents—Anti-Masonry and the Workingmen's Parties, 94-95. The Yankee Abolitionists—

Slavery Becomes an Issue, 96.   Texas Becomes a Nation—Dawn at the Alamo, 98.   Van Buren and His Hard Times, 100.

THE UPS AND DOWNS OF THE WHIGS   PAGE 103

The Log Cabin and Hard Cider Campaign, 104.   "Old Tippecanoe" Passes On—"Tyler Too" Becomes President, 106.   Riders on the Oregon Trail—Fremont and Marcus Whitman, 107.   The Great Daniel Webster in His Prime, 108.   James K. Polk and the Coon-Skinners of 1844. Manifest Destiny in Oregon and Texas, 111.   War in Mexico—The Halls of Montezuma, 113.   Daguerreotype History, 114.   Conscience Whigs—Congressman Abraham Lincoln Puts Polk on the Spot, 117.   George Caleb Bingham Paints Great Scenes of Western Politics, 118-120.   "Rough and Ready" Zachary Taylor Elected President, 122.   The Cheerful 1840's —Mormons, Shakers, Bloomers and the Polka, 124.   The Penny Papers Enlarge American Journalism, 126.   The Know-Nothings Enter Politics, 127.   "Ten Nights in a Bar-Room"—Prohibition Becomes an Issue, 128.   The Gold-Diggers of 1849 and After, 131.   California Becomes a Free State—Clay's Last Compromise, The Union Preserved, 133.   The South in Sullen Fury—Calhoun's Last Speech, and the Doughface Presidents, 135.   Uncle Tom's Cabin—The Underground Railroad, 136-137.   Commodore Perry Opens Japan, 139.   The End of the Whigs—Clay and Webster Die, 140.   The North Wins Control of Congress, 142.

THE FREE SOIL REPUBLICANS   PAGE 143

Stephen Douglas and His Nebraska Bill—The Anti-Nebraskans Found a New Republican Party Opposed to Slavery Extension, 145.   Bleeding Kansas and "Bully" Brooks—Near-Murder of a Senator, 146-147. The Fremont Campaign of 1856—Free Speech and Free Soil, 148.   James Buchanan, the Last Doughface President, 149.   The Slave and the Old Chief Justice—The Dred Scott Decision, 150.   The Illinois Debates—Lincoln vs. Douglas, 153.   John Brown Declares Personal War Against Slavery, 154.   Labor Struggles—The Lady Strikers of Lynn, 156.   Honest Abe, the Rail Splitter—Republicans Win the Presidency, 158.   The Deep South Secedes, 160.   Lincoln Goes to Washington, 163.   The Cannon Speak at Charleston, 165.   Johnny Rebs and Blue Bellies—South and North Rush to War, 166-167.   From Bull Run to Gettysburg, 169.   The Camera Record of the War, 170.   Lincoln's Master Strokes—Emancipation and the Gettysburg Address, 172-173.   The Disloyal Opposition—Copperheads and Anti-Draft Riots, 174.   "Long Abe" Beats "Little Mac" in 1864—Don't Swap Horses Crossing a Stream, 176.   "War . . . Is All Hell"—The Last Battles and Generals, 179.   Black Friday—Lincoln Murdered, 180.   Hanging of the Conspirators, 182.   Stanton, the Post-War Dictator, 184.   Andrew Johnson, the New President, 185.   Radical Republicans in the Saddle—The Vengeful Thaddeus Stevens and Impeachment of the President, 187.   Freeing the Freedmen—Reconstruction of the South, 188.   The Ku Klux Klan—Martyrs of Andersonville, 190-191.   Seward Buys Alaska—"God Bless the Russians," 192.   The Boys in Blue Elect Grant President, 194.   "Let Us Have Peace"—Grant's Administration, 196.   Railroads and the Vanishing Western Frontier, 198.   The Working People and Their Problems, 201.   The Robber Barons of Wall Street—Jay Gould and Jim Fisk, 202.

Reformers, Thieves and Congressional Grafters, 204-205. The Tammany Tiger at Bay—Downfall of Boss Tweed, 206. "Turn the Rascals Out"—Greeley's Campaign for the President, Its Comic and Tragic Aspects, 208. Panic of 1873 Sweeps Wall Street—Unemployment Hits the Nation, 211. Uncle Sam and Russian Ivan Grapple for Pacific Empire, 212.

THE BIG BUSINESS REPUBLICANS   PAGE 213

The First Hundred Years of American Progress Celebrated at the 1876 Centennial, 214. Women Demand the Vote and Run for President, 216. Thomas Nast's Political Zoo—He Makes the Elephant and Donkey Famous, 218. The Stolen Election of 1876—Tilden Wins, but Hayes Becomes President, 220. Hayes Frees the South—Conkling Eats Crow, 223. Greenbackers and Grangers Get into Politics, 224. Troops Kill Strikers in Baltimore, 226. Labor in the Melting Pot—Anti-Immigration Laws, 228. Job-Hunter Guiteau Kills President Garfield, 230. The Elegant Chester A. Arthur, 232. Vanderbilt's Boner—"The Public Be Damned!" 234. James G. Blaine, the Plumed Knight of 1883, 237. Grover Cleveland Tells the Truth—"Ma, Ma, Where's My Pa?", 239. Rum, Romanism and Mugwumps—The Feast of Balshazzar Blaine, 241. President Cleveland Alone in the White House—He Takes a Pretty Young Bride, 242. Cleveland's Slogan—"Public Office Is a Public Trust," 244. The Last Days and Death of U. S. Grant, 247. The Haymarket Bomb, 248. Reaction Against Labor, 250. Free Trade and the Tariff—Election of Benjamin Harrison, 253. The Billion Dollar Congress—Czar Reed of Maine, 254-255. The 65 Billion Dollar Country—What It Looked Like in the Early 1890's, 257. The Revolt of the Midwestern Populists, 259. The Gay Nineties—The Chicago Fair, "Little Egypt" and the Great Ferris Wheel, 260-261. A Gymnastic Debate in the Senate Over Silver, 262. Coxey's Army Invades Washington. 265. The Pullman Strike—"Nothing To Arbitrate," 266. Communism and the Supreme Court—Income Tax Outlawed, and Anti-Trust Laws Ignored, 268. William Jennings Bryan—The Cross of Gold and the Crown of Thorns, 271. The Bryan-Haters of 1896, 272. Mark Hanna and His Man, McKinley, 274. Sea Power and Sugar—Admiral Mahan, Hawaii and *Cuba Libre*, 276. "Remember the Maine, To Hell with Spain!" 278. McKinley and the Warmongers, 281. The Ten Weeks' War Against Spain—Teddy and His Rough Riders, 282. The Three Years' War to Conquer the Philippines—"Damn the Filipinos!" 285. The American Imperialists, 287. The Full Dinner Pail Campaign of 1900, 288. Uncle Sam Learns His Lesson, 290.

A PORTFOLIO OF CARTOONS IN COLOR   PAGE 291

The Cinderella of the Republican Party, 293. James G. Blaine, the Tattooed Man, 295. Little Roosevelt Puts On His Armor, 296. Conkling Blows Up, 298. Benjamin Harrison Hears the Raven Croak, 299. The Bosses of the Senate, 301. The Political Darius Green, John Sherman, 302. Sour Grapes and Leo XIII, 303. Cleveland and the Administration Typewriter, 305. Bryan, the Sacrilegious Candidate, 306. Bryan Slips Over the Cliff, 307. Uncle Sam in His Tariff Tub, 308. Mark Hanna and His Dollar Tracks, 310. McKinley and His Big Cigar, 311.

THE BIG STICK REFORMERS PAGE 313

The Men Who Owned the Country —Competition Eliminated, 315. Theodore Roosevelt, the Great American Boy, Becomes President, 313, 316. Teddy Revives the Anti-Trust Laws, Bats Down the Railroad Kings and Snubs J. P. Morgan, 319. The Christian Men of Property, and the United Mine Workers, 320. "I Took the Isthmus"—Roosevelt Gets the Panama Canal Started, 323. Teddy Everywhere—The Photogenic President, 324. Swinging the Big Stick, 327. "An Alphabet of Joyous Trusts," 328. Boodlers and Muckrakers—The Smell of Chicago, 330. Hearst, the Wizard of Ooze, 333. Big Will Taft Succeeds Roosevelt, 335. The Old Guard Back in the Saddle, 336. The Progressive Insurgents in Congress, 338. Socialists and Wobblies, 341. The End of a Beautiful Friendship—Roosevelt Fights Taft and the Old Guard, 342. Birth of the Bull Moose— "We Stand at Armageddon," 345. Woodrow Wilson, a Democratic Professor, Becomes President and Takes Over the Big Stick of Reform, 347. Mexico Boils Over—The Elusive Villa, 348. August, 1914—The Start of the Great War, Wilson Tries to be Neutral, 350. U-Boat 20 Sinks the Lusitania—"Too Proud to Fight," 353. "He Kept Us Out of War," 354. Charles Evans Hughes in 1916—"Just Tell Him He Isn't President," 355. Germany Resumes Submarine Warfare, and the U. S. Declares War, 356. Doughboys in Action in France, 358. Fighting the War on the Home Front, 360. The War of Words—The Fourteen Points, 362. Germany Gives Up—Armistice Day, 365. Wilson the Savior in Europe, 367. Wilson and the Troops, 368. Wilson and the Treaty-Makers, 371. The Willful Men of the U. S. Senate Block Wilson's League of Nations—Wilson's Physical Breakdown, 373. Strikers and Red-Baiters, 374. The Wall Street Explosion— Debs Runs For President From a Federal Prison, 376-377. Women Finally Get the Vote, 378. Prohibition, a Blue-Nosed King, Mounts His Throne, 380.

NORMALCY AND THE NEW DEAL PAGE 381

"We Drew to a Pair of Deuces"—Election of Warren G. Harding, 383. The Unhappy President—His Disgrace and Death, 384. Teapot Dome—The Smear of Oil, 386. Divided Democrats of 1924, 389. Calvin Coolidge and the Runaway Bull Market, 390. The Tempo of the Twenties—Lucky Lindbergh and Rudolph Valentino, 392. Top Hats and Red Tape—Treaties of the 1920's, 394-395. Al Smith, the Happy Warrior of 1928, 397. Herbert Hoover, the Great Engineer—"A Chicken in Every Pot," 399. Nightmare in Wall Street—The Stock Market Crash of 1929, 400. Prosperity "Just Around the Corner"—"The Fundamental Business of the Country . . . Is Sound," 402. Some Faces of the 1930's, 405. The End of the Treaties—Japan Starts a New War, Mussolini and Hitler Take Over Their Countries, 406. The Bonus Boys Camp in Washington and Are Burned Out by Hoover, 408. "The Skies Above Are Clear Again"—Democrats Nominate Franklin D. Roosevelt, 410. "An Amiable Man . . . Who Would Like to be President"—Roosevelt's Family and Career, 413. Roosevelt Smiles and Hoover Scowls—Campaign of 1932, 414. FDR in the White House—"Action, and Action Now," Fireside Chats and Brain Trusters, 416-417. The First Hundred Days of the New Deal, 418. Labor's Giant and Morgan's Midget, 420-421. Father Coughlin and

Huey Long—The Perspiring Priest and the Dixie Dictator, 422-423. The Nine Old Men Kill the Blue Eagle, 424. FDR at His Peak in 1936—The Faded Kansas Sunflower, 426-427. The Kickback Against the Court-Packing Bill, 428. Drought and the CIO, 430. TVA—The Yardstick, 432. The March of Aggression Abroad —"War Is Contagion," 434. "We Want Willkie"—The Rise of a Great Campaigner, 436. "Mister Third Term Candidate"—Roosevelt Beats Willkie, 438. The Atlantic Charter—"The Arsenal of Democracy," 440-441. Kurusu and Pearl Harbor, 442. The March of Death, and the Long Road to Victory, 444-445. The War in the Pacific and in Europe, 446. The Roving Commander in Chief—Big Power Politics During the War, 448. The End of the New Deal in 1944—"Old Doctor Win-the-War"—Roosevelt Beats Tom Dewey, 450. Roosevelt Dies on the Eve of Victory—"Let Us Move Forward," 452. Harry Truman Takes the Oath as President, 454. The Mushroom Cloud—End of the War, 456. The Bomb and the Diplomats, 458.

ATOMIC PEACE AND COLD WAR   PAGE 459

"It Is No Secret"—How the U. S. Got the Bomb, 460. Missions to Moscow—The Iron Curtain, 462-463. Harry Truman, the Man from Missouri—His Life and Hard Times, 464. The Whistlestop Campaign—Truman Confounds the Experts and Beats Dewey in 1948, 466. Spies and Un-Americans—The Red Menace and the Loyalty Program, 469. Chambers and Hiss—The Papers in the Pumpkin, 470. Aggression in the East—Communist Sneak Attack in Korea, the U. S. and UN Fight Back, 472. "Old Soldiers Fade Away"—MacArthur's Return, and an American Retreat, 474-475. The Republicans Nominate General "Ike" Eisenhower in 1952—"The Kind of a Guy We Like," 477. Adlai Stevenson Talks Sense, 478. Eisenhower Promises to Go to Korea—"Ike" Elected by a Landslide, 479. The Dick Nixon Story—A Soap Opera Spectacular, 480. What's Good For General Motors—Tidelands Oil, Dixon-Yates and "Conflict of Interest," 483. Joe McCarthy, Man with a Meat-Ax—His Rise and Fall in Cartoons, 484. The Death of Stalin and a Falling Out Among His Pall-Bearers, 486. Four Times to the Brink of War—The Perils of John Foster Dulles, 489. The Ultimate Hell-Bomb—Debate Among the Scientists, 491. The Unanimous Decree of the New Supreme Court—No Segregation in Public Schools, 492. "What a Belly-Ache" —Eisenhower's Health Becomes an Issue, 494. Eisenhower Re-elected in 1956— Adlai Stevenson's Test Ban Idea Falls Flat with the Voters, 496-497. The Human Sputnik—Nikita Khrushchev, the Star of the Cold War, 498-499. The Democrats Nominate a Catholic-Protestant Ticket in 1960, 500.

THE YEARS OF KENNEDY AND JOHNSON   PAGE 501

Young Man at the Top—Jack Kennedy Brings the New Frontier to the White House, 502. The Family and the Fortune Behind Kennedy—East Boston to Capitol Hill, 504. Kennedy's Political Rise—the Making of a Candidate, 506. Profiles in Politics—The Great TV Debates of 1960—Kennedy Wins by a Whisker, 508. The Kennedy Style in the White House—"Mr. Wonderful"—Jackie's Charm, 510. Education of a President—Peace Corps—Bay of Pigs—Berlin Wall

—South Vietnam, 512. The Missile Crisis in Cuba—Eyeball to Eyeball with Khrushchev—The Test-Ban Treaty and Cold War Thaw, 514. The Nonviolent Negro Revolution—Second Reconstruction of the South, 516. Kennedy's 1963 Travels, 518. The Unbelievable Event—Assassination of Kennedy in Dallas—Jack Ruby Kills Lee Harvey Oswald, 520. Lyndon Johnson's Wild Ride—He Becomes President—"I Will Do My Best," 522. Johnson's Background, Career, and Ambitions—LBJ, the Wrangler, 524. High Noon at the Cow Palace—Goldwater Nominated by the Republicans, 526. Johnson Swamps Goldwater in 1964—The Personal Touch in American Politics, 528. LBJ Speaks His Mind —Credo of a Strong-Minded President, 531.

ACKNOWLEDGMENTS   **PAGE 532**

PICTURE CREDITS   **PAGE 532**

INDEX   **PAGE 536**

THE AMERICAN PAST

The Declaration of Independence on the opposite page has been reproduced from the official printed copy attached to the Journals of the Continental Congress for July 4, 1776. This basic American manifesto was conceived in anger but phrased with cold determination. It states that all men are created equal, that they have certain inalienable rights as human beings, that constitutions and governments exist to secure those rights, and that whenever they fail to do so, the people may rebel and set up new constitutions and governments.

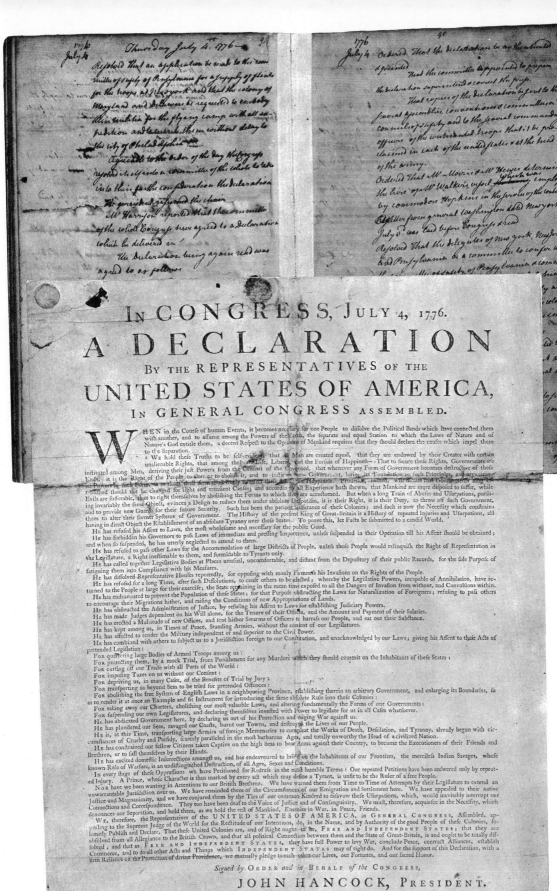

"The Reconciliation Between Britania and Her Daughter America" was a British propaganda cartoon of 1782, intended to aid the peace talks which were then going on. Before Uncle Sam was invented, cartoonists pictured the United States as a wild red Indian, a rattlesnake, an eagle, or a bucking horse.

CHAPTER 1

THE AGE OF THE FEDERALISTS

THE LUSTY IMPRESSION which young America made in the family of nations at the close of the Revolution is shown in the cartoon on the opposite page. The United States is the naked Indian girl with tobacco leaves around her hips and a liberty pole over her shoulder, leaping forward to buss her dear mama England. Some Americans may have felt this way about England in 1782—a great many more wanted no part of their erstwhile mother country. But they all shared the same aggressive desire to do what they wanted, when they wanted, without interference from friend or foe.

This fact is a good starting point for a book on the American past, in terms of people and politics. For politics is simply the means by which people try to get what they want, and Americans have always wanted liberty first of all. The songs and catchwords of the Revolution were all about liberty—liberty for the people, liberty for the thirteen "Free and Independent States"—liberty, in fact, for all mankind. In 1782, in a world which was still run largely by kings and other privileged persons, the Americans had more liberty than anyone else.

But liberty was about all they did have. They had no economic security, no system of defense, not even any government worthy of the name. The so-called "United States of America" was not a nation at all. It was a loose alliance of thirteen little nations which had managed to stick together long enough to fight off the British armies. Now that the big war was practically over, those thirteen nations were raising tariff walls, strengthening their military forces, and threatening little wars among themselves.

In this situation there appeared in several states a group of men who wanted to transform the United States into a single, strong, united nation. These men became known as Federalists, and they formed the first important American political party. The plans they put forward stirred fierce opposition, for they meant that each state and every individual American would have to give up a certain amount of liberty. They meant more tax collectors, more public officials and judges, and a national army and navy. Americans generally hated these things more than they hated the Indians or the British.

The Federalists won their early battles by sheer force of intellect and reason, and by playing clever, hardheaded politics. They captured many votes by wrapping their projects in the name of George Washington, who was one of them. They adopted as their political badge the black cockade which had been worn by the soldiers of the Revolution—a shrewd appeal to American patriotism. Most of the wealthy merchants, landowners, and lawyers were Federalists. They had plenty of money and almost complete control of the press.

The Federalists always pretended, however, that they were not politicians at all. They carried on their organization work and made their nominations in secret caucuses from which rank-and-file voters were excluded. The typical Federalist thought it was unseemly and even indecent to be caught playing politics: John Marshall, a leading Federalist, once declared that nothing "more debases or pollutes the human mind" than political parties. This hypocritical attitude had much to do with the eventual downfall of the Federalist party.

On the whole the Federalists were more interested in protecting their money and property than in giving their fellow Americans any more liberty. Their slogan, as expressed by John Jay, was: "Those who own the country ought to govern it." In their pictures they appear as stern, dignified men, obviously filled with a sense of their own virtue, and dressed to the hilt in silk stockings, silver-buckled shoes, and powdered wigs. But it would be wrong to think of them as mere political antiques. They wrote our Constitution, wangled its adoption in most of the states, organized the Federal Government, and ran it with much success during its first twelve precarious years. They built the platform on which American history has been enacted ever since.

THE FIRST INAUGURATION

THE PRECISE MOMENT of the Federalists' greatest triumph is pictured above. On a balcony of Federal Hall in Wall Street, New York City, General George Washington has just heard the President's Oath administered for the first time: "I do solemnly swear that I will faithfully execute the Office of the President of the United States, and will to the best of my ability, preserve, protect and defend the Constitution

of the United States." With one hand on his heart and the other on an open Bible he is about to reply, "I swear—so help me God!"

To encourage the infant textile industry on this great occasion, the new President wore a dark brown suit which was 100 per cent made-in-America. His calm majesty was so impressive that people in the streets blinked away tears and shouted "Huzza!" in choked voices. Washington was the greatest symbol of patriotism and unity that the Americans had. But inwardly he was not at all calm. He had predicted for years that the thirteen states would fly apart in civil war and economic chaos. If the new Federal Government could be held together for just twenty years, he believed, the country would be safe. That was to be the underlying aim of his administration.

At 17 Washington *(standing)* was official surveyor for Culpeper County, Virginia.

"FIRST IN THE HEARTS OF HIS COUNTRYMEN"

WASHINGTON'S RISE to the position of No. 1 American was due in part to a political bargain. The Revolution had started in 1775 as a Massachusetts war, but the Massachusetts men in the Continental Congress knew they could never win unless the other states joined in. So they decided to throw their votes behind a Southerner for Commander in Chief. This made Washington a logical choice, for he was a Southerner from the largest American state—Virginia—and he already had a wide reputation as a military man. He was also a member of Congress, and American Congressmen have always preferred to give important jobs to one of their own, when they could.

Fortunately Washington was well equipped for the job. He had been a soldier since he was 20. At 22 he had led troops against the French in western Pennsylvania. At 23 he was commander of the whole Virginia army along the Indian frontier. He had traveled on horseback over thousands of miles of wilderness. He had a natural love of action, a handshake like hard steel, and had never known physical fear. The portrait on the opposite page by Charles Willson Peale shows him as the Army knew him: a superb six-foot two-inch specimen of vigorous and commanding manhood.

Washington was born February 22, 1732, on this site overlooking Pope's Creek, Westmoreland County, Virginia.

At 21 Washington *(right)* was sent west to interview the French. His raft almost capsized in the icy Allegheny.

At 23 he fought with Braddock's ill-fated army near Pittsburgh, and got four French bullets through his coat.

At 26 he married Martha Custis, a rich widow, and acquired two stepchildren. He never had children of his own.

The British retreat from Concord, April 19, 1775, is pictured at the right. Minutemen are firing on the British rear. Some redcoats have jumped the fences to fire back.

WASHINGTON LEADS
THE REVOLUTION

Washington took command at Cambridge, July 3, 1775, soon after Bunker Hill. Lacking powder for an attack, he besieged Boston until the British sailed away to New York.

Beaten at New York by superior enemy forces, Washington retreated to the Delaware River in the winter of 1776. Here he launched his Christmas night attack on Trenton.

WASHINGTON's political opinions were largely formed by his experiences in the Revolution. As Commander in Chief he had to take orders from a government which had no power to enforce its decisions and often showed no inclination to help him or save itself. In a country of 2,200,000 people, with at least 250,000 able-bodied men, Washington never had more than 8,000 well-trained Continental troops to fight in a single battle. These were augmented by the state militia who came and went almost as they

At Valley Forge in 1777-78 Washington pondered the failures of Congress while his army froze and starved. A few months later he struck the foe a savage blow at Monmouth.

Canvas-topped supply wagons arrive at Washington's camp and are greeted with cheers. During most of the eight years' war his men got no uniforms, shoes, or steady pay.

pleased, but who never mustered more than about 20,000 under Washington's command. Such "Minutemen" fought bravely when their own villages were invaded *(above)*. But they were too fond of their personal liberty to submit to the whipping-post discipline of the Continental Army. It is no wonder that Washington decided, as he wrote to a Federalist friend, that men must sometimes be forced to do things for their own good.

Yet when some of his own officers came to him with plans to make him a dictator, Washington turned them back in disgust. "The mass of citizens in these United States *mean well*," he wrote, "and I firmly believe they will always *act well* whenever they can obtain a right understanding of matters." In the end it required the aid of a large French army and naval squadron to win the Revolution. This humiliating fact gave Washington his basic political principle: that the United States must by all means be strong enough to stand on its own feet in the future.

At Yorktown in 1781 Washington received the surrender of a whole British army under Cornwallis, virtually ending the war. But Yorktown was largely a French victory.

Washington bade good-by to his officers December 4, 1783, after squelching an attempt to set up a military dictatorship. Then he returned to his farm at Mount Vernon.

A NEW METHOD OF MACARONY MAKING AS PRACTISED AT BOSTON

For the Custom House officer's landing the Tea
They Tarr'd him and feather'd him just as you see
And they Drench'd him so well both behind and before
That he begg'd for God's sake they would drench him no more

Pub.d Oct.r 16 1774 by Fran.t Adams

The feud between American Tories and the Sons of Liberty was older than
the Revolution. This cartoon shows what happened to John Malcomb, a Tory
exciseman who collected the British tea tax in Boston in 1774. He was tarred
and feathered and forced to drink the health of the royal family in scalding tea. ("Macarony" was a nickname for a feather-wearing dandy.)

TORIES AND MUTINEERS

THE REVOLUTION against Great Britain was not just a simple fight for liberty—it was also a complicated civil war among the Americans themselves. Tory American troops and traitors like Benedict Arnold burned cities in Connecticut and Virginia and massacred the frontier dwellers of New York and Pennsylvania. The patriots swung the Tories on liberty poles, smeared them with tar and feathers, and confiscated all their possessions. More than 70,000 Tories escaped from the country, but many more stayed right where they lived, and most of them became Federalists after the war.

Toward the end of the Revolution another kind of civil strife broke out inside the Army. The mutiny of the Pennsylvania line *(below)* was led by former Philadelphia workingmen and might be called the first successful American strike. Later mutinies were put down with great severity. In May 1781 twelve soldiers who incited their fellows against accepting pay in worthless paper were led out on a parade ground and shot. When one of them failed to die quickly an officer ordered his comrade to run a bayonet through him. In 1783 another group of unpaid soldiers surrounded the government buildings in Philadelphia and drove Congress to seek refuge in Princeton. The grievances of these men were severe and their complaints not easy to suppress.

Outside a country alehouse, somewhere in Revolutionary America, a Tory is swung from a liberty pole while another defiantly waits his turn. Youngsters are busy stripping a goose for the tar-and-feathering to come.

On New Year's Day, 1781, 1,300 veteran Pennsylvania troops swarmed out of their barracks at Morristown and started a march on Congress to demand twelve months' overdue pay and their discharge. They killed one officer and roughly handled General Anthony Wayne *(above)*. A Congressional committee met the mutineers at Princeton and granted some of their demands.

SHAYS' REBELLION

A scene during Shays' Rebellion: a blacksmith in a Massachusetts town refuses to accept a writ of attachment for his debts.

This $20 bill issued by the Continental Congress in 1775 was "not worth a continental" by the end of the Revolution.

BY THE END of the Revolution the paper money issued by the Continental Congress had depreciated to one-fortieth of its face value. But soldiers who had lived through Valley Forge could not collect even their pitiful army pay of 22 cents a day. Veterans returning home were thrown into prison for debt and lost their homes at public sales. On the other hand, many large creditors went into hiding to avoid being paid in worthless paper. These money troubles swept the whole country and caused one political crisis after another.

In the summer of 1786 organized groups of Massachusetts farmers and veterans invaded county courthouses and made the judges stop foreclosures for debt. They were led by a Revolutionary captain named Daniel Shays, and their announced program was to close the courts until the legislature granted them relief. The Massachusetts authorities treated them as armed rebels. When 2,000 ragged "Shaysites" marched on the Continental arsenal at Springfield in January 1787, a militia force killed three of them and dispersed the others (below). Ten days later General Benjamin Lincoln, a friend of Washington's, smashed the movement by seizing the main Shays camp at Petersham.

The newspapers attacked the rebels as desperadoes and vagabonds, but most of them were decent American citizens who had been driven to desperation by want and injustice. Most of the relief they asked was granted by the Massachusetts legislature. Shays himself went to the frontier of western New York State and died a peaceable farmer.

Shays' Rebellion was all over in a few months, but its effects went deeper than any event since the Boston Tea Party. It sent a shiver down the spines of conservatives and Federalists. And it showed that the leaders of the first American Revolution would shoot down anybody who tried to start another.

Shays' attack on the Springfield arsenal (right) failed because his men were poorly armed and exhausted from marching through the deep snow. Even so they twice charged the well-armed militia.

THE FEDERAL CONVENTION

The troubles in Massachusetts threw a glaring light on the weakness of the Articles of Confederation which had been adopted by the thirteen states in 1781. Under the Articles the national Government consisted solely of a Continental Congress which had no power to enforce its "laws." The Congress was "abused, laughed at & cursed in every Company," according to Dr. Benjamin Rush, and some of the states did not even bother to send delegates to it. Of course it had been unable to check Shays' Rebellion. The situation made General Washington especially gloomy. "I feel," he wrote to General Knox, "infinitely more than I can express to you, for the disorders which have arisen. . . . Good God! who, besides a tory, could have foreseen, or a Briton predicted them?" And to his young friend, James Madison, he wrote: "What stronger evidence can be given of the want of energy in our government than these disorders? If there is not power in it to check them, what security has a man for life, liberty, or property?"

Others who felt the same way were already doing something about it. During Shays' Rebellion delegates from five states met at Annapolis to settle interstate squabbles over navigation and commerce. Madison, who was present for Virginia, and Alexander Hamilton, representing New York, persuaded the others that these problems could not be solved by a few states. They recommended that a convention of all the states be called "for the sole and express purpose of revising the Articles of Confederation."

The Federalists in Congress lost no time in putting this suggestion into effect. And so, on May 25, 1787, the Federal Convention went into session at the State House in Philadelphia. Only nine states were present to begin with. Three came late, and Rhode Island refused to come at all. Yet this was, without a doubt, the most important political meeting ever held in the United States. Its leading members, including Washington, were determined to go much further than mere revision. They had plans for an entirely new constitution: a sweeping agreement in black and white which would bind all Americans and their posterity into a single nation. They were well aware of the tremendous significance of their task, which was, as Madison said, "to decide forever the fate of republican government."

The Convention went to work first on the so-called Virginia Plan, drafted by Madison and others, which provided three equal branches in the new Government: an executive, a judiciary, and a legislature of two houses, both elected on the basis of population from the various states. This latter provision roused violent opposition from delegates of the smaller states, who rallied behind the New Jersey Plan for a single legislative body in which each state would cast an equal number of votes. After seven weeks of debate and deadlock, a special committee drew up what became known as the Connecticut Compromise. This provided a Senate elected solely on the basis of state equality, and a House of Representatives elected on the basis of population. (Negro slaves, who could not vote, were counted as three-fifths of a person each.)

This first great political compromise was the basis of the Constitution as finally adopted, and as it is today. While distinctly favorable to the smaller states, it contained one provision that the large-state men and Federalists wanted desperately. This was the simple but profoundly important declaration that all laws and treaties of the national Government "shall become the supreme law of the respective States . . . anything in the respective laws of the individual States . . . notwithstanding." Once this was agreed to, all other problems became relatively minor.

Since the finished Constitution was a compromise, it did not fully satisfy anybody. Hamilton, one of the most aggressive Federalists, called it a "shilly-shally thing of milk and water which could not last." He proposed a plan which would practically wipe out state lines and establish a lifetime executive who would be about the same as a king. On the other hand, libertarians like Thomas Jefferson thought the Constitution paid too much attention to the rights of the moneyed and propertied men, and too little to the needs of ordinary Americans. It did nothing, for instance, to correct state election laws which allowed only men with considerable property to vote. And although it professed to be written by "We the People," it actually prevented the people from electing their own President and Senators, by setting up a complicated machinery of electors and balloting in state legislatures.

Another phase of the Convention's proceedings was as distasteful to Americans of the time as it would be today. Meeting in secret session, with sentries on guard, the 55 delegates gave "We the People" no information at all about their work until the Constitution was signed, sealed, and delivered to the various states for ratification. Even during the great political debate which followed, the records of the Convention were not made public. This undemocratic secrecy, and the take-it-or-leave-it manner in which the Constitution was presented for ratification, were vigorously attacked when it emerged into the open arena of American politics.

Washington presides over the Federal Convention.

We the People of the United States, in order to form a more perfect Union, establish justice, insure domestic Tranquility, provide for the common defense, promote the general Welfare, and secure the Blessings of Liberty to ourselves and our Posterity, do ordain and establish this Constitution for the United States of America.

Article. I.

Section. 1. All legislative Powers herein granted shall be vested in a Congress of the United States, which shall consist of a Senate and House of Representatives.

James Madison

THE PREAMBLE to the Constitution *(above)* said that "We the People" were establishing the new Government. Yet the people generally knew nothing about it, and had to be sold on the whole idea. The best brains of the Federalist party were assigned to this task. Madison, Hamilton, and John Jay together wrote 85 propaganda articles under the title *The Federalist* for the New York newspapers. Their masterful editorials were aimed not at the average voter, but at the educated and propertied classes who controlled the country. Their language was somewhat formal, but taken all together they made the most thorough and convincing political platform that has ever appeared in America. In the excerpt below James Madison, a great theorist, discusses the causes and control of political parties.

MADISON SAYS THE UNION WILL CURB POLITICAL STRIFE

"Among the numerous advantages promised by a well-constructed Union, none deserves to be more accurately developed than its tendency to break and control the violence of faction. . . . The latent causes of faction are . . . sown in the nature of man. . . . A zeal for different opinions concerning religion, concerning government, and many other points . . . an attachment to different leaders ambitiously contending for pre-eminence and power . . . have, in turn, divided mankind into parties, inflamed them with mutual animosity, and rendered them much more disposed to vex and oppress each other than to co-operate for their common good. . . .

"But the most common and durable source of factions has been the various and unequal distribution of property. Those who hold and those who are without property have ever formed distinct interests in society. Those who are creditors, and those who are debtors, fall under a like discrimination. A landed interest, a manufacturing interest, a mercantile interest, a moneyed interest, with many lesser interests, grow up of necessity in civilized nations, and divide them into different classes, actuated by different sentiments and views. . . .

"A pure democracy, by which I mean a society consisting of a small number of citizens, who assemble and administer the government in person, can admit of no cure for the mischiefs of faction. A common passion or interest will, in almost every case, be felt by a majority . . . and there is nothing to check the inducements to sacrifice the weaker party or an obnoxious individual. Hence it is that such democracies have ever been spectacles of turbulence and contention; have ever been found incompatible with personal security or the rights of property; and have in general been as short in their lives as they have been violent in their deaths. . . .

"A republic, by which I mean a government in which the scheme of representation takes place, opens a different prospect, and promises the cure for which we are seeking. . . . The two great points of difference between a democracy and a republic are: first, the delegation of the government, in the latter, to a small number of citizens elected by the rest; secondly, the greater number of citizens, and greater sphere of country, over which the latter may be extended. . . . It is this circumstance, principally, which renders factious combinations less to be dreaded. . . . The influence of factious leaders may kindle a flame within their particular States, but will be unable to spread a general conflagration through the other States. A religious sect may degenerate into a political faction in a part of the Confederacy; but the variety of sects dispersed over the entire face of it must secure the national councils against any danger from that source. A rage for paper money, for an abolition of debts, for an equal division of property, or for any other improper or wicked project, will be less apt to pervade the whole body of the Union than a particular member of it; in the same proportion as such a malady is more likely to taint a particular county or district, than an entire State.

"In the extent and proper structure of the Union, therefore, we behold a republican remedy for the diseases most incident to republican government. And according to the degree of pleasure and pride we feel in being republicans, ought to be our zeal in cherishing the spirit and supporting the character of Federalists."

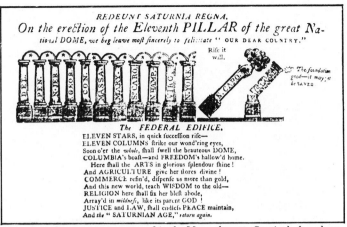

REDEUNT SATURNIA REGNA.

On the erection of the Eleventh PILLAR of the great National DOME, we beg leave most sincerely to felicitate "OUR DEAR COUNTRY."

Rife it will.

The foundation good—it may yet be SAVED

The FEDERAL EDIFICE.

ELEVEN STARS, in quick succession rise—
ELEVEN COLUMNS strike our wond'ring eyes,
Soon o'er the *whole*, shall swell the beauteous DOME,
COLUMBIA's boast—and FREEDOM's hallow'd home.
Here shall the ARTS in glorious splendour shine !
And AGRICULTURE give her stores divine !
COMMERCE refin'd, dispense us more than gold,
And this new world, teach WISDOM to the old—
RELIGION here shall fix her blest abode,
Array'd in *mildness*, like its parent GOD !
JUSTICE and LAW, shall endless PEACE maintain,
And the " SATURNIAN AGE," *return again.*

This triumphant cartoon appeared in the Massachusetts *Centinel* after eleven states had ratified. North Carolina waited until Washington had been President for seven months. Rhode Island was the last to·sign, on May 29, 1790.

THE CONSTITUTION RATIFIED

WHEN THE AMERICANS finally got a look at their new Constitution the immediate reaction of most of them was that they didn't like it. The new central Government looked just like the old British tyranny in an American disguise. It had the same power to organize standing armies and levy taxes from a distant capital which they had fought against in the Revolution. The opposition to the Constitution was especially strong in the rural districts, where most Americans lived. A backwoods preacher in North Carolina told his flock that the proposed federal capital city would undoubtedly become "a fortified fortress of despotism . . . [where] an army of 50,000 or perhaps 100,000 men will be finally embodied and will sally forth and enslave the people who will be disarmed!" In Massachusetts 18 old Shays rebels were elected to the state ratifying convention. One of them predicted that the new Congress would be as bad as the Spanish Inquisition. "Racks and gibbets," he shouted, "may be amongst the most mild instruments of their discipline!"

Against this kind of electioneering the wealthy Federalists staged giant rallies in the cities, with cheese and biscuits and drinks for everybody. In Philadelphia 17,000 persons assembled for a Federalist jamboree at which there was not a single drunken quarrel because, said a reporter, "They drank nothing but BEER and CYDER." The skilled city workmen, like the shipwrights of Boston and the pewtersmiths of New York, were Federalists because they believed the new Government would mean steadier work.

The Federalists had the best writers, the most money, and practically all the newspapers at their disposal. The Anti-Federalists made the most political noise, and if the matter had been put to a popular vote the Constitution probably would have been defeated. But "We the People" never did vote on it directly. Under the Federalist scheme special ratifying conventions were held in each state. When nine states ratified it, the Constitution went into effect. Less than a third of the eligible voters took part in electing the state conventions.

Delaware was the first state to ratify, followed by Pennsylvania, where an Anti-Federalist mob attacked James Wilson, one of the principal authors of the Constitution, and nearly killed him with barrel staves. New Hampshire was the decisive ninth, in June 1788. The most exciting fight was in New York, where Alexander Hamilton, by personal magnetism and smart political maneuvering, persuaded a hostile convention to ratify. Three of the ratifying states demanded immediate amendments to guarantee human as well as property rights.

The Federalists put the new machinery to work with great speed. George Washington was unanimously elected President, and within a year the first ten amendments (the "Bill of Rights") were passed.

Two of the busiest streets in the nation were Wall Street, New York, where the new Government had temporary headquarters in the remodeled City Hall *(above)*, and Second Street, Philadelphia, which was the shopping center of the largest city in America *(below)*.

THE NEW NATION

On April 16, 1789, President-elect George Washington made the following entry in his diary: "About ten o'clock I bade farewell to Mount Vernon, to private life, and to domestic felicity; and with a mind oppressed with more anxious and painful sensations than I have words to express, set out for New York...." Washington had to borrow money for this trip to his first inauguration—like many prominent Americans he was land-poor, and his farm at Mount Vernon, which was worked by slaves, often failed to meet expenses.

It took him seven days to make the 235-mile journey to Federal Hall, New York City. The country he traveled through was still a land of farms and small villages, hemmed in by forests. The first census in 1790 gave the United States a population of four million, of whom only 3 per cent lived in the six largest cities: Philadelphia, New York, Boston, Charleston, Baltimore, and Salem. The national territory was 900,000 square miles, of which more than half was still occupied by the Indians. Nine out of ten Americans worked on farms, raising small crops which barely fed their own families. Practically all of them attended church on Sunday, and once or twice a year they gathered for elections or militia musters. They read a surprisingly large number of books, political pamphlets, and newspapers.

The inhabitants of America, wrote a European traveler, "pass their lives without any regard to the smiles or frowns of men in power." The Federal Union and all its concerns seemed very remote to most of them. Soon after his inauguration Washington began his grand tours of the country *(below)*, to convince the provincial Americans that they really had a national government, and that it was worth taking an interest in.

Washington hated to leave Mount Vernon, where he watched every chore.

Pittsburgh the largest settlement of the West, looked like this in 1789.

Soapmaking and laundering were typical barnyard tasks in New England.

Nassau Hall at Princeton *(left)* was the largest building in the nation.

President Washington inspects a New England cotton mill.

The last lap of Washington's trip was a triumphant ride across New York Bay in a satin-trimmed barge *(right)*.

Thomas Jefferson, the lone idealist in Washington's Cabinet, was 47 when he became Secretary of State. In the portrait at the right his red hair is hidden by the formal powdered wig which he wore as American envoy to France in the 1780's.

JEFFERSON
AND
HAMILTON

As SECRETARY OF STATE in the new Government President Washington appointed Thomas Jefferson of Virginia, the principal author of the Declaration of Independence. For Secretary of the Treasury he chose Alexander Hamilton of New York, the spark plug of the Federalists. Hamilton was a tireless, brilliant, hard-boiled realist in politics. He believed that money made the wheels go round—or, as he put it in more elegant language, "Money is, with propriety, considered as the vital principle of the body politic."

Hamilton was convinced the Government would not last unless the wealthy people of the country could make money by it. His reasoning went like this, and these are his words: "All communities divide themselves into the few and the many. The first are the rich and well born, the other the mass of the people. The voice of the people has been said to be the voice of God; and however generally this maxim has been quoted and believed, it is not true in fact. The people are turbulent and changing; they seldom judge or determine right. Give therefore to the first

class a distinct, permanent share in the government. They will check the unsteadiness of the second, and as they cannot receive any advantage by a change, they therefore will ever maintain good government."

The permanent share which Hamilton proposed to give his privileged group was the opportunity to profit by speculations in government-improved lands, government-guaranteed securities, and government-protected industries. He foresaw a country of big cities and banks, with factory jobs for everybody, including wives and young children. This idea was horrifying to Jefferson, who wanted the United States to remain a land of small farmers and craftsmen.

The debates between these two strong men raged hotly at Cabinet meetings, but Hamilton usually had his way with the President. He always had a specific plan for getting things done, which was a valuable thing in a new government. But Jefferson understood the American people better than Hamilton did, and he soon developed his own plan of action through political organization and pressure.

Alexander Hamilton, Washington's favorite, was 32 when he entered the Cabinet. He was short, dapper, and efficient, with ruddy cheeks and bright blue eyes. He dominated the Government so completely that he was called "the Prime Minister."

Edmund Randolph, the Attorney General, was a born fence-sitter who tried to stay neutral in the Cabinet fight, but often sided with his fellow Virginian, Jefferson. Randolph helped to write the Constitution and then refused to sign it.

General Henry Knox, the 300-pound Secretary of War, had been Washington's artillery expert during the Revolution. Knox was all for Hamilton and the Federalists. He speculated in Western lands and profited directly from Hamilton's program.

John Adams, the Vice President, was a staunch Federalist who liked to wear silk stockings and velvet pants. As presiding officer of the Senate he often decided tie votes in favor of Hamilton's projects, though he hated Hamilton personally.

HAMILTON WINS THE FIRST ROUND

THE FIRST important bill passed by the First Congress was a tariff law which gave financial help to American shipowners, iron, glass, and rum manufacturers. Next came the vital issue of the public debt, which consisted of $52 million in bonds and warrants issued by the Continental Congress, and $18 million more issued by the states to help pay for the Revolution. Most of it was in default.

Secretary of the Treasury Hamilton told Congress that the entire debt should be funded at full face value by the Government. It was, he said, a matter of national faith and credit—the United States must start its career with an A-1 financial standing. He did not deny the fact that most of the original security holders and old soldiers had long since sold their certificates at depression prices, and that speculators would reap an enormous profit from his policy. Even before his recommendation was made public New York capitalists heard about it and sent agents scurrying through the country to buy depreciated certificates. A number of Congressmen did the same thing.

Congress quickly agreed to pay the national part of the debt. But the assumption bill, which provided for payment of $18 million in state debts, met fierce opposition and was defeated in the House. Some states had already paid their own debts and saw no reason to help pay the others'.

At this point Hamilton conceived and carried through a famous political bargain with his Cabinet foe, Thomas Jefferson. One afternoon the two leaders met at dinner and talked about the assumption bill. They also talked about the future location of the national capital, which was then a red-hot issue between several states. They reached the following agreement: Jefferson and his friend Madison would persuade some of the Virginia Congressmen to change their votes and pass the assumption bill. Hamilton, in turn, would see that the New York members supported a site on the Potomac River for the new "Federal City." And to get the necessary vote in the Senate, where the rich Philadelphia merchant, Robert Morris, pulled the strings, both sides agreed to make Philadelphia the temporary capital until 1800.

This masterly piece of logrolling was a great victory for Hamilton. It secured his whole program, and gave the big-money men and speculators behind him $40 million clear profit. Jefferson realized this later and angrily claimed he had been hoodwinked.

Robert Morris, the rich Pennsylvania Senator, clutching a moneybag, drags Congress to its new Philadelphia home.

HAMILTON'S BANK

The rest of Hamilton's program slipped through Congress easily. A tax was levied on whisky, and a national mint was established to coin American money. The first Bank of the United States was organized, to issue paper money and control the nation's credit. The Bank bill started the first great debate over "constitutionality." Jefferson argued that the Bank was illegal because the Constitution did not specifically authorize it. Hamilton rested his case on the famous Section Eight, which gives Congress power to provide for "the general Welfare." President Washington agreed with Hamilton and soon the Bank began to do business in a handsome building in Philadelphia *(left)*. A boom in Bank stocks followed, and many friends of Hamilton's got rich. This convinced Jefferson and his followers that "stock-jobbers" and profit-hungry "parasites" were having their way with the Government.

FRENCH FIASCO

At the start of Washington's second term the French revolutionists guillotined their king and proclaimed a world-wide war against the British empire. Washington promptly proclaimed American neutrality, although we still had a military alliance with France, and most Americans were for the revolution. In April 1793 Citizen Edmond Charles Genêt *(left)* arrived as the first minister from the French Republic. Genêt decided to go around "old man Washington," as he called him, and appeal directly to American voters. He hired soldiers, outfitted French fighting ships, set up French courts on American soil, and helped organize political clubs to fight "pride of wealth and arrogance of power" in the United States itself. These insolent tactics swung American opinion away from France, and Genêt was fired by his Government. His fiasco was a big help to the Federalists, who were anti-French and pro-British.

BRITISH LUCK

In 1794 President Washington's special envoy, John Jay, made an unfortunate treaty with England. Jay was a narrow-minded Federalist who was easily blinded by British glitter. He agreed not to export cotton in American ships, since he did not even know cotton was an American product. In return for a long list of such concessions which he gave, the British promised only to evacuate their Northwest forts on American territory — which they had already promised to do in 1783. Jefferson's followers attacked the treaty as "the death warrant of American liberty" and burned Jay in effigy *(left)*. The Treaty was saved in Congress by Fisher Ames, a Federalist orator from Massachusetts. Ames shed great crocodile tears for the "widows and orphans" who would be created if the British and their Indian allies were not given this opportunity to quit the Northwest forts. "I can fancy that I listen to the yells of savage vengeance, and the shrieks of torture," he cried. "Already they seem to sigh in the west wind—already they mingle with every echo from the mountains." His Federalist colleagues from the East wept openly during Ames' speech, but Westerners were not impressed. Andrew Jackson of Tennessee said President Washington should be impeached for signing such a cowardly treaty.

The Cannibals are landing

Volunteers

Stop de wheels of

de gouvernement

Triumph Government: perish all its enemies.__
Traitors, be warned: justice, though slow, is sure.

Presented to the New York State Historical Society. By Geo. B. Reed. Montpelier, Vermont.

This Federalist cartoon shows Washington and his federal chariot heading off an invasion by French Republican "cannibals." At right Jefferson and friends try to block the wheels and a dog lifts his leg on a Republican newspaper.

THE RISING OPPOSITION

IN THE FINE spring weather of 1791 Thomas Jefferson and James Madison rode northward from Philadelphia on what they called a "botanizing excursion." They wrote letters home about strawberries in blossom, the speckled trout they caught, and the blue laws of Vermont, where they were arrested for riding in a carriage on Sunday. But not a word did they say about politics. Actually their journey was the beginning of a well-organized political opposition to Hamilton and all his Federalist works.

At Albany the distinguished travelers called on Governor George Clinton, an old-time and embittered Anti-Federalist. In New York City they paid their respects to Aaron Burr, the ambitious young lawyer who was closely linked with the Sons of Saint Tammany. This quaint society with its Indian rigmarole had been started before the Revolution, as an antidote to the British Sons of Saint George. Its members were city workmen and small merchants who despised the Federalist "nabobs."

The results of the Jefferson-Madison expedition showed up in the election of 1792. Washington was re-elected unanimously. But John Adams, running again for Vice President, was beaten by Governor

Republican cartoon shows "Peter Porcupine," a ferocious Federalist editor, spewing out hatred of America. "Porcupine" was an ex-British soldier named William Cobbett.

Another Federalist cartoon of 1793 shows the Republicans as a mob of cutthroat anarchists consorting with the devil.

Jefferson stands on a bench and declaims wildly while Republican astronomer David Rittenhouse stargazes at left.

Clinton in New York, Virginia, and North Carolina. The alliance between Jefferson's Southern planters and Tammany soon burgeoned into a full-fledged political party, taking in Genêt's radical Democratic Societies, the discontented farmers and Western frontiersmen, and old opponents of the Constitution. Jefferson's followers thought Hamilton and other leading Federalists were working toward a monarchy and an hereditary privileged class in the United States. So they took the name "Republicans," to show they were for pure republican government.

The Federalists seemed to think there was something monstrously immoral and illegal about this rising opposition. Their cartoons pictured the Republicans as cannibals, drunkards, and pirates. President Washington suggested that "self-created" political societies were a menace which the Government should annihilate by force, if necessary.

The Republicans replied with a cartoon showing David Humphreys, the President's close friend, leading an animal on which Washington was seated. The caption read, "The glorious time has come to pass, When David shall conduct an ass." Another Republican cartoon showed Washington being placed on a

guillotine. This was shown to the President at a Cabinet meeting one day, and he flew into a violent passion, according to Jefferson. He swore that "by God he had rather be in his grave than in his present situation; that he had rather be on his farm than to be made emperor of the world." No copies of these Republican cartoons are known to exist today; perhaps they were all destroyed by outraged Federalists.

Jefferson's alliance with Tammany put practical politics into the Republican party at an early date. This contemporary engraving shows a Tammany brave of 1800 being fondled by admirers on a Broadway corner.

In the East, Lady Washington's Friday night parties were top social events. They were always over by 9 o'clock, which was bedtime for the President.

In the West, tar and feathers entered politics again in 1794. Here a group of Whisky Rebels escorts a federal tax collector from his burning home.

WASHINGTON
UNDER ATTACK

DURING WASHINGTON'S second term the Republican newspapers plagued him continually about his kingly habits. The President, said one editor, prefers levees, drawing rooms, stately nods instead of shaking hands, and seclusion from the people. Washington had no desire to be a king, but he often acted like one. When his close friend, Gouverneur Morris, walked up to him one day and slapped him on the back, Washington froze him with an angry glare. He did not think that a President of the United States should be subject to such familiarities. The portrait at the right shows him in a kingly mood, wearing on his coat lapel the jeweled insignia of the Society of the Cincinnati.

Washington believed, with good reason, that prestige was important in world affairs. The United States was a very shaky young nation and Washington wanted to give it dignity. His Presidential coach was as splendid as an emperor's—a gorgeous canary-colored affair decorated with gilt cupids and nymphs, and drawn by six perfectly matched white horses. His grooms rubbed white marble paste on the horses at night and let it dry to a shiny gloss. Then the horses' hoofs were painted black and their teeth scoured before they went out to haul the President.

On Tuesdays when Congress was in session Washington received visitors at formal levees. On these occasions he wore black velvet knee breeches and yellow gloves, and held a cocked hat ornamented with the Federalists' black cockade. To each guest he gave a stiff bow and a few words. On Friday evenings Mrs. Washington held her "drawing-rooms," which were cozier affairs, where the President was often surrounded by pretty girls.

All this Presidential pomp was far removed from the hills of western Pennsylvania, where an armed revolt against Washington's administration broke out in the summer of 1794. The cause was the tax which Hamilton had put on whisky. The Western farmers all made whisky to sell in the East: it was the best way they had to transport their grain, for there were no roads and the Mississippi River was kept closed by its Spanish rulers. The whisky tax worked to the advantage of the New England rum industry, which was largely owned by Hamilton's Federalist friends. So the "Whisky Rebels" refused to pay the tax, and tarred and feathered the tax collectors.

Washington was convinced the Republican politicians were backing the Whisky Rebellion, and he was not far wrong. Making the first test of his constitutional power to mobilize state troops under federal command, he assembled an overwhelming force of 15,000 men and assigned Hamilton to supervise them. By November the government forces were in control around Pittsburgh, and the whisky tax was being collected once more. A few bedraggled "Whisky Boys" were captured and paraded in triumph through the streets of Federalist Philadelphia. But the victory was an expensive one politically, for practically all the West went over to Jefferson and his Republicans.

THE
FAREWELL ADDRESS

of President Washington was partly written by Hamilton, and was published in a Philadelphia newspaper September 19, 1796. It offered some stately Federalist advice to Americans:

"Indignantly [frown] upon the first dawning of every attempt to alienate any portion of our country from the rest or to enfeeble the sacred ties which now link together the various parts. . . . Let me now . . . warn you in the most solemn manner against the baneful effects of the spirit of party generally. . . . It serves always to distract the public councils and enfeeble the public administration. It agitates the community with ill-founded jealousies and false alarms; kindles the animosity of one part against another; foments occasionally riot and insurrection. It opens the door to foreign influence and corruption, which find a facilitated access to the government itself through the channels of party passion. . . .

"There is an opinion that parties in free countries are useful checks upon the administration of the government, and serve to keep alive the spirit of liberty. This within certain limits is probably true; and in governments of a monarchical cast patriotism may look with indulgence, if not with favor, upon the spirit of party. But in those of the popular character, in governments purely elective, it is a spirit not to be encouraged. . . .

"As a very important source of strength and security, cherish public credit. One method of preserving it is to use it as sparingly as possible. . . .

"Observe good faith and justice toward all nations. Cultivate peace and harmony with all. . . . Europe has a set of primary interests which to us have none or a very remote relation. Hence she must be engaged in frequent controversies, the causes of which are essentially foreign to our concerns. Hence, therefore, it must be unwise in us to implicate ourselves by artificial ties in the ordinary vicissitudes of her politics or the ordinary combinations and collisions of her friendships or enmities. . . .

"It is our true policy to steer clear of permanent alliances with any portion of the foreign world. . . . Taking care always to keep ourselves by suitable establishments on a respectable defensive posture, we may safely trust to temporary alliances for extraordinary emergencies."

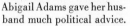

Adams was born in a salt-box house *(left)* in Braintree, Massachusetts. The house at right was his later residence.

Abigail Adams gave her husband much political advice.

Their son John Quincy was Minister to Holland at 26.

Washington, D. C. *(above)*, became the capital in 1800, and Abigail hung her laundry in the White House East Room.

STOUT
JOHN ADAMS

JOHN ADAMS, the second President of the United States, was fat, fussy, hot-tempered, warm-hearted, and got into fights with almost every prominent American of his time. He hated Hamilton, the leader of his party, so viciously that he once called him "the bastard brat of a Scotch pedlar." He was openly jealous of Washington. He had been a friend of Jefferson's but now despised his "democratical" thinking. "There never was a democracy that did not commit suicide," he snorted.

Twenty years before he came to the Presidency Adams was the political wheel horse of American independence. He got Washington elected Commander in Chief, helped draft the Declaration of Independence, and lobbied it through Congress. During the peace negotiations he went to Holland and obtained loans which saved the Government. He was the first American Minister to be received by King George III after the Revolution was won. But he looked upon his eight years as Vice President as a great humiliation. "My country," he wrote to his wife, "has in its wisdom contrived for me the most insignificant office that ever the invention of man contrived or his imagination conceived."

When Washington declined to seek a third term, John Adams was the logical Federalist candidate. But Hamilton secretly tried to knife him in the election by backing Thomas Pinckney of South Carolina. This scheme diverted enough Federalist votes to give the Vice Presidency to Jefferson, the leader of the opposition. Hamilton continued to interfere by advising the members of Adams' Cabinet and even wrote reports which they gave to the President. When Adams discovered this he fired two Cabinet members and started a feud which wrecked the Federalist party. Personal vanity was his weakest point; personal courage and integrity were among his strongest.

As a young Boston lawyer in the 1760's John Adams was a staunch American patriot. But when the British Captain Preston was unjustly charged with murder after the Boston Massacre *(right)*, Adams defended him and won his acquittal.

24

"NO; NO; NOT A SIXPENCE!"

Cartoon of 1799 shows the Hydra-headed French Government demanding money from Americans at dagger's point.

General Charles Cotesworth Pinckney of South Carolina was the man who refused to give the French a sixpence.

THE CARTOON ABOVE provides a complete documentation, from the Federalist point of view, of Washington's farewell warning against European intrigues. The three honest-looking men in broadbrimmed hats are United States commissioners who were sent to France in 1797 to reach an agreement about American shipping. (France and England were at war and both countries were seizing American ships when they felt like it, but France was causing the most trouble at the moment.) The five-headed monster with the dagger is the five-man Directory which was then ruling revolutionary France. While he demands "Money, Money, Money!!" from the Americans various Frenchmen in the background are robbing each other and chopping off heads.

All of this relates to the fact that when the American commissioners arrived at Paris they were confronted by three French officials who demanded a $250,000 bribe, a $10 million loan from the United States to France, and threatened to declare war if both were not forthcoming. The Americans were prepared to pay a little bribe money but they would not submit to wholesale blackmail. "No; no; not a sixpence!" they finally told the Frenchmen, and broke off the negotiations.

When President Adams made this story public the newspapers changed the American reply to "Millions for defense but not one cent for tribute!" and a real shooting war broke out between French and American warships in the West Indies.

The brand-new American frigate *Constellation (left)* bears down on the French Navy's *L'Insurgente* off Nevis on February 9, 1799. *L'Insurgente* has been abusing American merchant ships and *Constellation* intends to chastise her.

After a raking fight in which 29 French sailors and one American were killed *L'Insurgente* hauls down her tricolor flag and surrenders. In 2½ years of this undeclared war the American Navy took 85 French ships and lost one.

THE FEDERALIST

AT THE HEIGHT of the French war fever the Federalists in Congress passed the Alien and Sedition Acts, which were intended to silence their Republican opponents forever. The Alien Acts gave President Adams the power to deport "dangerous" aliens, and made it more difficult for new arrivals to become voters. They were aimed especially at a sizable group of liberal-minded refugees from England and Ireland who had become ardent Jeffersonians. The Sedition Act practically made it a crime for anybody to be a Republican. It provided jail sentences up to five years and fines up to $5,000 for any person who spoke or wrote about the President, the Congress, or the Federal Government "with intent to defame [them] or to bring them . . . into contempt or disrepute."

Leading Republicans all over the country were promptly arrested on the basis of what they had said in newspaper articles or personal letters, and railroaded through the courts by Federalist judges like the coarse and vindictive Samuel Chase. One ailing Republican editor died from the mistreatment he received in the Boston jail. A Republican official of Otsego County, New York, was forced to travel 200 miles in manacles to the prison in New York City. In Newark, New Jersey, when a salute was fired in honor of President Adams, a man standing near by remarked that he wished the cannon wadding "had been lodged in the President's backsides." For this seditious statement he was fined $100.

The most notable victim was Congressman Matthew Lyon of Vermont, who was both a Republican and an Irishman. The Federalists hated Lyon for his aggressive disposition—one of their rhymesters once called him

> a strange, offensive brute
> Too wild to tame, too base to shoot.

One day in Congress a Connecticut Federalist named Roger Griswold made an

Federalist Supreme Court Justice Samuel Chase was a notorious courtroom bully.

THE KENTUCKY RESOLVES

Vice President Thomas Jefferson was shocked to the depths of his philosophical being by the Alien and Sedition Acts. But he saw at once that they constituted a grievous political mistake which could seriously damage the Federalist party. He quietly spread rumors through friends that the next items on the Federalist program were to make President Adams a king, establish a royal succession for his family, and install the Senators for life. Jefferson was exaggerating, but his predictions were widely circulated and made splendid campaign material. While the Federalists went merrily on tying more rope around their necks, Jefferson got ready to jerk the country out from under their feet.

Working in complete secrecy, he drew up nine resolutions which his followers put through the legislature of Kentucky. The Kentucky Resolves declared that the Alien and Sedition Acts were contrary to the letter and spirit of the Constitution, and were therefore null and void so far as Kentucky was concerned. Other states were invited to take similar action, but all declined except Jefferson's own Virginia.

The Kentucky Resolves were passed in a good cause, but they contained enough political dynamite to blow up the Union. Resolve No. 1 said that "the several States composing the United States of America, are not united on the principle of unlimited submission to their general government; but that by compact under the style and title of a Constitution for the United States and of amendments thereto, they constituted a general government for special purposes . . . and that whensoever the general government assumes undelegated powers, its acts are unauthoritative, void, and of no force." Resolves Nos. 3 and 4 declared that the Alien and Sedition Acts interfered with the powers of the states, and were "altogether void" within the boundaries of Kentucky. Out of these statements grew the gigantic doctrines of states' rights, nullification, and secession.

Republican John Breckinridge sponsored Jefferson's resolves in Kentucky.

REIGN OF TERROR

insulting remark about Lyon's Revolutionary record, and Lyon bristled up to him and spat in his face. Two weeks later Griswold worked up enough courage to attack Lyon with his cane, and Lyon hit back with a pair of tongs from one of the Congressional fireplaces. This was the first good fight that ever occurred on the floor of Congress.

Soon afterward Lyon was arrested for writing in a letter that President Adams had an "unbounded thirst for ridiculous pomp, foolish adulation, and selfish avarice." He was convicted of sedition and sentenced to four months in a dirty little jail at Vergennes, Vermont. But the Green Mountain Republicans held political rallies outside the jail and re-elected him to Congress by a majority of two to one. Jefferson helped to pay his $1,000 fine. Lyon was one of those indestructible Americans who loved rough-and-tumble politics and outdoor adventure equally well. From Vermont he moved to Kentucky, and then to the wilderness territory of Arkansas, and was elected to Congress from both those places.

The popular uproar against the Alien and Sedition Acts became so great that the naval war with France was almost forgotten. In March 1799 President Adams offered to begin peace talks. Napoleon, who had ousted the corrupt Directory, promptly agreed, and the shooting in the Caribbean soon came to an end. The extreme Federalists were wild with rage against the President for this "betrayal." They had organized a big army under Washington and "General" Hamilton, and were ready to invade Louisiana and Florida, and perhaps even liberate South America. When Adams left Washington later that year to spend some time at his home in Massachusetts, the Federalist Congressman Robert G. Harper said he hoped the horses would run away and break the President's neck. Nobody charged him with sedition for that remark.

Republican Matthew Lyon of Vermont was re-elected to Congress from jail.

Cartoon of 1798 *(below)* shows Lyon and Griswold slugging each other on the floor of Congress. Speaker Dayton *(in chair)* seems to be enjoying the fracas. This crude but spirited drawing indicates that Americans already regarded their Congressmen as semicomic characters.

On December 12, 1799, a day of rain and snow, General Washington caught cold while riding around his farm. Much bleeding, and a remedy of molasses, butter, and vinegar, failed to relieve him. On December 14 he died of a throat infection. The Federalists felt especially bereft, for he was their greatest man.

CHAPTER 2

THE

JEFFERSON

REPUBLICANS

WASHINGTON'S DEATH in 1799 probably saved him from the supreme humiliation of losing a political fight. He had planned to take part in the 1800 campaign to re-elect John Adams and a Federalist administration, but by then nothing could stop the triumphant surge of Jefferson's Republicans. The new party swept into power in 1800, captured the Presidency and control of Congress, and entrenched itself so strongly that it continued to run the Government for forty years.

The Republican party was born to answer the basic question which had divided the first Cabinet: Can the average run of mankind govern themselves by their votes, as Jefferson thought they could? Or must they *be* governed by a privileged class of "the rich, the well-born, and the good," as Hamilton and the Federalists sincerely believed? The Federalist viewpoint dominated the Constitution, which stressed the rights of government and the duties of its citizens. But the Republicans drew their inspiration direct from the Declaration of Independence, with its ringing emphasis on the right of men to revolt, if necessary, against an unjust government. They put the people first and the government second.

This contrast provided the philosophical background, but the 1800 election was not fought on any such lofty level. The Republicans broke the Sedition Law right and left, and called John Adams everything from the Duke of Braintree to a madman. They assailed the Federalists as monarchists, England-lovers, warmongers, and spendthrifts, and accused them of selling out the country to the moneylenders.

The Federalists replied that the Republicans were low radical scum and carriers of bloody class-war schemes from Europe—especially from Red France —and that their real aim was to set up an American military dictator like Napoleon. In New England the Federalist clergy spread word that Jefferson planned to confiscate all the Bibles in the country and substitute one he had written himself. From their pulpits they echoed President Timothy Dwight of Yale, who had said that Republicanism meant a nation-wide orgy: "our wives and daughters the victims of legal prostitution; soberly dishonored; speciously polluted. . . ."

The big campaign sensation was a pamphlet written by Alexander Hamilton in which he attacked Adams as a liar, an ingrate, and "unfit" for the office of President. This piece of intraparty treachery came on top of another indiscreet pamphlet which Hamilton had published, admitting that while he was Secretary of the Treasury he had paid blackmail to hush up "an amorous connection" with a Mrs. Reynolds of Philadelphia. These two publications destroyed Hamilton as a political figure and cost the Federalists many votes in 1800.

The election was won by a formidable political combination which Jefferson and his followers had been patiently putting together for years. Its strongest element was the mass of small farmers in all the states, for Jefferson believed that farmers were the perfect American citizens, and his program was aimed to make them especially happy. Also in the Republican phalanx were the frontier dwellers of the West; the rich planters of the South; the so-called "foreign vote," especially the Irish and rural Pennsylvania Germans; a growing number of city workmen who were attracted by Jefferson's attacks on "the aristocracy of wealth"; and the Tammany bosses of New York and Philadelphia, who were in politics strictly for profit.

These Jefferson Republicans comprised the first genuinely American political party, the first to adopt the revolutionary and humanitarian ideas of the Declaration of Independence, and the first to use machine methods. Their Federalist foes tried to smear them by calling them "democrats," which was a horrid word to most Americans in 1800. But the left-wing Republicans accepted and used this label, so that as time went on their party was called Republican-Democratic, and eventually just Democratic, which is its name today.

"Mad Tom in a Rage" was the title of this Federalist cartoon attacking Jefferson and his administration. The Federalists liked to picture Jefferson as a brandy-soaked anarchist tearing down the pillars of government.

BEWARE OF AARON BURR!

AT THE very moment of victory, the Republicans almost lost everything by an amazing blunder. Everyone knew that their candidate for President was Jefferson, and that their choice for Vice President was Aaron Burr, the suave political boss of New York City. But when the electoral votes were counted they showed the first and only tie for President in American history: Jefferson, 73; Burr, 73; Adams, 65; C. C. Pinckney, 64; and Jay, 1.

This result was possible because of the peculiar voting system in the Electoral College. (The system was changed in 1802 by a constitutional amendment.) Each elector voted for two men, and the man who got the most votes became President, while the second highest became Vice President. The Republicans planned to have a few electors split their ticket, so that Burr would come just behind Jefferson. But the Virginia electors thought the New York delegation would attend to this, and the New Yorkers left it up to Virginia, and so nobody did it.

The tie vote threw the election into the House of Representatives, where a group of lame-duck Federalists decided to elect Burr President. But Alexander Hamilton protested loudly and effectively. "If there be a man in this world I ought to hate, it is Jefferson," he wrote to his friends in Congress. "But the public good must be paramount to every private consideration." He still thought Jefferson a hypocrite and a political fanatic, but Burr was worse —"a cold-blooded Catiline"—"a profligate; a voluptuary ... without doubt insolvent." Burr was capable of selling out the country to a foreign power, or of starting a war for personal profit. "For heaven's sake," wrote Hamilton, "let not the federal party be responsible for the elevation of this man!"

The balloting started in the House on February 11, 1801. One critically ill Republican member was carried through a snowstorm, on his bed, to vote for Jefferson. The capital teemed with threats and rumors: that the Pennsylvania militia was on its way to force Jefferson's inauguration, that Chief Justice John Marshall might appoint a Federalist President, who would be assassinated if he tried to take office. Balloting was by single states. For six days and 35 ballots there was no majority. Jefferson had eight states; Burr, six; and two were divided. On the seventh day Federalist James Bayard of Delaware withheld his vote, which took one state away from Burr and made Jefferson President. Aaron Burr moved into second place as Vice President, hiding his disappointment behind a polite smile.

Black-eyed, hatchet-faced, unscrupulous Aaron Burr was the son of a president of Princeton University. Burr never became a member of Tammany Hall himself, but ran the Tammany machine through underlings.

Aaron Burr !

At length this Cataline stands CONFESSED in all his VILLAINY—His INVETERATE HATRED of the Constitution of the United States has long been displayed in one steady, undeviating course of HOSTILITY to every measure which the solid interests of the Union demand—His POLITICAL PERFIDIOUSNESS AND INTRIGUES are also now pretty generally known, and even his own party have avowed their jealousy and fear of a character, which, to great talents adds the deepest dissimulation and an entire devotion to self-interest, and self-aggrandizement—But there is a NEW TRAIT in this man's character, to be unfolded to the view of an INDIGNANT PUBLIC!—His ABANDONED PROFLIGACY, and the NUMEROUS UNHAPPY WRETCHES who have fallen victims to this accomplished and but too successful DEBAUCHEE, have indeed been long known to those whom similar habits of vice, or the amiable offices of humanity have led to the wretched haunts of female prostitution—But it is time to draw aside the curtain in which he has thus far been permitted to conceal himself by the forbearance of his enemies, by the anxious interference of his friends, and much more by his own crafty contrivances and unbounded prodigality.

It is time to tear away the veil that hides this monster, and lay open a scene of misery, at which every heart must shudder. Fellow Citizens, read a tale of truth, which must harrow up your sensibility, and excite your keenest resentment. It is, indeed, a tale of truth! and, but for wounding, too deeply, the already lacerated feelings of a parental heart, it would

be authenticated by all the formalities of an oath.

I do not mean to tell you of the late celebrated courtezan N———, nor U———, nor S———, nor of half a dozen more whom first his INTRIGUES have RUINED, and his SATIATED BRUTALITY has afterwards thrown on the town, the prey of disease, of infamy, and wretchedness—It is to a more recent act, that I call your attention, and I hope it will create in every heart, the same abhorrence with which mine is filled.

When Mr. Burr last went to the city of Washington about 2 months ago, to take the oath of office, and his seat in the August senate of the U. States, he SEDUCED the daughter of a respectable tradesman there, & had the cruelty to persuade her to forsake her native town, her friends and family, and to follow him to New-York. She did so—and she is now IN KEEPING in Partition-st. Vice, however, sooner or later, meets its merited punishment. Justice, though sometimes SLOW, is SURE. The villain has not long enjoyed this triumph over female weakness. The father of the girl has at length after a laborious and painful search, found out the author of his child's RUIN, and his family's DISHONOR.—HE IS NOW IN THIS CITY, and VENGEANCE will soon light on the guilty head!—— Fellow-citizens, I leave you to make your own comments on this complicated scene of misery and vice.— I will conclude with a single observation—Is that party at whose head is this monster, who directs all their motions and originates all their nefarious schemes worthy of your support?

After Burr became Vice President the New York Federalists published this handbill accusing him of a series of seductions. Burr's love affairs were numerous enough, but these statements were political fabrications.

"FOR JEFFERSON AND LIBERTY"

ON THE MORNING of March 4, 1801, President-elect Thomas Jefferson walked into the dining room of his Washington boardinghouse and took his usual place at the foot of the long table. His chair was the farthest from the fire and the room was chilly, but he smilingly refused a better seat. After working in his study for a few hours, he walked up the hill to the unfinished Capitol and read his Inaugural Address in a low, monotonous voice. It was not a call to arms, as many had expected, but a lofty appeal for national unity. "Every difference of opinion is not a difference of principle," said Jefferson. "We are all Republicans, we are all Federalists."

This sounded strangely mild from the leader who had once exclaimed, "God forbid that we should ever be twenty years without . . . a rebellion!" It caused the radical Republicans to grumble about a surrender, and the Federalists to sniff "Hypocrite." In truth Jefferson was a philosopher-politician who believed there was good in all men, except perhaps the most bullheaded Federalists. Now that Republican principles had triumphed, he said, only one thing remained to make Americans a happy and prosperous people: that was "a wise and frugal Government, which shall restrain men from injuring one another, shall leave them otherwise free to regulate their own pursuits of industry and improvement, and shall not take from the mouth of labor the bread it has earned."

His program called for less government spending, fewer taxes, less army and navy, fewer judges, factories, and banks (no banks at all if possible), less social snobbery, and no "entangling alliances" with other countries. But he wanted more schools, libraries, and newspapers, more American land, and especially more farmers. In theory he would have changed the Government into something resembling a national grange.

In practice he did not do this, for there were too many immediate problems which he had to meet with definite action. And Jefferson was a President of determined—even stubborn—action. Some indication of this may be seen in his picture on the opposite page—in the big, powerful, folded hands and the calm, weathered, strongly set features.

Jefferson abolished formal social affairs at the White House and received callers in his working clothes: an old brown coat, red waistcoat, corduroy breeches, wool hose, and heelless carpet slippers. Yet in spite of his occasionally sloppy appearance, he was the most sophisticated and versatile of our Presidents. He invented a plow and a swivel chair, sorted mammoth bones on the White House floor, imported seeds and books from Europe, edited his own version of the New Testament, played the violin, and was a gifted architect. He was as keenly aware of the weaknesses of human beings as any of the "practical" men who constantly denounced him. But he clung to the belief that the world could, and would, become better. "Cherish the spirit of our people," he once wrote to a fellow Republican, "and keep alive their attention. Do not be too severe upon their errors, but reclaim them by enlightening them. If once they become inattentive to public affairs, you and I, and Congress and Assemblies, Judges and Governors, shall all become wolves. . . . Experience declares that man is the only animal which devours his own kind; for I can apply no milder term to the governments of Europe, and to the general prey of the rich on the poor."

Jefferson designed Monticello with a billiard room in the dome. But before it was completed, Virginia outlawed billiards.

Jefferson lounged around the White House in his old clothes *(right)* to set an example of Republican simplicity.

"A LITTLE REBELLION NOW AND THEN

is a good thing, and as necessary in the political world as storms in the physical," was a well-known saying of President Thomas Jefferson's. And he had also said: "The tree of liberty must be refreshed from time to time with the blood of patriots and tyrants." But the revolution which Jefferson led in 1801 was fatal to no one, and his Republican followers confined their bloodletting to their song:

The gloomy night before us flies,
The reign of terror now is o'er;
Its gags, inquisitors, and spies,
Its herds of harpies are no more!
Rejoice! Columbia's sons, rejoice!
To tyrants never bend the knee,
But join with heart, and soul, and voice,
For Jefferson and Liberty.

No lordling here, with gorging jaws,
Shall wring from industry the food;
Nor fiery bigot's holy laws
Lay waste our fields and streets in blood!
Rejoice! Columbia's sons, rejoice!
To tyrants never bend the knee,
But join with heart, and soul, and voice,
For Jefferson and Liberty.

WRITER SNEERS AT REPUBLICAN AMERICA

During Jefferson's Presidency many foreign visitors traveled about the United States, seeing what had been accomplished by the American Revolution and the twenty-odd years that followed. Among them was the Irish poet and song writer, Tom Moore (*left*), who thought almost everything he saw was disgusting. One day in 1804 Moore called at the White House all dressed up in the latest London fashion, and sprinkled generously with perfume. Jefferson gave him a curious stare and a handshake, and turned quickly to someone else. Moore took revenge by writing a sneering poem about Washington, D. C., where

... nought but woods, and Jefferson they see,
Where streets should run, and sages ought to be.

Moore continued his travels around the country, and decided it might be all right for savages and Republicans to live in, but would never be fit for gentlemen. His letters constituted a "Report on the Americans" which was classic in its snobbery. "Such a road as I have come!" he wrote one day, "and in such a conveyance! The mail takes twelve passengers, which consists of squalling children, stinking negroes, and republicans smoking cigars. . . . Nothing could be more emblematic of the *government* of this country than its *stages*, filled with a motley mixture, all 'hail fellow well met,' driving through mud and filth, which *bespatters* them as they *raise* it, and risking an *upset* at every step. . . . As soon as I am away from them, both the stages and the government may have the same fate for what *I* care. . . ."

THE MILITANT REPUBLICANS

John Randolph of Roanoke was a unique figure in American politics. A mysterious disease had attacked him when he was about 19, leaving him with the beardless face and soprano voice of a choirboy. Yet no one could question his personal bravery or indomitable spirit. He fought in several duels and performed prodigious feats of horsemanship, such as riding 1,800 miles to Charleston and Savannah, killing one horse on the way. He was easily the most forceful member of Congress. When an opponent taunted him on his lack of virility, Randolph replied with withering scorn: "You pride yourself upon an animal faculty, in respect to which the negro is your equal and the jackass infinitely your superior!"

JEFFERSON's leader in the House of Representatives was John Randolph of Roanoke, the childish-looking creature whose picture appears on the opposite page. Randolph was a pure Republican, but he had no use for democracy. "I am an aristocrat," he once snapped; "I love liberty, I hate equality." He strode through the halls of Congress as though he owned them, booted and spurred, with a riding whip in his hand and a favorite hound at his heels.

A rich Virginia landowner and descendant of Pocahontas, Randolph was only 26 when he was first elected to Congress in 1799. He became notorious at once by attacking the American Army as a pack of "ragamuffins" and "mercenaries" who were trying to drag the country into war with France. Two Marine Corps officers followed him into a theater one night, climbed into his box, plucked at his cape, and did their best to jostle him into a fight. But Randolph haughtily faced them down and called them "puppies." Then he demanded a personal apology from President Adams for this affront to the dignity of Congress. No one in America could equal his gift for stinging invective in debate. It was he who said of Edward Livingston, a political antagonist: "He shines and stinks like rotten mackerel by moonlight!" He boasted that he would never vote to admit a new state to the Union, because that would impair the sovereignty of the thirteen original states. "Asking one of the States to surrender part of her sovereignty is like asking a lady to surrender part of her chastity!" he cried, in his shrill, flutelike voice.

Another key Republican in Congress was William B. Giles of Virginia, who was the special foe of Federalist judges. Giles thought that any judge who had the impudence to declare an Act of Congress unconstitutional should be immediately impeached and removed from office. This opinion was shared by other leading Republicans and, to some extent, by Jefferson himself. But the Republicans found it difficult to loosen the Federalist grip on the courts. The best they could do was to impeach a few judges like the drunkard Pickering, of New Hampshire, and the bully Chase, of Maryland. And even Chase was acquitted.

Jefferson's closest Cabinet advisers were Madison, his Secretary of State, and Albert Gallatin, the brilliant Swiss-born Secretary of the Treasury. Gallatin was the first naturalized American to become prominent in politics, and the Federalists groaned that the Government was being run by "foreigners." But no Republican was so viciously abused as old Tom Paine, who spent two weeks in the White House in 1803. When this became known, the shrieks of the Federalists filled the skies. Tom Paine—that sot, that "old battered bellwether of Jacobinism and infidelity"—setting foot in the house of the President! The Federalists tried to make everyone forget that Paine was the author of *Common Sense* and *The Crisis*—the greatest propagandist of the American Revolution. They smeared him as a brandy-fuddled atheist, hoping that some of their tar would stick to his friend, Thomas Jefferson.

Treasury Secretary Albert Gallatin

Congressman William Branch Giles

Tom Paine, White House guest

THE MIDNIGHT JUDGES

For many years after Jefferson's victory the real leader of the Federalist opposition was Chief Justice John Marshall of the United States Supreme Court. The Constitution had placed the federal courts out of reach of the voters, and they were staffed by 100-per-cent Federalist party men. In the last moments of the Adams administration Congress had rushed through a Judiciary Act creating jobs for 21 new Federalist judges. Marshall, who was also serving as Adams' Secretary of State, was still signing commissions for these "Midnight Judges" when the Adams administration died. The next day he calmly swore in Jefferson as President, and returned to his duties on the bench.

The Federalist Chief Justice was a tall, loose-limbed Virginian who had been raised on the log cabin frontier, and fought well in the Revolution. He was only 45 at the start of Jefferson's first term, and he was destined to outlast all the Republican administrations. In a series of strong judicial decisions he built an almost impregnable legal barricade around the Union and the business interests which benefited from it. His decisions established the right of the federal courts to annul an Act of Congress as "unconstitutional" (*Marbury vs. Madison*), to annul a state law because it conflicted with a federal law (*McCulloch vs. Maryland*), and to annul a state law which interfered with corporation contracts (*Dartmouth College vs. Woodward*). These great Federalist decrees were more important than any Presidential election between 1800 and 1828.

Chief Justice John Marshall made the Supreme Court into a Federalist fortress.

WINNING THE WEST

WHILE THE politicians fought their wars of words the history of the country was being decided by ordinary Americans, going west. The painting above shows Daniel Boone leading a group of settlers through the Cumberland Gap from Virginia into Kentucky in March 1775—just a few weeks before the Battle of Concord. Boone was among the first white hunters to penetrate the Gap, in 1769. He lived to see a million people pour across the mountains and found the states of Kentucky (1792) and Tennessee (1796). After helping to clean out the Indians Boone became a Kentucky real-estate operator and wound up his business

Western women cooked their meals out-
doors, except on the coldest winter days.
Abraham Lincoln was born in a log cabin
like this, while Jefferson was President.

career—like many another American speculator—with a surplus of 50 cents.

During Jefferson's Presidency other migrations drove up through the Northwest Territory, above the Ohio River, and down into the lands of the Creeks and
Cherokees, beyond the Old South. Ohio was admitted as a state in 1802; Indiana
became a territory in 1800, Michigan in 1805, Illinois in 1809. The American
push to the West was a continual adventure in self-reliance and personal liberty
—a constant renewal of the nation's youth. As long as there was a Western frontier,
Americans would be boundlessly optimistic about the future.

Boonesborough, Kentucky, was a typical
Western fort, built by Boone in 1775,
close to the Kentucky River. The Indians
attacked it many times but never took it.

Robert R. Livingston *(right)*, who bought Louisiana, was a Hudson River aristocrat. He later financed Fulton's development of the steamboat and tried to establish a monopoly of steamboat travel.

In his headquarters at the Louvre Napoleon *(center)* shakes hands with Americans who have just bought Louisiana. "You will fight England again," he told them.

JEFFERSON BUYS A

IN APRIL 1803, Dictator Napoleon Bonaparte of Europe made a deal with the envoys of President Thomas Jefferson. For $15 million—which he needed to finance his forthcoming war with England—Napoleon turned over to the United States the entire Louisiana Territory. This vast triangular domain began at the mouth of the Mississippi River and stretched west and north over 800,000 square miles to the Rocky Mountains and British Canada. Only a little while before, Napoleon had extorted Louisiana from Spain and had thought of making it the center of a great French-American empire. But when Jefferson sent word that he would like to buy

Meriwether Lewis *(left)*, Jefferson's secretary, explored Louisiana and the far Northwest with William Clark in 1804-1806. In 1809 he was mysteriously murdered in a backwoods tavern in Tennessee.

WESTERN EMPIRE

New Orleans and some of the land around it, Napoleon made a brisk decision. "I renounce Louisiana," he told his ministers, "the whole colony without reserve." To the Americans he said, in effect, "Take it all, or nothing."

Robert R. Livingston, Jefferson's Minister to France, gladly took it all. At one stroke, and without even a threat of war, the Louisiana Purchase doubled the nation's size, pushed back the frontier another 1,500 miles, and secured the Mississippi as a highway for Western commerce. It was by far the best bargain in American diplomatic history.

The Indian woman, Sacajawea, points a way through the mountains to Lewis and Clark, who reached the Pacific at the mouth of the Columbia in November 1805.

One of the pistols in this box (according to family tradition) fired the bullet that killed Alexander Hamilton. The other was in his hand when he fell. The same weapons were used in an earlier duel, in 1801, when Hamilton's eldest son Philip was killed following a political argument.

AARON BURR KILLS HAMILTON

A FEW minutes after 7 o'clock on the morning of July 11, 1804, Vice President Aaron Burr and General Alexander Hamilton stood ten paces apart on the wooded heights of Weehawken, New Jersey. Hamilton raised his long-barreled dueling pistol against the sun and then put it down. "I beg your pardon for delaying you," he said, "but the direction of the light sometimes renders glasses necessary." He then took out his spectacles and put them on.

A second cried the word "Present!" Burr fired at once and Hamilton pitched forward on his face, his pistol discharging in the air. Burr started toward him, a spasm of regret on his chiseled features, but his second hurried him away, covering his face with an umbrella. Hamilton was carried to the edge of the Hudson River and revived with spirits of hartshorn. He was then rowed across to New York in the bottom of a little boat. Burr's bullet had pierced his liver and lodged in his spine. After 31 hours of agonizing pain he died.

The causes of this dramatic event went far back into the lives of both men. Burr and Hamilton had clashed temperamentally when they were young Revolutionary army officers. They had been rivals for pre-eminence in the New York law courts. They had fought savagely in politics, yet they had always remained correct and outwardly friendly in their personal contacts. They dined together often and visited each other's homes. But all the time Hamilton was pouring his poisonous opinions of Burr into confidential letters to his friends—opinions which were reported back to Burr in exaggerated form.

In February 1804 Burr definitely broke with the Jefferson Republicans and made a lone race for Governor of New York. Again Hamilton played a major part in beating him, as he had for the Presidency in 1801. Six weeks after his defeat Burr was shown an old copy of an Albany newspaper in which the following sentences appeared, in a printed letter: "General Hamilton and Judge Kent have declared,

in substance, that they looked upon Mr. Burr to be a dangerous man, and one who ought not to be trusted with the reins of government. . . . I could detail to you a still more despicable opinion which General Hamilton has expressed of Mr. Burr."

Here, at long last, was something out in the open, something which no man of honor could overlook, especially if he harbored many old grudges against an implacable political foe. In his elegant but mortgaged mansion at Richmond Hill in New York City Burr picked up a quill and wrote the first of a series of formal letters, filled with expressions of gentlemanly indignation, and punctuated with "I have the honor to be, sir," and "You must perceive, sir," which led to the fatal glade of Weehawken.

The wave of public horror which followed Hamilton's death was amazing to Burr and to many other Americans. Almost everyone prominent in New York politics had fought in duels, including Mayor DeWitt Clinton, District Attorney Riker, and Judge Brockholst Livingston (who had killed his man). Yet now these officials joined with the outraged populace in shouting that Hamilton had been killed like a dog. A coroner's jury called for Burr's arrest for murder. Insulting poems were dropped on his doorstep:

> Oh Burr, oh Burr, what hast thou done,
> Thou hast shooted dead great Hamilton!
> You hid behind a bunch of thistle,
> And shooted him dead with a great hoss pistol!

In the midst of this uproar Burr fled to New Jersey in a small boat and made his way by foot and wagon to Philadelphia. There he dallied for a while with an old friend named Celeste, and then went on to Georgia and South Carolina, where he made a 400-mile trip through the swamps in a canoe. In January he was back at his post in Washington, presiding over the Senate.

Mrs. Alexander Hamilton was the former Elizabeth Schuyler, daughter of the rich Revolutionary General, Philip Schuyler.

"I NEED NOT TELL YOU OF THE PANGS I FEEL"

One week before the duel Hamilton and Burr were both at a Fourth of July banquet in downtown New York. After the meal Hamilton jumped up on the table and sang a rollicking Scots ballad, "The Drum." Burr sat, with his chin in his hands, gazing long and deeply into his enemy's face. At that time all the "arrangements" had been completed.

On the same day Hamilton wrote his farewell letter to his wife. "This letter, my dear Eliza," it read, "will not be delivered to you, unless I shall first have terminated my earthly career.... If it had been possible for me to have avoided the interview, my love for you and my precious children would have been alone a decisive motive— But it was not possible, without sacrifices which would have rendered me unworthy of your esteem. I need not tell you of the pangs I feel, from the idea of quitting you and exposing you to the anguish which I know you would feel.... Adieu best of wives and best of women. Embrace all my darling children for me. Ever yours— A. H."

Hamilton died in his prime, at the age of 47. He left seven children, $55,000 in debts, and an ever-growing fame.

BUT HAMILTON STILL LIVES

BURR'S BULLET took a strange course on that morning in Weehawken. For even as it pierced Hamilton's body it lifted his prestige to dazzling heights. And it killed Burr as dead, politically, as though it had turned around and struck between his eyes.

Before the duel Hamilton's influence had been sharply on the wane. The New England Federalists, whom he had enriched by favorable laws, had turned against him and were plotting secession from his beloved Federal Union. It is possible that Burr, if he had been elected Governor of New York, would have joined with the New Englanders and tried to form a separate northern confederacy. Hamilton was disgusted by such treachery, and by the general drift of things under Jefferson's Republican regime. "Every day proves to me more and more that this American world was not made for me," he wrote to a friend.

Yet Hamilton had probably done as much to form the American political world as any other man, and the shocking suddenness of his death made his significance loom larger than ever. Men realized again that it was Hamilton who had taken the Constitution as a sheaf of paper and transformed it into a strong, living government. He had formulated the famous doctrine of implied powers, and had furnished the first great example of executive initiative and daring.

Even Jefferson had followed Hamilton's example when he bought Louisiana—without any authorization from the Constitution or Congress, but knowing it was the best thing to do.

Hamilton could never have been President himself—he was too outspoken in his contempt for ordinary people. "Our real disease," he wrote on the night before he was shot, "is *democracy*." He certainly did not believe all the high-sounding words in the Declaration of Independence. His well-known remark on child labor—that "women and children are rendered more useful, and the latter more early useful, by manufacturing establishments, than they would otherwise be"—is a fair sample of his thinking about working people.

Yet it is probably true that no humanitarian could have accomplished the job which Hamilton did so efficiently at the beginning of the Government. In the words of Daniel Webster, "He smote the rock of the national resources and abundant streams of revenue gushed forth; he touched the dead corpse of Public Credit, and it sprang upon its feet." He made the United States a going concern. In every period of our history, and in all our political parties, there have been men who looked to Hamilton's vigorous realism for their first inspiration. In that sense, he continues to live.

AND BURR IS DEAD AND GONE

Aaron Burr's legacy to American history was the image of himself as a perfect scoundrel. For all his gracefulness and charm, his popularity and cleverness, he had no higher motives in public affairs than those provided by a boundless vanity and a bottomless pocketbook.

In 1804 the Republicans dropped him from their ticket and he lost his job as Vice President. In 1806 he made a mysterious expedition through Ohio and Kentucky and met a small body of armed men in Tennessee. He seems to have had several possible schemes in mind: to invade Spanish Florida; to start a revolution in Mexico; or to rouse the Western states to secede and elect him President. At any rate he was arrested and sent to Richmond to be tried for treason, on direct orders of President Jefferson. Chief Justice Marshall ran the trial along strictly Federalist lines and acquitted Burr single-handed. Burr then spent several years in Europe, where he wrote notes to Napoleon, offering to overthrow the American Government for a sum of money.

He returned to New York unmolested in 1812, and died there in 1836. His long last years were as painful as any Hamiltonian could wish. His beloved daughter Theodosia disappeared on an ocean voyage, and for years he haunted the Battery, waiting vainly for her lost ship to come in. At 77 he married his rich old mistress, Betsy Bowen Jumel, who soon threw him out of her house, and divorced him on a charge of infidelity. On his deathbed, according to the newspapers, he struggled frantically, crying, "I can't die; I won't die!" But the doctor replied, "Mr. Burr, you are already dying."

Burr lingered on until he was 80, turning into the toothless, spindle-shanked, forgotten old codger shown above.

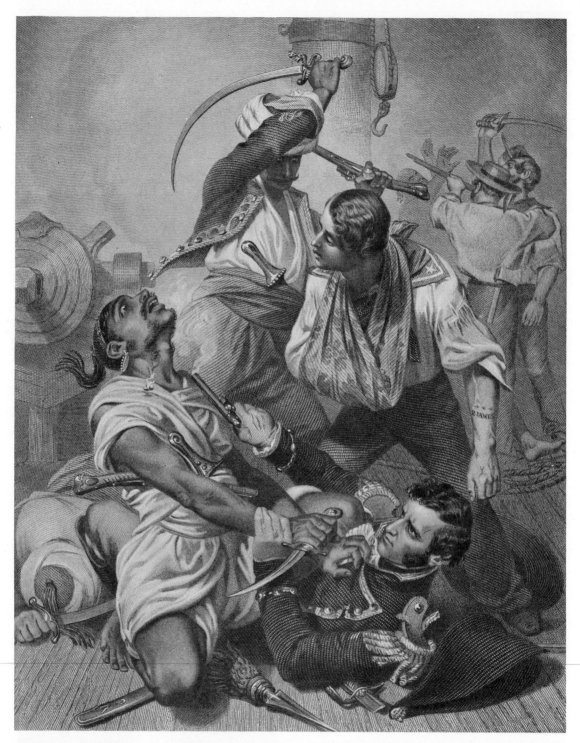

"TO THE SHORES OF TRIPOLI"

JEFFERSON WAS the first President to interrupt the long-standing American policy of appeasement and bribes to the pirate nations of North Africa. When the Pasha of Tripoli tried to extort more cash by chopping down the flagstaff of the United States Consulate, Jefferson sent the tiny American Navy to bombard Tripoli. This brought on a fight during which Lieutenant Stephen Decatur leaped on board an enemy gunboat with a cutlass in one hand and a pistol in his hip pocket. The Tripolitan captain knocked him down, but Decatur shot him dead *(above)*. During their struggle a wounded American seaman named Daniel Frazier put his head in the way of a scimitar stroke and saved Decatur's life. Tradition, and the tattoo marks shown in the picture, have wrongly attributed this heroic deed to another sailor named Reuben James.

The burning of the American frigate *Philadelphia* was a lurid exploit of the Tripoli war. The ship had been captured while stuck on a reef and was being refitted by the Tripoli-tans. On the night of February 16, 1804, Decatur and his daredevil crew slipped on board, knifed the guards, set the ship afire with gunpowder, and rowed safely away *(left)*.

In March 1805 the American Consul William Eaton *(in cocked hat)* started from Egypt with eight United States marines, 38 Greeks, 300 Arabs, and an unemployed pasha *(left)*, to attack Tripoli from the rear. The little army marched across 600 miles of desert and captured the port of Derne before Jefferson suddenly called off the war.

ISOLATION AND INSULTS

"PEACE IS our passion," Jefferson had written. But peace was lacking in most of the world in 1805, when Jefferson began his second term in the White House. Napoleon was master of Continental Europe and England was mistress of the seas. These two mighty antagonists were locked in a global war for supremacy, but the British Navy was bleeding more from desertion than from the blows of its enemy. In ten years of war with France 42,000 seamen deserted to escape the rotten food and galley-slave existence on British warships.

Many of the deserters came to the United States and sailed out again with American papers. The British captains did not stand on diplomatic ceremony about this. They simply stopped American ships and kidnaped their crews, not caring much whether they found real deserters or not. Other innocent victims were snatched by navy press gangs in British ports. All together an estimated 10,000 American citizens were manacled, lashed, thrown into filthy bunks, and converted into cheap cannon fodder by the process known as impressment. In addition, both France and England confiscated American merchant vessels whenever and wherever they felt like it, until 1,475 ships and many millions of dollars' worth of goods had been lost.

The crowning insult came on June 22, 1807, when the British naval frigate *Leopard* met the American Navy's *Chesapeake* just outside Hampton Roads, and insisted on searching her for deserters. Commodore Barron of the *Chesapeake* refused, whereupon the *Leopard* poured in a stiff broadside, killing three Americans and wounding 18. The *Chesapeake* was just departing on a peaceful mission to the Mediterranean; her guns, which had to be fired with log-gerheads and slow-burning matches, were not ready for action. Just one American shot was fired, by Lieutenant William Allen, who ran to the galley and brought back a hot coal in his bare hands. Barron struck his flag to avoid further bloodshed, and the British came aboard and carried off four men.

When the wounded *Chesapeake* limped back to Norfolk the American people experienced, for the first time, a truly national anger. They would have gone to war in a minute if Jefferson and Congress had asked it. But Jefferson did not ask it. He was no pacifist, as he had shown by his action against Tripoli. But he believed the United States could stay out of war and still get justice by following certain rules of economics and logic.

His policy, which he called "peaceable coercion," was a kind of controlled isolationism. At his request Congress had already passed a law barring some British goods from entering the United States. Now a more drastic measure, the celebrated Embargo, was imposed. This prohibited all exports from all American ports. Jefferson's theory was that American food and raw materials were so necessary to the warring countries that they would soon come to terms.

Unfortunately he was wrong. France and England laughed at the Embargo and got all they needed from American smugglers. Huge black markets sprang up on the Canada and Florida borders, while law-abiding American sailors were thrown out of work and American ships rotted at the wharves.

The Embargo was extremely unpopular. It split the Republican party and gave the Federalists a new lease on life. It was Jefferson's biggest mistake. In March 1809, just before he went out of office, he signed a bill repealing it.

Commodore Barron *(left)* of the battered *Chesapeake* offers his sword to British Capt. Humphreys, who refuses it.

American sailors with hands tied are led off to British slavery as the *Chesapeake's* flag droops on her deck.

Jefferson's peace policy was lavishly satirized in this cartoon, which shows him waving a quill-pen sword over a fortress of proclamations. Napoleon *(upper right)* blows the breath of war against the windmill on Jefferson's hat.

James Madison won an easy Republican victory in the Presidential election of 1808. He was 58 years old, a short, brisk man with apple-red cheeks, a dry wit, and mischievous manners with the ladies.

THE

CHARMING

MADISONS

THOMAS JEFFERSON was carefree and gay as he turned over the Presidency to his hand-picked Republican successor, James Madison. Then he mounted a horse and rode off to his hilltop home, Monticello, and never came back to Washington again. But little "Jemmy" Madison was not nearly so happy. He trembled and looked pale while he read his innocuous Inaugural Address. At the grand Inauguration Ball, the first ever held, he said he would rather be home in bed, although usually he enjoyed drinking champagne with his friends.

His wife Dolly was a greater attraction. She was 18 years younger and several inches taller than the President. She had long rippling black hair, dark blue eyes, and a creamy skin. For the ball she wore a pale yellow velvet gown with a long train, pearls on her arms, neck, and ears, and a velvet Paris turban with nodding bird-of-paradise plumes. So many people crowded in to look at her that several windows were broken.

Dolly Madison was the first pretty mistress of the White House, and American newspaper readers were interested in everything she did. Although born a Quaker, she played cards for money, dipped snuff, used rouge, and wore extravagant gold and silver slippers. As the nation's official hostess she gave big, hearty "harvest suppers" with plenty of wine, ice cream, macaroons, and fruit at the end. For some reason, everything she did made her popular, and her popularity was a valuable political asset to her husband.

Dolly Madison met her husband when he picked her up from a slippery Philadelphia sidewalk in the early 1790's. He was then a Congressman, and she was a recent widow being courted by Aaron Burr.

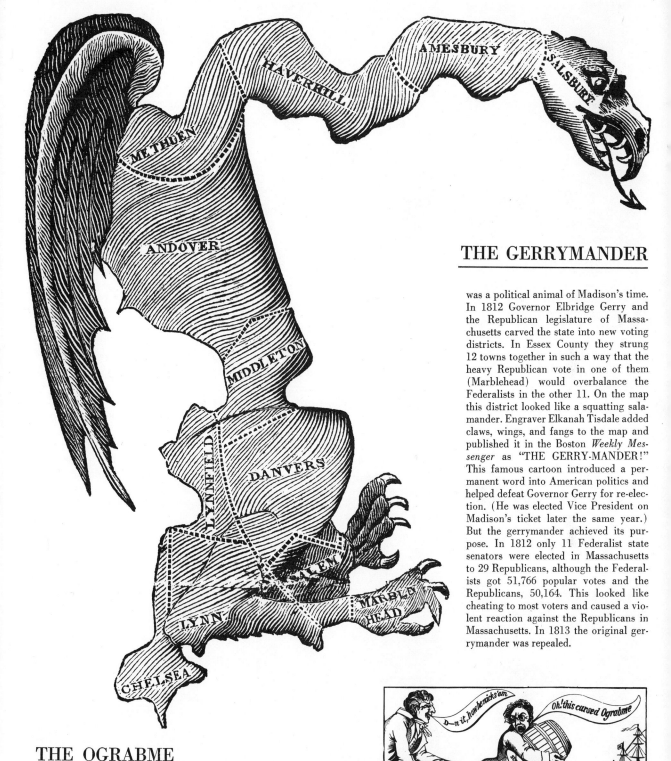

THE GERRYMANDER

was a political animal of Madison's time. In 1812 Governor Elbridge Gerry and the Republican legislature of Massachusetts carved the state into new voting districts. In Essex County they strung 12 towns together in such a way that the heavy Republican vote in one of them (Marblehead) would overbalance the Federalists in the other 11. On the map this district looked like a squatting salamander. Engraver Elkanah Tisdale added claws, wings, and fangs to the map and published it in the Boston *Weekly Messenger* as "THE GERRY-MANDER!" This famous cartoon introduced a permanent word into American politics and helped defeat Governor Gerry for re-election. (He was elected Vice President on Madison's ticket later the same year.) But the gerrymander achieved its purpose. In 1812 only 11 Federalist state senators were elected in Massachusetts to 29 Republicans, although the Federalists got 51,766 popular votes and the Republicans, 50,164. This looked like cheating to most voters and caused a violent reaction against the Republicans in Massachusetts. In 1813 the original gerrymander was repealed.

THE OGRABME

also called the Snapping Turtle, or Terrapin, was a favorite cartoon character. "Ograbme," of course, is "embargo" spelled backward. In 1811 a new embargo was proclaimed, and the cartoon at the right shows it working against a man who is trying to smuggle a barrel of tobacco onto a British ship. The Federalists, who did most of the illegal smuggling, made the turtle a symbol of government oppression and swore that

> *Down to the grave t' atone for sin*
> *Jemmy must go with Terrapin. . . .*

Langdon Cheves of South Carolina asked for 25,000 soldiers and 32 new warships.

Felix Grundy of Tennessee wanted revenge for brothers killed by the Indians.

Henry Clay boasted that the Kentucky militia could easily conquer all Canada.

THE WAR HAWKS

WHILE PRESIDENT MADISON fretted and fussed, and tried to enforce the new Embargo, the British continued their hostile acts at sea, and also promoted an Indian frontier war from bases in Canada. Madison was too timid and indecisive to deal with this emergency. For the first time, the leadership of the country passed to Congress, and particularly to the militant young Representatives shown above—the War Hawks of 1811. Their leader was Henry Clay, the strutting, crowing "cock of Kentucky," who had cried out a year earlier in Congress: "Sir, is the time never to arrive, when we may manage our own affairs without the fear of insulting his Britannic majesty? Is the rod of British power to be forever suspended over our heads? . . . No man in the nation wants peace more than I; but I prefer the troubled ocean of war . . . with all its calamities . . . to the tranquil and putrescent pool of ignominious peace!"

The War Hawks spoke for the new generation which had grown up since the Revolution. The Federalists might sneer at them as "young politicians, half hatched, the shell still on their heads," but their words and gestures thrilled the country. They talked, breathed, and dreamed of a glorious war which would end

At the Tippecanoe River in Indiana, November 7, 1811, 950 Americans dispersed an Indian horde led by the Prophet Tenskwatawa *(in white robe)*, who fled to British Canada.

Richard M. Johnson of Kentucky joined the Army and killed Chief Tecumseh.

Peter B. Porter of New York quit Congress and volunteered when war came.

John C. Calhoun of South Carolina stayed in Congress and raised money for the war.

with Canada, Florida, Mexico, and various points south all safely wrapped up in the American Union. They were supremely confident that Americans could lick anybody.

They also had a talent for getting things done. They elected Clay Speaker, and he bossed the House of Representatives as it had never been bossed before. Calhoun and Porter wrote a report on British-American relations and concluded that "open and decided war" was the only solution. Cheves drafted bills for a larger navy. Grundy and Johnson took up the cry "On to Canada!" after the Battle of Tippecanoe. Finally Madison made a bargain with the War Hawks: If they would back him for President again in 1812, he promised to send them a war message before the election. On June 1 he kept his word. On June 18, after two weeks of debate, Congress declared war. The vote was 79 to 49 in the House and 19 to 13 in the Senate, which showed that the War Hawks had considerable opposition. But even Jefferson was convinced by that time. "I believe . . . it is necessary," he wrote calmly; "war or abject submission are the only alternative left us. I am forced from my hobby, peace."

"BLOOD MUST FLOW!"

John Randolph, the great dissenter of Congress, fought the War Hawks at every turn, and in the end he was silenced only by Clay's imperious gavel. Then he dashed off a breathless manifesto to his Virginia constituents declaring that the war with England would deliver America to Napoleon—"Before these pages meet your eye, the last republic of the earth will have enlisted under the banners of the tyrant. . . . The blood of the American freemen must flow to cement his power . . . to establish his empire . . . over the land that gave our fathers birth—to forge our own chains!"

Randolph had broken with Jefferson in 1806 and was now the leader of a faction which considered itself more Republican, and more jealous of states' rights, than either Jefferson or Madison. His savage sarcasm made him a dangerous foe of every administration bill. When Jefferson was trying "peaceable coercion" Randolph sneered, "What is it? A milk-and-water bill! A dose of chicken broth. . . ." But he was opposed to naval preparedness too: "What! shall this great mammoth of the American forest leave his native element and plunge into the water in a mad contest with the shark? Let him beware that his proboscis is not bitten off. . . ." The truth was that Randolph never cared much for the American nation as a whole. He was, as the poet Whittier wrote,

Too honest or too proud to feign
A love he never cherished,
Beyond Virginia's border line
His patriotism perished.

John Randolph said the war would drag America "at the wheels of Bonaparte."

"ON TO CANADA"

THE WAR OF 1812, according to the War Hawks, was supposed to be an American military parade through Canada. But the Canadians and British didn't wait for the parade to start. Instead they marched to Detroit and confronted the American invasion army led by General William Hull, a doddering veteran of the Revolution. General Hull was already frightened into a state of incoherence by threats of an Indian massacre. He sat for a whole afternoon on the ground in a corner of his fort, drooling tobacco juice on his chin and vest. Then he surrendered his army without firing a shot. During the same week the Pottawatomie Indians captured Chicago and staged a ghastly slaughter of American soldiers and their wives and children.

American General William Hull *(right)* surrenders his army August 16, 1812.

These disasters almost paralyzed the American high command right at the start of the war. President Madison and his chief general, Henry Dearborn, were incompetent anyway, and seemed incapable of making effective plans. Most of the generals in the field were as bad, or worse. The nadir of military absurdity was reached in November, when the American General Alexander Smyth ordered 2,000 men into small boats on the Niagara River, and then ordered them out again, and repeated this three days later. On the second occasion the soldiers mutinied and fired their guns at the General's tent. He took to his heels and fled all the way to his home in Virginia, where he was legislated out of the Army.

The turning point came in 1813, when a collection of newly built ships under Captain Oliver Hazard Perry of the Navy won a slam-bang water fight on western Lake Erie, giving the Americans control of the beaches on both sides. General William Henry Harrison, the victor of Tippecanoe, promptly took his veteran troops across the lake and won an important battle at the Canadian Thames River. But the invasion of Canada was a failure on other fronts. One American army of 5,000 men marched all the way to the ramparts of Montreal, and then retreated when they heard the Canadian buglers sounding their calls.

"We have met the enemy, and they are ours," wrote Captain Oliver H. Perry *(standing)* after his Lake Erie victory.

At the Battle of the Thames in lower Canada the American cavalrymen wore tall black silk hats with fur plumes.

At Chippewa *(above)* and Lundy's Lane, along the Niagara front, American invaders fought bloody, indecisive battles.

At Lake Champlain Commodore Macdonough *(center)* turned back a British counterinvasion, capturing 7 ships.

The British frigate *Guerriere (right)* is a drifting, dismasted hulk after a 30-minute fight with the *Constitution (left).*

"FREE TRADE AND SEAMEN'S RIGHTS"

As soon as Congress declared war the haughty British Navy bore down to do its bit along the American coast. But there it received a very nasty shock. Three American frigates—the *Constitution,* the *President,* and the *United States*—were faster and threw a heavier broadside than any ships of their class in the world. The first Britisher to discover this was the frigate *Guerriere,* which ran into the *Constitution* August 19, 1812, about 600 miles east of Boston. While the British gunners stoked up on brandy and fired round after round of hot shot, the *Constitution* remained silent and worked in very close. Then it loosed a series of murderous broadsides which ripped the masts off the *Guerrière,* killed and wounded 79 of her crew, and tore big holes beneath her waterline. So many British cannon balls bounced harmlessly off the *Constitution's* thick hull that her sailors nicknamed her "Old Ironsides."

This brilliant sea victory, which was followed by several more, showed Americans—and the rest of the world—that British naval power was by no means invulnerable. It also helped to distract attention from the military disasters in Canada. Henry Clay, after shouting "On to Canada!" with the rest of the War Hawks, now gave the war an entirely different slogan. "Strike wherever we can reach the enemy, at sea and on land," he cried. "But if we fail, let us fail like men, lash ourselves to our gallant tars, and expire together in one common struggle, fighting for FREE TRADE AND SEAMEN'S RIGHTS!"

THE UNITED STATES

The Capitol looked like this after the British burned it. The House of Representatives roof *(left)* collapsed in flames.

IN 1814 the British Navy, by sheer force of numbers, drove American warships into hiding and took over the Atlantic coast. British sailors and marines swarmed into towns in Maine, on Cape Cod, in Maryland and Virginia. They forced the inhabitants to dig potatoes and cut corn for them, to hand over cattle and sheep and large "contributions" of cash. The American newspapers charged the invaders with raping American women and burning the houses of leading Republican politicians. The very effective British blockade stopped most American commerce and almost bankrupted the Government, which existed on loans from the foreign-born bankers Stephen Girard and John Jacob Astor.

The worst disgrace in American military history came in August 1814, when a British expeditionary force from Bermuda landed in Chesapeake Bay and marched on Washington, D. C. About 5,000 militia from Virginia and Maryland, together with 600 sailors and marines from a gunboat flotilla, met 1,500 of the British invaders at Bladensburg, five miles east of the capital. The Americans were well placed in low hills and had the advantage in cannon. But when the British fired their new rocket weapons in the air the American mules and militia both stampeded, and the battle was lost. The 600 American seamen kept firing their naval guns until they were surrounded. But the militia ran away so fast that only eight of them were killed.

President Madison, who had made no plans for defending Washington, bor-

" 'TIS THE STAR-SPANGLED BANNER"

The bombardment of little Fort McHenry *(center)* lasted 25 hours. But the flag was still there when it was over.

The panoramic view at the left shows the British fleet pouring bombs and solid shot into Fort McHenry, the gateway to Baltimore, on the morning of September 13, 1814. All that day and night the bombardment crashed down on 1,000 American defenders. They could not reply because their guns did not reach far enough. But when the British ships tried to sneak in closer, the cannon growled, and the enemy scuttled back, badly hurt. As long as McHenry's batteries held out, the British did not dare run past them into the narrow mouth of the Patapsco River.

On the morning of the fourteenth a Washington lawyer named Francis Scott Key, who was a temporary prisoner on one of the British warships, stared hopefully through the dawn at the silent fort. Yes, the flag was still there! The words of a triumphant song began to stir in Key's brain. He wrote part of it on the back of a letter, and finished it the next day when he was released and went to

TAKES A BEATING

The White House was consumed inside but rain preserved its walls. These two watercolor sketches were made in 1815.

rowed a pair of dueling pistols from the Secretary of the Treasury and drove to the battle in a carriage. But when he saw how things were going he hurried in the opposite direction. His wife, searching through crowds with a spyglass, finally caught up with him. She saved the White House silver plate, a Gilbert Stuart portrait of Washington which she broke out of its frame, a wagonload of official papers, and her parrot. Everything else was lost, including her velvet gowns and golden slippers.

When the enemy troops arrived at the White House they found a dinner for forty people all cooked and smoking on the kitchen spits. British Admiral Sir George Cockburn stole a cocked hat that belonged to the President and a cushion from Dolly's favorite chair as his personal souvenirs, and consigned the rest of "Jemmy's palace" to the flames. Fifty British sailors surrounded it and at a signal from an officer hurled balls of burning pitch through the windows. The same destruction was meted out to the Capitol (whose central dome had not been built), the newspaper offices, all the city's bridges, and several houses where snipers had hidden. While the burning was going on Admiral Cockburn rode around the city on a white horse, dangling Dolly Madison's cushion from his saddle and making jokes which a Washington lady declared were "too vulgar for me to repeat." The next night he and his army took to their boats and headed up the Bay to Baltimore, where a very different reception awaited them.

Baltimore. A printer set it in type and the war-excited crowds sang it to the tune of "Anacreon in Heaven," a famous old English drinking ditty:

And the rockets' red glare, bombs bursting in air,
Gave proof thro' the night that our flag was still there.

Within a few days "The Star-Spangled Banner" became a symbol of victory snatched from defeat. After the national humiliation at Washington, the defense of Baltimore roused and inspired the country. A fresh army of Maryland militia redeemed their state and fought off a British landing force of 9,000 men. The British General Ross, who had boasted that Baltimore would be his winter headquarters, was shot dead at the head of his troops. The British fleet turned sail and headed back down Chesapeake Bay, leaving Baltimore deliriously singing:

'Tis the star-spangled banner: O, long may it wave
O'er the land of the free and the home of the brave!

Heartily sick of war, British *(left)* and American diplomats signed the peace treaty of Ghent December 24, 1814.

THE TORY EDITOR and his APES Giveing their pitiful advice to the AMERICAN SAILORS

A disloyal Federalist editor *(above left)* fails to win over three American sailors. Below, the hardy war brides of 1812.

SOLDIERS on a march to BUFFALO.

The Hartford Convention or LEAP NO LEAP.

William Charles' cartoon shows three New England states *(on the ledge)* plotting to jump into the arms of King George III.

NEW ENGLAND TALKS TREASON

THE DARKEST political moment of the war came in December 1814, when delegates from Massachusetts, Rhode Island, and Connecticut met at Hartford to discuss secession from the United States and a separate peace with England. The Hartford Convention was arranged by leaders of the old Federalist party who gloated publicly over the burning of Washington and the misfortunes of "Madison's war." The New England Federalists refused to send their militia to the war and carried on a smuggling business with the British Army and Navy.

Commodore Stephen Decatur also accused them of hanging blue lanterns along the Connecticut shore to signal British ships. New England, with its worldwide maritime interests, actually made money during the war, and its bitter opposition was purely political. The treasonous secession movement was led by Timothy Pickering, boss of the reactionary Essex (County) Junto, who had been Secretary of State for both Washington and Adams. Pickering's scheme to break up the Union was temporarily shelved at the Hartford Convention by more moderate Federalists, who voted for a truce with the Madison government

until New England's "grievances" were looked into further. Three Massachusetts "ambassadors" then went to Washington to "negotiate," but were met by news of the Treaty of Ghent. This left them without much to negotiate, and they went home looking slightly ridiculous.

The amused contempt with which the rest of the nation came to regard this episode is shown in the cartoon above. The bald old man kneeling under the ledge is Pickering, praying that he will be made Lord of Essex by Great Britain. The three figures above are Massachusetts, Rhode Island, and Connecticut, debating whether they should leap into the embrace of King George, who is promising them lots of business in codfish and molasses. William Charles, who made the three drawings on these pages, was the first political cartoonist who drew for the amusement of average Americans, rather than in the interests of a particular party. Charles was strongly in favor of the war and the Republicans, but he could also poke fun at the York State soldiers who marched to the front encumbered by their women, babies, and all their household furniture *(opposite page)*.

THE BATTLE OF NEW ORLEANS

THE ENGRAVING above shows the final battle of the War of 1812, which was actually fought two weeks after the war was over. On January 8, 1815, a British army which had been sent to capture New Orleans marched bravely up to the entrenchments of General Andrew Jackson, in the Mississippi River swamps, a few miles east of the city. Jackson's Kentucky and Tennessee riflemen mowed them down in long scarlet rows, while his pirate-trained cannoneers ripped

through their ranks with grapeshot. In less than 30 minutes 2,000 British soldiers were killed or wounded. Among the dead was the British Commander in Chief, Sir Edward Pakenham, whose body was preserved in a cask of rum and carried back to England. The American loss was exactly 13. Weeks later both sides heard of the Treaty of Ghent.

The picture shows one line of Britishers advancing along the riverbank *(foreground)* while other regiments wait their turn in the fields above. The American trenches *(left)* bristle with bayonets and gunfire, and men from both armies are struggling in the water. The Battle of New Orleans showed that some British generals had not learned much since the days of Bunker Hill. It also showed that American riflemen were still among the world's best shots. And it wound up the war in such a blaze of glory that the Americans felt sure they had won it.

The first great painting of an American political scene *(right)* shows a city-wide election at the State House in Philadelphia, in the autumn of 1815. The voters lined up at the central building (later known as Independence Hall) are handing their ballots through the windows to the clerks inside. Each city ward was assigned a window of its own. In the center of the picture an infirm old voter can be seen descending from a carriage supplied by some friendly politicians, while a wagon full of cheering ward heelers is riding through Chestnut Street at the left. Voters who have already been to the polls are fighting, drinking, eating roasted oysters, and spilling down the steps of the hotel at the extreme left, which is also the headquarters for the city's Republican machine. John Lewis Krimmel, the German-born artist who painted this spirited picture, was known as the "American Hogarth." His works are scarce, for he was drowned in a millpond at 32.

THE ERA OF GOOD FEELINGS

THE END of the war brought a fresh surge of national pride which submerged old political differences. The Federalists had committed suicide at their Hartford Convention, and the nation was now entering a brief period of one-party rule. The secret caucus of Republican members of Congress was the most powerful political group in the country. It had arranged Jefferson's second nomination for the Presidency,

and both of Madison's. In 1816 it gave the nod to another member of the Virginia dynasty, James Monroe, who had served the usual apprenticeship as Secretary of State.

There was nothing inspiring about Monroe's lanky frame and slightly cynical blue eyes, but he suited the nation's relaxed postwar mood. After an easy election victory he set out on a northern tour by coach and steamboat, principally to persuade Federalist New England that a Republican President was not necessarily a devil with horns. New England was in a mood to be convinced; Monroe's tour was a personal and political triumph. The Boston *Centinel*, the leading Federalist daily, gave his administration the name by which it became generally known—"The Era of Good Feelings."

Andrew Jackson led his troops into Spanish Florida and put to death two Britishers.

"OUR COUNTRY! MAY SHE

THE AMERICAN ARMY and Navy came out of the War of 1812 in excellent fighting trim. And they still had plenty of fighting to do. In Florida, which was weakly ruled by Spain, a combination of warlike Indians and runaway Negro slaves had set up their own government and were raiding and plundering across the American border. In 1817 General Andrew Jackson was ordered to take his Tennessee militia into Florida and end the Indian menace. Jackson did that, and plenty more. He seized the Spanish capital at Pensacola, appointed one of his colonels to take the place of the Spanish Governor, and proclaimed the laws of the United States in force. His men caught two of the most troublesome Indian chiefs by running up a British flag on a gunboat offshore; the old Indians paddled out and came aboard, thinking they were among friends. Then the Americans took them to St. Marks and hanged them.

This incident convinced Jackson that the British were behind the Indian troubles in Florida. He caught a "noted Scotch villain" and munitions trader named Arbuthnot, and hanged him, and had a young British army officer shot for helping to command the Indians. There was a great international outcry over these two deaths, but

Two Seminole Indian chiefs, captured by Jackson's ruse, go ashore at St. Marks, Florida, to be hanged.

Stephen Decatur told the Algerians that they could have tribute from the cannon's mouth.

ALWAYS BE RIGHT"

Jackson made his point. English adventurers got out of Florida, and President Monroe soon bought it cheaply from Spain.

Meanwhile Congress had declared war on Algiers, which was up to its pirate tricks again, and Commodore Stephen Decatur went to work on his old African foes. After battering an Algerian fleet and killing its admiral off the coast of Spain, Decatur forced Algiers, Tunis, and Tripoli to pay $81,000 for American ships they had taken, and to sign new treaties giving up all future "tribute," or bribes. In Algiers the Dey's officials begged Decatur to continue paying just a small token tribute in gunpowder. "If you insist on receiving powder as tribute," he told them, "you must expect to receive BALLS with it." This blunt warning was enough, and the North African pirate nations made no more trouble for American ships. On his return Decatur was wined and dined as the nation's greatest naval hero. At a banquet in his honor at Norfolk he uttered the famous toast which became the watchword for the fighting forces of the militant young United States: "Our Country! In her intercourse with foreign nations may she always be in the *right*, and always *successful, right* or *wrong!*"

Decatur's Mediterranean squadron returns in triumph from victories over Algiers, Tunis, and Tripoli in 1815.

WEBSTER
AND THE
NORTH

DESPITE the placid appearance of the Era of Good Feelings some old political hates still smoldered under the surface. Young Daniel Webster of New Hampshire and Massachusetts was one who helped to keep them hot. A wily lawyer and an emotional orator who could shed tears at will, Webster was first elected to Congress in 1812. He immediately plunged into a fight to hamstring the Republican administration's war measures. He killed off a draft law, opposed bounties for army enlistments, and refused to vote taxes for the war. If President Madison wanted to fight, he said in a much-quoted speech, let him fight only on the ocean, for "our party divisions, acrimonious as they are, cease at the water's edge." (Victories at sea, of course, were a direct benefit to maritime New England.)

After the war "Black Dan" opposed the protective tariff of 1816—New England shipbuilders did not want a tariff on imported iron and hemp. But a few years later Northern manufacturers were more influential than shipbuilders, and Webster became an eloquent advocate of high tariffs.

Rowland's Steel Works in Philadelphia was typical of the North's new industries. Webster became their tariff champion in Congress.

CALHOUN AND THE SOUTH

Southern planters who lived in houses like this imported most of their supplies. They resented the higher prices caused by tariffs.

To MANY Americans John Caldwell Calhoun of South Carolina was the "young Hercules" of Congress who carried the War of 1812 on his shoulders. Though not so impassioned an orator as Webster, he was more logical and more learned. Under President Monroe he became Secretary of War and a leading spokesman of the new American nationalism, which greatly modified the Jeffersonian agrarian ideals of the dominant party. Jefferson himself had changed; in 1816 he wrote that "we must now place the manufacturer by the side of the agriculturist." In 1816 Calhoun and other latter-day Jeffersonians put through a high protective tariff and a new Bank of the United States which was copied after Hamilton's.

But when the tariff threatened to ruin South Carolina's cotton planters Calhoun made a drastic about-face. He became the bitter enemy of protectionism and the great exponent of sectionalism in politics. In a few years more he would be attacking the very existence of the Union, while Webster would be brilliantly defending it.

Handsome Harry Clay was called the "Great Pacificator," because of the many big political compromises he arranged. He loved good Kentucky whisky, horse races, card-playing for high stakes, and striped peppermint sticks, which he ate while listening to other speakers in Congress.

CLAY, THE MASTER

THE DOMINANT figure of postwar politics was Henry Clay of Kentucky. Clay had grown more suave since his War Hawk days, but his ego was still enormous. He believed he ought to be the next President, and he was eager to be appointed Secretary of State, which had been the usual steppingstone. But President-elect Monroe passed him by and appointed an experienced diplomat, John Quincy Adams. Clay's rage was so great that he refused to allow the House of Representatives (where he was still Speaker) to be used for Monroe's inauguration.

Thereafter Clay set out to build himself up on an unbeatable combination of political issues. He sought to bridge the growing split between North and South with what he called the "American System." This included high tariffs for Northern manufacturers, and a tender regard for the rights of slaveholders, in new territories as well as old. It also included the spending of millions from the Federal Treasury for roads, canals, and river improvements, an idea especially pleasing to voters in the undeveloped West. President Monroe thought such government spending was contrary to the Constitution, but Clay had the popular side of the argument.

With all his thirst for power and taste for compromises, Clay had a truly national vision of the American future. Once a petty Congressman asked him, with intended sarcasm, if he would build government roads all the way to the Rocky Mountains. "Not today," replied Clay, "nor tomorrow, but this government is to last, I trust, forever; we may at least hope it will endure until the wave of population, cultivation and intelligence shall have washed the Rocky Mountains. . . . Sir, it is a subject of peculiar delight to me to look forward to the proud and happy period . . . when circulation and association between the Atlantic and the Pacific and the Mexican Gulf shall be as free and perfect as they are at this moment in England or in any other country of the globe."

"The Mill-Boy of the Slashes" was an early Clay nickname. He was born in "the Slashes" of Hanover County, Virginia.

A familiar Clay argument for higher tariffs were the shelves of American stores, piled high with foreign goods.

Fairview Inn, near Baltimore, was a stopping place on the Cumberland wagon road, which was started by Jefferson and was passable as far as Wheeling, in 1817. Extension of this and other federally financed roads through the West was a valuable phase of Clay's "American System."

"A FIRE-BELL IN THE NIGHT"

TWO SHATTERING events made the year 1819 a turning point in American politics. One was a Western land panic, followed by a series of bank failures, which produced the first nation-wide depression. Thousands of settlers lost their partly cleared farms, the country's paper-money system collapsed, and the East's infant industries were mostly shut down. The other crisis came in Congress, where a bill admitting the newly organized state of Missouri was introduced, along with a state constitution adopted by Missouri voters. Missouri was part of the old Louisiana Territory that Jefferson had bought, and its richest farmlands had been settled by slave-owning Southerners. Naturally their new constitution made slavery legal and permanent in Missouri.

The home of Missouri's first Governor in 1820

But this involved a major change in national policy. By the Northwest Territory Ordinance of 1787 the Continental Congress had barred slavery from all new states north of the Ohio River. The admission of Missouri as a slave state would break that line and set up a huge obstruction against the westward spread of the free states.

Northern Congressmen proposed to solve this dilemma by gradually eliminating Missouri's slaves. They wrote amendments providing that no new slaves could be brought into the state, and that all children born there of slave parents should become free at the age of 25. With these changes the Missouri bill passed the House of Representatives but was turned down by the Senate. Neither House would give in, and Congress adjourned without settling the deadlock.

When the next session rolled around, a group of middle-of-the-road Northerners, with the powerful backing of Speaker Clay, offered a compromise. Let Missouri come in as a slave state, they argued, since she was already slave in fact. But let slavery be barred "forever" from all the rest of the Louisiana Territory north of the line 36° 30′ (now the northern boundary of Arkansas). And let Maine, which had recently applied for statehood, be admitted as a free state. This would keep the free and slave states balanced at 12 each.

The debate on this plan was the most bitter in years. Yankee Congressmen taunted the South with seeking to establish new markets for the flesh and blood of men "raised like black cattle and horses on plantations." Angry Southerners answered with threats of war. "You are kindling a fire which all the waters of the ocean cannot extinguish," cried Howell Cobb of Georgia; "it can be extinguished only in blood!" The Compromise passed, and Missouri was admitted with its slaves.

Stark fear had much to do with the passage of the Missouri Compromise. For the first time Americans had a good look at the ugly passions which lay just below the surface of the slavery question. The venerable Jefferson, on his hilltop at Monticello, was deeply stirred. "This momentous question, like a fire-bell in the night, awakened and filled me with terror," he wrote. "I considered it at once as the knell of the Union. It is hushed, indeed, for the moment. But this is a reprieve only, not a final sentence."

This Missouri tax collector rode around his district on an ox with brass knobs on its horns. If a taxpayer slammed his front door, the ox simply lifted the roof off his house.

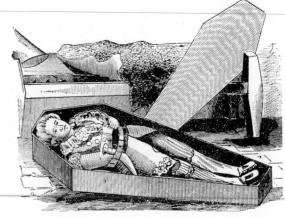
Daniel Boone, the old Kentucky Indian-fighter, moved to Missouri and died there in 1820. This woodcut is supposed to show him "trying on" his coffin shortly before he died.

John Randolph, Virginia's great irreconcilable, was so excited during the Missouri debates that he could eat nothing but crackers and gruel for days. He insisted the South should secede at once rather than accept any limitation on slavery. This silhouette of him was made at his stud farm, "Roanoke." A few years later he became insane.

THE MONROE-ADAMS DOCTRINE

Simón de Bolívar freed Bolivia, Colombia, Venezuela.

On December 2, 1823, President Monroe sent to Congress his annual message,
which contained the following sensational
announcements:

"The American continents, by the free
and independent condition which they
have assumed and maintain, are henceforth not to be considered as subjects for
future colonization by any European
powers. . . . The political system of the
allied powers [The Holy Alliance] is essentially different . . . from that of America. . . . We owe it, therefore, to candor
and to the amicable relations existing between the United States and those powers
to declare that we should consider any

José de San Martín led
revolts in Chile and Peru.

attempt . . . to extend their system to any portion of this hemisphere as dangerous to our peace and
safety. With the existing colonies or dependencies of any European power we have not interfered and shall not interfere. But with the Governments who have declared their independence . . .
we could not view any interposition for the purpose of oppressing them . . . by any European
power in any other light than as the manifestation of an unfriendly disposition toward the United
States."

This was the famous Monroe Doctrine, which was conceived and partly written by Monroe's
hard-working Secretary of State, John Quincy Adams. It was an extremely bold gesture, aimed
directly at three of the world's big powers: Spain, Russia, and France. Since 1809 several Spanish
provinces in America had revolted and declared their independence; in 1822 the United States
recognized five of them as nations: Chile, Colombia, Mexico, Peru, and La Plata (Argentina). But
in Europe the reactionary Holy Alliance (Russia, Austria, Bourbon Spain and France) was reported
to be organizing an army to take them back. And in Moscow Czar Alexander I had announced that
he was extending Russian sovereignty all the way down the Pacific coast to Oregon. The Foreign
Minister of England, George Canning, did not like any of these moves. He suggested that the

Czar Alexander I tried to
seize Oregon for Russia.

United States join England in a warning
against aggression in the Americas. But
Secretary Adams was too smart for this.
He saw no reason, he said, to "come in as
a cock-boat in the wake of the British man-
of-war." He proposed that the United
States issue its own warning, and include
England as one of the countries to be
warned.

He sold Monroe on his idea, and the
Doctrine which they wrote was regarded,
in time, as the most successful diplomatic
stroke in American history. The European
powers thought it the height of rudeness.
But they were too jealous of each other
to join together and chastise the United
States for its impudence.

Francis I of Austria was
part of the Holy Alliance.

Once when President Monroe was touring the country an effusive citizen asked him if he did not feel worn out by all his traveling. "Oh no," smiled the President. "A little flattery will support a man through great fatigue." But by 1824 Monroe had grown somewhat tired of his job, and the country was decidedly tired of him and of the fading Virginia dynasty which he represented. It was true that he had been re-elected in 1820 by the largest majority since Washington. It was also true that he was the "Last of the Cocked Hats"—the last Revolutionary officer and constitutional "Father" to head the Government. But for all that, most Americans were ready for a change.

John Quincy Adams was a canny diplomat and a sophisticated judge of Madeira wines. But he was suspicious, cold in manner, and lacking in personal charm. He had no close friends, and spent his lonely hours in the White House reading the Bible, writing in his massive diary, and toiling incessantly at the job of being President.

Cartoon of 1824 shows Candidates Adams, Crawford, and Jackson toeing the mark for the White House race. Clay scratches head *(right)*.

THE PRESIDENTIAL FOOT RACE OF 1824

THE ERA of Good Feelings blew up with a bang in the Presidential election of 1824. For 20 years the winning nomination had been passed around on a platter by the Republican caucus in Congress. But now there were too many new leaders, and the mass of voters was tired of caucus rule. Four candidates, all Republicans, lined up at the Capitol end of Pennsylvania Avenue *(above)* as the race to the White House began: William H. Crawford of Georgia, the official caucus candidate; General Andrew Jackson of Tennessee, who had stormed back into politics to vindicate his actions in Florida; bald John Quincy Adams of Massachusetts; and handsome Harry Clay of Kentucky. When the race was over Jackson had 99 electoral votes; Adams, 84; Crawford, 41; and Clay, 37. Since no candidate had a majority, the election (as provided in the Twelfth Amendment) was thrown into the House of Representatives, where Clay was Speaker and boss. Jackson and his followers insisted that the House was duty bound to select him because he had received more popular votes. But Clay put his finger on Adams—and Adams got the plum. Clay had a cold-blooded motive for this. He figured that Adams would not be too popular as President, and that he—Clay—would find it easy to succeed him.

But when Adams turned around and named Clay Secretary of State, the Jacksonians raised a great shout of "corrupt bargain." Instead of fixing a nice soft succession for himself, Clay made "Old Hickory" Jackson the most aggrieved, determined, and popular man in the United States.

THE WHITE HOUSE

in the 1820's had its front yard on the Potomac River. President Adams slipped down there every warm morning between 4 and 6 o'clock, left his clothes under a tree, and plunged in for a quick dip. Visitors to Washington often saw the portly President, who was an excellent swimmer, sporting about on his back in the water. Coming out, he would dry himself with napkins, put on his clothes, and stroll back to his study to read the Bible and the newspapers before his 9 o'clock breakfast. Once a drowned Revolutionary veteran was taken out of the river while he was swimming near-by. Another time a lady reporter sat on his clothes and obtained an interview which he had been trying to avoid. But he continued to enjoy his swims.

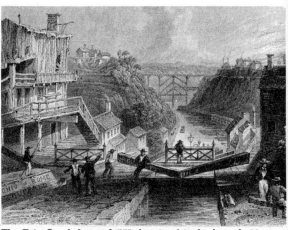

"The Wedding of the Waters," with DeWitt Clinton presiding, married the Great Lakes to the Atlantic. It also cemented economic unity between the Middle West and North.

The Erie Canal dropped 571 feet in altitude through 82 locks. This picture at Lockport, N. Y., shows lock gates of heavy timber and a hotel *(left)* for boat passengers.

"A cent and a half a mile, a mile and a half an hour," summed up the cost and speed of a ride on the Erie Canal. Horses walking along the towpath drew the flat, heavy arks smoothly across the muddy water. Passengers could sit out on top during the day (ducking down frequently for bridges) and sleep on shelflike wooden berths at night.

The first American railroad cars were drawn by horses.

This river steamboat ran from Trenton to Philadelphia.

AMERICANS ON THE MOVE

ONE DAY IN 1825 Governor DeWitt Clinton was towed through the harbor of New York City on a long flat canalboat named *Seneca Chief*. When he reached a point near Sandy Hook he picked up a small keg with a bunghole in the center and poured 5 gallons of water into the Atlantic Ocean. Then he said with great solemnity: "May the God of the heavens and the earth smile propitiously on this work and render it subservient to the best interests of the human race." From other boats around him a great cheer and a roar of cannon boomed out.

This was the official opening of the Erie Canal, which was said to be the largest engineering work ever completed by any government in the world. The Canal was, in effect, an enormous ditch, 363 miles long, 40 feet wide and 4 feet deep. More than half of it was cut through forests or swamps. Its entire cost of $7 million had been borne by New York State, for the Virginians in charge of the Federal Government had declined to contribute. The state raised part of the money by lotteries and part by a $1 tax on all persons who traveled 100 miles or more by steamboat.

Boats on "Clinton's Ditch" traveled at the exact speed that a team of horses would walk, so that a trip from New York to Buffalo took about 5 days. But even so, the Canal offered the fastest and cheapest route for east-west freight, and the most comfortable passenger ride as well. The Canal put New York City far ahead of Philadelphia in trade and population. Boston, Baltimore, even distant Charleston, felt the pinch of its competition. A wave of boosterism and building swept these rival cities and states: Pennsylvania alone built almost 1,000 miles of canals before 1840. Baltimore started the first trans-mountain railroad track, the Baltimore and Ohio. But to most Americans the word "railroad" was still a mystery. "What is a railroad?" asked the editor of a Pennsylvania newspaper. "Perhaps some correspondent can tell us." But no one did.

President Adams, who was more progress-minded than his predecessors, extended the Cumberland Road and wanted to build other national highways. Meanwhile individual Americans were trying other ways to move faster and farther. A Philadelphia mathematician built a flying machine in his back yard and petitioned Congress for the exclusive right to navigate the American skies. A more useful invention was the elliptical steel spring for carriages and stage-coaches, which came into use around 1825. This made possible long cross-country journeys without the awful jolting which had cracked the bones and soured the temper of many a Congressman coming into Washington, D. C.

This American of 1827 satisfied his urge for speedier travel by straddling and shoving a two-wheeled velocipede.

"Jackson is to be President, and you will be HANGED."

This campaign cartoon of 1828 threateningly recalled Jackson's many executions of army deserters and enemies.

JACKSON GETS HIS REVENGE

A LARGE AMOUNT of political mud was slung around the country in the bitter Presidential election of 1828. The opposing candidates, once again, were

John Quincy Adams, who can write,
And Andrew Jackson, who can fight.

Secretary of State Henry Clay, who had been eliminated from the race by the continual din of "corrupt bargain" from the Jackson men, supported Adams. Perhaps he was responsible for circulating the old scandal of Jackson's unlucky marriage—the General, it seems, had married his devoted wife Rachel before she was legally divorced from another man, and then, when he discovered his mistake, had to marry her a second time. The Adams propagandists tried to make this seem like a monstrous act of immorality. One pro-Adams pamphlet asked the question: "Ought a convicted adulteress and her paramour husband to be placed in the highest offices of this free and christian land?"

Clay and the other Adams men were hoping, of course, that Jackson would fly off the handle and try to kill somebody in the midst of the campaign. But for once Old Hickory managed to control himself. "How hard it is to keep the cowhide from these villains," he raged, but his friends talked him out of challenging Clay to a duel. Then came the notorious Coffin Handbills *(opposite page)*, which pictured the General as a raving bully who had killed his own Tennessee militiamen in cold blood. The Jackson men fought back with the ridiculous charge that Adams, while serving as Minister to St. Petersburg, had surrendered a beautiful American servant girl to the lustful Russian Czar.

The voting results were strikingly like those of 1800. Adams carried the same states his father had carried and, like him, lost the election. Jackson swept the old Jeffersonian states (New York, Pennsylvania, and the South) and won all the West as well.

Jackson on a man-eating Western alligator and Adams on the Embargo turtle stage a political tug of war in 1828.

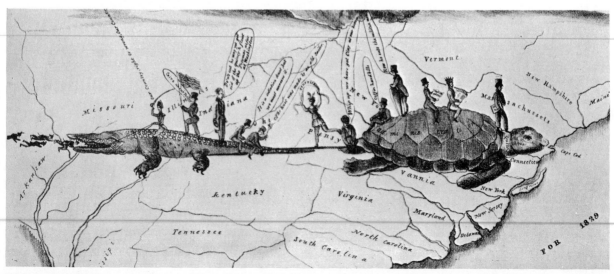

Some Account of some of the Bloody Deeds
OF
GENERAL JACKSON.

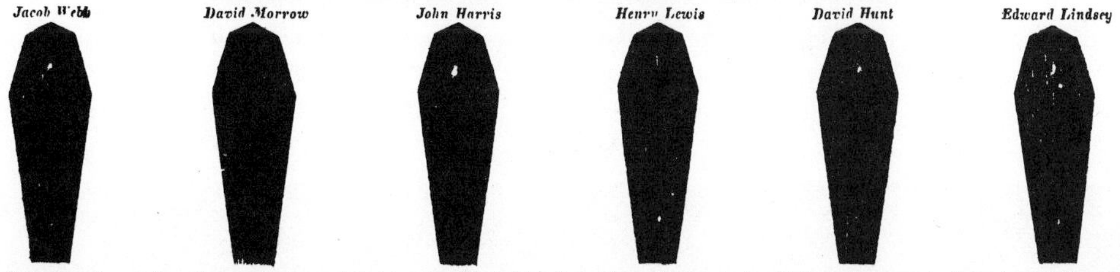

Jacob Webb   David Morrow   John Harris   Henry Lewis   David Hunt   Edward Lindsey

A brief account of the Execution of the Six Militia Men.

As we may soon expect to have the *official* documents in relation to the Six Militia Men, arrested, tried, and put to death, under the orders of General Andrew Jackson, this may not be an improper time to give to the public some of the particulars of their execution, as we have them from—"AN EYE WITNESS," who appeals to Col. Russell, for the truth of every word he relates.

Harris was a Baptist preacher, with a large family. He had hired as a substitute for three months. This was the case with most of them. They were ignorant men, but obstinate in what they believed right, and what they had been told by their officers was right.—They were all sure they could not be kept beyond three months, and they gave up their musquets, and had provisions dealt out to them, from the public stores, before they left the camp.—This confirmed their convictions that they were right and doing what was lawful.

Col. Russel commanded at the execution. The Militia men were brought to the place in a large wagon. The military dispositions being made, Col. Russell rode up to the wagon and ordered the men to descend. Harris was the only one who betrayed feminine weakness. The awfulness of the occasion; his wife and nine children; the parting with his son; and the fear of a quickly approaching ignominious death! quite overcome him, and he sunk in unmanly grief. No feeling of military pride could brace him up.

Col. Russel, doubtless, felt as a man, but he felt also for the pride of the army, and desired to animate the men with fortitude. "You are about to die, said he, by the sentence of a Court Martial—die like men; *like soldiers.* "You have been brave in the field—you have fought well—do no discredit it to your country, or dishonour to the army, or yourselves, by any unmanly fears. Meet your fate with courage." Harris attempted to make some apology for his conduct, but while he spoke, he wept bitterly. The fear of death, the idea that he should never again behold his wife and little ones, and his son weeping near him, had taken such entire possession of his mind that it was impossible he should rally.

Lewis, the gallant Lewis, said in a clear and manly tone, "Colonel, I have served my country well. I love it dearly, and would, if I could, serve it longer and better. I have fought "bravely—*you know* I have, and here "I have a right to say so MYSELF. I

"would not wish to die in this way"—here his voice faltered, and he passed the back of his right hand over his eyes —"I did not expect it: But, I am now "as firm as I have been in battle, and "you shall see that I will die as becomes a soldier, you know I am a "brave man." "Yes, Lewis, said the Colonel, you have always behaved like a brave man." Other sentences were uttered, other declarations were made, and words of comfort spoken, but they were lost on me: my attention, says an Eye Witness, being chiefly directed to Lewis.

Six coffins were ranged as directed, and on each of them knelt one of our condemned American Militia Men—Such a sight was never seen before! I trust to God it never will be seen again! Six soldiers were detailed and drawn up to fire at each man. What an awful duty! Their white caps were drawn over the faces of the unhappy men.—Harris evidently trembled, and I could almost persuade myself that the heart of Lewis was enlarged, and that his bosom rose with manly courage to meet death. The fatal word was given and they all fell.

As we approached the scene of blood and carnage, Lewis gave signs of life; the rest were all dead—he crawled upon his coffin. After the lapse of a few

minutes he said—I give his very words: "Colonel"—the Colonel was close to him—"Colonel, I am not killed, but I am sadly cut and mangled." His body was now examined and it was found that but four balls had wounded him. "Colonel," said he, "did I behave well." "Yes, Lewis"—said the Colonel in the kindest tone of voice—"like a man." "Well sir," said he, "have I not atoned for this offence? *Shall I not live?*" The Colonel was much agitated, and gave orders that the Surgeon should, if possible, preserve his life. They did all that skill and humanity could do—it was all of no avail. Poor Lewis expressed a great desire to live—"not," said he at one time, "that I fear death, "but I would repent me of some sins, "and I desire to live yet a little longer in the world." He suffered inconceivable agony, from his wounds, and died on the fourth day.

Many a soldier has wept over his grave. He was a brave man and much beloved. He suffered twenty deaths. —I have seen the big drops chase each other down his forehead with pain and anguish. There was much sensibility and sympathy throughout the camp.—I would not have, unjustly and unnecessarily, signed this death warrant for all the wealth of all the Indies. The soldiers detailed to shoot Lewis had,

from strong feelings of sympathy, or mistaken humanity failed to shoot him —but four balls had entered his body.

"An Eye Witness" appeals to Col. Russell, who he thinks now lives in Alabama, for the perfect truth of this sketch. He does not fear but the Colonel will keenly recollect and faithfully depict the horrors of the day on which six Americans were shot to death under his command—but not by his orders.

The order bears date the very day after *General Jackson* returned in triumph to New Orleans, and the day before he joyfully went, under triumphal arches, to the Temple of the living God; where, says the historian, "they crowned their adored General with laurels." The order for the execution of these six unhappy men bears date January 22, 1815. His crown of laurels had not yet withered, when blood, the life's blood of his countrymen, of his fellow soldiers, flowed plentifully by his order. May that order and its consequences, sink deep into the hearts of the American people and steel them against him who had no flesh in his obdurate heart; who did not feel for Man; in the midst of Joy and Revelry, almost in the more immediate presence of his Creator, who issued the fatal order to put his fellow creatures to death, and to make their wives & children, widows and orphans.

MOURNFUL TRAGEDY;

Or, the death of Jacob Webb, David Morrow, John Harris, Henry Lewis, David Hunt, & Edward Lindsey—six militia men, who were condemned to die, the sentence approved by Major General Jackson, and by his order the whole six shot.

O! DID you hear that plaintive cry
Borne on the southern breeze?
Saw you JOHN HARRIS earnest pray
For mercy, on his knees?

Low to the earth he bent, and pray'd
For pardon from his chief;
But to his earnest prayer for life
JACKSON, alas! was deaf.

"Spare me"—he said—"I mean no wrong,
"My heart was always true:
"I'or for my count's cause it beat,
"And next, great Chief, for you.

"We thought our time of service out—
"Thought it our right to go:
"We meant to violate no law,
"Nor wish'd to shun the foe.

"Our officers declared that we
"Had but three months to stay;
"We served those three months faithfully,
"Up to the latest day.

"No one suspects intended wrong;
"The judgment only erred—
"In such a case, O noble Chief,
"Let mercy's voice be heard.

"At home an aged mother waits
"To clasp her only son;
"A wife, and little children—this arm
"Alone depend upon.

"Cut me not off from those dear ties;
"So soon from life's young bloom;
"O 'tis a dreadful thing to die,
"And moulder in the tomb!

"Sure mercy in a noble gem
"On every Chieftain's brow
"More sparkling than a diadem—
"O exercise it now.—"

'Twas all in vain, John Harris' pray'r,
'Tis past the soul's belief!
Hard as the flint was Jackson's heart;
He would not grant relief.

He order'd Harris out to die,
And five poor fellows more!
Young, gallant men, in prime of life,
To welter in their gore!!

Methinks I hear the muffled drum,
And see the column move;
Lo here they come—how sad their looks
Farewell to life and love!

See six black coffins rang'd along—
Six graves before them made;
Webb, Lindsey, Harris, Lewis, Hunt,
And Morrow kneeled and prayed.

They kneel'd and pray'd, and tho' of NONE,
And all its dear delights.
The deadly tubes are levell'd now—
The scene my soul affrights!

Sure he will spare! Sure JACKSON yet
Will all reprive but one—
O hark! those shrieks! that cry of death!
The dreadful deed is done!

All six militia men were shot;
And O! it seems to me
A dreadful deed—a bloody act
Of needless cruelty.

A short time before the execution of the militia-men, seven regular soldiers were shot near Nashville, by a band of regulars scarcely sufficient to guard the prisoners.—They were confined in a house, and taken out and executed one at a time, there being scarcely enough men for the purpose of executing and guarding at the same moment. An eighth soldier was to have been executed at the same time. He was a young man, who had deserted one month before his time had expired. General Jackson doomed him to die with the others. He was saved by a writ of habeas corpus from Judge M'Nairy, who fell under Jackson's displeasure for snatching this one victim from his blood-stained hands. If Jackson's army had been at hand, no doubt M'Nairy would have shared the fate of Judge Hall and Judge Fromentin. Capital punishments in an army, are designed for example as well as for penalty; but in this case it was a transaction of horror to peaceful citizens: no army was there to witness the bloody tragedy. He has ever been a man of "blood and carnage."

Do not be startled, gentle reader at the picture before you. It is all true and every body ought to know it. Gen. Jackson having made an assault upon Samuel Jackson, in the streets of Nashville, & the latter not being disposed to stand still and be beaten, stooped down for a stone to defend himself. While in the act of doing so, Gen. Jackson drew the sword from his cane and run it through Samuel Jackson's body, the sword entering his back and coming out of his breast. For this offence an indictment was found against Gen. Jackson, by a grand jury, upon which he was subsequently arraigned and tried. But finding means to persuade the petit jury that he committed the act in self-defence, he was acquitted. Gentle reader, it is for you to say, whether this man, who carries a sword cane, and is willing to run it through the body of any one who may presume to stand in his way, is a fit person to be our President.

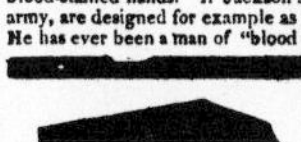

Poor JOHN WOODS, he was a generous hearted, noble fellow as ever lived, who had volunteered in the service of his country. He was on guard one day at Fort Strother—the officer of the guard had permitted him to go to his tent, and snatch a hasty breakfast; whilst disposing of his scanty meal, seated on the ground beside his skillet, an upstart little officer, who was not Woods' equal at home, ordered him to pick up and carry off some bones that lay scattered about the place —Woods refused, and the little officer attempted to compel him. At this instant, Gen. Jackson, having heard the dispute, came out of his tent, and without knowing any thing of the merits of the case, repeatedly vociferated—"Shoot the damn'd rascal!—Shoot the damn'd rascal." For this offence, the unfortunate, the gallant Woods, was tried, condemned and shot. Before his trial, Gen. Jackson used this language to the court-martial. "By the immortal God! if you find him guilty I will not pardon him!" And he kept his promise; though he did offer a pardon provided he would enlist in the regular service—Thus perished as noble a fellow as ever lived, for as trifling an offence as ever took the life of man!!!

On the 27th day of March, 1814, General Jackson had found at an Indian village, at the bend of the Tallapoosie, about 1000 Indians, with their *squaws* and *children,* "running about among their huts." The following is an account of the sanguinary massacre which took place —it is Gen. Jackson's own, and therefore must be received as sufficient evidence against himself. He says :—"DETERMINING TO EXTERMINATE them, I detached Gen. Coffee with the mounted men, and nearly the whole of the Indian force, early in the morning of yesterday, to cross the ensuing the tragedy we speak of, awoke in river about two miles below the encampment, and to surround the bend in such a manner as "five hundred and seventy" fellow creatures, that none of them should escape by attempt to cause, by way of worthy afterpiece, axing to cross the river." The result he then details :—"*Five hundred and fifty seven were* left dead on the Peninsula, and a great number *of them were killed by the horsemen in attempting to cross the river*; it is BELIEVED THAT NO MORE THAN TEN ESCAPED. We continue

to DESTROY many of them who had once *called themselves under the bands of the river,* *until we were prevented by the night.* THIS MORNING WE KILLED 16 WHICH HAD BEEN CONCEALED."

We ask you to pause and reflect that the above tragic narration of cold-blooded and merciless cruelty, is taken from an official communication made by General Andrew Jackson.

The General, after sleeping (with what composure, we cannot say) thro' the night succeeding we killed sixteen which had been concealed"—and the man who acts and speaks thus; who has half as much blood upon his conscience, as he has upon his hands,—he, forsooth, is to be called the peer and *like* of Washington, the happy warrior,—

"he
Whom every man at arms could wish to be!"

But it is time to have done with the unpleasant subject. We will observe in addition to the details already given, that the village was burnt, and several women and children killed. In conclusion, we ask our fellow citizens, whether Genl. Jackson, though he has contributed largely to the military reputation of our country, has not done enough to disqualify him, in the eyes of the people as virtuous as they are free, for the office he seeks at their hands.

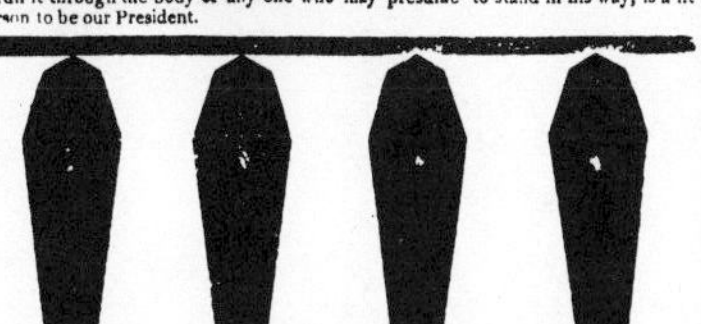

Gen. Jackson, detailing his progress among the Indians, in the course of which men, WOMEN and CHILDREN, were indiscriminately "exterminated," their towns burnt and their country laid waste, with the utmost complacency and *sang froid,* says, in his letter dated, "Camp before St. Marks, April 9, 1818"—"Capt. M'Ever having hoisted English colours on board of his boats, *Francis the Prophet,* Hocomochemotehe and *two others,* were *decoyed* on board. *These have been hung to-day*;" Reader, mark the perfect indifference with which Gen. Jackson, hangs or stabs his fellow beings, with or without trial, and the more than callous, aye, even exulting composure, with which he detains his horrid and bloody deeds! If the Indians, according to the customs of their nation, put to death a prisoner, all the feelings of our nature rise into indignation against them. With what feelings then should we contemplate the *decoying* and the cold-blooded murder of prisoners, by a civilized man, in the face of the laws and customs of his country!

FRANKLIN, Tenn. September 10, 1813.

A difference which had been for some months brewing between Gen. Jackson and myself, produced on Saturday, the 4th inst. in the town of Nashville, the most outrageous affray ever witnessed in a civilized country. In communicating the affair to my friends and fellow-citizens, I limit myself to the statement of a few leading facts, the truth of which I am ready to establish by judicial proofs.

1. That myself and my brother, Jesse Benton, arriving in Nashville on the morning of the affray, and knowing of General Jackson's threats, went and took lodgings in a different house from the one in which he staid, on purpose to avoid him.

2. That the General and some of his friends came the house where we had put up, and commenced the attack by levelling a pistol at me, when I had no weapon drawn, and advancing upon me at a quick pace, without giving me time to draw one.

3. That seeing this, my brother fired upon General Jackson, when he had got within eight or ten feet of me.

4. That four other pistols were fired in quick succession; one by me and by me at the General; and one by Col. Coffee at me. In the course of this firing, General Jackson was brought to the ground; but received no hurt.

5. That daggers were then drawn. Col. Coffee and Mr. Alexander Donaldson made at me, and gave me five slight wounds. Captain Hammond and Mr. Stokeley Hays engaged my brother, who being still weak from the effect of a severe wound he had lately received in a duel, was not able to resist two men. They got him down; and while Capt. Hammond beat him on the head to make him lie still, Mr. Hays attempted to stab him, and wounded him in both arms, as he lay on his back parrying the thrusts

with his naked hands. From this situation a generous hearted citizen of Nashville, Mr. Sommer, relieved him. Before he came to the ground, my brother clapped a pistol to the breast of Mr. Hays, to blow him through, but it missed fire.

6. My own and my brother's pistols carried two balls each; for it was our intention, if driven to arms, to have no child's play. The pistols fired at me were so near that the blaze of the muzzle of one of them burnt the sleeve of my coat, and the other aimed at my head at a little more than arms length from it.

7. Capt. Carroll was to have taken part in the affray, but was absent by the permission of General Jackson, as he has proved by the General's certificate, a certificate which reflects I know not whether less honor upon the General or upon the Captain.

8. That this attack was made upon me in the house where the Judge of the District, Mr. Searcy, had his lodgings! Nor has the civil authority yet taken cognizance of this horrible outrage.

These facts are sufficient to fix the public opinion. For my own part, I think it scandalous that such things should take place at any time; but particularly so at the present moment, when the public service requires the aid of all its citizens.—As for the name of *courage,* God forbid that I should ever attempt to gain it by becoming a bully.—Those who know me, know full well that I would give a thousand times more for the reputation of Croghan in defending his post, than I would for the reputation of all the duellists and gladiators that ever appeared upon the face of the earth.

THOMAS HART BENTON, Lieut. Col. 39th Infantry.
And now a member of the Senate of the United States.

Thomas Jefferson died on the fiftieth anniversary of independence, July 4, 1826. The previous year, aged 82, he let the sculptor John Browere coat his head with plaster and make the life mask below. The plaster dried too quickly and had to be removed with chisel and mallet, almost tearing off his ears.

CHAPTER 3

THE

JACKSON

DEMOCRATS

ANDREW JACKSON rode into the White House on a wave of protest votes. In 1824 only 356,038 Americans had voted for President; in 1828 the number swelled to 1,155,340—an increase of 224 per cent. What had caused this outpouring?

It was, to a large extent, the climax of a struggle which had been going on for 40 years between the people and their various state legislatures. Under the old Federalist scheme of things no individual citizen was supposed to vote for President; the legislatures met every four years and named each state's Presidential electors. But states where the Federalists were not in control, like Virginia, granted popular suffrage as early as 1789. Most of the new Western states permitted it as soon as they were admitted. Elsewhere the issue was fought out, over and over, in state elections, and in conventions to draft new state constitutions.

In 1828, for the Jackson-Adams contest, New York, Vermont, Georgia, and Louisiana allowed their citizens to vote for President for the first time. Only two of the older legislatures—Delaware and South Carolina—still clung to their Federalist prerogative, and Delaware yielded in 1832.

This long battle for the simple right to vote gave many ordinary Americans the feeling that there was something fraudulent about the whole political system. They blamed whichever group was in power, and during the 1820's their suspicions helped to split the Republican party into hostile fragments.

One large fragment, which included most of the new voters, rallied around Jackson, who had the extra advantage of being the nation's foremost military hero. This formidable bloc of voters accepted and even gloried in the name of Democrats. The General himself praised the once-horrid word—he said that he was for "the Democracy of Numbers" as against "the moneyed aristocracy" of the few. With his powerful sanction "democracy" became an indispensable word in American politics.

The opposition, led by Henry Clay, took the more traditional name of National Republicans. They stood for all the things that Jackson disliked and fought: government aid to banks and business, increased powers for the Federal Government, federal spending for local improvements. But they too claimed descent from the "pure Republican principles" of Jefferson—which had, as a matter of fact, been greatly modified by Jefferson's successors.

During Jackson's Presidency these two parties met head-on in the most spectacular political clash since the days of Hamilton and Jefferson: the fight to recharter the Bank of the United States. The Bank was a privately owned corporation which was swimming in money and politics. It kept Daniel Webster and lesser statesmen on its payroll, subsidized newspapers all over the country, and maintained the most aggressive lobby in Washington. Through special privileges granted to it by the Madison Administration, it held a virtual monopoly of American and foreign credit transactions. Jackson did not like the way the Bank behaved, and he thought it was unconstitutional besides. When Congress approved a new Bank charter in 1832 the President rejected it in a veto message which expressed in memorable words the philosophy of his adherents:

"It is to be regretted that the rich and powerful too often bend the acts of government to their selfish purposes. . . . When the laws undertake . . . to make the rich richer and the potent more powerful, the humble members of society—the farmers, mechanics, and laborers—who have neither the time nor the means of securing like favors to themselves, have a right to complain. . . . If we cannot at once . . . make our Government what it ought to be, we can at least take a stand against all new grants of monopolies and exclusive privileges, against any prostitution of our Government to the advancement of the few at the expense of the many. . . ."

A few days before writing this Jackson told Martin Van Buren, "The bank, Mr. Van Buren, is trying to kill me, *but I will kill it.*"

President Jackson in a white beaver hat and steel-rimmed
spectacles was painted by his close friend, Ralph Earl.

OLD HICKORY TAKES OVER

Mrs. Andrew Jackson

Andrew Jackson *(foreground)* lost his mother, two brothers, and South Carolina home during the Revolution.

Taken prisoner at 14, Jackson *(center)* refused to black a British officer's boots even when struck with a sword.

The Hermitage, near Nashville, was Jackson's beloved plantation home. Here he returned after all his battles.

A typical small-town crowd inspects the President-elect as he journeys to Washington for his inauguration in 1829.

THE NEW DEMOCRATIC President was 62, lean and taut, with the look of a frontier fighting man and the manners of a frontier aristocrat. His soldiers in 1812 had nicknamed him "Old Hickory," after the toughest thing they could think of. His head, under the fountain-shaped crest of white hair, still bore the ugly scar inflicted by a British sword in 1781. One bullet from an old duel was lodged in his chest, near the heart. Another rested in a bone of his left arm.

He could not spell words very well, but he had been a successful lawyer and judge and a wealthy cotton planter. He owned slaves and believed in the slavery system. His political ideas were like the cane he carried—straight up and down, with a sharp steel sword inside. His actions sprang from an intense— even fanatical—patriotism, a razor-edged sense of honor, and an instinctive belief in the American common man.

He was haggard and ill when he arrived in Washington in February 1829. His wife had died since the election—she was hounded to death, he thought, by the slanderous lies of his political opponents. He refused to make a courtesy call on President Adams, and grimly took the oath of office from the aged Federalist Chief Justice, John Marshall, who was just as grim. Then he rode to the White House on horseback, at the head of a happy mob of partisans who tore down the curtains, smashed glasses, climbed over the tapestried chairs in muddy boots, and smeared the carpets with liquor and food. The capital had never seen the like of this Democratic debacle. Jackson fled through a back door and somebody put tubs of punch on the lawn to draw the hilarious Democrats outside, where they dispersed when the tubs were empty.

Amos Kendall, a semi-invalid, was Jackson's confidant and "thinking machine."

"TO THE VICTOR

THE SCRAMBLE for cakes and wine at Jackson's inauguration party was soon surpassed by a fiercer scramble for jobs. The government offices were filled with Republican hacks who had grown old, slovenly, and careless with public funds. They had all supported Adams, and it was easy to persuade Andrew Jackson that they were a treacherous crew and ought to be replaced. While the Democratic newspapers kept up cries of "Cleanse the Augean stable!" and "The Barnacles Shall Be Scraped Clean from the Ship of State!" a steady procession of deserving Jacksonians filed into office.

The opposition shrieked that this was "tyranny," "proscription," a new "reign of terror." They found a better name for it after Senator William L. Marcy, a New York Democrat, rose to defend his administration colleagues. "They see nothing wrong," he blandly said, "in the rule, that to the VICTOR belongs the spoils of the ENEMY." After that Jackson's name was linked forever with the "spoils system."

The headquarters for spoils and everything else in the Government was at the White House, where the President usually lounged before a fireplace in his shirt sleeves, smoking a corn-cob pipe. Here the famous "Kitchen Cabinet" conferred with him and decided matters of state. This inner circle of advisers was the first Presidential brain trust, and wielded far more influence than the regular Cabinet. Its smartest members were Amos Kendall, a former Kentucky newspaper editor who wrote many Jackson messages, and Martin Van Buren, boss of the smoothly running Democratic machine of New York State, who also happened to be Secretary of State. Another White House intimate was Major John H. Eaton of Tennessee, who had been Jackson's colleague in the Army and the Senate. Eaton was not too bright, but he had just married a lively young widow, and wished to embark on a social career in the capital. Jackson obliged him by

Mrs. Emily Donelson, Jackson's niece and hostess, fled from the White House when her uncle asked her to be nice to Peggy Eaton.

Mrs. John C. Calhoun led the social boycott against Peggy Eaton, and helped ruin her husband's chances of becoming President.

BELONGS THE SPOILS"

making him Secretary of War.

This appointment touched off a tempest of petticoat politics which was too destructive to be funny. Eaton's bride was the celebrated (or notorious) Peggy O'Neale Timberlake, an innkeeper's daughter of much beauty and boldness. Her whims had already driven one man to suicide and her previous husband to a mysterious death at sea. When Peggy Eaton realized that other Washington wives would not entertain her because of her reputation, she jostled against them at formal dinner parties, and got into a fight with Jackson's pretty niece over a bottle of Cologne water.

The gossip quickly made the rounds that Peggy had allowed Eaton to woo her while her first husband was alive, that she had traveled to New York with him on several occasions, and that she had suffered a timely miscarriage as the result of a fall. This kind of talk scraped deep wounds in Andrew Jackson's chivalrous soul. He begged the other members of his Cabinet to intercede with their wives—but when he gave a White House banquet the tension between Peggy and the other ladies was so obvious that nobody had a good time. He called a special session of the Cabinet and refuted, point by point, and date by date, the charges against her honor. Still the ladies refused to have anything to do with her. While the country snickered over his dilemma, Old Hickory's anger blazed forth. He kicked out his whole Cabinet and appointed a new one.

The big loser by this was Vice President John C. Calhoun, whose wife had led the anti-Peggy forces. Calhoun had been the logical No. 2 man among the Democrats, but now the crafty Van Buren moved up and took his place. On a morning horseback ride with the President, "Little Van" had suggested the scheme for ending the Cabinet crisis by ending the Cabinet. He lost his own place in the State Department, but henceforth he was Jackson's most trusted adviser.

The scandalous past of Peggy Eaton *(center)* wrecked Jackson's first Cabinet.

The only Cabinet meeting ever held to discuss a woman's virtue is satirized in this cartoon. Peggy (who did not attend the real meeting) is pictured as a ballet dancer. Van Buren peers through a lorgnette. Jackson's verdict: "She is as chaste as a virgin!"

Robert Young Hayne, Senator from South Carolina, fronted for Calhoun in the Congressional debates on nullification.

THE CHIEF NULLIFIER

was the stern spokesman for the slave-and-cotton kingdom of the South, Vice President John C. Calhoun *(right)*. At a Jefferson birthday banquet in 1830 Calhoun and Jackson met face to face on this issue, in a scene which thrilled the nation. The dinner was under way and the diners had already heard a long string of toasts when the President was called upon. He rose and, looking straight at Calhoun, said in a commanding voice: "Our Union: It must be preserved!" Abruptly the clatter of conversation and glasses ceased; everyone stood and drank. Calhoun's hand was shaking so that the yellow wine ran down the side of his glass. In a hesitating tone he offered the next toast: "The Union, next to our liberty, most dear!" and then added a little speech: "May we all remember that it can only be preserved by respecting the rights of the States and by distributing equally the benefits and burdens of the Union." But it was Jackson's sharp words that rang in the nation's ears the next day, and for a long time afterward.

"I WILL HANG JOHN C. CALHOUN!"

RUMBLING OUT of a routine Senate debate in the first winter of Jackson's Presidency, an old and terrifying issue suddenly confronted the nation. Could a state, as an individual member of the Federal Union, nullify the Union's laws within its own territory? In South Carolina, where the cotton planters writhed under Clay's new "Tariff of Abominations," a determined drive for nullification was already under way. As a first step the nullifiers planned to stop the collecting of federal duties at Charleston.

In the Senate an ardent South Carolinian named Robert Y. Hayne expounded the nullification doctrine. When Hayne attacked the North, and dragged up spiteful memories of the Hartford Convention, Senator Daniel Webster of Massachusetts rose to reply. For two days the giant of New England hurled his thunderbolts, crushing Hayne under a sheer weight of eloquence. But everyone, including Andrew Jackson, knew that Hayne was only a figurehead, and that the leader of the nullifiers was Vice President Calhoun. When South Carolina finally passed an ordinance of nullification Jackson prepared to call out 35,000 troops and lead them against his native state himself. As a first step, he announced, he would try Calhoun for treason and, if convicted, "hang him as high as Haman." When Calhoun heard this he trembled and turned pale. Henry Clay, the Great Pacificator, arranged a compromise on the tariff, and South Carolina took back her nullification law.

Years later, when asked if he had any regrets in his life, Andrew Jackson admitted that he had **two:** that he had been unable to shoot Henry Clay, or to hang John C. Calhoun.

WEBSTER REPLIES TO HAYNE AND DEFENDS THE UNION

Daniel Webster's second speech in reply to Senator Hayne, delivered on January 26, 1830, has been called the greatest recorded American oration. Webster first replied at length to Hayne's aspersions against New England and demolished with ponderous logic the constitutional argument for nullification. Then he closed with his famous peroration to the Union:

I profess, Sir, in my career hitherto, to have kept steadily in view the prosperity and honor of the whole country, and the preservation of our Federal Union. It is to that Union we owe our safety at home, and our consideration and dignity abroad. It is to that Union that we are chiefly indebted for whatever makes us most proud of our country.

That Union we reached only by the discipline of our virtues in the severe school of adversity. It had its origin in the necessities of disordered finance, prostrate commerce, and ruined credit. Under its benign influences, these great interests immediately awoke, as from the dead, and sprang forth with newness of life. Every year of its duration has teemed with fresh proofs of its utility and its blessings; and although our territory has stretched out wider and wider, and our population spread farther and farther, they have not outrun its protection or its benefits. It has been to us all a copious fountain of national, social, and personal happiness.

I have not allowed myself, Sir, to look beyond the Union, to see what might lie hidden in the dark recess behind. I have not coolly weighed the chances of preserving liberty when the bonds that unite us together shall be broken asunder. I have not accustomed myself to hang over the precipice of disunion, to see whether, with my short sight, I can fathom the depth of the abyss below; nor could I regard him as a safe counselor in the affairs of this Government, whose thoughts should be mainly bent on considering, not how the Union may be best preserved, but how tolerable might be the condition of the people when it should be broken up and destroyed.

While the Union lasts we have high, exciting, gratifying prospects spread out before us, for us and our children. Beyond that I seek not to penetrate the veil.

God grant that in my day at least that curtain may not rise! God grant that on my vision never may be opened what lies behind! When my eyes shall be turned to behold for the last time the sun in the heavens, may I not see him shining on the broken and dishonored fragments of a once glorious Union; on States dissevered, discordant, belligerent; on a land rent with civil feuds, or drenched, it may be, in fraternal blood!

Let their last feeble and lingering glance rather behold the gorgeous ensign of the Republic, now known and honored throughout the earth, still full high advanced, its arms and trophies streaming in their original lustre, not a stripe erased or polluted, not a single star obscured, bearing for its motto, no such miserable interrogatory as "What is all this worth?" nor those other words of delusion and folly, "Liberty first and Union afterward;" but everywhere, spread all over in characters of living light, blazing on all its ample folds, as they float over the sea and over the land, and in every wind under the whole heavens, that other sentiment, dear to every true American heart,—Liberty *and* Union, now and forever, one and inseparable!

Webster's reply to Hayne inspired this famous painting by George Peter Alexander Healy. The setting is the little semicircular chamber where the Senate met until 1860. The gallery is thronged with lady visitors, including the second Mrs. Daniel Webster, a bride of six weeks. The familiar figure of Webster, his massive body thrust forward, one hand clenched upon his desk, dominates the scene. For this triumphant occasion he is wearing a dark blue swallow-tailed coat with brass buttons, a buff waistcoat, and

a white cravat. Senator Hayne, who provoked the torrent, is seated at left center, just to the right of an old Senator with long gray curls. Standing with his back to a pillar in the rear is Senator Thomas Hart Benton of Missouri, who once fired two bullets at Andrew Jackson during a street brawl in Nashville. Vice President Calhoun leans attentively over his desk at far left. Soon after this Calhoun quit the Vice Presidency and was elected to the Senate for the sole purpose of trying to answer Webster.

"The Downfall of Mother Bank" shows the effect of Jackson's removal of the government deposits. "Nick" Biddle *(with horns)* and his newspaper hirelings scurry for their lives. Jack Downing, symbolizing the people, hurrahs.

JACKSON KILLS THE BANK

THE BANK OF THE UNITED STATES was a rich and powerful institution when Jackson entered the White House. By the end of his first term it was the tumbling wreck, the deathly sick old lady, the thrashing dragon shown in these three cartoons. The American people watched this transformation in breathless suspense. At first they applauded the President in his battle with the "money power." But toward the finish they felt as though they were being dragged through a ghastly dream. In these cartoons their conflicting emotions are expressed by Major Jack Downing, a comic philosopher who stands beside Jackson and speaks the mind of the man in the street.

The Bank began the fight with a monopoly of government deposits, totaling nearly $10 million, and a capitalization of $35 million. Its discount activities ran to $40 million a year, its profits as high as $11½ million. Its president was Nicholas Biddle, a Philadelphia patrician who smiled condescendingly on the old backwoodsman in the White House. "As to mere power," Biddle once confided, "I have been for years in the daily exercise of more personal authority than any President."

It was the arrogant Biddle who insisted on an early showdown. The Bank's charter did not expire until 1836, and Jackson was willing to wait until then. But in 1832 Biddle applied to Congress for a new 15-year charter with the same monopoly features the Bank had long enjoyed. Henry Clay, who was running against Jackson for President that year, seized upon this as a campaign issue. When the charter was granted by Congress, and Jackson vetoed it in his famous "poor against the rich" message, Biddle could scarcely restrain his glee. "As to the Veto message I am delighted with it," he wrote to Clay. "It has all the fury of a chained panther biting the bars of his cage. It is really a manifesto of anarchy." He predicted—rather naïvely—that the voters would punish the President for his presumption. The Bank poured more money into Clay's campaign than had ever been spent on a Presidential election.

In the White House Old Hickory stiffened. After the election was over and Clay had been soundly beaten, Jackson issued an order withdrawing all government deposits from the "monster." That sealed the Bank's doom, but it died slowly and painfully, dragging down the country's credit by a series of revengeful measures.

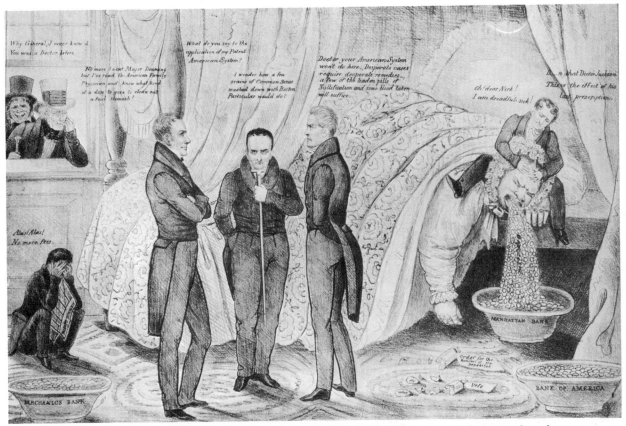

"The Doctors Puzzled" shows Mother Bank disgorging the Government's funds into smaller banks. Biddle sits on her neck, while Clay, Webster, and Calhoun consult on the sad case. Jackson and Downing peek through the window.

"Political Quixotism" shows Jackson as the victim of an anti-Bank nightmare. Downing, representing the public, tries to haul him back to bed by his suspenders. This cartoon appeared when people were tired of the Bank war.

THE REIGN OF

"King Andrew the First," a typical opposition cartoon, shows Jackson trampling on the Constitution and federal court decisions. Once when the Supreme Court handed down a decision he didn't like, Jackson declared: "John Marshall has made his decision, now let him enforce it."

JACKSON had to remove two Secretaries of the Treasury before he found one who would carry out his order to withdraw the government deposits. Meanwhile the Bank's champions raised a nation-wide hue and cry against "King Andrew the First." Tyrant, usurper, dictator, destroyer of the liberties of his country, detestable, vain, ignorant, malignant—these were a few of the epithets hurled at the man in the White House. Reports of genuine business distress— often caused by the dying Bank's deliberate policy— were magnified in the Bank's kept press. In the Senate, where Martin Van Buren had succeeded Calhoun in the Vice President's chair, a magnificent piece of political play-acting took place. Henry Clay had the floor. With touching pathos he begged Van Buren to intercede and change the President's "fatal" course.

"Depict to him," he begged, "the heart-rending wretchedness of thousands of the working classes cast out of employment. Tell him of the tears of helpless widows, no longer able to earn their bread, and of unclad and unfed orphans who have been driven, by his policy, out of the busy pursuits in which

Senator John C. Calhoun (right) was "the cast-iron man" of Congress in the middle 1830's. Plunged into icy bitterness by his defeat during the nullification crisis, Calhoun now charged that Jackson had made himself a Caesar, striving "to choke and stifle the voice of American liberty."

KING ANDREW

but yesterday they were gaining an honest liveli-
hood. . . ." Van Buren sat quietly until Clay was all
through. Then, without batting an eye, he destroyed
the whole effect by strolling over to Clay's desk and
borrowing a pinch of snuff.

In March 1834, under Clay's prodding, the Senate
passed a resolution of censure which charged that
the President had "assumed upon himself authority
and power not conferred by the Constitution and
laws, but in derogation of both." This was an unprecedented action, and Jackson regarded it as a grave
reflection on his honor. Senator Tom Benton of Missouri, who had become Jackson's ardent disciple
after trying to kill him in a free-for-all, fought for
three years to erase the resolution from the Senate
journal. In 1837 Benton finally succeeded—a thick
black line was drawn around the record of Clay's
resolution, and the word "expunged" was written
across it. After eight years of battling with the giants
of American finance and politics, "King Andrew"
was still their master when he quit the Presidency
and retired to the Hermitage.

"Symptoms of a Locked Jaw" shows Clay sewing up Jackson's mouth after the passage of the famous censure resolution. Jackson had sent a thundering protest message to
the Senate and Clay prevented it from being recorded. But
Old Hickory was too tough for this kind of needlework.

Senator Thomas Hart ("Old Bullion") Benton *(left)*
fought Jackson's battles in the Senate. Benton's special
hobby was getting rid of "shinplaster" paper money.
When the Treasury, at his insistence, issued new gold coins
in 1834 the people called them "Benton's mint drops."

M.—" Murder! Murder! ——"
L.—" Nic, gag him! Stuff a 'kerchief down his throat, for ——'s sake."
N.—" I'll fix him," [*Crams a handkerchief into his mouth.*]—" Lend a hand, Colonel."

K.—" There comes the wretch, bound, hoodwinked, and under guard."
L.—" Hold him up, Sheriff."
M.—" Do, for mercy, give me a little water, before I choke."
S.—" Yes, yes; silence! you shall have some water."

M.—" Gentlemen, I am your prisoner; show your magna——"
L.—" Do you feel that? [*Pushing against Morgan's breast with a pistol.*] Another word, and I will shoot you."

THE ENEMIES OF MASONRY

THE ANTI-MASONIC PARTY was a political nuisance which grew to serious proportions during Jackson's Presidency. It had started back in 1826, after the unsolved disappearance of William Morgan, a brick-and-stone mason of Batavia, New York. Morgan was a Royal Arch Mason who got into debt and decided to make some money by publishing a book describing secret Masonic rituals. He took out a copyright for the book, but before it appeared in print he vanished. The popular belief was that he was whisked away in a carriage and thrown into the Niagara River by the Masons. His body was never found.

This weird episode led to a national outcry against the Masons—who denied everything—and the organization of a separate political party to agitate for their suppression. In the early 1830's the Anti-Masons were thick as hornets in the rural "Yankee Belt," from Maine to the Ohio Western Reserve. In Pennsylvania their fiery leader was Thaddeus Stevens of Gettysburg, who made a speech denouncing the Masonic Grand Lodge as "a chartered iniquity, within whose jaws are crushed the bones of immortal men, and whose mouth is continually reeking with human blood, and spitting forth human gore." The Masons themselves, said Stevens, were a "feeble band of lowly reptiles" who shunned the light and retired to "midnight dens" to perpetrate their "blasphemies."

The Anti-Masons were the first American party to hold a Presidential nominating convention, at Baltimore, in September 1831. Strangely enough, their candidate, William Wirt, was a Mason. In 1832 Wirt and the Anti-Mason ticket carried Vermont, and ran ahead of Jackson in Massachusetts.

These woodcuts from the *Anti-Masonic Almanac* for 1833 show the alleged fate of William Morgan at the hands of the Masons. In the bottom picture Morgan, blindfolded, is about to be pushed into the river. His widow later became one of the wives of Joseph Smith, the Mormon Prophet. At right, the Masons celebrate Morgan's death.

H.—" The enemies of Masonry—may they find a grave, six feet deep and six feet long, due east and west."

The message of this crude Workie cartoon could be grasped by the most untaught mechanic of the 1830's. While the devil and the millionaire conspire to buy up an election, the honest workingman fights back with his ballot.

THE REVOLT OF THE WORKIES

IN 1829 ANOTHER new political party polled 5,600 votes in New York City and elected the president of the Carpenters' Union to the state assembly. The official name of the new organization was the Working Men's Party, and its members were commonly called the "Workies." Aided by Jackson's obvious bias toward the common man, the Workies won some modest victories in industrial centers like Philadelphia, Albany, and New London. Among their "radical" demands were a ten-hour day for factory workers, abolition of imprisonment for debt, and more and better public schools for their children. Their votes were mostly recruited from the small and struggling trade-unions.

This debut of the American labor movement in politics was greeted with hysterical abuse by the conservative newspapers, whose editors called the Workies the "Infidel Party," the "Dirty Shirt Party,"

a "ring-streaked and speckled rabble." Their leaders, said the New York *Commercial Advertiser*, were "lost to society, to earth and to heaven, godless and hopeless," and deserved nothing better than to "die like ravenous wild beasts, hunted down without pity." The Workies' propaganda was also violent. "Great wealth," said one Workie philosopher, "ought to be taken away from its possessors on the same principle that a sword or a pistol may be wrested from a robber."

The Working Men's party faded rather quickly from the national scene. Most of the Workies joined the left wing of Jackson's Democracy, and sang in the campaign of 1834:

Mechanics, Carters, Laborers
  Must form a close connection
And show the rich Aristocrats
  Their powers at this election. . . .

THE YANKEE

EVER SINCE the beginning of the Government a movement for gradual emancipation of the Negro slaves had been winning converts in the South. Washington, Jefferson, Clay, even John Randolph, the high priest of Southern rights, had favored it. They were willing to have a tiny trickle of blacks purchase their freedom, or receive it from benevolent masters, provided there was no interference with the touchy institution of slave "property."

But the Puritan conscience of the North had now grown tired of waiting. At least 300 slaves were born each year for every one that was freed. In 1831, from the Yankee capital of Boston, a disturbing new voice was heard. William Lloyd Garrison, writing in the first number of his weekly paper, the *Liberator*, demanded the total, unconditional, immediate abolition of American slavery. "On this subject," wrote Garrison, "I do not wish to think, or speak, or write, with moderation. No! No! Tell a man whose house is on fire, to give a moderate alarm; tell him to moderately rescue his wife from the hands of the ravisher ... but urge me not to use moderation in a cause like

William Lloyd Garrison called the American Constitution "an agreement with hell" because it sanctioned slavery.

This slave store in New Orleans specialized in domestic servants, who stood around outside wearing their best clothes and trying to attract buyers. The men in the silk hats at left sold for between $600 and $800 each.

ABOLITIONISTS

the present. I am in earnest—I will not equivocate—
I will not excuse—I will not retreat a single inch—
AND I WILL BE HEARD."

Later that same year the Nat Turner slave insurrection broke out in Virginia, causing the senseless
slaughter of 55 whites and more than 100 blacks.
Although such revolts were nothing new, the whole
South blamed this one on Garrison. A virtual state
of siege went up in the Southern states: Garrison's
paper was banned and burned in the streets; a wave
of lynchings swept the back country; white Northerners were beaten; and all discussion of slavery
was forbidden, even in the national Capitol. When
the abolitionists sent in the Declaration of Independence as a petition to Congress, the Southern members refused to allow it to be read.

In the North, too, the abolitionists were treated
as dangerous fanatics. Their meeting places were
burned by mobs, Garrison himself was beaten on a
Boston street, and his disciples were murdered. The
abolition issue was too hot for the orthodox politicians of the 1930's, so it was left to mob violence.

Prime field hands like these sugar-cane cutters were the
most valuable slaves, selling for as high as $1,300 apiece.

THE FIRST MARTYR

of the abolitionists was the Reverend Elijah Parish
Lovejoy, 35, of Alton, Illinois, whose printing press
is pictured above, in the hands of a proslavery mob.
Lovejoy was born in Maine, educated at Waterville
College, and settled in Alton as a Presbyterian minister and as editor of the Alton *Observer.* In an editorial dated July 20, 1837, he gave the following
concise statement of the abolitionist creed:

"Abolitionists hold that 'all men are born free and
equal, endowed by their Creator with certain inalienable rights, among which are life, LIBERTY, and the
pursuit of happiness.'

"They do not believe that these rights are abro-
gated, or at all modified by the colour of the skin,
but that they extend alike to every individual of the
human family.

"As the above-mentioned rights are in their nature
inalienable, it is not possible that one man can
convert another into a piece of property, thus at once
annihilating all his personal rights, without the most
flagrant injustice and usurpation. . . .

"Abolitionists, therefore, hold American Slavery
to be a *wrong,* a legalized system of inconceivable
injustice, and a SIN . . . against God. . . ."

Some time after he published this, the Reverend
Lovejoy was cornered in his newspaper office by a
drunken "posse" who dumped his press into the Mississippi River and fired the building *(below).* Lovejoy was shot five times with rifle balls. The next day,
as his corpse was carried through the streets, the
slavery men stood on the sidewalks and jeered.

THE TEXANS
AT THE ALAMO

Texas was a province of Mexico until the American settlers there proclaimed their independence in 1835. At dawn on March 6, 1836, an invading army of 3,000 Mexicans wiped out 183 Texans in an old Spanish mission called the Alamo. The Texas wounded were shot by order of General Antonio

Lopez de Santa Ana. All the dead bodies were then stripped, thrown into a pile, and burned. Among them were James Bowie, inventor of the bowie knife, and Davy Crockett, the famous frontiersman and ex-Congressman from Tennessee. Six weeks later the Texans under their great leader, Sam Houston, inflicted a shattering revenge at the Battle of San Jacinto. Santa Ana was taken prisoner, his army fled back across the Rio Grande, and the Lone Star flag waved in triumph over the free Republic of Texas. But the Texans—and their kinsmen in the United States—never forgot the Alamo.

President Martin Van Buren inaugurated a ten-hour day on federal public works.

LITTLE VAN AND HIS HARD TIMES

No PRESIDENT ever had so many revealing nicknames as Martin Van Buren—he was the "Flying Dutchman," the "Red Fox of Kinderhook," the "Little Magician," the "American Talleyrand." He "rowed to his object with muffled oars," in the phrase of John Randolph. He was the smartest out-and-out politician of the Democratic party. His enemies said he was so vain that he wore the carpet threadbare in front of his study mirror. In 1837, with Jackson's powerful blessing, he moved into the White House.

But Little Van was doomed to suffer the full brunt of another financial panic which soon broke loose in Wall Street as the result of a wild land- and stock-speculation boom. The businessmen blamed the depression of 1837-1840 on Jackson's anti-Bank policy, while the Democrats blamed Nick Biddle. The hard times split the Democratic party: one night in Tammany Hall there was a fight in which the conservatives turned off the gaslights and the left-wingers seized control at a meeting lit by locofoco friction matches. Thereafter the radical Democrats, who wanted to abolish banks and the paper-money system, were called "Locofocos."

While the panic was at its peak a fresh disaster struck the administration. Samuel Swartwout, the Tammany collector of the port of New York, ran off to Europe after stealing $1,225,705.69 from the Government. A Congressional committee absolved Van Buren from any personal blame. But the Swartwout affair led to new outbursts against the Democrats and their spoils system.

"The Times" depicts the depression of 1837. Wives are begging and sleeping in the street, jobless workmen go without shoes *(right)*, and a broken bank draws a crowd *(rear)*.

"A Select Committee of Enquiry Hard At Work" shows Democratic Congressmen white-washing Van Buren in the Swartwout investigation. This was the opposition viewpoint.

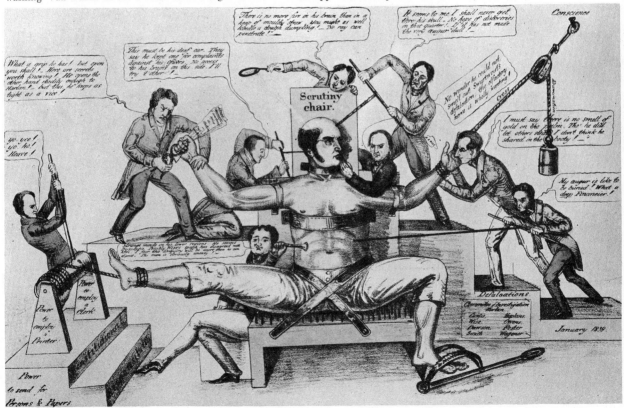

"Worse Than a Spanish Inquisition" gives a Democratic view of the same investigation. The committee has Van Buren strapped to a torture seat and is putting the screws to him.

"I had rather be right than be President," said Henry Clay in 1839. But Americans were skeptical. Clay and the rest of Jackson's old foes were trembling with desire to take over the White House and its luxuries, including the 20 East Room spittoons which Old Hickory had bought for $12.50 each.

CHAPTER 4

THE UPS AND DOWNS OF THE WHIGS

THE POLITICAL CAMPAIGN of 1840 began early in the year when Congressman Charles Ogle of Pennsylvania turned the ancient charge of White House extravagance against President Van Buren. Let us, he urged in a famous speech, make a trip to the Executive Mansion and its "Blue Elliptical Saloon"—let us see how Little Van lives in luxury while Americans starve—"Let us survey its spacious courts . . . its sumptuous drawing rooms, its glittering and dazzling salons, with . . . French bronze lamps, gilt framed mirrors of prodigious size . . . gilt and satin settees, sofas, bergeras, divans, tabourets and French comfortables, elegant mahogany gilt eagle mounted French bedsteads, gilt plateaus, gaudy artificial flowers, rich blue and gold bonbons, tambours, compotiers, ice cream vases . . . olive boats . . . silver tureens . . . golden goblets, table spoons, knives and forks. . . ."

Mr. Ogle's speech did credit to his imagination, and to the superior tactics of the new Whig party, whose principal purpose at the moment was to place its own man in the Blue Elliptical Saloon. The Whigs had absorbed almost all the anti-Jackson elements in the country, including Clay's National Republicans, the Anti-Masons, a remnant of old-fashioned Federalists, and some conservative Democrats. They took their party's name from the patriots of the Revolution, and their political technique from the Democrats themselves, improving it as they went along. The Whigs were the new party of business and property, but they carefully suppressed—in public, at least—the old Federalist prejudice against "the people." Since Jackson had won his political battles by appealing to the common man, the Whigs announced that they were common men too, and their campaign posters showed them with their shirt-sleeves rolled up, hammering at a forge or following a plow. In 1840 the Whigs cleverly played both ends against the middle to discomfit Van Buren. First they publicized the golden forks and spoons at the White House until they made the President look like an insufferable snob. Then they turned around and stressed his close connections with the Democratic Locofocos, who were the champions of class war and the proletariat.

The Whigs also played smart politics in their choice of a candidate for President. Of course Henry Clay was their biggest man and should have had the nomination. When the Whig convention met at Harrisburg Clay stayed in Washington, waiting eagerly for the good news. While he waited he made numerous trips to a large decanter on the sideboard. Finally word came that the Whigs had passed him by and chosen General William Henry ("Old Tippecanoe") Harrison, an aged nonentity from North Bend, Ohio. Clay jumped up and stamped back and forth across the room, exclaiming wildly: "My friends are not worth the powder and shot it would take to kill them! . . . I am the most unfortunate man in the history of parties: always run by my friends when sure to be defeated, and now betrayed for a nomination when I, or any one, would be sure of an election."

The lesser Whig politicians had decided on Harrison because he had no ideas that could either interest or infuriate anybody. The pattern of their campaign was set by Nicholas Biddle, who ordered Harrison to say nothing at all to anybody. "Let no Committee, no convention—no town meeting ever extract from him a single word, about what he thinks now, or what he will do hereafter," Biddle had warned, in an earlier campaign, and his instructions were followed to the letter.

The Whigs made a rousing start in 1840, but they had trouble keeping up the pace. Their own ranks were seriously divided by the disagreements of the North and South, especially on slavery. Over the widening sectional chasm the Whig leaders skipped nimbly for a dozen years, contriving newer and more desperate compromises to hold the Union together. "Peace in our time" might have been said to be their motto.

THE LOG CABIN CAMPAIGN

Soon after the Whigs nominated Harrison the Baltimore *Republican* reported that the General was financially embarrassed. "Give him a barrel of Hard Cider," suggested the *Republican*, "and settle a pension of $2,000 a year on him, and my word for it, he will sit the remainder of his days in his Log Cabin." Harrison's real home was a stately white mansion beside the Ohio River which he called the "Log Cabin," in sentimental memory of a cabin that had once stood there. But the Whig publicity experts, including young Horace Greeley, did not bother to explain this. Instead they flooded the country with pictures, stories, and songs *(above)* about Old Tippecanoe and his imaginary cabin. They sang:

> Let Van from his coolers of silver drink wine,
>   And lounge on his cushioned settee;
> Our man on his buckeye bench can recline,
>   Content with hard cider is he!

When the Democrats tried to mention the "issues" the Whigs drowned them out with their hypnotic marching chant:

> Tippecanoe—Tippecanoe—
> Tippecanoe and Tyler too.

In some cities the Whigs built log cabins 40 feet long, with real raccoons scrambling on the roofs, and plenty of free cider (hard) inside.

The Whigs won in a landslide: 234 electoral votes to 60. But according to the Philadelphia *Public Ledger* the Log Cabin campaign was a "national drunken frolic," and a disgrace. The worst part of it was, said the *Ledger*, that many ladies went to the open-air meetings, strained their voices shouting "Huzza," drank hard cider from gourd shells, and devoured baked beans with their fingers from barrels. "Was this the proper sphere of women?" demanded the editor of the *Ledger*. "Was this appropriate to her elevating, refining influence? Did such things improve men? No. They merely degraded women, and made men still more degraded than they were before. . . ."

William Henry Harrison was a simple country gentleman who kept a pet South American macaw on his estate and served his house guests 365 hams a year.

A "Tippecanoe and Tyler Too" parade gets ready to start from Harrison headquarters in one of Philadelphia's northern wards. The band is riding in a wagon decorated with a log-cabin painting. In 1840 the Whigs even called themselves "Democratic" to get votes.

The Whigs rolled a paper ball from city to city and on to Washington, chanting, "As rolls the ball Van's reign doth fall, And he may look to Kinderhook."

John Tyler *(right)* was the first Vice President to win promotion by a death.

—AND TYLER TOO

Explosion of a big navy gun killed two of Tyler's Cabinet but gave him a bride.

PRESIDENT HARRISON liked to slip out of the White House very early in the morning and buy his own meat and vegetables in the Washington markets. One morning he walked out in the rain and caught cold. His health had already been undermined by the job-hunters who swarmed into the Executive Mansion and thrust their papers into his hands and pockets—they pursued him so closely, he said, that he could not attend to "the necessary functions of nature." Now, at the age of 68, his cold turned into pleurisy. The doctors cupped him, someone read the 103rd Psalm, and on April 4, 1841, after 30 days in office, Old Tippecanoe passed on. His last delirious words were addressed to the office-seekers: "I cannot stand it. . . . Don't trouble me. . . . These applications, will they never cease . . . ?"

The Presidency now went to the other end of the "Tippecanoe and Tyler Too" combination. John Tyler was an old-fashioned states' rights Republican-Democrat of the Jeffersonian school. The Whigs had put him on their ticket to draw votes from among the conservative Democrats, but as President, Tyler opposed many things that the Whigs wanted, including a new national bank and government roads. He also looked down his long nose at the Jackson Democrats and the radical Locofocos. During his four years in the White House he tried to build up a middle-of-the-road political party of his own, but with no success. The Whigs drummed him out of their party as an ingrate of the worst sort, and the Democrats would scarcely speak to him. He was the President nobody wanted.

Personally, Tyler was an affable aristocrat who solaced himself with early-morning mint juleps and a pretty White House bride. In February 1844 he was in a cabin of the U.S.S. *Princeton*, talking to Miss Julia Gardiner of New York and some others, when the Navy's biggest gun exploded on the deck above. The Secretary of State, Secretary of the Navy, and three other leading friends of Tyler's, including Miss Gardiner's rich father, were killed. Soon afterward the President and the young lady were married, and in 1845 they retired to "Sherwood Forest," his Virginia estate, and raised a family of seven children.

John Charles Frémont

Jessie Benton Frémont

Dr. Marcus Whitman

RIDERS ON THE OREGON TRAIL

In 1842 two men, one riding west and one riding east, helped to shape the nation's destiny. The one who rode west wore the blue and gold uniform of a second lieutenant in the United States Army Topographical Corps. His name was John Charles Frémont; he was 29, impulsive and gay, and already a seasoned explorer of America. His father was a French-born dancing master, his mother a young Richmond, Virginia, matron who ran away from her aged husband and bore John Charles without benefit of a marriage ceremony. But young Frémont was so attractive and talented that he had just won as his bride the most gifted girl in Washington—Jessie Benton, the 17-year-old daughter of the veteran Democratic Senator.

Starting from Missouri with a well-equipped party of soldiers and guides, Frémont rode west and north along the Oregon Trail, an old fur-trapper's path which had already been widened and beaten down by covered wagons. He scouted through the Rocky Mountain passes with the help of Kit Carson, climbed a 13,730-foot peak which he named for himself, and returned to Washington burning with enthusiasm for the distant West. During the following winter he and Jessie together wrote a book about his trip which became a national best seller.

Meanwhile the other man had started east from Oregon itself, on a journey that has no equal in history. His name was Marcus Whitman; he was 40 years old, a sober, quiet-spoken doctor and missionary of the Congregational church, who had been born in New York

A train of emigrant wagons on the Oregon Trail

State of Yankee stock. In 1836 he had taken his pregnant wife to the Oregon country in the first wagon that ever crossed the Rockies. He founded a tiny log-cabin settlement called Waiilatpu by the Indians, whom he converted to Christianity and taught to read and write. In 1842 he and the other scattered American settlers in Oregon heard that the British Hudson's Bay Company was about to obtain permanent possession of the whole Oregon Territory—a vast area which then included everything from Mexican California to Russian Alaska. Dr. Whitman was going east anyway to report to his missionary board. He decided to hurry his trip and make an appeal to "save" Oregon.

Starting on horseback late in the year, he was caught by snow in the mountains and floundered through the drifts until he reached the unexplored waters of the Grand River in Colorado. He swam his horse across through broken ice and rode south all the way to Mexican Santa Fe, 1,500 miles from Oregon. Then he turned east and went on for 2,000 more miles, reaching Washington in March 1843. He got no encouragement from Secretary of State Daniel Webster, but he had an important talk with President Tyler, who promised that his administration would not abandon the Americans in Oregon. Then he went on to New York, where he started a backfire of Oregon publicity in Horace Greeley's New York *Tribune*. When he headed west again in the spring he found himself riding alongside the greatest emigrant wagon train that had ever followed the Oregon Trail.

WEBSTER IN HIS PRIME

DANIEL WEBSTER was the only big Whig who would associate with President Tyler. He stayed on as Secretary of State after Harrison's death and did some famous work on the Webster-Ashburton Treaty with England in 1842. Lord Ashburton, the British negotiator, was a man of Webster's own mold — portly, solid, and much addicted to the pleasures of the table. The two statesmen engaged in a contest of cooks: one night they had Parisian potages, ragouts, and casseroles at the Englishman's house, and the next night there were New Jersey oysters, Maine salmon, Virginia terrapin, and South Carolina rice-birds at Webster's. The champagne, Madeira, claret, and Burgundy were the finest to be had, and all at the expense of the two Governments.

Webster's treaty ended a number of irritating questions, including a Northeastern boundary dispute which had caused a bloodless "war" between Maine farmers and Canadian lumberjacks in 1838. But the Oregon boundary was left up in the air, for Webster never felt much interest in the voterless Far West. "What do we want with . . . this region of savages and wild beasts, of deserts of shifting sands and whirlwinds of dust, of cactus and prairie dogs?" he once asked.

He was the most prominent man in the Government, and the most sought-after guest at Washington dinner parties, where even in his cups he could always be roused to a speech. Let someone mention "national debt" and Webster was on his feet: "Gentlemen, there's the national debt—it should be paid [loud cheers]; yes, gentlemen, it should be paid [cheers], and I'll be hanged if it shan't be—[taking out his pocketbook]—I'll pay it myself! How much is it?" Since his pocketbook was notoriously flat, this last always drew laughter and more cheers.

In 1843, having seen his treaty and a new tariff through Congress, the "Great Blue Light" of the Northern Whigs resigned from the Cabinet and retired for an interval to his seaside estate at Marshfield, near Boston, which had been paid for—in part —by the textile manufacturers of New England.

"Daniel in the Lion's Den" is a Democratic satire on Webster's negotiations with England. In 1842 he gave away a large chunk of Maine and made other concessions which angered Anglophobes. After his Presidential hopes grew dim in the 1840's, Webster became careless about appearances. He was seen at a public dinner hiding a bottle under his waistcoat, and he gratefully accepted $20,000 from Northern industrialists whom he had served politically.

James Knox Polk was the "Young Hickory" from Tennessee who led a Democratic comeback in 1844. Polk was the first "dark horse" candidate, and the first whose election was reported by telegraph. He was a hard-working President who told secrets only to his diary.

COON-SKINNERS OF 1844

Blow the trumpet, beat the drum,
Run Clay Koons, we come. We come,

sang the resurgent Democrats in the Presidential election of 1844. The Whigs had finally nominated Henry Clay, and adopted as their mascot the raccoon which climbed around their log cabins in 1840. But this time the Democrats were ready for them with tricks of their own: bands of "Koon-Skinners" paraded the streets, blowing the Whig Coon from a cannon's mouth, hanging him, carving out his gizzard, and stripping him down to his bones—all in effigy, of course *(right)*. The Democratic candidate was James K. Polk, a protégé of Andrew Jackson. The big campaign issue was the projected annexation of Texas to the United States: Jackson, Polk, and the South were strongly for it, the Northern Whigs were opposed, and Clay tried to straddle the issue. In this election, abolitionists had their own militant third party—the Liberty party—and nominated James G. Birney, a repentant Alabama slaveholder, for President. Birney took away enough Whig votes in New York State to cost Clay the state, which in turn cost him the election, and his last chance at the White House.

"**Times ain't now as they used to was.**" This sage and time-honored saying of the "Roman Consul, in the early days of that celebrated

Coon of 1810.

Coon of 1844.

Sic transit gloria coonery!

Well, and truly has the poet said,
"That 'coon is the leane-t of all the lean squad,
And totters a furlong while marching a rod."

"FIFTY-FOUR FORTY OR FIGHT!"

ENGLAND   AMERICA

Polk's election forced a quick showdown with England over the Oregon boundary line. During the campaign Senator William Allen, known to reporters as "the Ohio gong," coined the Democratic slogan "Fifty-four Forty or Fight!" This meant the United States insisted on taking everything up to the Alaskan border, including all the Canadian Pacific ports and the whole Western fur trade. Sir Robert Peel, the British Prime Minister, was quite willing to fight over this, as shown by the English cartoon at the left. (The little man with a slave whip in his pocket is Brother Jonathan, the cartoon ancestor of Uncle Sam.) President Polk was not scared either—he told one Congressman that "the only way to treat John Bull is to look him straight in the eye." After doing this for some time, however, Polk calmly arranged a compromise which set the Northwestern boundary of the United States at the 49th degree, where it has remained ever since. Polk never intended to fight for all of Oregon, although he let the Western Democrats shout themselves hoarse for "Fifty-four Forty or Fight!"

THE WATCH ON THE RIO GRANDE

In 1845 the Democratic editor of the New York *Morning News,* John L. O'Sullivan, gave Americans a dynamic new slogan. It was, he said, "our manifest destiny to overspread and to possess the whole of the continent which Providence has given us for the ... great experiment of liberty." President Polk was a great believer in Manifest Destiny, and he also believed in helping it along by every possible means. The outgoing Tyler administration had robbed him of some glory by annexing Texas two weeks before he was inaugurated. But Polk had his cool gray eyes fixed on California, an even greater prize. The Mexican Republic still had California. In order to get it, Polk was prepared to buy it for cash, or to start a revolution there, or to take it away in a war. An old unsettled argument over the Texas-Mexico border line gave him an opening. Early in 1846 he ordered General Zachary Taylor *(right)* and 3,900 troops (including the Texas Rangers) to enter the disputed territory. Taylor promptly marched to the north bank of the Rio Grande and trained his cannon on the Mexican town of Matamoras, on the other side of the river. And soon the war was on.

THE HALLS OF MONTEZUMA

At Resaca de la Palma, second skirmish of the war, Captain May's dragoons charge and silence the Mexican guns.

At Churubusco, just outside Mexico City, American infantrymen swarm over a stone fort defending a key bridge.

At Buena Vista, 4,700 Americans fight a stubborn defensive battle against 20,000 Mexicans, and drive them back.

General Scott, in gold epaulets and a helmet with a snow-white plume, enters Mexico City September 17, 1847.

A navy squadron under Commodore Sloat takes California July 7, 1846. Bluejackets are landing in a stream of boats.

Wolves prowl among the dead. Of 80,000 Americans who invaded Mexico, 12,830 died. Mexicans lost many more.

War news from Mexico was speeded to the excited home front *(right)* by the newly invented "electro-magnetic telegraph." Reporters who visited the Army were especially fond of sending back anecdotes about General Taylor, who slept in the sand, like his men, and rarely wore a proper uniform. General Scott, on the other hand, was always dressed to kill. The newspapers called Scott "Old Fuss and Feathers," while Taylor was "Old Rough and Ready."

MEXICO was no military pushover in 1846. She was, in population and in territory, the second-largest republic in the world. Her special pride was her regular Army, which was twice as big as ours. On the Rio Grande the Mexican commander had 5,700 confident troops against Taylor's isolated 3,900.

There the Mexican cavalry made the first attack, surrounding a scouting party of 60 American dragoons, killing ten and capturing the rest. The incident was a godsend to President Polk, who was planning to make war anyway. Now he solemnly told Congress that "the cup of forbearance has been exhausted," that Mexico "has invaded our territory and shed American blood upon the American soil." Congress declared war May 13, 1846, and appropriated $10 million to pay the initial expense. A call for 50,000 volunteer soldiers was issued, and quickly met. (Women were allowed to join the Army as laundresses, at the rate of one laundress to every twenty men.)

General Taylor had already crossed the Rio Grande and won revenge in two small skirmishes. After receiving large reinforcements he pushed on across 500 miles of semidesert, took the important town of Monterey in three days of hard street fighting, and defeated the main Mexican armies at the Battle of Buena Vista. These solid victories were due in large part to the superiority of American ordnance, which included Colt revolving pistols and long-range howitzers. The Mexicans' smooth copper cannon balls were so ineffective that our troops often watched them come bouncing across the ground and then dodged them.

In March 1847 General Winfield Scott was sent by sea with another American army to pierce the heart of Mexico. Landing near Vera Cruz under the protection of the Navy's big guns, Scott's forces hacked their way into Mexico City in six months of tough fighting. Two young West Point graduates, Captain Robert E. Lee and Lieutenant Ulysses S. Grant, were with Scott, and Grant also saw some hot fighting under Taylor.

Meanwhile California, which was the real American goal, was seized by John Charles Frémont, the Navy, and 100 dragoons, who made an epic overland trek from Kansas by way of Santa Fe.

Gen.ˡ Wool & Staff
Calle Real to South

The daguerreotype above is one of the first photographs of American military men in wartime. It shows Brigadier

General John E. Wool and his staff at Saltillo, which Wool captured in 1846 after a 900-mile march from San Antonio.

Lieut. U. S. Grant was photographed during the war. He wrote home that he saw a shell "nock one man's head off."

DAGUERREOTYPE HISTORY

THE FIRST photographs of American soldiers and statesmen were made in the 1840's, by the process invented by Louis Jacques Mandé Daguerre of France. In politics this new art of "painting with sunbeams" had an important effect: for the first time everyone could see what the great men of the nation really looked like. Andrew Jackson was 78 years old when the daguerreotype on the opposite page was made, April 15, 1845. But even as he sat propped up in his chair, almost suffocated by tuberculosis, his unbeatable spirit was mirrored and perfectly preserved on the photographer's plate. In June Old Hickory died, after telling his weeping slaves, "I hope and trust to meet you all in Heaven, both white and black—both white and black."

John Quincy Adams, the grand old man of the Whig party, sat for this daguerreotype portrait in 1847. After leaving the Presidency, Adams served for 17 years as a Congressman from Quincy, Massachusetts. For eight years he fought, and finally overthrew, the "gag rule" which Southerners had imposed to prevent Congress from receiving petitions against slavery. In 1848, aged 80, he collapsed at his desk and died on a couch in the Speaker's office.

CONSCIENCE WHIGS

To THE Northern Whigs and the enemies of slavery generally, the war against Mexico was the most monstrous, guilty, oppressive conflict ever fought. They called it a bloody Southern junket to steal territory and find "bigger pens to cram with slaves." In the Senate "Black Tom" Corwin of Ohio compared President Polk to Tamerlane sitting on a throne of 70,000 skulls. "If I were a Mexican," he shouted, "I would tell you, 'Have you not room in your country to bury your dead men? If you come into mine we will greet you with bloody hands, and welcome you to hospitable graves!' " These debates widened the intraparty split between the Northern "Conscience Whigs" and the Southern "Cotton Whigs," who stood by slavery to the end. President Polk himself never admitted that slavery had anything to do with the war. "I put my face alike against Southern agitators and Northern fanatics," he noted primly in his diary.

Thomas Corwin of Ohio

LINCOLN PUTS POLK ON THE SPOT

In December 1847 Congressman Abraham Lincoln, aged 38, a Conscience Whig from Illinois, introduced his "spot resolutions" in the House of Representatives. These asked President Polk to describe the exact spot where American blood was first shed, and to say whether or not that spot was on soil rightfully claimed by Mexico. Lincoln's resolutions had little effect on the war, but they provided more embarrassment for the Democratic administration. The House had already passed the famous Wilmot Proviso, which prohibited the introduction of slavery into any new territory acquired by the war. This measure was sponsored by David Wilmot, an antislavery Democrat from Pennsylvania, and was the first important rider ever attached to a routine Congressional bill. The Democratic Senate tried to bury the proviso but it became a big political issue in later years.

Abraham Lincoln of Illinois

THOREAU GOES TO JAIL

Henry Thoreau, the literary recluse of Walden Pond, did not approve of slavery or the Mexican War. So in 1846 he refused to pay his one-dollar poll tax in the town of Concord, because the money might go eventually to buy "a man or a musket to shoot one with." For this wartime act of defiance Thoreau was arrested, locked up in a whitewashed jail cell, and released the next day when Ralph Waldo Emerson paid his tax. The experience helped to produce Thoreau's essay on "Civil Disobedience," which opened up a new line of attack on the American system of majority government. "There will never be a really free and enlightened State," he wrote, "until the State comes to recognize the individual as a higher and independent power . . . and treats him accordingly." This was an American form of anarchy, which Thoreau and his disciples continued to practice, sometimes quietly, and sometimes with violence.

Henry Thoreau of Walden Pond

BINGHAM PAINTS WESTERN POLITICS

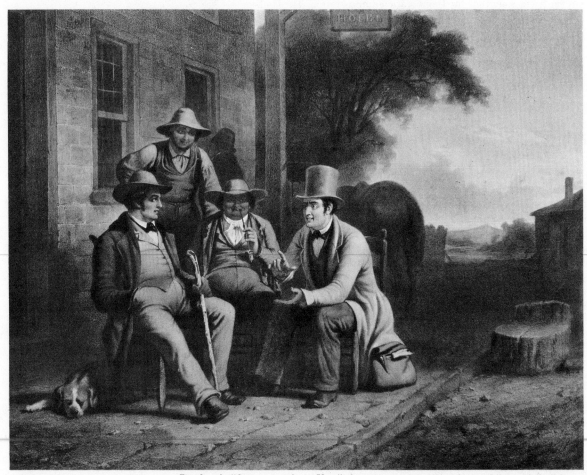

George Caleb Bingham, a self-portrait

GEORGE CALEB BINGHAM of Missouri painted these great political scenes out of his own personal experience. In 1840 Bingham broke into politics as an enthusiastic young orator for "Tippecanoe and Tyler Too." When the Whigs went to Washington, Bingham set up his studio in the Capitol itself and painted portraits of Whig celebrities. In 1846, when he was 35, the Whigs in his home county nominated him for the Missouri House of Representatives. He was elected by a plurality of three votes, according to the Whigs, but the Democrats in the legislature charged fraud and refused to seat him. Two years later Bingham ran again and won by 26 votes. This time there was no complaint, and he took his place at Jefferson City. During his term he wrote a legislative report which upheld slavery and states' rights, but promised to stand by the Union, "come what may, whether prosperity or adversity, weal or woe."

But eventually Bingham became disgusted with elections and politicians, though he continued to paint the most charming pictures of them. "It will be a glorious time for the country when the present party organizations shall be broken up entirely," he wrote. "We need not expect until then to have a revival of the good old times, when honesty and capacity, rather than party servility, will be the qualifications for office."

Bingham's "Canvassing for a Vote" shows a campaigner with a saddlebag full of literature *(right)* setting forth his arguments to a skeptical group outside a highway tavern.

"Verdict of the People" shows a clerk reading election results aloud from the steps of a Missouri courthouse. In the center a man is jotting down figures on the top of his hat.

"County Election" shows voters lined to cast spoken ballots in a Western town. The candidates stand on the steps and tip their hats politely. At left is the inevitable cider barrel.

"STUMP SPEAKING"

BINGHAM'S MASTERPIECE shows a rural Missouri crowd listening to a speaker in the long white alpaca coat and black silk tie which were frequently worn by frontier statesmen in the 1840's and '50's. Bing- ham described this painting as follows: "In my orator I have endeavored to personify a wiry politician grown gray in the pursuit of office and the service of party. His influence upon the crowd is quite

manifest, but I have placed behind him a shrewd clear-headed opponent who is busy taking notes, and who will, when his turn comes make sophisms fly like cobwebs before the housekeeper's broom." The fat man at the far left is a portrait of a former Governor of Missouri, the Hon. Meredith Miles Marmaduke. He was so incensed when he saw this picture that he challenged Bingham to a duel.

The Whigs wrote no platform in 1848, and Taylor declined to discuss any issues *(right)*. "I am a Whig, *but not an ultra Whig*," was about all he would say.

ROUGH AND READY

The special Whig talent for playing both ends against the political middle was beautifully displayed in the 1848 election. After attacking the Mexican War from every possible angle they turned around and nominated its most popular hero, General Zachary Taylor *(opposite page)*, for President. The campaign was a noisy repetition of 1840, with "Old Rough and Ready" in place of "Old Tippecanoe," and battle pictures of Buena Vista and Monterey substituting for log cabins. General Taylor was the crudest specimen yet of a Presidential candidate. His soldiers in Mexico adored him because he rode around the front lines wearing a battered straw hat and a blue-checked gingham coat, chewing and spitting, and getting into the thick of every fight. At Buena Vista a bullet cut through the sleeve of his shirt and another ripped his coat lining. A few minutes later he pulled up beside an artillery crew and casually ordered, "Double-shot your guns and give 'em hell."

Among his qualifications was the fact that he had never cast a vote in his life. When the Whigs mailed their nomination to him he refused to pay ten cents postage due, and sent the letter back unopened. But the people were in the mood for a rough-and-ready President, and "Old Zack" Taylor was their man.

Antislavery votes in 1848 went to a Free Soil party ticket headed by old Martin Van Buren, shown about to fall in Salt River.

The defeated Democratic candidate was Lewis Cass of Michigan, a "doughface" whose head is being baked in this Whig cartoon.

THE CHEERFUL FORTIES

American couples danced the foreign polka with gusto in 1848, to show their sympathy with the revolutionists in Europe.

To THE 17 million Americans of the 1840's politics was by no means all-important. Only a small number took seriously the elections and the debates in Congress. Nor did they worry about such things as wars. "The world has become stale and insipid," cried a respectable New York newspaper in 1845, "the ships ought to be all captured, and the cities battered down, and the world burned up, so that we can start again. There would be fun in that."

And so, while they fought with Mexico and pushed back the Western frontier again, they also danced the European polka and sang the latest hit tunes

This happy family is ready for an evening of culture. More books were read in the forties than ever before.

The persecuted Mormons took their wagons far to the West in the forties, and founded a polygamous empire in Utah.

These rural New York Shakers were pledged to a life of life of religious celibacy, but they enjoyed a good rousing barn dance.

from the minstrel shows. "Humbug" and "reform" were among their favorite words. They laughed and called it "humbug" when P. T. Barnum made suckers out of them with the fakes in his New York City Museum. But they invented the telegraph, ether anesthesia, rubber-soled shoes, periscopic spectacles, spiritualism, envelopes, air-conditioning, and the Eccaleobion, or automatic egg-hatching machine. They were bursting with energy and self-esteem, these Americans of the forties, and they felt that their future was bright despite anything the politicians might—or might not—do.

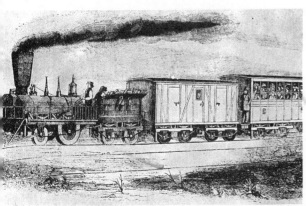

Railroads crisscrossed the East and headed toward the Mississippi River. Horse-drawn omnibuses invaded the cities.

In Seneca Falls, New York, Mrs. Amelia Bloomer furthered the woman's rights cause by inventing these female pants.

Bennett of the *Herald* was a canny Scot who tirelessly tooted his own bagpipe.

Walter Whitman of the *Eagle* advised his fellow Democrats to be bold and "radical."

Greeley of the *Tribune* wanted to give every poor citizen a piece of public land.

THE PENNY PAPERS

IN THE 1840's the biggest and richest newspaper in the country was James Gordon Bennett's one-cent New York *Herald*, which had reached a daily circulation of 50,000 by sensational reporting of sexy murders, Wall Street panics, and cross-eyed Publisher Bennett himself. When another newspaper editor beat him up one day Bennett hastened to describe the fracas in his own paper, adding, I "may have knocked down his throat some of his infernal teeth for anything I know." Bennett was "neutral" in politics, although he once accepted some of Biddle's tainted Bank money.

The most influential paper, politically, was Horace Greeley's New York *Tribune*, which spoke for the Conscience Whigs and antislavery men. Rival publishers called the disheveled, absent-minded Greeley a crackpot because he supported communistic societies in the United States, belonged to a printers' union, and hired Karl Marx as a foreign correspondent. Meanwhile, for the Brooklyn *Eagle*, a young Democrat named Walter Whitman wrote dreamy editorials about Manifest Destiny and the sacred right of "Yankeedoodledom" to expand all over the map. In 1848, disgusted by doughface Democrats, Whitman gave up his newspaper job and began writing free verse.

"LANGUAGE IS HARDLY ADEQUATE..."

THE GREAT FIRE.

The first woodcut news pictures appeared in the penny papers of the late 1830's and '40's. The example at the left was printed in the Philadelphia *Spirit of the Times* on the day the fire occurred, an achievement which led the editor to boast as follows: "We reached the scene about 9 o'clock, this morning—drew a hasty picture of it, and by 12 o'clock, Johnson, the artist, had the representation ready for the press. So much for enterprize!"

Bennett's *Herald* printed the first pictures of murder victims and murder trials, which was denounced by the conservative press as "A VILE PRACTICE." But when the *Herald* ran a picture of Sarah Mercer, whose brother was on trial for killing her lover on a ferryboat, the opposition editors really let loose. "And she must bear all this, to enable such vile prostitutes of the press to put a few pence in their purses!" raged one. "Language is hardly adequate to express our scorn of such creatures and their detestable practices."

Many other developments helped the penny papers out-

In 1844 an anti-Catholic political party called the "Native Americans" provoked a series of riots in Philadelphia and elected James Harper, of the famous publishing firm, Mayor of New York. The lithograph above shows a "Native" mob wearing tall beaver hats fighting the state militia in Philadelphia. Twenty-four persons were killed and two famous old Catholic churches burned in these riots. The Natives wanted to bar all naturalized citizens from office and extend the waiting time for citizenship to 21 years. By 1850 they were absorbed in a much larger antiforeign movement which took the form of a secret society. Members were pledged to vote exactly as their leaders told them to, and to answer "I know nothing" to all questions about their organization. The "Know-Nothings" elected governors in Kentucky, Maryland, Delaware, and four New England states. Vice President Millard Fillmore later became one of them.

THE KNOW-NOTHINGS

strip their predecessors: the electro-magnetic telegraph, which spread news faster and farther; the cylindrical Hoe presses, which printed it more quickly; a better-educated population, in which, for the first time, a majority of Americans had gone to school. A great increase in advertising made the newspapers financially secure and produced "singing commercials" like this one of 1849:

> Where'er Consumption's victims are,
> In palaces or halls,
> Or in the rural cottages,
> With neatly white-washed walls,
> Sink not into despondency,
> There's naught for you to fear,
> By the pale and flickering taper,
> Or the brilliant chandelier;
> But drink the draught, 'twil save you,
> That bids Consumption fly,
> Take DR. SWAYNE'S WILD CHERRY,
> And do not, do not die!

The Know-Nothings charged that Irish and German immigrants were stealing American elections and running the big city political machines.

Leading New Yorkers, including Mayor Fernando Wood *(shaking hands, right)*, frequented the Gem Saloon at Broadway and Worth Street, which had the city's largest mirror.

"TEN NIGHTS IN A BAR-ROOM"

"I MUST TRY old Morrison's remedy for cold weather," remarked James Latimer, a hard-working mechanic, as he finished dinner one night in 1842. He drew a cork, poured out a glass of cordial, and drank it off. "It does warm—that's a fact. Come try some of it, Polly." And he filled the glass again and handed it to his wife. . . . And so began the sad story of "The Bottle and the Pledge," by Timothy Shay Arthur, who also wrote the best-selling *Ten Nights in a Bar-Room* and hundreds of other temperance tales. The moral war against drinking was at its peak in the forties. President Zachary Taylor was a "teetotal" temperance man, as were Abraham Lincoln and Horace Greeley. Even Walter Whitman, who loved the "foaming ale" in the Pewter Mug tavern in New York, picked up some easy money writing a temperance yarn called *Franklin Evans; or, The Inebriate*. Meanwhile, bands of reformed drunkards traveled

Illustrations from "The Bottle and the Pledge" show how liquor ruined a happy home. James Latimer persuades his wife to drink.

Too many bottles of cordial and brandy have lost Latimer his job. Now Mrs. Latimer pawns her clothes to buy more bottles.

Represen... ...s a drunken spectacle of himself on a... ...d suicide with a bowie knife.

from on... ...leagues to take the pledge; angry w... ...s "Cold Water Army" was on the... ...oasted one newspaper, the numbe... ...00,000 to 125,000, and the moder...

But... ...s, who turned from persuasion to... ...s passed in 1838 in Tennessee, an... ...n stricter one took effect in Maine... ...ng Mayor of Portland. Although... ...o get back their rum, and bootle... ...on became an institution in Maine... ...the country.

Neal Dow, the "Cold Water Mayor"

Lati... ...reless apar... ...time.

Latimer is locked up in a madhouse, where he is visited by his delinquent children. When they leave he will suffer further torment.

129

The first gold hunters were equipped only for dirt and gravel digging. Some made $750 a week, some made $10 in all.

Mining companies which could turn whole rivers through their sluiceways soon took over the most valuable claims.

Chinese diggers stuck together in little groups, eating rice with chopsticks and cutting each other's hair for relaxation.

San Francisco in 1848 was a village of 50 adobe huts. In 1849 it was the makeshift city shown above, with a floating population of 20,000, and a harbor full of deserted ships which sometimes caught fire (right) and sank uncared for.

THE GOLD DIGGERS

On the rainy afternoon of January 28, 1848, a workman in a stained serape rode into Sutter's Fort near Sacramento and unwound a wet cotton rag, out of which fell shiny dust and flakes. "I believe it is gold!" the man whispered to Captain John Sutter. "But the people at the mill laughed at me—said I was crazy!" Sutter peered closely at the particles. "Yes, it looks like gold," he said. "Come, let us test it. . . ."

It was gold, and a large part of the world went wild at the news. Soon a bigger army of Americans than ever marched on Mexico was heading west by ship and prairie schooner—

> Oh! California,
>   That's the land for me;
> I'm off for Sacramento
>   With my washbowl on my knee.

To meet them at the diggings came Russians, Mexicans, Hawaiians, "Sydney ducks" from Australia, and thousands of pigtail-wearing Chinese. California's new army and navy posts were stripped bare as all ranks left to dig gold; ships deserted by their crews rotted and sank to the bottom of San Francisco Bay. From the East Yankee traders sent out barrels of cheap metal spelter on the same ships with the gold diggers; when this stuff was dumped into a stream by a California promoter, it formed flakes like gold and started a stampede for claims.

The first big rush for gold gave California a rough, predominantly masculine population of 250,000 or more, which lived turbulently under the rule of the disorganized United States Army.

A California gold digger, from an on-the-spot sketch

CALIFORNIA GOES FREE SOIL

For more than two years Congress was deadlocked over the Wilmot Proviso and could not organize California or any other new states in the territory wrested from Mexico. So in September 1849 the Californians took matters in their own hands. They elected a governor and legislature, adopted a free-soil (no slavery) constitution, and announced they were ready to become a state at once. When this news reached Washington it provoked another great political tug of war between the Northern and Southern members of Congress. But meanwhile the Californians went on ruling and improving themselves. The jack-boot miners of '49 quickly gave way to multimillion dollar mining corporations. Handsome stagecoaches *(left)* dashed through the mountains. San Francisco grew into a roaring boom town where ham and eggs cost $3 a plate and a gambling tent on the Plaza rented for $40,000 a year. But Jim Marshall, who found the first gold flakes, died poor—and crazy.

131

THE CALIFORNIA COMPROMISE

THE SCENE at the left, painted by Peter Frederick Rothermel, shows the start of the greatest Senate debate since 1830. All the old giants are still there. Henry Clay, the Great Pacificator, has the floor. Two rows behind him sits Daniel Webster, with his head resting on his left hand. Calhoun is standing *(third from right)*, his iron-gray hair falling down about his ears. Tom Benton appears with his nose realistically portrayed *(seated, second from right)*.

The battle was precipitated by California's request to enter the Union as a free-soil state. To the South this seemed to be the most dangerous attack on slavery since the Missouri Compromise. The Northern Free Soilers, both Democrats and Conscience Whigs, were again demanding that the Wilmot Proviso be passed. If this were done, said the Southerners, their states would band together and resist its enforcement "to any extremity."

On the morning of February 5, 1850, the 72-year-old Clay walked up the Capitol steps to offer his last compromise. "Will you lend me your arm?" he asked a friend. "I feel myself quite weak and exhausted this morning." But when he began to speak his old-time fire and charm were strong as ever. Let California enter as a free state, he argued, since her people had already made this choice. Let two more future states, New Mexico and Utah, be formed into territories without any restrictions as to slavery. Let the slave trade (but not slaveholding) be abolished in the District of Columbia, as the abolitionists had long demanded. And finally, let the North agree to enforce a drastic new fugitive slave act, to return all runaway slaves to their owners.

This was the Compromise of 1850: a middle-of-the-road solution which would at least hold the Union together for a while. Calhoun attacked it bitterly; Webster supported it in a sensational speech which was widely denounced in the North. By September it had all been passed, and the newspapers were headlining their Washington reports: "Most Glorious News"—"The Country Saved"—"The Closing of the Drama."

John C. Calhoun of South Carolina waged a relentless battle against the Declaration of Independence during the closing years of his life. "Nothing can be more unfounded and false," he declared, than "the prevalent opinion that all men are born free and equal . . . [for] it rests upon the assumption of a fact which is contrary to universal observation."

THE SOUTH
IN SULLEN FURY

ON MARCH 4, 1850, John C. Calhoun sat in an armchair on the Senate floor, his neck swathed in flannels. His voice was stifled by catarrh, but he had written one last speech to oppose Clay's California Compromise. While his words were read by Mason of Virginia the old nullifier glared proudly around the Senate: in his eyes there burned the implacable resentment and defiance of the South.

It was not enough, Calhoun warned, to pass a more stringent fugitive slave act—every Northern citizen must cease to agitate the slavery question forthwith. The admission of California or any other free-soil state was clearly illegal, for it interfered with the personal right to hold slaves, which had been granted by the Federal Constitution. The North was going ahead of the South too fast in population and resources, and Congress must act to restore the "equilibrium" between the two sections. Calhoun's plan for doing this was to pass a constitutional amendment dividing the executive power between two Presidents, one from the South and one from the North!

Calhoun had long since lost interest in compromises. He was convinced the Union must break up soon, and he had prepared for that event a rigid political creed which exalted slavery as "a positive good" and a practical necessity. There has never existed, he said, a "civilized society in which one portion of the community did not, in point of fact, live on the labor of the other." Was it not better, then, to have the inferior blacks labor in paternalistic slavery for the Southern whites, than to imitate the factory "wage slavery" of the North, with its capital-labor strife and seasonal starvation? The abolitionists, he warned, would not stop at freeing the slaves: they would also try "to raise the Negroes to a social and political equality with the whites, and, that being effected, we would soon see the present condition of the two races reversed. They, and their Northern allies, would be the masters, and we the slaves."

Four weeks after his last speech Calhoun died of lung disease in a Washington lodginghouse.

"The South, the poor South," he murmured toward the end.

Jefferson Davis of Mississippi (photographed with his youthful second wife) inherited Calhoun's Southern leadership.

THE DOUGHFACE PRESIDENTS

Millard Fillmore

It was John Randolph who coined the word "doughface" to describe a Northern politician with Southern ideas about slavery. In 1850 the Presidency suddenly fell under doughface control when Zachary Taylor died. Old Rough and Ready had survived many a hard campaign, but a series of Fourth of July speeches at the Washington Monument was too much for him. After sitting all afternoon in a broiling sun, he returned to the White House and tried to cool off by eating cherries and drinking iced milk. Five days later he was dead of cholera morbus.

The pliable Millard Fillmore from Buffalo, New York, succeeded him, and soon ordered a rigorous enforcement of the new Fugitive Slave Act. In 1852, in a listless campaign, the Democrats elected as President Franklin Pierce of New Hampshire, a classic specimen of a doughface. The South ran Pierce's administration, through Jefferson Davis, his strong-willed Secretary of War.

Franklin Pierce

135

Eliza's race across the Ohio River, shown in an *Uncle Tom's Cabin* theater poster, was often duplicated in real life. One Negro woman who was caught on the Ohio side cut her baby's throat as they were carried back to slavery.

"LIFE AMONG THE LOWLY"

In June 1851 the *National Era* of Washington, D. C., began publishing a 36-part serial story called *Uncle Tom's Cabin; or, Life Among the Lowly*, by Mrs. Harriet Beecher Stowe. No American novel ever had such far-reaching political effects. "It penetrated the walls of Congress," wrote a contemporary, "and made the politicians tremble. It startled statesmen, who scented danger near." Senator William H. Seward of New York urged his Southern colleagues to read it and learn the error of their ways. But Southern critics thought the book was a "criminal prostitution of the high functions of the imagination." Its authoress, they said, "must be either a very bad or a very fanatical person."

Yet as propaganda *Uncle Tom's Cabin* was not all one-sided. Early scenes in the story depicted Colonel Shelby and Augustine St. Clare as kind-hearted Southern gentlemen who took good care of their slaves. But it was Simon Legree, with his whips and bloodhounds, who made the most lasting impression. When he stalked, black-mustached and villainous, across a thousand theater stages of the North, he became the very personification of the Fugitive Slave Act and all its hated results.

The martyrdom of gentle Uncle Tom, the sad death of little Eva, and Eliza's dash for life across the ice, with baying bloodhounds close behind her, became fixed in millions of Northern minds as true pictures of life in the slaveholding South.

Harriet Beecher Stowe was the first professional author since Tom Paine to strongly influence American history.

THE UNDERGROUND RAILROAD

These fugitive slaves are fleeing from the Maryland Eastern Shore to an Underground Railroad depot in Delaware.

Methods of escape were many. One woman slave simply put on her master's suit and hat and took a train north.

THE FUGITIVE SLAVE ACT of 1850 rubbed the unsavory aspects of slavery into Northern nostrils in a very vigorous way. An alleged runaway could be seized and shackled wherever found, could not have a trial by jury, could not testify or summon witnesses for himself, and could be shipped south to his master no matter how long he had been free. James Hamlet, a peaceable resident of New York City, was the first to feel the law's effect. He was taken at his work by a federal officer and sent to Baltimore in irons.

In 1850 there were at least 20,000 Negroes in the North who had escaped through an abolitionist network known as the "Underground Railroad." These people now started a wild stampede for Canada, and many Northerners did all they could to help them, and to block the enforcement of the law. "This filthy enactment," wrote Ralph Waldo Emerson, "was made in the nineteenth century, by people who could read and write. I will not obey it, by God!"

At Christiana, Pennsylvania, in 1851, local Negroes fought off a party of slave-hunters from Maryland and killed one.

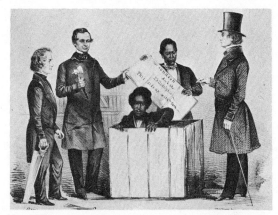

Henry Brown escaped from Richmond to Philadelphia via Adams' Express, in a box labeled "This side up with care."

Two accredited artists accompanied Perry to Japan and their sketches were published in his official report to Congress. The one above shows Perry and his staff arriving at an imperial tent during the 1854 negotiations. The one below, which shows Japanese men and women bathing together, caused a Congressional furor and was later suppressed. According to Perry, the lower-class people of Japan had lax morals and enjoyed looking at obscene pictures.

PERRY OPENS JAPAN

In 1852 Commodore Matthew Calbraith ("Old Bruin") Perry sailed with a squadron of United States warships on a ticklish mission to Japan. The Japanese had opened their country for a while in the sixteenth century, but they were so annoyed by foreign missionaries and cheated by foreign traders that they slammed the door again. Perry's delicate job was to pry it open without starting a war.

His four steam-propelled men-of-war entered Yedo Bay July 8, 1853, belching black smoke as they moved steadily against a strong head wind. The Japanese had never seen ships of this type before. An old and ominous folk song came to their minds as they watched:

> Thro' a black night of cloud and rain,
> The Black Ship plies her way—
> An alien thing of evil mien—
> Across the waters gray.

The local officials ordered Perry to get out of the Bay, but he put up a stiff diplomatic front and disobeyed. He announced he was carrying a letter from President Millard Fillmore to the Emperor, and that the United States would be insulted if the letter was not received. A Japanese dignitary finally accepted it, and Perry sailed away, leaving word he would be back the next year for an answer.

He returned in February 1854, this time with seven powerfully armed "Black Ships." Meanwhile, the Japanese had completely reversed their policy. They greeted Perry warmly, agreed to sign a trade treaty, and happily accepted such gifts as a telegraph instrument and a miniature American locomotive which traveled along the shore at 20 miles an hour. The high spot was reached at a banquet on the U.S.S. *Powhatan,* when a tipsy Japanese official threw his arms around Perry, crushing a pair of gold epaulets and repeating in Japanese, "Nippon and America, all the same heart!" Perry's door-opening mission was a spectacular success. But as Mr. Dooley later remarked, "We didn't go in; they came out."

Commodore Perry treated the Japanese with stern, gold-braided dignity. A brother of the hero of Lake Erie, Perry had already seen service on American ships off Norway, Liberia, Cuba, Naples, Greece, Smyrna, and Vera Cruz.

Japanese wrestlers entertained Perry at Yokohama. He responded by staging a banquet under American big guns.

Japanese soldiers at Yokohama had expensive saddles but were armed with old-fashioned matchlock rifles and spears.

THE END OF THE WHIGS

No American party leader was ever more frantically loved by his followers than Henry Clay, shown at left in a daguerreotype with his wife Lucretia. In 1844, when he lost his last chance at the Presidency, Clay sobbed in his wife's arms.

THE WHIG PARTY died three times in 1852—first with Henry Clay, then with Daniel Webster, and finally in the November election for President. The Whig candidate was General Winfield Scott, another Mexican War hero. But the country had almost forgotten the Mexican War, and the attempt to popularize Old Fuss and Feathers was a dismal failure.

In June the noise made by the Whig convention delegates disturbed the dying moments of Henry Clay, who succumbed to a racking cough in the National Hotel at Washington. Webster, who had hoped to get the nomination himself, lingered glumly at his Massachusetts seaside home until October. A remarkable story was printed of his passing:

On his last afternoon he heard the doctor say, "Give him a spoonful of brandy in fifteen minutes, another in half an hour, and another in three quarters of an hour, if he still lives." These directions were followed until the time came for the third spoonful, when the attendants could not decide whether he was alive. While they deliberated the dying statesman suddenly raised his head and said feebly, "I still live." The brandy was given to him, and he sank into his final sleep.

Daniel Webster died disgraced in the eyes of the Conscience Whigs and his own New England. He had supported the Fugitive Slave Act, and had told Massachusetts to conquer her "prejudices" to preserve the Union. So far as the abolitionists were concerned he was an "apostate," a "falling star," "Lucifer descending from Heaven!"

On February 2, 1856, a Massachusetts Free Soiler
was elected Speaker of the House of Representatives
over a South Carolina slaveowner, after a nine-week,
133-ballot deadlock. This was the first naked test
of strength between North and South. Below, Northerners in the gallery cheer wildly as their man wins.

CHAPTER 5

THE
FREE SOIL
REPUBLICANS

THE PASSING of the Whigs left behind a whirlpool of sectional rivalry and political hate. Senator Ben Wade, a fierce Free Soiler from Ohio, described it accurately when he said: "There is really no Union now between the North and the South. . . . No two nations upon earth entertain feelings of more bitter rancor toward each other. . . ."

This feeling was not based solely on slavery and its extension into the territories—although these had become the dominant issues. It went back to the ancient struggle between the two sections for economic and political supremacy. The North, with its factory system based on free labor, was already far ahead in the 1850's. The South was so involved in its slave and cotton-growing investments that it could not change peaceably if it wanted to. So it tried every political trick to hem in and restrain the North, while extending slavery as fast and far as possible.

The logic of the situation called for the formation of two new political parties: one for the South and one for the North. Calhoun's successors almost achieved this by tightening the historic Southern grip on the Democratic party machinery. But although they found many Northern doughfaces to do their bidding, they did not succeed in converting Andrew Jackson's Democracy into a 100-per-cent proslavery party.

It was the North which produced the first truly sectional party in American politics. Its beginnings were so widespread and spontaneous that no one man can be called its founder. But in February 1854 Alvan Bovay, a young lawyer in Ripon, Wisconsin, wrote a letter to Editor Horace Greeley of the New York *Tribune*, asking for help in organizing the opponents of slavery extension in a new party. "Urge them to forget previous political names and organizations, and to band together under the name I suggested to you in 1852," Bovay wrote. "I mean the name REPUBLICAN."

Greeley responded without much enthusiasm. "I am a beaten, broken-down, used-up politician, and

have the soreness of many defeats in my bones," he wrote. "However, I am ready to follow any lead that promises to hasten the day of Northern emancipation."

Bovay and his neighbors went ahead. In March they held a meeting in the Ripon schoolhouse and appointed a committee to organize the new party in their own home town. The committee was composed of three Conscience Whigs, one antislavery Democrat, and one man who had voted for Van Buren in 1848 on the Free Soil (third party) ticket. This little group was typical of hundreds of others which sprang up in the Northern states during the next few months.

The new party snowballed into power with unprecedented speed. In May 1854 thirty Congressman members met in Washington and officially adopted "Republican" as its name. By thus reviving the name of Jefferson's original party, they announced, they were asserting again the pro-Union and antislavery views of the founders of the Republic. In July the first state Republican convention was held in Jackson, Michigan, followed shortly by one at Saratoga Springs, New York. When the next Congress convened the Republicans elected the Speaker, Nathaniel P. Banks of Massachusetts, after a bitter contest which blocked all other House business for two months. Banks was a former bobbin boy in a New England cotton mill; his Democratic opponent, William Aiken of South Carolina, was the owner of 1,100 slaves.

Seasoned politicians like Lincoln and William H. Seward stayed aloof from the new party for a while. They thought it contained too many radicals, socialists, and outright abolitionists, whose motto, "Free Soil, Free Speech, Free Labor, and Free Men," it quickly took for its own. But the Republican movement gathered so much strength in the North that the "practical" leaders were soon forced to join it, and take the party helm themselves, to prevent the rank and file from steering straight into civil war.

Senator Stephen Arnold Douglas of Illinois was a fountain of tobacco juice and spread-eagle oratory and the last of the great compromisers. He spoke for a large number of "Go Ahead" Americans who wanted to forget about the slavery problem and continue expanding all over the Western Hemisphere. "I do not care whether slavery is voted up or voted down," he said.

DOUGLAS AND THE ANTI-NEBRASKANS

IN THE SENATE a shaggy, thick-necked, miniature bull of a man fought with bluster and cunning to hold the North and the South together. Stephen A. Douglas, the "Little Giant," was a Vermont-born Democrat who married the daughter of a North Carolina slave-holder. But his opinions were formed on the Western frontier, where he had made good as a lawyer, judge, and rough-and-tumble politician. In private life he was deeply involved with Chicago capitalists in a scheme to build a railroad to the Pacific coast from Chicago through Council Bluffs. This project had been stalled by Jefferson Davis and other Democrats, who wanted to build a rival line from Memphis, through Texas and Santa Fe.

Douglas had a simple but explosive plan for ending the slavery crisis. Let the country forget all the old compromises, and write a new one: let the people of each territory decide for themselves whether they would have slavery, and let Congress accept their decision. This was really nothing more than the squatter law of the pioneers, but Douglas dressed it up under the title of "Popular Sovereignty." In January 1854 he introduced his famous Nebraska bill, which led to the creation of two new territories, Nebraska and Kansas, and gave the inhabitants of each the privilege of deciding on slavery.

Douglas was eager to get these territory governments started to speed his railroad plans, and he was perfectly willing to conciliate his business rivals in the South by opening up a new outlet for slavery. After a sharp debate his bill was passed and signed by the doughface President, Franklin Pierce.

In the North Douglas' bill meant just one thing: the deliberate, final betrayal of the promises made in the Missouri Compromise, which had stood for 34 years against the westward spread of the "slave power." It was to protest against the "wicked" Nebraska bill that Alvan Bovay and his neighbors held their first meeting in the Ripon schoolhouse, in a movement that spread like wildfire, and led directly to the rapid rise of the Free Soil Republicans. The protesting Northerners called themselves "Anti-Nebraska men" before they adopted the name "Republican." The three Senators at the right were "Anti-Nebraska men" who flung hot words of scorn and hate at Stephen Douglas.

During one of the debates Senator George E. Badger of North Carolina was bemoaning the fact that, if the North had its way, he could never take his "old black mammy" to Nebraska. He loved his "old black mammy," he said, and she loved him. Turning to Senator Wade of Ohio, he exclaimed, "Surely you will not prevent me from taking my old black mammy with me?"

"It is not that he cannot take his old black mammy with him that troubles the mind of the Senator," sneered hard-boiled Ben Wade, "but that if we make the territories free, he cannot sell the old black mammy when he gets her there."

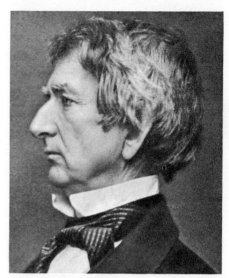

Senator William Seward of New York charged the South was forcing "an irrepressible conflict."

Senator Salmon Chase of Ohio called Douglas' bill "a criminal betrayal of precious rights."

Senator Charles Sumner of Massachusetts called Douglas a skunk and slavery a Southern harlot.

Missouri "Border Ruffians" on their way to "vote" in Kansas. Their leader was Missouri's ex-Senator David Atchison.

BLEEDING KANSAS...

IN MARCH 1855 the new territory of Kansas held an election under the "Popular Sovereignty" plan. Across the border from Missouri rode 5,000 slavery men armed with bowie knives and revolvers. These "Border Ruffians," as the Northern newspapers

The ruins of the Free State Hotel at Lawrence, Kansas, after the Missourians burned and looted the town in 1856.

called them, took charge of the Kansas polls, barred Free Soil men from voting, and elected a proslavery legislature. Then they rode back to Missouri.

The North replied to this by sending to Kansas organized colonies of tough, determined abolitionists. With them came wagonloads of Sharp's breech-loading rifles, paid for by collections taken up in Northern churches. Soon a small-scale civil war was flaming along the Kansas frontier. On May 21, 1856, an invading force of Missourians plundered and burned the Free Soil capital of Lawrence. On May 25 a band of Free Soil fighters led by John Brown dragged five proslavery settlers from their cabins on the Pottawatomie and killed them in cold blood.

The "Kansas War" cost only a few hundred lives, but the whole country watched it with breathless excitement, for almost everyone realized it was a rehearsal for something bigger. On May 19, 1856, Senator Charles Sumner of Massachusetts delivered a powerful Republican philippic on "The Crime

"Southern Chivalry" shows Congressman Preston Brooks trying to kill Senator Sumner. Democratic Senators are laughing.

... AND "BULLY" BROOKS

Against Kansas," in which he sought to place all blame on the South. In his speech he made some coarse remarks about the elderly Senator Butler of South Carolina, suggesting that Butler must have chosen "the harlot, Slavery," to be his "mistress."

Three days later, Butler's nephew, Congressman Preston Brooks of South Carolina, walked into the Senate chamber and tried to murder Sumner. The Senator, a tall man with long legs, was sitting at his desk writing when Brooks approached. As he looked up Brooks brought his heavy gutta-percha cane crashing down on Sumner's bare head. Sumner's desk was fastened to the floor and his legs were tangled underneath; in his agonized struggle to rise he tore the desk loose from the floor and then fell over on his back. Brooks continued to batter his skull until the cane broke. Senators Douglas and Robert Toombs of Georgia were standing near by but did not interfere.

Sumner's injuries disabled him for three years and almost blinded one eye. But "Bully" Brooks became the hero of the South. Admirers sent him scores of canes and a gold-handled cowhide whip to use on other abolitionists. And a Washington magistrate let him off with a $300 fine.

South Carolina militia in a Missouri camp in 1856. They were sent west to fight for slavery in the "Kansas War."

FREE SPEECH, FREE SOIL, FREE MEN —AND FRÉMONT!

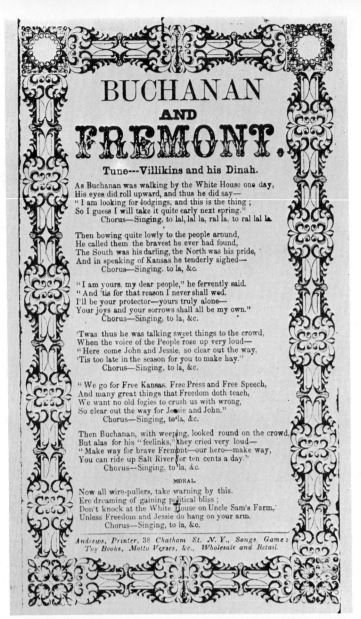

BUCHANAN AND FRÉMONT.

Tune---Villikins and his Dinah.

As Buchanan was walking by the White House one day,
His eyes did roll upward, and thus he did say—
"I am looking for lodgings, and this is the thing;
So I guess I will take it quite early next spring."
Chorus—Singing, to lal, lal la, ral la, to ral lal la.

Then bowing quite lowly to the people around,
He called them the bravest he ever had found,
The South was his darling, the North was his pride,
And in speaking of Kansas he tenderly sighed—
Chorus—Singing, to la, &c.

"I am yours, my dear people," he fervently said.
"And 'tis for that reason I never shall wed.
I'll be your protector—yours truly alone—
Your joys and your sorrows shall all be my own."
Chorus—Singing, to la, &c.

'Twas thus he was talking sweet things to the crowd,
When the voice of the People rose up very loud—
"Here come John and Jessie, so clear out the way,
'Tis too late in the season for you to make hay."
Chorus—Singing, to la, &c.

"We go for Free Kansas, Free Press and Free Speech,
And many great things that Freedom doth teach,
We want no old fogies to crush us with wrong,
So clear out the way for Jessie and John."
Chorus—Singing, to la, &c.

Then Buchanan, with weeping, looked round on the crowd,
But alas for his "feelinks," they cried very loud—
"Make way for brave Frembnt—our hero—make way,
You can ride up Salt River for ten cents a day."
Chorus—Singing, to la, &c.

MORAL

Now all wire-pullers, take warning by this.
Ere dreaming of gaining political bliss;
Don't knock at the White House on Uncle Sam's Farm,
Unless Freedom and Jessie do hang on your arm.
Chorus—Singing, to la, &c.

*Andrews, Printer, 38 Chatham St. N.Y., Songs, Games
Toy Books, Motto Verses, &c., Wholesale and Retail.*

Republican song of 1856 featured Jessie along with John. Republicans also claimed that Buchanan would reduce Northern wages to 10 cents a day.

John Charles Frémont at 43 was the youngest-looking man who had yet run for President.

Frémont *(holding flag)* proclaimed a California revolution against Mexico in 1846. In 1849 he was elected one of California's first Senators.

In 1856 the Republicans made their first attempt to capture the Presidency. "Bleeding Kansas" was their principal issue, and John Charles Frémont, the California glamour boy who had become a red-hot Free Soiler, was their candidate. For the first time sex appeal was brought directly into a Presidential campaign when Frémont and his pretty wife Jessie appeared side by side on campaign banners and cartoons. "Frémont and Jessie" seemed to be the Republican ticket, instead of Frémont and William L. Dayton. "We go for our country and Union, and for brave little Jessie forever," ran one Republican ditty.

In the North and Middle West the Frémont campaign became a moral crusade against slavery, with preachers, professors, poets, and young people in the lead:

> Arise, arise, ye braves,
> And let our war-cry be,
> Free Speech, Free Press, Free Soil, Free Men,
> Fre-mont and Victory!

But the solid banking and industrial interests of the Eastern cities did not join this idealistic stampede. Wall Street was frightened by Southern threats to secede from a Republican government; August Belmont and other conservative financiers poured out money until the Democrats had $10 to spend for every dollar the Republicans could raise. The Know-Nothing vote was turned against Frémont by false whispers that he was a practicing Catholic; Democratic orators raked over the old scandal of his illegitimate birth. The sneering term "Black Republicans" was invented by the opposition to describe the aggregation of "nigger-lovers," "red" radicals, prohibitionists, cigar-smoking women, and free-lovers who were supposed to make up the Republican party.

The unkindest cut of all came when old Tom Benton, Jessie's father, turned against them and supported the Democratic ticket in Missouri. On the morning after the election, as the telegraph ticked out the news of their defeat, Jessie remarked, with a wry smile, "Colonel Benton, I perceive, has the best of the family argument."

Yet the Republicans took 42 per cent of the major-party vote of the nation, a fact which made James Buchanan, the incoming Democratic President, look even older and more depressed than usual. The cartoon below emphasizes the contrast between the wrinkled "Old Buck" and the blooming "Young America" represented by the Frémonts.

THE LAST DOUGHFACE

to occupy the White House was James Buchanan *(above)* of Lancaster, Pennsylvania, a rich, worldly-wise gentleman of 65 who habitually carried his head cocked to one side like a listening parrot. Old Buck was the first and only bachelor President—a lover's quarrel in his youth had robbed him of the only girl he ever wanted to marry. His official hostess and constant companion was his niece, Harriet Lane, a beautiful blonde with auburn hair and violet eyes.

Buchanan's bland exterior and half-baked thinking on slavery made him a perfect example of a doughface statesman. Early in his career he had been a Middle States Federalist. When Missouri was admitted as a slave state he called a meeting in his home town to protest. But when the Federalists disappeared in the 1820's Buchanan slipped over to the Jackson side and became a Democrat. By 1830 he was saying that slavery was wrong but nothing could be done about it. He despised the Yankee abolitionists for their crudeness and fanaticism, and thoroughly enjoyed the aristocratic Southern flavor of Washington social life. In the 1840's and '50's he was an expansionist diplomat and Secretary of State, who schemed to conquer Cuba and Central America for slavery.

He was a minority President—he got 1,800,000 votes to Frémont's 1,300,000 and 900,000 for the Know-Nothing candidate, ex-President Fillmore. In his Inaugural Address he let slip a hint that he had been tipped off in advance on a Supreme Court decision which was supposed to settle the vexing slavery question forever—a decision to which, as he said, "all good citizens" should cheerfully submit.

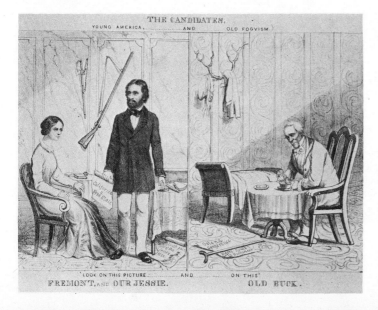

THE CANDIDATES.

YOUNG AMERICA, AND OLD FOGYISM.

LOOK ON THIS PICTURE AND ON THIS

FREMONT AND OUR JESSIE. OLD BUCK.

THE SLAVE AND THE OLD CHIEF JUSTICE

In 1857 the most famous slave in America was Dred Scott, who did odd jobs and part-time janitor work around St. Louis. Dred was born on a Virginia plantation about 1795 and taken in 1827 to Missouri, where he was sold to Dr. John Emerson, an army surgeon, who used him as a valet and barber. Dr. Emerson took Dred to Rock Island, Illinois, for two years and Fort Snelling, Minnesota, for two more; in both these places slavery was illegal by state law or by act of Congress. Dr. Emerson died and Dred passed to his widow, who moved to the free state of Massachusetts and remarried. (Her second husband was an abolitionist Congressman.) She left Dred and his family in St. Louis, where an agent hired him out for five dollars a month. Like many slaves who had passed their prime, Dred was not a hard worker and the demand for his services was small. He was also afraid that he might be sold away from his wife and daughters.

In 1846 Henry T. Blow, the son of his first owner, persuaded Dred to sue for his freedom on the ground that he had lived for four years on free soil. At that time there was general reciprocity between free and slave states, and the lower Missouri court quickly gave Dred his liberty. But the Missouri Supreme Court reversed this decision and turned Dred back into a slave. The case was then taken to the Federal Circuit Court, which declined to interfere. All of this ran through several years, during which the Republican party appeared in Missouri and decided to make Dred a test case. Late in 1856 the case of "Dred Scott, *Plaintiff in error . . .*" reached the Supreme Court of the United States. Dred Scott would never have become famous if Chief Justice Roger B. Taney could have left his case alone. But after a short routine ruling was written, denying Dred's appeal, the Southern members of the Court persuaded Taney to rewrite it into something much broader. Taney was an old-line Democrat and Maryland slaveholder who was greatly disturbed by the political debates over slavery. His Dred Scott opinion threw the whole weight of the federal courts onto the Southern side of the question.

It is useless and mischievous, wrote the 79-year-old Chief Justice, for the opponents of slavery to quote the Declaration of Independence, for its great words were never intended to include Negroes. In 1776 the "unhappy black race" was excluded from civilized governments "by common consent," and "had no rights which the white man was bound to respect." This condition was carried over into the United States Constitution, and must stand as long as the Constitution stands. Congress has never had any right to legislate against slavery; the Northwest Ordinance of 1787, the Missouri Compromise, and all other federal restrictions on slavery are therefore null and void. Of course no slave can ever become a citizen of the United States, or sue in a federal court. Slaves are "articles of merchandise" and their owners can take them into any state and keep them there, or take them out, as they please.

Aside from its faulty history and reactionary tone, Taney's judicial manifesto was a political blunder of the first magnitude. Up to this time many voters in the North and West were not deeply excited over the issue of slavery extension in the territories. But now they began to believe that the federal courts would force slavery down their throats, in states that were already free. That was certainly what Taney's decision seemed to threaten. The Dred Scott decision was, in fact, a lifesaver to the Republicans.

Chief Justice Roger Brooke Taney handed down his Dred Scott decision March 6, 1857, but obligingly "leaked" its important contents in advance to President-elect Buchanan.

Dred Scott was set free by his owner soon after the Supreme Court decision. He got a job as porter in Barnum's Hotel, St. Louis, but died of tuberculosis the next year.

The Dred Scott decision jolted ex-Congressman Abraham Lincoln out of the political doldrums and into the active leadership of the Illinois Republicans. In 1858 he accepted the Republican nomination for Senator in Illinois in a speech that became famous. "A house divided against itself cannot stand," he said, and the words "House Divided" made headlines all over the country. Lincoln's Democratic opponent was Senator Stephen A. Douglas of Nebraska bill fame. The redoubtable "Little Giant" and the gawky "Rail Splitter" barnstormed across the state in a series of debates which covered every angle of the slavery question. Douglas won the election by shameless appeals to "white supremacy," and by labeling Lincoln a warmonger. But in their debate at Freeport Lincoln trapped Douglas into saying that the voters of a territory could, if they wanted to, invalidate the Supreme Court decision in the Dred Scott case by their local police powers. This bit of backtracking became widely known as Douglas' "Freeport Doctrine." It enraged the Southern "fire-eaters," split the Democratic party, and probably cost Douglas the Presidency in 1860.

THE ILLINOIS DEBATES

The debates began when Lincoln made his "House Divided" speech at Springfield June 17, 1858. Douglas answered him at Chicago July 9. At Ottawa, on August 21, they began their joint debates, which closed at Alton October 15. Some highlights follow:

Lincoln, at Springfield: "A house divided against itself cannot stand." I believe this government cannot endure permanently half slave and half free. . . . I do not expect the house to fall; but I do expect it will cease to be divided. It will become all one thing, or all the other.

Douglas, at Chicago: Mr. Lincoln advocates boldly and clearly a war of sections, a war of the North against the South, of the Free States against the Slave States. . . . He objects to the Dred Scott decision because it does not put the Negro in the possession of citizenship on an equality with the white man. I am opposed to Negro equality. . . . I am in favor of preserving, not only the purity of the blood, but the purity of the government from any mixture or amalgamation with inferior races.

Lincoln, at Chicago: I protest, now and forever, against that counterfeit logic which presumes that because I do not want a Negro woman for a slave, I do necessarily want her for a wife. My understanding is that I need not have her for either, but, as God made us separate, we can leave one another alone, and do one another much good thereby. . . . The Judge regales us with the terrible enormities that take place by the mixture of races. . . . Why, Judge, if we do not let them get together in the Territories, they won't mix there.

Douglas, at Freeport: The last time I came here to make a speech . . . I saw a carriage—and a magnificent one it was—drive up and take a position on the outside of the crowd; a beautiful young lady was sitting on the box-seat, whilst Fred Douglass *(a celebrated ex-slave)* and her mother reclined inside, and the owner of the carriage acted as driver. I saw this in your own town.
A Voice: What of it?
Douglas: All I have to say of it is this, that if you, Black Republicans,

think that the Negro ought to be on a social equality with your wives and daughters, and ride in a carriage with your wife, whilst you drive the team, you have a perfect right to do so.

Lincoln, at Quincy: I suggest that the difference of opinion, reduced to its lowest of terms, is no other than the difference between the men who think slavery a wrong, and those who do not think it wrong. The Republican party think it wrong; we think it is a moral, a social, and a political wrong. . . . We propose a . . . policy that shall deal with it as a wrong.
Douglas, at Quincy: I hold that, under the Constitution of the United States, each State of this Union has a right to do as it pleases on the subject of slavery. . . . It is none of our business whether slavery exists in Missouri or not.

Lincoln, at Freeport: I now proceed to propound to the Judge the interrogatory. . . . Can the people of a United States Territory, in any lawful way, against the wish of any citizen of the United States, exclude slavery from its limits prior to the formation of a state constitution?
Douglas, at Freeport: I answer emphatically . . . slavery cannot exist a day or an hour anywhere, unless it is supported by local police regulations. . . . Hence, no matter what the decision of the Supreme Court may be on that abstract question, still the right of the people to make a Slave Territory or a Free Territory is perfect and complete. . . .

At Ottawa some of Lincoln's admirers carried him off the platform on their shoulders. This was referred to as follows:

Douglas, at Jonesboro: I wish to say to you that whenever I degrade my friends and myself by allowing them to carry me on their backs along through the public streets . . . I am willing to be deemed crazy.
Lincoln, at Jonesboro: Let the Judge go on; and after he is done . . . I want you all, if I can't go home myself, to let me stay and rot here; and if anything happens to the Judge, if I cannot carry him to the hotel and put him to bed, let him stay here and rot. . . .

Lincoln speaks while Douglas waits his turn behind.

JOHN BROWN'S BODY

WHILE OTHER WHILE OTHER men debated slavery the experienced guerrilla fighter John Brown invaded the South and provoked a state of war.

John Brown was a Connecticut Yankee, born in 1800. He had been a drover, tanner, and traveling salesman before he went to Kansas in 1855 and organized a band of abolitionist irregulars. He directed the famous massacre of proslavery settlers on Pottawatomie Creek, in Kansas, and also raided into Missouri, stealing horses and slaves, and killing one slaveholder. In 1858 he led a few followers into Canada and organized a revolutionary "government" for the South, with himself as Commander in Chief.

On the night of October 16, 1859, after a long period of planning and spying, he rode into Harpers Ferry, Virginia, with a wagonload of pikes and an "army" of 18 men. A local Negro and an Irish railroad hand were killed in an early exchange of shots. Brown then set up headquarters in the United States armory, which his men had captured, and waited for the near-by slaves to revolt and join him. Instead he was surrounded by swarms of militia and a company of marines under Colonel Robert E. Lee. On the morning of the eighteenth a marine lieutenant pushed into the armory and beat Brown to the floor with his sword. By that time ten of his men, including two of his sons, were dead or dying.

John Brown, the Kansas guerrilla, is shown in the photograph at the top of the page. John Brown of Harpers Ferry is shown directly above. He grew his huge beard as a disguise.

154

Marines, rushed to Harpers Ferry from Washington, smash the enginehouse door behind which Brown is trapped.

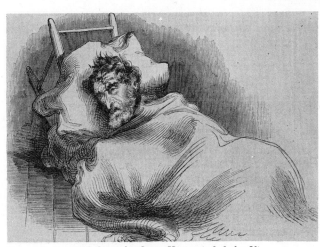

Brown lies wounded on the floor. He reminded the Virginia Governor of "a broken-winged hawk with talons set."

JOHN BROWN'S FINISH

was vividly reported by the newspapers, and by sketch artists from the new picture weeklies. After his capture Brown was left lying on the floor, his hair and clothes smeared with blood, while various persons badgered him with questions. The following exchange was reported by the New York *Herald:* "*Bystander:* Upon what principle do you justify your acts? *Mr. Brown:* Upon the golden rule. I pity the poor in bondage that have none to help them.... *Bystander:* To set them free would sacrifice the life of every man in this community. *Mr. Brown:* I do not think so. *Bystander:* I know it. I think you are fanatical. *Mr. Brown:* And I think you are fanatical."

This steady courage and moral certainty accompanied Brown to the gallows, to which he was quickly condemned for murder and treason. He welcomed his execution as good publicity for the antislavery cause. "I have been whiped...," he wrote in one of his last letters to his wife, "but am sure I can recover all the lost capital occasioned by that disaster; by only hanging a few moments by the neck."

An artist from *Leslie's* weekly drew this picture of John Brown ascending the gallows December 2, 1859. As the body dropped through the trap the commanding colonel exclaimed, "So perish all such enemies of Virginia!"

ON MARCH 7, 1860, eight hundred women shoemakers of Lynn, Massachusetts, went on strike for an increase in pay. Carrying parasols and wearing their best hoop skirts, they paraded through a snowstorm behind the Lynn City Guards, while an artist for *Leslie's* sketched the picture which appears above. Two weeks later the strike was still on, and the ladies all went to an outdoor chowder party, which was followed by dancing and kissing games. A riot almost occurred when a boss machinist named Piper boasted that he had persuaded two girls to go back to work. A committee of strikers escorted Piper

THE LADY STRIKERS OF LYNN

off the grounds, while the band played the "Rogue's March."

Labor unions had existed in Eastern cities since before the Revolution, but their right to strike was first established in 1842, by a decision of Chief Justice Lemuel Shaw of Massachusetts. Yankee mill girls like those shown above were famous for their fighting spirit during strikes. At Lowell they captured their mill superintendent and ducked him under a pump. At Dover, New Hampshire, when asked to take a wage cut, they pelted their boss with wads of cotton and walked off the job.

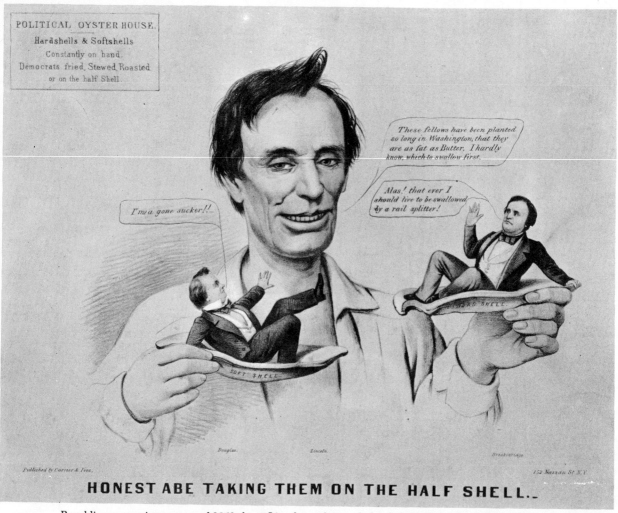

*These fellows have been planted
so long in Washington, that they
are as fat as Butter, I hardly
know, which to swallow first.*

*Alas! that ever I
should live to be swallowed
by a rail splitter!*

I'm a gone sucker!!

Published by Currier & Ives,   152 Nassau St. N.Y.

Douglas.   Lincoln.   Breckinridge.

SOFT SHELL   HARD SHELL

HONEST ABE TAKING THEM ON THE HALF SHELL._

Republican campaign cartoon of 1860 shows Lincoln ready to gulp his Soft Shell and Hard Shell Democratic opponents.

THE REPUBLICANS passed over their best-known men in 1860 and nominated Abraham Lincoln of Illinois for President. "Honest Abe" is his nickname, said the Republican newspapers, and he has won it by a lifetime of fair dealing—he is just what this sorely swindled nation needs—born in a log cabin, springing fresh from the people, his life and character should touch the popular heart. The Republican publicity machine played down Lincoln's "House Divided" speech and played up his youthful exploits as a fence-rail splitter.

Southerners sneered that Lincoln looked like an African gorilla and talked like a third-rate slang-whanging lawyer. "We know old Abe does not look very handsome," replied a Republican, "but if all the ugly men in the United States vote for him, he will surely be elected!" Thousands of Lincoln voters organized Wide Awake Clubs and tramped the

Rail splitting was the favorite cartoon theme in 1860. Here Rail Splitter Lincoln heedlessly splits the Union.

"The 'Nigger' in the Woodpile" shows Greeley and Lincoln trying to hide the Negro problem under a pile of rails.

HONEST ABE, THE RAIL SPLITTER

THE RAIL CANDIDATE.

Democratic cartoon shows Lincoln riding one of his own rails, supported by radical Editor Horace Greeley and a Negro.

streets at night, wearing military caps and capes, and carrying torches over their shoulders like guns.

Northern big business was still against the "radical" Republicans, but Northern workers flocked to the party. Lincoln himself went out of his way to address a meeting of striking shoemakers. "I am glad," he said, "to see that a system of labor prevails in New England under which laborers can strike when they want to . . . and wish it might prevail everywhere."

Meanwhile the Democrats split wide open on slavery. The moderate, "Soft Shell" branch of the party nominated Stephen A. Douglas for President. The proslavery "Hard Shells" repudiated Douglas and his Freeport Doctrine and put up John Breckinridge of Kentucky. The two Democrats together polled 2,226,738 votes to Lincoln's 1,866,452. But Lincoln carried the Solid North and won the Electoral College.

"Storming the Castle" shows Lincoln in Wide Awake costume, rushing to bar his rivals from the White House.

"The Political Gymnasium" shows Lincoln, Douglas (boxing), and other politicians performing in a maze of rails.

THE SOUTH

LINCOLN'S ELECTION set the nightmare in motion. The Union began to break up. South Carolina, where the dead Calhoun still reigned, was the first to go. On December 20, 1860, her people in convention assembled declared "that the union . . . between South Carolina and other States under the name of the United States of America is hereby dissolved." By February 1 six other cotton states—Florida, Mississippi, Alabama, Georgia, Louisiana, and Texas—had seceded. As they went they flung charges at the people of the North: "They have enticed our slaves from us . . . insulted and outraged our citizens . . . encouraged a hostile invasion of a Southern State to excite insurrection, murder and rapine." Seasoned Southern statesmen like Jefferson Davis of Mississippi, and Georgia's "Little Wizard," Alexander H. Stephens, tried to block outright secession. "The people are run mad," complained Stephens. "They are wild with passion and frenzy, doing they know not what."

The planters and courthouse politicians of the Deep South were indeed intoxicated by visions of a new "Manifest Destiny." Now that they were free, they said, they would build a slaveholding empire all the way down to the Amazon Valley. Eventually the moderate Northern states might rejoin them, and Washington could be the capital again. But they would never take back the "nigger-loving" Yankees!

Confederate President Jefferson Davis disliked his job. He would have preferred to command the Southern armies.

At his inauguration in Montgomery Davis said the South would not shirk "the final arbitrament of the sword."

South Carolina militia captured this federal post, Castle Pinckney, from one U. S. Army officer December 27,

WALKS OUT

The first step toward this dream was taken February 8, 1861, at Montgomery, Alabama, when the seven seceded states formed a new union—the Confederate States of America—with a constitution guaranteeing the perpetual existence of slavery. Jeff Davis was elected President and Stephens was named Vice President, both somewhat against their will.

In Washington a weird state of confusion and treachery prevailed. A Senator from seceded Florida, still drawing his federal pay, stayed at the capital and sent home advice for capturing the United States forts near Pensacola. Secretary of War Floyd, a Virginian, withdrew 115,000 army rifles and muskets from Northern arsenals and sent them to various Southern cities. President Buchanan, a lame duck in the White House, could only weep and wring his hands. When South Carolina demanded the federal forts in Charleston Harbor Buchanan started to yield, then changed his mind and did nothing.

Meanwhile a federal steamship, the *Star of the West*, tried to enter the harbor with food and reinforcements for the 75 United States soldiers who were marooned on the island Fort Sumter. South Carolina shore guns opened fire and drove the ship away. On the Senate floor Louis Wigfall of Texas, whose state had already seceded, flung this taunt at the North: "Your flag has been insulted; redress it if you dare. You have submitted to it for two months, and you will submit forever."

Vice President Alexander H. Stephens, an old friend of Lincoln's, secretly believed the Confederacy was doomed.

1860. The Stars and Stripes was hauled down and the red palmetto flag of South Carolina was run up in its place.

The day before, Major Robert Anderson withdrew his tiny federal force to the heavily armed island Fort Sumter.

Another *Vanity Fair* cartoon shows President Abe doing the Highland fling while waiting for a train to Washington.

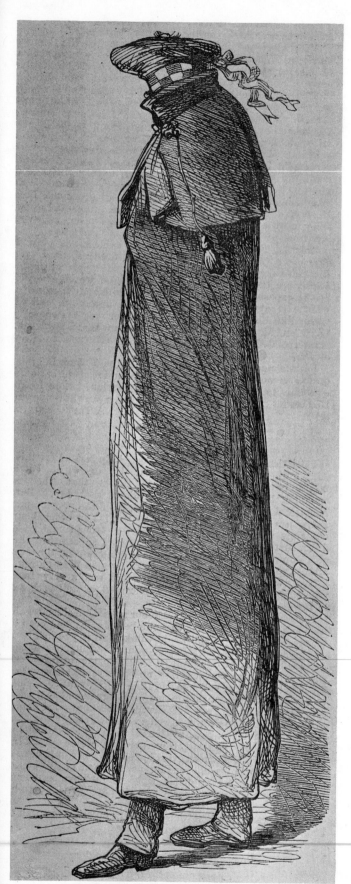

"A Fugitive Sketch" in *Vanity Fair* perpetuated the false rumor that Lincoln disguised himself in Scotch costume.

Confederate cartoon by Adalbert Volck shows Lincoln arriving in a boxcar and being greeted by a scared cat.

LINCOLN GOES TO WASHINGTON

IN SPRINGFIELD, Illinois, Abraham Lincoln sat and thought and grew the first beard ever seen on a President. Lincoln and the whole North seemed weak and uncertain in the face of the South's bold action. Lincoln was making no commitments or statements, and definitely stalling for time. Virginia and seven more slave states were still in the Union—the Republican strategy was to keep them in, at least until Lincoln could get to Washington and be inaugurated.

On February 11, 1861, "Old Abe" left Springfield for a long roundabout railroad trip which would end at the capital. In speeches along the way he gave expression not so much to his own views as to the alternating fears and hopes of the North. At Indianapolis he asked a simple question: Would it be "invasion" or "coercion" (as Jeff Davis had charged) if the Federal Government should try to hold and retake its own forts and other property? At Cleveland he told a laughing throng that the crisis was all artificial—"Let it alone and it will go down of itself." In Philadelphia, in a more serious tone, he pledged himself to uphold the promise of the Declaration of Independence—that "the weights would be lifted from the shoulders of all men, and that all should have an equal chance." That night, after going to Harrisburg, he suddenly dropped out of sight. Telegraph wires along his route were cut and nothing was heard of him until he turned up at Willard's Hotel in Washington 24 hours later. The New York *Times* printed a false rumor that he had sneaked into the capital disguised in a Scotch plaid cap and a long military cloak. Actually he arrived in an ordinary sleeping car, wearing a soft wool hat and his usual shawl around his shoulders. The fears of some prominent officials that he might be murdered by proslavery mobs in Baltimore were responsible for the 24 hours of secrecy.

On March 4 Lincoln delivered an Inaugural Address which was conciliatory but perfectly firm. "In your hands, my dissatisfied fellow countrymen, and not in mine, is the momentous issue of civil war. . . ," he told the seceded South. "You can have no conflict without being yourselves the aggressors. . . . We are not enemies, but friends. We must not be enemies."

Two days later President Davis called for 100,000 Confederate volunteers.

This photograph, taken the day Lincoln arrived in Washington, shows how he really looked—tired and dignified.

Early arrivals gather at the Capitol to hear Lincoln's Inaugural Address. The great dome was still being built.

163

AT 4:30 A.M. April 12, 1861, a dull boom and a spurt of flame broke the misty silence over Charleston Harbor. A big mortar shell soared up from the shore and plunged down on Fort Sumter, where it exploded with a thunderous roar. This first shot from the Confederate battery at Fort Johnson was fol-

lowed by a rain of shells from four directions against Sumter, which remained strangely silent for several hours, and then began firing sporadically in reply. As the cannon spoke in Charleston, more than 40 years of political compromises went up in smoke, and the Civil War between North and South began

The picture at the left from *Harper's Weekly* shows the final stages of the bombardment of Fort Sumter *(center)* on the morning of April 13. Fort Johnson, where the first shot was fired, is in the foreground. In the background at the right are the tiny silhouettes of the federal relief ships, which never came any closer because they were outgunned by the Confederate shore batteries.

The federal garrison on Sumter consisted of 65 soldiers, 10 officers, and one New York City police sergeant in mufti. They had little ammunition, less food, and were completely surrounded by heavy guns and 8,800 hostile troops. Major Anderson, the federal commander, would not let his men go to the ramparts and fire their biggest cannon for fear they might be hurt. After 34 hours of Confederate shelling, during which the inside of the fort was smashed and set afire, Anderson surrendered and boarded a ship for New York, carrying with him Fort Sumter's riddled flag. No one on either side was killed until the final moments of the evacuation, when Anderson's men fired a 50-round salute. At the 50th discharge a premature explosion killed one federal soldier.

THE CANNON SPEAK

Both sides had maneuvered to have it happen this way. Lincoln had sent supplies to Sumter, though he knew this would lead to shooting. Jefferson Davis had ordered the shooting, although it was obvious the supplies could not be delivered. The Confederate military commander knew that Sumter's garrison had nothing left to eat but salt pork and water, and planned to surrender by April 15. But already the Southern politicians were saying that the Confederacy would break up "unless you sprinkle blood in the face of the people." The South fired the first shot because the South felt the need for war.

Southern volunteers try to look very tough and bloodthirsty in front of a Richmond photographer. The young man at upper left is brandishing a bowie knife at the camera.

JOHNNY
REBS...

THESE ARE some of the young Americans who rushed to join their respective colors after they heard about Sumter. The Southerners shown directly above doubtless pictured their foes as a horde of fanatical John Browns, while the blue-clad Yanks on the opposite page expected to fight an army of Simon Legrees. Both these misconceptions vanished quickly on the battlefield, where the fighting men got to know each other well.

Lincoln's first call for troops was issued on April 15, the day after Sumter surrendered. Virginia seized this as a pretext to secede and join the Confederacy, taking with her the ablest professional soldier in America, Colonel Robert E. Lee. Arkansas, Tennessee, and North Carolina (which had previously voted

Northern volunteers attend a religious service somewhere in Virginia. The occasion is supposed to be serious, but the boy sitting at the far right has trouble stifling a grin.

to stay in the Union) also went "Secesh." But Virginia's western counties seceded from Virginia and became a new loyal state. And Unionists took control of Maryland, Kentucky, and Missouri, the remaining slave states. To prevent Washington itself from going Confederate, Massachusetts, New York, and Rhode Island rushed in crack regiments to garrison the Treasury, the Patent Office, and the Capitol itself. By the end of May two well-defined enemy nations faced each other across a line from Chesapeake Bay to the southern boundary of Kansas. Their rival capitals, Richmond and Washington, were only 110 miles apart. In the space between, the two armies bivouacked, drilled, fattened on beef and concentrated milk, sharpened bayonets, prayed, wrote letters home, and waited.

AND BLUE BELLIES

"Farnsworth's Charge at Gettysburg" was a minor incident in the war's biggest battle, July 1-4, 1863. The Union General Farnsworth *(right)* was killed at the head of his men by a Texas sharpshooter, and the charge was a failure.

Harper's Weekly, in this atrocity picture, accuses the "Rebs" of bayoneting Union wounded *(right)* at Bull Run.

Cavalry of Lee's Army of Northern Virginia fords the Potomac in the first invasion of the North, September 1862.

Steam-driven warships with armor plate and revolving gun turrets were used effectively in the Civil War. This picture shows a big steamboat battle off Memphis, June 6, 1862, soon after the Union Navy took New Orleans.

FROM BULL RUN TO GETTYSBURG

IN JULY the Army of the Potomac, 36,000 strong—the biggest army ever assembled on American soil—moved out from the vicinity of Washington to begin its grand invasion of the South. Its immediate mission was to capture Richmond and disperse the rebel Government; after that it was supposed to clean up what was left of the Southern armies. At Bull Run, a little stream 30 miles west of the White House, it collided with a Confederate force of 30,000 men. The confident Yanks pushed smartly ahead and the Southern front line gave way. On a near-by hill General Thomas Jonathan Jackson stood "like a stone wall" and let the Northern wave come on. At the last possible moment his well-drilled Shenandoah brigade jumped up from the underbrush, fired one crashing point-blank volley, and charged with fixed bayonets. "Yell like furies when you charge!" Jackson told them, and for the first time the ear-piercing rebel yell was heard on a battlefield. The federal onslaught faltered, fell back, and turned into an avalanche in reverse. Its remnants never stopped running until they reached the muddy streets of Washington.

For three years after Bull Run the eastern end of the war surged back and forth between Washington and Richmond, with wide circles around and behind them. The battles grew bigger and bloodier every year, but none of them were decisive. In the West and along the seacoast, the federals had definitely the best of it. Middle West farm boys with rifles over their shoulders invaded Tennessee, broke the Deep South's inner defenses at Shiloh, and pushed into Mississippi and Louisiana. When they reached Vicksburg, the great Confederate stronghold on the Mississippi River, they unslung shovels and dug miles of trenches and canals around it. Vicksburg fell after a 43-day siege, cutting the Confederacy in two. On the same day Lee's final invasion of the North was smashed at Gettysburg.

From the strictly military standpoint the American Civil War was the mightiest spectacle of the nineteenth century. More than 2,300,000 men fought in it. More than 600,000, or one out of four, were killed. In order to win it the North had to subdue an empire of 749,000 square miles, which was more territory than Napoleon's armies had conquered in 15 years. The North had more soldiers (1,556,000 to the South's 800,000), more factories, railroads, ships, and money. But the South had smarter generals, a more united home front, a sharper sense of grievance, and a stronger urge to fight.

Union reserves at Fredericksburg watch fearfully as wounded are brought back and treated December 13, 1862.

The North had 7,000 casualties in this major defeat. The picture was drawn by Thomas Nast for *Harper's Weekly*.

THE CAMERA RECORD

THE CIVIL WAR was the first in history to be photographed on a large scale. Mathew Brady, Alexander Gardner, T. H. O'Sullivan, and others followed the Union troops and took pictures of everything from generals to army mules. They got some of their most striking shots by driving out after a battle with the wagons that collected the dead. They used big box cameras on tripods, and collodion-coated wet glass plates which had to be sensitized in one kind of chemical bath immediately before exposure and developed immediately after in another. The process was painfully awkward but it produced a magnificent record of the war.

Union wounded rest in the sun after the big battle at Chancellorsville, May 3-5, 1863.

Dead men from both armies strew the field of Gettysburg at dawn July 5, 1863. Here the North and South each lost about 5,000 killed.

This was a Confederate battery at Antietam, September 17, 1862. Federal shells smashed horses and men, riddled the Dunker church.

This young Southerner was bayoneted in the federal rush for Petersburg, April 2, 1865, while trying to reload the rifle beside him.

President Lincoln, with an unaccustomed haircut, sits for his photograph in 1863.

LINCOLN'S MASTER STROKES

FROM THE BEGINNING of the war the abolitionists brought great pressure on Lincoln to abolish slavery by the exercise of his extraordinary wartime powers. The impetuous Horace Greeley wrote a passionate public "Prayer of Twenty Millions," demanding that the President do this in the summer of 1862. Lincoln replied in a widely reprinted letter. "If I could save the Union without freeing *any* slave I would do it," he wrote to Greeley, "and if I could save it by freeing *all* the slaves, I would do it; and if I could save it by freeing some and leaving others alone I would also do that. . . . I intend no modification of my oft-expressed *personal* wish that all men everywhere could be free." Very soon after writing this letter Lincoln decided to free *most* of the slaves.

His Emancipation Proclamation, which went into effect January 1, 1863, gave technical freedom to 3,063,392 slaves, worth approximately $2 billion, in ten seceded states. (It could only be enforced, of course, where the invading Northern armies were in control.) But it gave no freedom at all to 441,702 slaves in the five border states which had stayed in the Union. Tennessee and certain counties in Virginia and Louisiana were also allowed to keep their slaves, because they had already submitted to federal rule.

Despite these compromise provisions, the Emancipation Proclamation was the most telling political stroke of the war. World opinion, which had previously favored the underdog South, switched decisively to the liberating North. Mass meetings of English workers forced the British Cabinet to stop the building of Confederate naval vessels in England. The Czar of Russia, who had freed his serfs peaceably in 1861, sent squadrons of warships on a friendly visit to New York and San Francisco. Emancipation also weighed heavily in the military scales, by adding 50,000 Negro troops and many more Negro laborers to the Union Army. It worked so well, in fact, that President Davis and the Confederate Cabinet later offered to abolish slavery themselves in return for European recognition. But by the time they made this decision, it was too late.

Meanwhile, at Gettysburg, Lincoln had won another great victory with words. The brief statement of Northern aims which he made there, November 19, 1863, was the best propaganda speech of the war.

BY THE PRESIDENT OF THE UNITED STATES OF AMERICA.

A Proclamation.

Whereas, on the twenty-second day of September, in the year of our Lord one thousand eight hundred and sixty-two, a proclamation was issued by the President of the United States, containing, among other things, the following, to wit:

[remainder of proclamation text]

By the President:

Abraham Lincoln

A million copies of Lincoln's Proclamation were distributed in the South.

These runaway slaves made their way across the Union lines before emancipation, and got jobs as army teamsters. General Benjamin F. Butler called them "contraband of war."

THE GETTYSBURG ADDRESS

was a five-minute, ten-sentence statement of what the war was about, from the Northern point of view. It was spoken by Lincoln at the dedication of a cemetery for the Union soldiers who had died at Gettysburg four months earlier. It did not assail the South, or exult in the victory which had cost so much. But it struck the exact keynote of Northern feeling. It became, in time, the most famous single utterance of any President.

At the right is Lincoln's manuscript; following are his words:

"Four score and seven years ago our fathers brought forth, upon this continent, a new nation, conceived in Liberty, and dedicated to the proposition that all men are created equal.

"Now we are engaged in a great civil war, testing whether that nation, or any nation, so conceived, and so dedicated, can long endure.

"We are met here on a great battlefield of that war. We have come to dedicate a portion of it as a final resting place for those who here gave their lives that that nation might live. It is altogether fitting and proper that we should do this.

"But in a larger sense we can not dedicate—we can not consecrate—we can not hallow this ground. The brave men, living and dead, who struggled here, have consecrated it far above our poor power to add or detract.

"The world will little note, nor long remember, what we say here, but can never forget what they did here.

"It is for us, the living, rather to be dedicated here to the unfinished work which they have, thus far, so nobly carried on. It is rather for us to be here dedicated to the great task remaining before us—that from these honored dead we take increased devotion to that cause for which they here gave the last full measure of devotion—that we here highly resolve that these dead shall not have died in vain; that this nation shall have a new birth of freedom; and that this government of the people, by the people, for the people, shall not perish from the earth."

Before the speech a parade moved through Gettysburg toward the cemetery. Lincoln rode a chestnut horse, "the largest in the Cumberland Valley."

This crowd saw the President put on his steel-rimmed spectacles, rise, and deliberately read his speech.

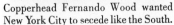
Copperhead Fernando Wood wanted
New York City to secede like the South.

Copperhead Clement Vallandigham was
banished from the North by Lincoln.

THE DISLOYAL OPPOSITION

COILED behind Lincoln's back, ready to strike if the North should weaken, was a vast fifth column of Southern sympathizers, "nigger-haters," draft-dodgers, peace-at-any-price Democrats, embittered editors, and ambitious politicians. The loyal newspapers called them "Copperheads," and they accepted the name, wearing the head of Liberty, cut from a copper United States cent, as their badge.

The leading Copperhead of New York City was Mayor and Congressman Fernando Wood, whose newspaper, the *Daily News*, helped stir up the Draft Riots of 1863. The national idol of the Copperheads was Congressman Clement L. Vallandigham of Dayton, Ohio, who led the fight against every measure to carry on the war. In May 1863 Vallandigham was arrested for publicly expressing sympathy with the enemy, and Lincoln ordered him turned over to the South. Even the Confederates snickered when Vallandigham stalked across no man's land and announced to an astonished private: "I surrender myself to you as a prisoner of war." The next year he sneaked back into the United States with a pillow tucked under his pants and vest, and fake whiskers pasted to his jaw. But Lincoln ignored him.

Northern cartoon of 1863 shows the Union threatened by political reptiles with hats of Midwest Democratic Congressmen.

THE ARREST

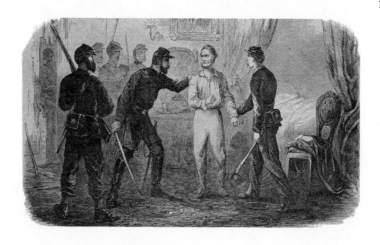

of Vallandigham caught the No. 1 Copperhead in a pair of long white drawers. Union soldiers chopped down the door of his house and seized him in his bedroom after shots had been fired at them from a window. Later, after the troops had gone, a mob of Dayton Copperheads stormed through the city, burning a newspaper office and other buildings belonging to Union men. Vallandigham was arrested for saying that the North was waging "a wicked, cruel and unnecessary war . . . for the freedom of the blacks and the enslavement of the whites. . . ."

Antiwar mob, inflamed by Copperhead propaganda, fights New York police during the Draft Riots of July 13-16, 1863.

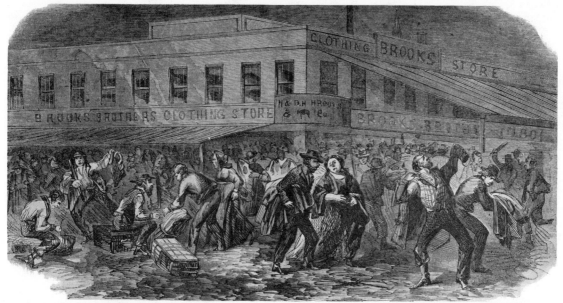

Brooks Brothers' clothing store is looted by some of the 50,000 draft rioters. At least 75 people were killed in the riots.

DON'T SWAP HORSES
CROSSING A STREAM

Republican cartoon shows Lincoln and McClellan *(in the bushes)* as the political nags of 1864. Brother Jonathan, on Lincoln, tells John Bull why he does not intend to swap.

The 1864 election made "Long Abe" look longer than ever in *Harper's Weekly*.

Lincoln is a confident giant, McClellan a political pygmy, in this cartoon. The spade in Little Mac's hand refers to the campaign charge that his army dug more than it fought.

Little Mac, little Mac, you're the very man,
  Go down to Washington as soon as you can . . .
Democrats, Democrats, do it up brown,
  Lincoln and his Niggerheads won't go down,

sang many a Northern voter in the bitterly fought wartime election of 1864. The melody was supposedly written by Stephen Foster before his death early in the year. But the words came from the Copperheads on the Democratic national committee. Northern morale was low and the Democrats played politics accordingly. Their platform had a plank written by Vallandigham himself, calling for an immediate truce and a negotiated peace. Their candidate for President was General George B. McClellan, who combined defeatism with a dash of military glamour. McClellan had led the Army of the Potomac for 15 seesawing months before Lincoln fired him as a chronic staller.

President Lincoln was renominated by the newly formed National Union party, composed of most of the Republicans and a large bloc of War Democrats. When a delegation went to the White House to congratulate him, Lincoln told them one of his famous little jokes. The situation of the country, he said, reminded him of an old Dutch farmer who once remarked that "it was not best to swap horses when crossing a stream." "Don't swap horses" made a neat campaign slogan for the Unionists. But what really re-elected Lincoln in 1864 was a pair of great Northern victories: Sherman's capture of Atlanta in September, and Sheridan's sweep through the Shenandoah Valley in October. In November McClellan, the little general without an army, trailed Lincoln by half a million popular votes, and got only 21 electoral votes to Lincoln's 212.

General George B. McClellan, candidate for President, strikes a Napoleonic pose.

The soldier vote went heavily for Lincoln, as most army commanders openly boosted the Union ticket. The drawing above shows men of the Army of the Potomac lined up to cast their ballots while a visiting politician does a little persuading at the left.

"If the people [of Georgia] raise a howl against my barbarity and cruelty, I will answer that war is war, and not popularity-seeking," said General William T. Sherman.

"It is well that war is so terrible—we would grow too fond of it," said General Robert E. Lee to Longstreet, as he watched the federals dying in heaps at Fredericksburg.

"I . . . propose to fight it out on this line if it takes all summer," said General U. S. Grant *(center with slouch hat)* after losing 17,000 men in the Wilderness. It took all summer, all winter, and 43,000 more men. Grant was tobacco-stained, sometimes drunk, and wore a sloppy private's blouse. But, as Lincoln said, "he fights!"

Two women in widow's black wander through the ruins of Richmond in April 1865. Fleeing Confederates blew up the city.

"WAR...IS ALL HELL"

IN VIRGINIA, Tennessee, Georgia, and the Carolinas, the war ground on, leaving its mark on the faces of generals and cities. Two rugged Westerners were now in charge for the Union. Major General William Tecumseh Sherman, tall, testy, and red-whiskered, carved his way through the South's heart from Chattanooga to the sea—wrecking, smashing, and burning in a campaign of deliberate attrition. Sherman believed that the quickest way to end the war was to destroy the South's productive capacity and crush Secesh morale. He could see no glory in war anyway—"It is all hell," he said.

On the main front before Richmond Lieutenant General Ulysses Simpson Grant pounded Lee's army with massive strokes. Each stroke killed thousands of men, but the North had plenty of men, and the South did not. Richmond fell April 3, 1865. On April 9 Lee was surrounded by solid walls of federal infantry at Appomattox Court House. Donning a spotless light gray uniform and a jeweled sword, he rode through Grant's lines and surrendered. The federals began to cheer but Grant stopped them, saying: "The war is over—the rebels are our countrymen again."

BLACK FRIDAY

Two NIGHTS after Lee's surrender President Lincoln stepped out on a White House balcony and faced a victory-celebrating crowd. A secretary held a candle over his shoulder as he carefully read his terms for peace. There would be no wild rampage of revenge so far as the President was concerned. Each Southern state could return to the Union with full privileges as soon as 10 per cent of its white citizens took the oath of allegiance and formed a new state government. The problem of Negro voting would be left to the states, both South and North. But the President hoped that "very intelligent" colored men, and those who had served the Union as soldiers, would be permitted to vote.

Down on the grass a young man with a handsome, sallow face and a black mustache turned to his companion. "That means nigger citizenship," he exclaimed. "Now, by God, I'll put him through!" The man who said this was John Wilkes Booth, an unemployed actor who had been hanging around Washington for months, plotting to kidnap the President. Somewhere on the lawn a band suddenly struck up "Dixie," the Confederate national air, and Booth walked off angrily into the night.

Washington was still in a holiday mood three days later, on Good Friday, April 14. In the morning Lincoln told his Cabinet again that he would take no part in hanging the rebels—"even the worst of them." "Frighten them out of the country . . . scare them off," he said, making motions as though he were shooing sheep. "Enough lives have been sacrificed." In the evening he drove with his wife to Ford's Theatre to see a play called *Our American Cousin*. It was not a good play and he didn't want to go. But his appearance had been advertised, and Mrs. Lincoln had invited guests, so he went.

At some point during the performance his bodyguard, a befuddled Washington policeman, went out into the alley for a drink of whisky. What happened after that was sheer, lurid melodrama. Through the unguarded rear door of the President's box stepped Booth, with a small brass pistol in one hand and a dagger in the other. He fired one shot into the back of Lincoln's head, slashed the other man in the box with his dagger, and leaped from the box railing to the stage. The spur of his boot caught in a flag so that he fell crookedly on one foot, fracturing his left leg. But he staggered to his feet, waved his bloody dagger at the audience, shouted, *"Sic semper tyrannis*—Virginia is avenged!"* and escaped before anyone realized that he had just murdered the President.

John Wilkes Booth, the actor-assassin, was a monomaniac on the race question.

Leslie's weekly shows how Booth sneaked up on Lincoln and fired from behind. Mrs. Lincoln sits beside the President. At right are their two guests, Major Rathbone and his fiancee.

Lincoln's last photograph, taken April 9, the day of Appomattox, shows no elation over Northern victory. Four years of war had cut deep lines of sadness on the Rail Splitter's face, but they had not made him hate the South. "With malice toward none; with charity for all . . . ," he had urged in his second Inaugural Address in March, "let us strive . . . to bind up the nation's wounds." Booth's bullet cut him down before he could fairly begin.

From a scaffold in the Washington jailyard, on the hot morning of July 7, 1865, dangled four of John Wilkes Booth's accomplices. Mrs. Mary Surratt *(left)* kept a boardinghouse where Booth's gang met. David Herold was Booth's personal aide and companion. Lewis Paine, a Confederate deserter, was assigned to kill Secretary of State Seward on the night of April 14. He got into Seward's home and cut Seward's throat with a bowie knife, but did not quite kill him. George Atzerodt, a middle-aged Confederate spy, was supposed to kill Vice President Andrew Johnson, but lost his nerve and didn't try.

Booth himself had been dead for months when this photograph was taken. On April 26 federal troops and Secret Service agents trapped the assassin in a Virginia barn. A soldier fired through the door and Booth was dragged out with a wound through his neck. He lay conscious all night on a farmhouse porch, bleeding to death and sucking noisily on a rag soaked in brandy. Toward morning he asked to see his hands—he could no longer feel or move them. A soldier lifted them up and Booth muttered, "Useless, useless." Those were his last words. His corpse was buried secretly under an arsenal floor.

STANTON, THE DICTATOR

FOR A FEW WEEKS after Lincoln's death this moon-faced man with sprouting whiskers and baggy pants was the virtual dictator of the United States. Edwin M. Stanton was Secretary of War and boss of an army of 900,000 men. He decided—without any real evidence—that President Davis and the Confederate Cabinet had something to do with Lincoln's assassination. After the Southern armies collapsed Davis tried to escape to Mexico, but federal cavalrymen caught him in Georgia, wearing his wife's cloak and shawl. Stanton put him in a stone cell at Fortress Monroe, Virginia, and kept him there under a charge of treason for two years. One day the ex-President of the Confederacy threw a dish of food in a soldier's face, and for this he was held down by force while chains and an iron ball were riveted around his ankles. One reason Stanton was so rough was that his conscience bothered him. It was his job to protect Lincoln's life, and he had made a complete botch of it at Ford's Theatre.

Soldiers guard ex-President Davis in his military cell. He was freed in 1867.

JOHNSON, THE NEW PRESIDENT

President Johnson defends his policies on a "swing around the circle" in 1866.

ANDREW JOHNSON, who succeeded Lincoln as President, was a "poor white" from the Tennessee hills who went around Washington with a revolver on his hip. He was put on the Union ticket in 1864 because he was the fightingest War Democrat that the friends of Lincoln could find. At his inauguration as Vice President he took three large drinks of undiluted whisky, and made such a loud, maudlin speech that his predecessor tried to pull him back to his chair by his coattails. Later he told a Washington street crowd that he would hang Jeff Davis and all the "diabolical" crew at Richmond if he ever got the chance. But once he was in the White House, President "Andy" softened his tune. He hanged almost nobody, proclaimed a general pardon for the Confederate rank and file, and followed Lincoln's "10 per cent plan" for restoring the Southern states. This mild policy brought him into a disastrous collision with the Republican Radicals in Congress, who wanted to kill "white supremacy" in the South.

In this harsh and unforgiving face the beaten South could now see its worst enemy. Thaddeus Stevens of Pennsylvania, boss of the Republican House of Representatives, had no sympathy for any ex-Confederate. He planned to have Congress carve up the "damned rebel provinces" and fill them with new settlers, as though the whole South were conquered Indian land. The estates of "leading rebels" would be divided into 40-acre farms and sold to the former slaves at $10 an acre. If the Southerners did not like this, he implied, they could go to any other country they liked and stay there.

"I have never desired bloody punishments to any great extent," said Thad Stevens, "but there are punishments quite as appalling and longer remembered than death. They are more advisable, because they would reach a greater number. Strip a proud nobility of their bloated estates; reduce them to a level with plain republicans; send them forth to labor and teach their children to enter the workshops or handle a plow, and you will thus humble the proud traitors."

War Secretary Stanton defies the President and camps all night in his office.

THE RADICALS IN THE SADDLE

Congressman Ben Butler reads impeachment evidence against the President.

THE LINCOLN PLAN to "restore" the South limped along for more than a year under the clumsy sponsorship of President Johnson. Meanwhile came published reports that the Southern Negroes were being "restored" to virtual slavery by organized terror, lynchings, and "Black Laws" which forced them to work wherever they lived, and to accept wages and working conditions imposed by their old owners. Whipping and other penalties prescribed by these laws recalled the unhappy days of Uncle Tom. "We tell the white men of Mississippi," cried the Chicago *Tribune*, "that the men of the North will convert the State of Mississippi into a frog pond before they will allow any such laws to disgrace one foot of soil in which the bones of our soldiers sleep and over which the flag of freedom waves." The *Tribune* spoke for the Radical Republicans who wanted to "reconstruct" the South, to change it completely from what it had been.

The Radicals swept the Northern Congressional elections in 1866, despite a feeble effort by Andy Johnson to rouse the voters against them. And in March 1867, nearly two years after Appomattox, Thad Stevens and other Radical Congressmen passed two Reconstruction Acts which wiped out everything that Johnson and Lincoln had done.

The Radical Acts set up five military districts in the South, with a major general of the United States Army as the ruler of each district. Twenty thousand federal troops, along with Negro militia, were mobilized to carry out the will of Con-

Thad Stevens, too sick to walk, is carried to an impeachment committee meeting.

gress. The Acts directed that ten Southern states must abolish their old constitutions and adopt new ones permitting Negroes to vote before they could send representatives to Congress. Tennessee was exempted because she had already submitted to Congressional dictation and framed a new constitution.

President Johnson vetoed the first Reconstruction Act but Congress passed it right back over his veto. The Radicals also shoved two more insults down the President's throat: they passed laws forbidding him to dismiss his own Cabinet members, or to transfer the commander of the Army (General Grant) without Congressional consent. Johnson, who was personally pugnacious, immediately replaced Stanton, the Radical Secretary of War. Stanton refused to give up his office and Congress soon afterward impeached the President—the first, and last, time this indignity was ever inflicted on a Chief Executive.

Thad Stevens, who was old and almost dead, planned the impeachment. "We had better put it on the ground of insanity or whisky," he growled one day to his fellow committee members. But the eleven "high crimes and misdemeanors" which were finally charged against the President were surprisingly mean and trivial. The trial was staged before Chief Justice Chase and the whole Senate, and resulted in a solemn vote of 35 to 19 for conviction. But it needed a two-thirds vote (or 36) to convict. So, by one vote, Andy Johnson was acquitted. Radical rule passed its high-water mark, and the Presidency was spared further humiliation by Congress.

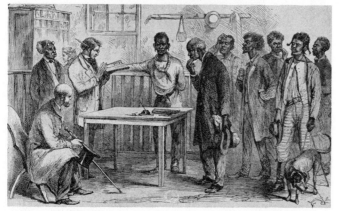

A black-and-white jury in a Southern courtroom in 1867. Negroes could also demand trial in special army courts.

Freedmen registering to vote in Macon, Georgia, during the first registration under army rule, September 1867.

A Freedmen's Bureau school in Richmond in 1866. Southern foes of Reconstruction burned many of these schools.

THE FREEING OF THE FREEDMEN

WITH FEDERAL BAYONETS prodding them from behind, the Southern states "reconstructed" themselves with great haste. In South Carolina, in 1866, the Black Laws required all freed Negroes to go to bed early, rise at dawn, speak respectfully to their employers, and perform no skilled labor without a license. But in 1867, under Reconstruction, the former slaves controlled the South Carolina legislature, and it was against the law to call a man a "nigger" or a "yankee" in that state.

The Radical program for the Negro freedmen was broad and definite. First came the Thirteenth Amendment, which made emancipation a part of the Constitution. Then came the Freedmen's Bureau, a branch of the Army, which opened Negro schools and relief centers and held special courts for Negroes throughout the South. Then came Negro suffrage under army protection, abolition of the Black Laws, and the Fourteenth Amendment, which gave full-scale citizenship to Negroes and took it away from many former "rebels." Finally, in 1869, came the Fifteenth Amendment, which barred the states from ever interfering with the Negro's right to vote. These later amendments forced Negro suffrage on Michigan, Ohio, Kansas, and other Northern states which had rejected it after the Civil War.

Thus, only five years after Lincoln's Proclamation, the four million ex-slaves were politically dominant in the South and held the balance of power in the nation. Lacking leaders and largely uneducated. they fell easily under the influence of Northern "carpetbaggers" and Southern white "scalawags" who used them for all kinds of schemes, both good and bad. Their legislatures were often corrupt and extravagant, though no more so than Northern legislatures during the same period. They set up the first public school systems in several Southern states, liberalized the South's antique election system, and carried on an effective revolution in behalf of the underprivileged of both races.

They also saved the Republican party. The Republicans had been a minority in 1860, in 1864, and, without the Negroes, they were still a minority. Thad Stevens used this as his clinching argument: What was the use, he asked, of having fought the war if Jeff Davis and the other enemies of the Union could march right back and take over the Senate and, maybe, the White House?

The Freedmen's Bureau, started by Republicans, was the Federal Government's first big venture in relief *(left)*.

"The First Vote," from *Harper's Weekly*, shows a Southern polling place during the state elections of 1867. In that year the Army's figures for the reconstructed states showed 703,000 Negro voters to 627,000 qualified whites.

A Prospective Scene in the "City of Oaks," 4th of March, 1869.

"Hang, curs, hang! * * * * * *Their* complexion is perfect gallows. Stand fast, good fate, to *their* hanging! * * * * * If they be not born to be hanged, our case is miserable."

The above cut represents the fate in store for those great pests of Southern society—the carpet-bagger and scallawag—if found in Dixie's Land after the break of day on the 4th of March next.

The genus carpet-bagger is a man with a lank head of dry hair, a lank stomach and long legs, club knees and splay feet, dried legs and lank jaws, with eyes like a fish and mouth like a shark. Add to this a habit of sneaking and dodging about in unknown places—habiting with negroes in dark dens and back streets—a look like a hound and the smell of a polecat.

Words are wanting to do full justice to the genus scallawag. He is a cur with a contracted head, downward look, slinking and uneasy gait; sleeps in the woods, like old Crossland, at the bare idea of a Ku-Klux raid.

Our scallawag is the local leper of the community. Unlike the carpet-bagger, he is native, which is so much the worse. Once he was respected in his circle; his head was level, and he would look his neighbor in the face. Now, possessed of the itch of office and the salt rheum of Radicalism, he is a mangy dog, slinking through the alleys, haunting the Governor's office, defiling with tobacco juice the steps of the Capitol, stretching his lazy carcass in the sun on the Square, or the benches of the Mayor's Court.

He waiteth for the troubling of the political waters, to the end that he may step in and be healed of the itch by the ointment of office. For office he 'bums' as a toper 'bums' for the satisfying dram. For office, yet in prospective, he hath bartered respectability; hath abandoned business, and ceased to labor with his hands, but employs his feet kicking out boot-heels against lamp-post and corner-curb, while discussing the question of office.

"HANG, CURS, HANG!"

THE KU KLUX KLAN, said the editor of the Tuscaloosa, Alabama, *Independent Monitor*, had its origin in "the galling despotism that broods like a night-mare over these Southern States . . . a persistent prostitution of all government, all resources and all powers, to degrade the white man by the establishment of a negro supremacy." Actually the Klan was started at Pulaski, Tennessee, in 1865, very soon after the war, and almost two years before Reconstruction. The first Klansmen rode around the countryside at night wearing white robes and masks, frightening freedmen by pretending to be the ghosts of Confederate soldiers. During Reconstruction, when most of the property-owning Southern whites could take no part in their own government, they joined the Klan and other underground groups like the Knights of the White Camelia and the Order of the White Rose. These secret societies worked very effectively to restore white supremacy by whippings, murders, and such crude warnings as the newspaper cartoon printed above.

The whipping of Phillis, a young North Carolina freedwoman, took place because she struck a white girl. Six of the whippers were jailed by military authorities.

Ku Klux costumes included white masks with red-braid holes for eyes, nose, and mouth. Some Kluxers wore false heads which they removed and gave to Negroes.

THE MARTYRS OF ANDERSONVILLE

and other Confederate prison pens were widely publicized during the Reconstruction period to justify the Radical policy toward the South. These drawings of living skeletons rescued from the prison at Belle Isle were published in a book by the Radical Congress. Yet General Grant himself had refused to save these men by exchange because—as he said—the South needed its soldiers back to carry on the war, while the North could always get new ones. Almost as many Southerners (25,976) died in Northern prisons as Northerners in the South (30,218).

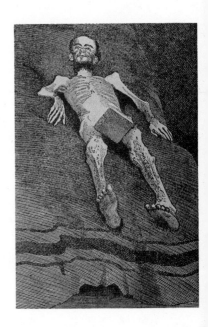

Americans thought Seward got a bad bargain when they saw this picture of Fort Yukon, one of the principal Russian posts in Alaska.

"GOD BLESS THE RUSSIANS"

IT WAS LINCOLN'S Secretary of the Navy who jotted down this remark in his diary when the Russian fleet dropped in at New York in 1863; this supposed gesture of friendship cheered up the North during a dark moment of the Civil War. One night in 1867 the Russian Minister in Washington dropped in on Secretary of State Seward with another pleasant surprise. He had just learned, he said, that Czar Alexander II would sell Russian America (Alaska) for $7,200,000. Seward stopped playing whist and offered to close the deal at once. "But your Department is closed," said the Russian. "Never mind that,"

Seward told him. "Before midnight you will find me at the Department, which will be open and ready for business." And so, before the next sun rose, Seward bought 4,000 miles of Pacific coastline and 375 million acres of new American territory for less than two cents an acre.

During the same year "Uncle Billy" skillfully untangled another phase of Manifest Destiny. In 1864 a French army had installed the Austrian Archduke Maximilian as "Emperor" of Mexico. Seward forced the French to get out of Mexico, and Maximilian was promptly shot by the Mexicans.

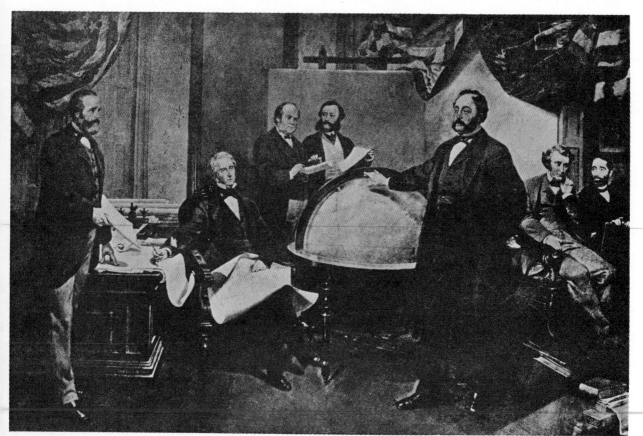

The Alaska purchase agreement was completed at 4 A.M., March 30, 1867. This painting shows Russian Minister Baron de Stoeckel standing in front of the large globe while Seward (seated, left) is pointing with his pen, as though asking the Russian to sign.

Leslie's weekly shows an American politician trying to find voters in uninhabited Alaska.

A cartoon sketch of "Uncle Billy" Seward

A firing squad of Mexican republicans disposes of Archduke Max-imilian, June 19, 1867. His flimsy "empire" lasted less than three years and was the last attempt of European royalty to appropriate American soil. Two of his Mexican generals were shot beside him.

Republican poster of 1868 boasts of reduced national debt since the war's end.

Grant's nomination starts a happy stampede at the Republican convention in Chicago. He was nominated by General John A. Logan of Illinois *(center)*, originator of Memorial Day.

THE BOYS

IN BLUE

IN THE PRESIDENTIAL campaign of 1868 the country got its first look at the solid masses of Union veterans who were now lined up as Republican voters. General Ulysses S. Grant was the Republican candidate, and the "Boys in Blue" whooped up their old commander with an enthusiasm that drowned out all discussion of political issues. The Democrats nominated former Governor Horatio Seymour of New York, an able but comparatively colorless man. Grant's Electoral College majority was overwhelming: 214 to 80. But in the popular vote he got only 3,015,071 (including 700,000 Negroes) to Seymour's 2,709,613.

A gigantic rally of Republican "Boys in Blue" from all over the North was staged October 2 in Philadelphia. Here the veterans march up Broad Street past the Union League *(right)*.

The 1868 Democratic convention met in Tammany Hall's brand-new $300,000 Wigwam.
Two ex-Confederate generals and the Grand Wizard of the Ku Klux Klan were delegates.

Some Union veterans carried torches for Seymour, as in this parade in New York. The Democratic platform called for lower taxes, less Reconstruction, and more greenback money.

"LET US HAVE PEACE"

This rare photograph of Grant without a beard shows a dimpled but stubborn chin.

PRESIDENT ULYSSES S. GRANT was short, round-shouldered, and slouchy, but he had a resolute blue eye and the look of a man who could not be trifled with. During the war he was called "Grant the Butcher" because he sent tens of thousands of men to death without a flicker of emotion. Yet he could not bear to kill an animal or bird, and he would go white with fury if he saw a man beating a horse. When his daughter Nellie was married in the White House Grant went off to her room after the ceremony and sobbed like a child.

The truth was that Grant was a well-intentioned, rather stodgy family man who could deal fairly well with facts but was baffled by ideas. He once summed up the Civil War in two typical sentences: "It is probably well that we had the war when we did. We are better off now than we would have been without it." His sole contribution to his own Presidential campaign was the four-word slogan, "Let us have peace."

During most of his life Grant was a failure at everything he tried: he failed as a farmer, as a businessman, and as a peacetime army officer. Strangely enough, this was because he lacked an aggressive personality—the conqueror of Lee was really a reticent man who hated to push himself forward. Poverty had greatly influenced his life—at one time it made him a drunkard, but he had conquered this failing before he became President. Poverty had also driven him, in St. Louis in the 1850's, to try to sell his wife's two slaves for cash to live on. At that time Grant could not get excited over slavery or any other political issue. But when the war came along he drifted into it, like millions of other plain citizens, with a mingled desire to serve his country and to forget his private troubles. He bore no grudge against the Confederates, then or later.

As President, Grant showed a conspicuous liking for expensive presents, such as Hambletonian colts, blooded bull pups, and gold-tipped cigars. His wife accepted free dresses, perfumes, and jewelry worth a great deal of money from men who did business with the Government. Grant could see nothing wrong with this. He looked upon rich men with a respect amounting to awe, regardless of how they made their money. He put a notorious war profiteer in his Cabinet and made friends with the most celebrated thieves in Wall Street. And he let his old army friends steal millions from the Government, simply because he could not believe that anyone he liked was personally dishonest.

THE PRESIDENTIAL SPEEDSTER

During Grant's two terms the White House stables flourished as never before. The President had a glistening assortment of carriages and at least a dozen horses, including a natural pacer named "Jeff Davis." He also enjoyed fast driving *(right)*. One day as he whirled along M Street a Negro policeman ran out from the sidewalk, grabbed the horse's bridle, and was dragged half a block before he stopped it. When he saw who his prisoner was the policeman apologized profusely, but Grant stepped down with a smile. "Officer, do your duty," he said, so the embarrassed policeman took the Presidential rig to the nearest station house. Grant walked back to the White House, but the speeding charge was never pressed.

This was the closest any President ever came to being arrested, except for Franklin Pierce, whose horse once ran down an old woman. Theoretically a President cannot be arrested on any charge unless he submits voluntarily.

The photograph at the left shows Grant shortly after he became President. He never swore, hated politics and political talk, disliked military parades and martial music, and, unlike Lincoln, refused to listen to off-color stories. Once when an army officer glanced around a table and remarked, by way of introduction, "I see there are no ladies present," Grant quieted him by saying, "Ah, but there are gentlemen present."

Before the Pacific railroad was finished trains from San Francisco ended their run at Cisco *(above)*, where stagecoaches took over.

The wedding of the locomotives in 1869

RAILROADS AND THE

ON MAY 10, 1869, at Promontory Point, Utah, a silver sledge drove a gold-headed spike into a laurel railroad tie, and out over the telegraph went an exultant message: "The last rail is laid! The last spike driven! The Pacific railroad is completed!" Then two locomotives, one from the East and one from the West, nosed forward until their pilots touched *(left)*, and their crews doused them with champagne. The Pacific railroad had been built in a little

Gambling tents and dance-hall shacks followed the hard-living railroad gangs. The photograph above shows Promontory, Utah, in 1869.

A dead trapper, scalped by Indians, is found by two army scouts. Indians sometimes killed the railroad workers to get their whisky.

VANISHING FRONTIER

over three years by more than 20,000 workmen across 1,775 miles of mountains and plains. The Republican administrations at Washington had helped by giving the promoters 23 million acres of land, plus $64 million in easy loans. The Republicans also made good another pledge by giving 160-acre Western farms to all comers (except former Confederates). Soon the buffaloes and Indians were being eliminated, while homesteaders' houses dotted the landscape.

Dead buffaloes, killed for their hides

A homesteader and his sod house in Kansas in 1872. Only the poorest land was free to homesteaders—a good farm cost around $1,000.

Silver miners picking ore from Nevada's Comstock Lode, the richest vein of silver in the world. Discovered just before the Civil War, the Lode yielded nearly $320 million before 1882. The miners earned $3 to $4 per day.

THE WORKING PEOPLE

"Bell-Time," drawn by Winslow Homer in 1868, shows workers pouring out of the mills at Lawrence, Massachu- setts, at the end of their 13-hour day. They worked from 5 A.M. to 7 P.M., with two half-hour periods off to eat.

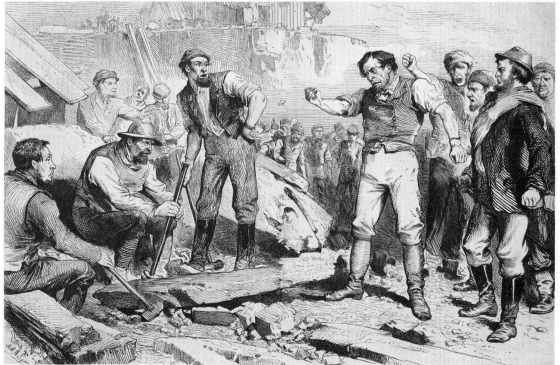

After the Civil War labor unions started a national drive for an eight-hour day with no cut in pay. This sketch from *Leslie's* weekly shows eight-hour strikers threat- ening nonstrikers on a New York City construction job.

BARONS OF

JAY GOULD and Jim Fisk were typical of thousands of smart young Northerners who stayed home and made a lot of money instead of fighting in the Civil War. Foxy, whispery little Jay Gould began his career by cheating two partners out of a leather factory, and then became an expert manipulator of railroad stocks on the New York Stock Exchange. Big, brassy Jim Fisk was a former circus barker who bought and sold war contracts, went south after the war, and made a fortune in confiscated cotton.

In 1867 this up-and-coming pair was befriended by old Daniel Drew, the onetime cattle drover, who had become a great figure in Wall Street. Drew made them directors of the Erie Railroad, which Commodore Cornelius Vanderbilt, the steamboat king and principal owner of the New York Central railroad, was also trying to acquire. Gould and Fisk secretly printed large blocks of illegal Erie stock and put them on the market, where Vanderbilt kept buying them in the hope of getting control. "If this printing press don't break down, I'll be damned if I don't give

Jay Gould kept his $23 million loot from Erie and gold, and bought the Union Pacific Railroad, Western Union, and New York City's "El" lines.

The "Erie War" — Gould escapes from process servers breaking into his office.

The "Erie War"—Gould and Fisk catch a New Jersey ferry with $6 million cash.

The gold corner—Fisk hides under counter from "suckers."

The gold corner — brokers wrangle in the street as prices collapse on Black Friday, September 24, 1869.

The "Erie War"—a new board of directors pries open Gould's office door in 1872. Gould was finally ousted from Erie by its English stockholders.

WALL STREET

the old hog all he wants of Erie!" Fisk said one day. When Vanderbilt discovered the fraud and got an order for their arrest they fled to New Jersey with the Erie books and $6 million in greenbacks. Gould went to Albany and bribed the legislature into legalizing all the Erie stock unloaded on Vanderbilt, plus a lot more. Then the partners came back to New York in triumph and opened luxurious offices in Pike's Grand Opera Palace, where Fisk also supported a bevy of actresses and staged rowdy musical shows.

The next year, at the age of 33, Gould bribed President Grant's brother-in-law to act as his spy in the White House while he cornered the $15 million worth of gold which was in circulation, and squeezed up its price. Fisk tried to involve Grant himself in this coup, but the President stayed out. The gold corner violently disturbed the whole currency structure of the country, and ended only when the Treasury stepped in and sold government gold. Gould's government contacts tipped him off in time, and he sold out at a profit, betraying his own partners.

Jim Fisk squandered his gains on wine, women, and diamonds. He was murdered in 1872 by a man who had cheated him in business and love.

Fisk, dressed as "Admiral" of the Fall River steamship line, toasts President Grant and pumps him about gold.

Fisk *(with champagne)* gets set for a cozy summer evening at Long Branch. This was after Josie Mansfield left him.

Josie Mansfield won Fisk's heart and about $200,000 in presents.

Josie lived in this brownstone love nest, not far from Fisk's office.

Edward Stokes, who also worshiped Josie, traps Fisk on hotel stairs and kills him.

THE REFORMER

IN WASHINGTON the Grant administration was packed with little robber barons. The Secretary of the Navy banked $320,000 in four years from his profits on naval contracts. There was stealing and graft in the War Department, the Treasury, both Houses of Congress, the District of Columbia Government, and even on the White House staff. Grant's Minister to Brazil varied the pattern slightly by stealing $100,000 from the Brazilian Government.

Many good Republicans were distressed by this corruption and organized a new wing of the party to reform the civil service. Their fiery spokesman was Senator Carl Schurz of Missouri *(right)*, a onetime revolutionist in Germany and a personal friend of Lincoln's. Schurz's "Liberal Republicans" gave Grant a few gray hairs, but the bulk of the party continued to vote "regular."

A GALLERY OF GRAFTERS

"You can't use tact with a Congressman! A Congressman is a hog! You must take a stick and hit him on the snout!" said a member of Grant's Cabinet in 1869. In Washington the Congressional hogs fed on what was thrown them by big business and its lobbyists. Collis P. Huntington of the Central Pacific Railroad spent from $200,000 to $500,000 at every Congressional session, and barely succeeded in outbribing his rivals. The Crédit Mobilier, a railroad construction company which siphoned off $23 million from the Treasury, was run by a Congressman. He bribed his colleagues with free stock which paid 625 per cent in dividends in a year. Pictured at the right are a few of the Washington grafters.

War Secretary William Belknap got $25,000 in bribes from Indian post storekeepers.

Congressman Oakes Ames was head lobbyist and pay-off man for Crédit Mobilier.

AND
THE THIEF

IN NEW YORK CITY the Democratic "Ring" made Grant's Republicans look like pikers. Grand Sachem William Marcy Tweed *(left)* and a few Tammany insiders stole $75 million from the city in two years, and their total take from 1865 to 1871 has been estimated as high as $200 million. Tweed bribed the Governor, legislature, Mayor of New York City, and countless small-fry officials. In 1869 he decreed that all contractors doing business with the city must add 100 per cent to their bills and hand back the overcharge in cash to the Ring. Later the fraudulent percentage was raised even higher. Under this scheme New York paid $1,826,-278.35 for plastering one city building, and $170,729.60 for 40 chairs and tables. Tweed was a director of Erie, along with Gould and Fisk, and supplied them with corrupt judges and legislators.

White House Secretary Orville Babcock was in on a $2½ million whisky tax fraud.

Vice President Schuyler Colfax squelched a Crédit Mobilier probe after being bribed.

Congressman James Brooks, the Democratic leader, also got Mobilier stock.

THE
TIGER
AT BAY

IT WAS THE pencil of a great cartoonist which finally broke the Tweed Ring. Thomas Nast, of *Harper's Weekly*, began his attacks on Tammany in 1869, when Tweed was at the height of his power. The Boss had never cared what the newspapers said, but Nast's merciless drawings got under his skin. Even if his followers could not read, he complained, they could "look at the damn pictures." When Nast drew Tweed in prison clothes the Boss predicted that if people got used to seeing him in stripes, they would eventually put him there—which they did!

The downfall of the Ring came after its financial officer, the city auditor, was killed in a sleighing accident in Central Park. Through carelessness the man appointed to his place was a henchman of Tweed's only important political enemy, ex-Sheriff James O'Brien. Thus O'Brien secured the Ring's secret accounts and took them to the New York *Times*, which began to publish them in July 1871. The Ring's lawyers offered the *Times* $5 million and Nast $500,000 to stop their attacks. When this failed the leading members scattered to foreign countries. Tweed escaped to Spain, disguised as a sailor. But even there a Nast cartoon followed him and led to his identification and arrest. He died in a New York jail in 1878.

Nast's most famous cartoon, "The Tammany Tiger Loose—'What are you going to do about it?'", was published in *Harper's* two days before the city election of November 1871. Earlier in the year, when a mass meeting of New Yorkers denounced Tweed, the Boss had smiled and asked, "What are you going to do about it?" The voters answered with ballots. The Ring officials were swept out, and Tweed was indicted for grand larceny. The Tammany tiger was invented by Nast. He derived it from a tiger's head painted on the engine of the old Americus fire company, where Tweed started his political career.

"TURN THE RASCALS OUT"

In 1872 the Liberal Republicans split off from the rest of the party and nominated Horace Greeley, the veteran editor of the New York *Tribune*, for President. The regular Republicans nominated Grant again, and the Democrats endorsed Greeley. The veteran reformer, with his baby-pink face and fuzzy chin whiskers, made a spirited campaign against Republican graft, using the slogan "Turn the rascals out!" But the Radical press (of which he had long been the bellwether) now turned and called him an accomplice of Jeff Davis, the Ku Klux Klan, and Boss Tweed. Cartoonist Nast pilloried him so viciously that Greeley said he didn't know whether he was running for President or the penitentiary. On Election Day he was snowed under by Grant, who had the Boys in Blue, the Negro vote, and a lavish campaign fund contributed by big business and the "Whisky Ring."

Horace Greeley was "a sublime old child" of 61 when he ran for President. He had spent his life promoting a mixture of causes: prohibition, spiritualism, socialism, Free Soil Republicanism, labor unions, high tariffs, the Civil War, and reconciliation with the South.

Campaign picture of Greeley shows him surrounded by "friends of the forest" near his home at Chappaqua, New York.

"Let Us Clasp Hands Over the Bloody Chasm" was drawn by Thomas Nast to illustrate a sentence in one of Greeley's campaign statements. Because Greeley attacked the evils of Reconstruction, Nast pictured him as a friend of Southern assassins and lynch mobs.

One of Nast's ugliest cartoons pictured Greeley and Tammany swallowing each other during the 1872 campaign. Nast was a loyal Republican and never attacked the corruption of Grant's regime as he did Tweed's.

A pro-Greeley cartoon of 1872 shows Grant doing a tipsy dance while Tweed (right) applauds his political trickery. Each side used Tammany scandals to smear the other.

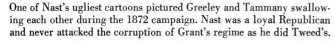

NEW SERIES. NEW-YORK, WEDNESDAY, NOVEMBER 6, 1872. DEAR AT ANY PRICE

Nast's final cartoon of the campaign shows Greeley being carried home dead, under a caricature heading of Greeley's paper. This was especially cruel, for Greeley's wife had just died, and

Greeley himself was very ill. Three weeks later he died of a brain fever, brought on by shame over his defeat, the sudden loss of his editorial post at the *Tribune*, and disgust with politics in general.

The New York *Daily Graphic* greeted the crash with this cartoon of a giant scavenger, whose foot is planted in front of J. P. Morgan's office. The caption read, "Panic, as a health officer, sweeping the garbage out of Wall Street."

PANIC SWEEPS WALL STREET

GRANT'S SECOND TERM had just begun when Jay Cooke & Company, the most famous banking firm in the United States, went bankrupt. Cooke was a kind of financial P. T. Barnum who had sold millions of dollars in government bonds during the Civil War by high-pressure advertising. Later he tried to finance the peace as he had the war, but overextended himself in promoting the Northern Pacific Railroad. His failure dragged down scores of Wall Street houses and paralyzed credit all over the country. In the next three years more than 23,000 business firms, mostly small ones, were wiped out. But the panic was a boon to big combinations like Standard Oil and Carnegie Steel, which bought out their competitors cheap. In New York the British-backed house of Drexel, Morgan & Co. quietly took Jay Cooke's place at the top of the banking heap.

An unhappy speculator reads his fate in ticker tape. Automatic stock tickers came into use soon after the Civil War.

Shabby "tramps," part of the unemployed army created by the panic of 1873, line up for dinner at the New York City poorhouse on Randall's Island. The dining room is already full and they are waiting for the second table.

In the 1870's, when Manifest Destiny was in a mild decline, a New York Daily Graphic artist drew this cartoon entitled "The Two Young Giants. Ivan and Jonathan Reaching For Asia by Opposite Routes." The United States had just made a commercial deal with Hawaii and Russia was expanding into China.

CHAPTER 6

THE
BIG BUSINESS
REPUBLICANS

THE ELECTION of 1872, in which the greatest Republican editor of all time went down to defeat and death, showed how much the Republican party itself had changed in 20 years. The primitive Republicans of the 1850's had been the party of free soil and idealism; in the 1860's they were the party of the Union and the patriotic war. But now they were, in effect, a new party: the party of Northern big business, which had flourished on Civil War profits and already had a firm grip on the nation's resources.

The men who ran the United States from 1865 to 1900 made more money than the world had ever seen. They had little respect for government or public opinion, which they bought and sold as they pleased. "Law? What do I care about law? Hain't I got the power?" cried Commodore Vanderbilt to one of his associates. Vanderbilt bribed legislatures and corrupted courts, engaged in the biggest stock-watering operations of his time, made $94 million in a little more than ten years—and left behind a work of great value to the country. Before he took over the New York Central railroad all passengers and freight had to change trains seventeen times between New York and Chicago. Vanderbilt consolidated tracks and terminals, cut the 900-mile running time from 50 hours to 24, and made the company pay 8 per cent dividends even on its watered stock. In the areas where he had no competition he charged "all that the traffic could bear," manipulating his freight rates so as to ruin some shippers and favor those with whom he made secret deals.

Other hard-driving men like Vanderbilt consolidated oil companies, steel mills, sugar refineries, and similar vital industries into centralized monopolies or "trusts." The panic of 1873 was actually helpful to the trust-builders, for it eliminated thousands of their small competitors.

Most Americans of the 1870's accepted the rule of big business as a natural and desirable thing. The Civil War and its aftermath had exhausted the nation's emotions and considerably tarnished its ideals. Yet its strength was greater than ever, and was now channeled entirely into money-making. Even the poet Walt Whitman, who hoped that America would distribute its democracy to the whole world someday, accepted the spirit of these times. "I perceive clearly," he wrote, "that the extreme business energy, and this almost maniacal appetite for wealth prevalent in the United States, are parts of amelioration and progress, indispensably needed to prepare the very results I demand. My theory includes riches, and the getting of riches. . . ."

At the very top of the big-business heap sat men who believed that everything they did was justified by God and the new Darwinian theory of evolution. John D. Rockefeller, Jr., expressed this concept perfectly when he told a Sunday school class: "The growth of a large business is merely a survival of the fittest. . . . The American Beauty Rose can be produced in the splendor and fragrance which bring cheer to its beholder only by sacrificing the early buds which grow up around it. This is not an evil tendency in business. It is merely the working-out of a law of nature and a law of God."

By this analogy Standard Oil and Carnegie Steel and the American Sugar Refining Company were the fragrant roses for which hundreds of lesser firms and thousands of individuals were clipped away and thrown on the nation's compost heap. Progress, said the Wall Street philosophers, required victims, and the victims should realize this and not complain. In the nation at large big business was the prize flower; and all Americans whose welfare did not coincide with the profits of large corporations were fulfilling a valuable function as victims of progress. This applied especially to the farmers, who were at the mercy of railroad monopolies, and the urban workers. Whether these large groups of citizens would always be content with their sacrificial role in Mr. Rockefeller's hothouse was a question which was still unsettled, however.

THE FIRST HUNDRED YEARS

On July 4, 1876, millions of Americans picnicked, listened to patriotic speeches, and enjoyed the fruits of freedom.

Southern boom: cotton at New Orleans

IN 1876 the nation celebrated its hundredth birthday by holding a centennial world's fair in Philadelphia. On opening day the Emperor Dom Pedro of Brazil stood beside the exhibit of Alexander Graham Bell and held the newly invented telephone to his ear. "My God, it talks!" he exclaimed, and from then on the Centennial was a great success. But even as the fountains played and the colored lights swung gaily in Fairmount Park, a very different

Making hay on a Midwest farm was a semimechanized job in 1876. Farm machines were swallowing the frontier.

Making hay on an Eastern estate was a summer sport for beaux and belles, who also made love while the sun shone.

These giant stationary engines designed by George H. Corliss formed the most striking exhibit at the 1876 Centennial.

scene was enacted in far-off Montana. There the Sioux Indians were on the warpath against white gold-thieves in the Black Hills. On June 25 the redskins surrounded 212 federal cavalrymen under General George A. Custer and killed and mutilated every man. After the battle Chief Rain-in-the-Face cut out Captain Tom Custer's heart and ate it. The United States was getting more sophisticated in 1876, but it was still rugged in spots.

Northern taste: Grant's seaside home

Lunch hour in the city. At the end of their first 100 years Americans ate more and faster than most people.

"Romance on the Hudson" shows a cadet at West Point in June 1876.

"Reality on the Plains" shows the same cadet after Custer's stand.

Susan B. Anthony of Rochester was fined $100 for voting in 1872. "I will never pay a dollar," she said, and she didn't.

The National Women's Suffrage Association sent organizers to all major party conventions. They argued that former Negro slaves could vote, so why couldn't white women?

WOMEN DEMAND THE VOTE

THE CAMPAIGN to obtain American citizenship for American women made a little headway in the 1870's. Militant ladies occasionally visited the polls and insisted on voting, even though they were spattered with rotten eggs and dirty words. The newspaper attacks were relentless: the New York *World* said that Miss Susan B. Anthony had "the proportions of a file and the voice of a hurdy-

These Boston women could vote in their city elections. "Mixed" polling places were considered slightly scandalous, however.

Wyoming women got the vote in the constitution of 1869. Wyoming later refused to enter the Union without women suffrage.

A Congressional committee hears impassioned suffrage arguments in 1871. The speaker is Mrs. Victoria Claflin Woodhull, sometimes known as "the terrible siren."

Victoria Woodhull, the first woman candidate for President, campaigned for equal rights and a single moral standard.

AND RUN FOR PRESIDENT

gurdy," and her fellow suffragettes were "mummified and fossilated females." But the men of the wide open West were more chivalrous. The territory of Wyoming was first to grant women suffrage, followed by Utah, where the Mormon women almost outnumbered the men. In 1872 and 1884 there were women candidates for President, although most American women still could not vote.

In 1884 Mrs. Belva Lockwood, a prominent woman lawyer, ran for President on an Equal Rights ticket. The men of Rahway, New Jersey, tried to ridicule her by parading in Mother Hubbards and striped stockings. But everyone laughed at the men instead.

"A Live Jackass Kicking a Dead Lion" *(left)* was Nast's first use of the Democratic donkey, which had appeared in cartoons as early as the 1830's. This drawing shows the Democratic press abusing ex-Secretary of War Stanton after his death in 1869. "Fine-Ass Committee" *(right)* is a typical Nast portrait of a group of Democratic Congressmen, blowing financial bubbles after the panic of 1873. "Caught in a

NAST'S
POLITICAL
ZOO

THOMAS NAST, who drew the first Tammany tiger, also created the Republican elephant, whose first appearance in a Nast cartoon is shown above. The lesser animals, braying and squealing, are stampeding the elephant into a pit labeled "Southern Claims" and "Chaos." The ass in the lion's skin represents the Democratic New York *Herald*, the prancing unicorn is the Republican New York *Times*, and the little fox peering out of the shrubbery is the Democratic party itself.

This complicated drawing appeared in *Harper's Weekly* in 1874, when the Republicans were put in a hole by charges that President Grant had a "Caesar" complex, and was planning to run for a third term in 1876. Later Nast cartoons showed the

Trap—The Result of the Third-Term Hoax" *(left)* shows the Republican elephant plunging into the pit as the smaller animals jeer. "The Trunk in Sight" *(right)* shows him feeling his way out after an 1875 victory in New Hampshire. When Nast got a good idea he used it week after week. And, since he was rock-ribbed Republican himself, his elephant was a likable, if skittish, animal.

elephant falling into the "third term trap," then sticking out his trunk a little, and finally escaping when Grant repudiated the third term *(above)*.

Even Americans who took little interest in politics were constantly entertained by the antics of Nast's cartoon zoo. His Democrats were donkeys, foxes, wolves, and tigers—sometimes hypocritical two-faced tigers with heads on both ends of their bodies. Grant and other important Republicans were drawn as dignified lions. Horace Greeley was a monkey in a long white coat, begging for pennies. Labor appeared as the goat.

By his skill at such conceits Nast earned $20,000 a year and was one of the country's best-known men. At the right is one of his many self-portraits.

THE STOLEN ELECTION

SAMUEL JONES TILDEN *(above)*, the Democratic candidate for President in 1876, was a rich corporation lawyer, a reform Governor of New York, a cold, calculating man who never married because, as one of his friends explained, "he never felt the need of a wife. . . . Women were, so far as he could see, unimportant to his success." Tilden habitually looked as though he smelled something bad, and in the election of 1876 he smelled something very bad.

On November 8, the morning after Election Day, Tilden woke up the winner. He had 4,300,590 popular votes and 196 electoral votes to 4,036,298 and 173 for his Republican opponent, Governor Rutherford B. Hayes of Ohio. Yet when the Electoral College met, Hayes was elected President. This result was achieved by Republican bribery, forgery, and perjury in Louisiana and Florida, where federal troops were still stationed under the Reconstruction Acts. The Republican election boards in these two states voided about 14,000 ballots and switched their 12 electoral votes to Hayes, giving him an Electoral College majority of one—185 to 184. The steal was so brazen that Tilden could scarcely believe it was happening. By the time his friends got around to bribing some election officials themselves, it was too late.

Lucy Hayes, the new President's wife, banished alcohol from the White House.

"His Fraudulency," President-elect Hayes, strikes a pose of dignified innocence. Hayes took no part in the steal himself. But he rewarded the conspirators with government jobs.

RUTHERFORD BIRCHARD HAYES

was a good and honest President, even though his election was crooked. He weeded grafters out of the Government, improved the civil service, defied the Republican spoilsmen, and stood up strongly for the church, the home, and the American gold standard. He also liked to play croquet on the White House lawn, but even there the Democrats would not let him alone. They charged that he had squandered six dollars of the taxpayers' money for a set of fancy boxwood croquet balls. "Lemonade Lucy" Hayes, his strong-minded wife, banned wine and liquor from the White House, and served fruit juices and cold water at formal dinners. This led her into a spat with the Secretary of State, who refused to invite foreign diplomats to banquets without wine. Mrs. Hayes never learned that her servants were supplying some of her guests with frozen rum punch, concealed in oranges. This phase of her dinners became known in Washington as the "Life-Saving Station."

The President was an expert baby-kisser. Here he performs at Steubenville, Ohio.

221

A hand-to-hand struggle between black and white legislators was a rare occurrence during Reconstruction. The incident pictured at the right took place in the Louisiana legislature in 1875, when the Conservatives (Democrats) seized power illegally for a few hours. The Conservative Speaker, L. A. Wiltz (center), snatched the gavel from the Negro Republican clerk and pushed him off the platform. Soon after this the federal troops arrived and the Republicans took charge of the state again.

Hiram Rhoades Revels, Negro Senator from Mississippi, was part Indian, educated by Midwest Quakers, was a barber, teacher, Union soldier, and preacher. He turned Democrat and helped oust carpetbaggers from Mississippi in 1875.

Joseph Hayne Rainey of South Carolina, the first Negro Congressman, was part white, also a barber by trade, served in the Confederate Navy, and escaped to the West Indies before Emancipation. He opposed harsh measures against the whites.

Jonathan Jasper Wright, Supreme Court Justice in South Carolina, was born of free parents in Pennsylvania, became a lawyer there, and went south to organize schools. He signed the order which brought the Democrats back in 1877.

THE SOUTH RESTORED

THE SOLID SOUTH was born in 1877, and Republican Rutherford B. Hayes was its fairy godfather. After the Electoral College named him President, Hayes' friends made a deal with the Southern Democrats. If they would keep quiet and not try to upset his inauguration, it was agreed, Hayes would withdraw the last federal troops from the South. Hayes was inaugurated without any trouble March 4, 1877, and promptly kept the bargain. On April 10 the troops moved out of the State House at Columbia, South Carolina, and the Democrats moved in. On April 24 the last federal garrison left New Orleans. The Southern Republicans and carpetbaggers who had stolen the Presidency for Hayes were rewarded with comfortable places on the federal payroll. With surprising ease the Southern states annulled the Fifteenth Amendment so far as Negro voting was concerned, and became solidly Democratic for the next 50 years.

Caption: Wade Hampton, planter and Confederate cavalry hero, led the "Bourbon Democrats" back to power in South Carolina.

Hayes' action rang down the curtain on the long and painful drama of Reconstruction, and gave the South back to the people who had owned it before the Civil War. Most Americans were either pleased or indifferent. The old bitterness between North and South was almost forgotten except at election time, when Republican orators faithfully waved the bloody shirt and rallied the Boys in Blue. But with the end of Reconstruction one fact stood out with startling clearness. Despite all the Southern propaganda about "Negro supremacy," the South had remained under white leadership during the entire postwar period. (The Southern grievance, of course, was that the white leaders were mostly Republicans.) There was never a Negro governor in the South. Only one legislature, in South Carolina, ever had a Negro majority in both houses. Two Negro Senators and 20 Negro Representatives were elected to Congress from the Southern states during Reconstruction—a very small number considering the fact that qualified Negro voters were actually in the majority.

The Negroes who attained to important offices during Reconstruction were, to a large extent, dignified, intelligent, and conciliatory in their political views and activities. Some of them worked hand in hand with the Democrats to restore white rule to the South.

CONKLING EATS CROW

Senator Roscoe Conkling *(left)*, the Republican boss of New York State, had the finest torso and the biggest appetite for patronage in Congress. When President Hayes began to improve the civil service, Conkling blocked the President's appointments and sneered at his "snivel service reform." But Hayes continued his fight for better government, and eventually forced Conkling to swallow some disagreeably honest appointments *(right)*.

Conkling kept his handsome body in trim by boxing and walking around Capitol Hill with his stomach sucked in. He was so vain that ordinary political sarcasm never bothered him. But when his Republican rival, Congressman James G. Blaine, jeered at his "turkey-gobbler strut," and likened him to a singed cat and a dunghill, Conkling's feelings were hurt. His feud with Blaine became a serious split in the Republican party, and his feud with President Hayes almost wrecked the administration.

GREENBACKERS

Benjamin Franklin Butler, cockeyed former Union general, once known as the "Bluebeard of New Orleans," was a Massachusetts Greenback Congressman.

MONEY IS at the root of a great deal of politics. In the 1870's a national Greenback party was organized with the general aim of distributing more money to more of the American people. The Republicans and Democrats tried to stamp the new party down, but it grew and caused serious trouble for both of them.

Abraham Lincoln gave the Greenbackers their big idea. In 1862 his administration began to issue $450 million in greenbacks to pay for the Civil War. Ever since Hamilton's time, all government paper money had been backed by a supply of precious metal which the Treasury bought and stored in various places. But Lincoln's greenbacks were based only on the Government's credit—a promise to pay. During the war they fell in value but continued to be legal tender. Banks and large investors bought them up cheap and turned them in at their face value for government bonds. As soon as the war was over these speculators demanded that the Government pay specie (gold) for the interest and redemption of their bonds. A few "soft money" politicians opposed this with the slogan "The same currency for the bondholder and the plowholder." But "hard money" Democrats like Samuel Tilden were in complete accord with the Republicans on this issue. After a long fight in Congress and the courts, specie payment was resumed by Hayes in 1879.

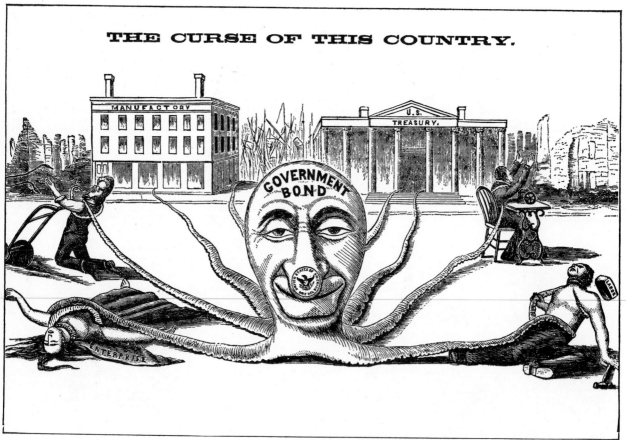

A Greenbacker cartoon of the 1870's shows a gold-nosed government octopus strangling labor, farmers, and small business. The Greenbackers fought gold payments on bonds.

AND GRANGERS

Meanwhile there had been a national slump in farm prices, with wheat falling from $1.50 to 67 cents a bushel, corn from 75 to 38 cents, cotton from 31 to 9 cents a pound. The Order of the Patrons of Husbandry, better known as the Grange, was started as a secret society to act politically for the farmers. The Grangers aimed their attacks at railroad monopolies and high freight rates. In 1876 many Grangers joined the Greenbackers in demanding that the Government withdraw all existing bank notes and substitute a copious supply of "fiat" paper money, "based on the faith and resources of the nation." In 1878 the Greenbackers, Grangers, and labor unions teamed up in a political coalition, electing 15 Congressmen and polling a million votes.

In 1878 also the soft-money members of Congress passed the Bland-Allison Act, which obliged the Treasury to buy and turn into coin at least $2 million worth of silver bullion each month. This plan for inflating the currency became increasingly popular: most of the Greenbackers and Grangers eventually became ardent Free Silverites. Oceans of oratory were spilled in debating these money schemes. But they all boiled down to a fight between big business, which had found the fixed gold standard most favorable to its operations, and the farmers and wage earners, who had to bear the brunt of each successive depression.

Peter Cooper of New York, the country's leading glue manufacturer, was Greenback candidate for President in 1876. He also built the first U. S. locomotive.

THE GREAT WESTERN EXPERIMENTAL MONEY-DOCTOR, AFTER INFINITE PAINS AND STUDY, SUCCEEDS IN MAKING A RAG-BABY. HE BREATHES INTO IT THE BREATH OF LIFE.

"BLESS ITS DEAR LITTLE HEART, IT IS AS GOOD AS GOLD!"

BUT THE LITTLE PET GROWS RAPIDLY, AND BECOMES TOO HEAVY TO CARRY;

SO HE DROPS IT AT A NEIGHBOR'S DOOR, AND FLIES.

BUT THE CREATURE HE HAS CREATED ARISES AND PURSUES ITS PARENT, AND—

FINIS.

Greenbacks were often called "rags," and cartoonists pictured the Greenback scheme as a rag doll. This comic strip of 1876 shows the doll turning into a Frankenstein monster.

On July 16, 1877, the Baltimore and Ohio Railroad cut wages 10 per cent—the third such wage cut it had imposed on its employees within three years. That evening a strike started on the B. & O. at Martinsburg, West Virginia, and spread quickly through Baltimore itself. On July 20 the Sixth Maryland militia, marching through the streets to the railroad station, fired on a hostile crowd and killed 12 people *(above)*. Meanwhile the strike had spread to Pittsburgh, where the Pennsylvania Railroad had also cut wages. There 57 strikers, soldiers, and

TROOPS KILL STRIKERS

rioters were killed in pitched battles, and $3 million worth of railroad property, including 126 locomotives, was destroyed. Every important city in the country was affected eventually, and most of the nation's railroad traffic was halted. The "Great Strike" of 1877, which grew out of the depression of 1873, was the bloodiest labor disturbance the United States had ever seen. President Hayes put a stop to it by sending regular troops into Maryland, West Virginia, Pennsylvania, Illinois, and Missouri to prevent picketing and interference with trains.

Ten million eager immigrants entered the U. S. between 1860 and 1890.

Latest arrivals dance and sing at the Castle Garden receiving station.

Slavic recruits for the coal mines wait for their train in Pennsylvania.

Russian Mennonite families in temporary barracks in central Kansas.

LABOR IN THE MELTING POT

IN 1870 a New England shoe manufacturer named Calvin T. Sampson fired his unionized workers and imported 75 Chinese laborers from the Pacific coast. The Chinese signed a contract to work for three years at $26 a month, and settled down in North Adams, Massachusetts, where they attended the Methodist Sunday school, saved their money, and reduced Mr. Sampson's costs $840 a week. A writer in *Scribner's* magazine hastened to praise this experiment, saying, "If for no other purpose than the breaking up of . . . labor combinations and 'Trades Unions' . . . the advent of Chinese labor should be hailed with warm welcome by all who have the true interests of . . . the laboring classes at heart."

Despite such opposition the labor unions grew phenomenally after the Great Strike of 1877. The Noble Order of the Knights of Labor, which sought to gather all American workers into one big union, had 700,000 members by the mid-1880's, when it forced Jay Gould to come to terms in a strike against his Western railroads. The American Federation of Labor was formed in 1881 by the representatives of 250,000 craft-union members. Left-wing unions led by socialists also appeared. In 1882 the labor unions persuaded Congress to stop the immigration of Chinese. But an endless supply of low-cost labor still poured in from Europe.

"Supply and Demand" shows an American employer using immigrant labor to outweigh his striking employees.

Agitation against Chinese labor was especially vicious in the Far West, where mobs smashed Chinese homes, cut pigtails off Chinese men, and committed many cowardly lynchings. The scene above occurred in Denver in 1880.

JOB-HUNTER KILLS PRESIDENT

James Abram Garfield was the last President born in a log cabin, and the first to be killed by the spoils system.

In 1880 the Republican "Stalwarts" abandoned the milk-and-water Hayes and tried to bring back their hero, General Grant, for four more years in the White House. At the Republican convention Senator Roscoe Conkling placed Grant in nomination with a poem that brought down the house:

> When asked what state he hails from
> Our sole reply shall be,
> He comes from Appomattox
> And its famous apple-tree.

But a majority of delegates feared the third-term trap, and compromised on a dark-horse candidate: Representative James A. Garfield of Ohio. The Democrats nominated General Winfield Scott Hancock, who was described in the New York *Sun* as "a good man, weighing 250 pounds." The popular vote was very close—Garfield 4,449,053, Hancock 4,442,035—but the Republicans were well ahead in the Electoral College. Garfield was an inoffensive President who planned to make a few mild reforms. But on July 2, 1881, he was fatally shot at the Washington railroad station by a job-hunter who had been hanging around the White House for months, stealing the President's stationery and begging for appointment as consul in Marseille.

General Hancock, as a fat political Samson, defies the Republican hosts with the jawbone of the suffering Democratic donkey. Republican newspapers jeered at Hancock because he said, "The tariff question is a local question."

The handcuffed assassin Guiteau arrives for his murder trial November 14, 1881.

Charles J. Guiteau shoots President Garfield, while Secretary of State Blaine stands amazed at right. One bullet lodged behind the spine and caused blood poisoning. Below, the wounded President's bedding is shifted at the White House. After suffering for weeks in the Washington heat, he was moved to the seashore at Elberon, New Jersey, where he died September 19. Garfield had been in wonderful spirits the day he was shot. In the morning his son ran into his room and made a flying leap across his bed. "*You* can't do that!" he cried, but the President jumped up in his nightshirt and did it. Then he got dressed and went off to catch a train for a reunion at Williams College, his alma mater.

Guiteau entertains the jury with a comic speech. His behavior suggested insanity.

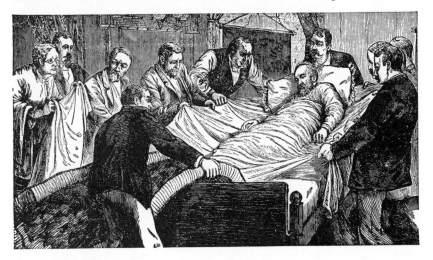

Guiteau hangs June 30, 1882. His skeleton went to the Army Medical Museum.

THE
ELEGANT
ARTHUR

CHESTER ALAN ARTHUR, who moved up from the Vice Presidency when Garfield died, looked more like a President of the United States than any man since Washington. Six feet two, with a well-rounded figure and full side whiskers, Arthur dressed like a gentleman, slept late in the morning, and spent from two to three hours at dinner. Before he moved into the White House he installed modern plumbing and held a rummage sale of such leftover relics as Nellie Grant's bird cage and Abraham Lincoln's old pants. Arthur had once been a minor cog in Senator Conkling's New York Republican machine, but he amazed the country by doing an honest and competent job as President. He set up a civil service merit system, prosecuted Republicans in the Star Route postal frauds, vetoed a big river-and-harbor "pork barrel" bill, started building a new steel Navy, and acquired Pearl Harbor, Hawaii, for an American naval base.

President Arthur was rich and accustomed to fashionable society. Here he is shown in his elegant carriage on Bellevue Avenue, Newport, where he was spending his vacation.

Arthur the sportsman was rated "one of the best salmon fishers in the country."

Arthur made the Navy his hobby, and the Navy staged gun drills for him at Newport (above). He started the first modern U. S. warships—the *Chicago, Boston,* and *Atlanta.*

This caricature of Vanderbilt appeared in the New York *Daily Graphic* a few days after he said "The public be damned!" Outside his car window one of his trains is smashing up.

VANDERBILT'S BONER

William Henry Vanderbilt, son of the old Commodore, inherited $90 million in 1877. In eight years he ran it up to $200 million, despite depression and strikes.

On October 8, 1882, William Henry Vanderbilt, the richest man in the world, was in a private railroad car outside Chicago when two reporters came aboard for an interview. They asked about the new Nickel Plate railroad—was it true it had been built only to blackmail Vanderbilt's great New York Central system? "It's no good; poorly built," Vanderbilt growled. They asked about the new fast train he had just put on to cut the New York–Chicago running time—did it pay? "No, not a bit of it," snapped the railroad king. "We only run the limited because forced to by the action of the Pennsylvania Railroad." "But don't you run it for the public benefit?" insisted one reporter. "The public be damned!" Vanderbilt exploded. "What does the public care for the railroads except to get as much out of them for as little consideration as possible!"

The next day every newspaper reader in the country knew that Vanderbilt had said "The public be damned!" (Except readers of the Chicago *Tribune*, which altered his words to "Nonsense!") Editors, ministers, politicians, labor leaders, even his fellow millionaires, denounced him. "I never said it, and that's all," he grumbled to reporters when he returned a week later to New York. In 1883 he resigned from all his railroad presidencies and laid down a rule that henceforth Vanderbilts should serve as board chairmen only, and let active railroad men run their railroads. In 1885 he died and was buried in a $300,000 mausoleum on Staten Island, where watchmen looked into his crypt every fifteen minutes to make sure his corpse was not kidnaped.

"The Grange Awakening the Sleepers" was inspired by the Vanderbilt system of secret rebates. The farmer is trying to rouse the country to the onrushing railroad menace.

"THE PUBLIC BE DAMNED!"

expressed with too much frankness the attitude of big business—the oil and steel trusts, the railroads with their under-cover rebates to corporations and their "squeeze" on farmers, the coal monopolists, meat packers, Western mine owners, and large employers of labor generally. But Vanderbilt's words were a boon to Democrats in 1882. In New York State they gave hundreds of thousands of votes to elect a new Democratic Governor, Grover Cleveland of Buffalo.

Vanderbilt's Fifth Avenue mansion was the most expensive private home in America. Above, reporters and critics examine his painting collection at a press reception in 1884.

BLAINE, THE PLUMED KNIGHT

James G. Blaine became the "Plumed Knight" in 1876, when Robert G. Ingersoll first presented his name for President. Blaine lost the nomination then, but Ingersoll's speech lived on. In 1884 the Republicans went to the polls with Ingersoll's words still ringing in their ears: "Like an armed warrior, like a plumed knight, James G. Blaine marched down the halls of the American Congress and threw his shining lance full and fair against the brazen foreheads of the defamers of his country and the maligners of her honor. For the Republican party to desert this gallant leader now is as though an army should desert their general upon the field of battle."

In 1884 the question which raged across the nation and stirred the angriest passions since the Civil War was this: Was James Gillespie Blaine the leader of leaders, the prince of politicians, and the Republican party's greatest man? Or was he a slippery liar who had prostituted his public position to make a private fortune? The answer was that Blaine was all these things.

His story is a tragedy of the gilded age of politics. He was brilliant, brainy, and immensely popular. As a boy of 17 he sat at the feet of Henry Clay and took notes on his speeches, and his personal charm was much like Clay's. He was born in Pennsylvania and taught school in Kentucky, but he became "Blaine of Maine" in 1854, when he moved to Augusta and became part owner of the *Kennebec Journal*. He was one of the first Eastern editors to nail the name "Republican" to the masthead of his paper. He was a delegate to the first Republican convention and a Lincoln-before-Chicago man in 1860. He was thus a genuine founder of his party.

In 1869, after serving an apprenticeship under Thad Stevens (whom he disliked), Blaine became Speaker of the House. In 1876, when the corruption of Grant's regime threatened to wreck the Republicans, Blaine turned the tide by making a fierce "bloody shirt" speech about the horrors of Andersonville Prison. This should have earned him the nomination for President that year. But then disaster struck him.

In revenge for his slurs on Jeff Davis the Democrats located some letters showing that he had sold his influence in Congress to various business firms. In one deal he received $110,150 in bonds and cash for performing various services, including the saving of a federal land grant, for the Little Rock and Fort Smith Railroad. The incriminating evidence was in the possession of a Boston bookkeeper named James Mulligan. When the storm broke Blaine went to Mulligan's hotel room in Washington, asked for a look at the letters, put them in his pocket, and walked out. A few days later he rose in the House and flung the package on his desk. "Thank God Almighty, I am not afraid to show them!" he cried, and read parts of the letters aloud. His superb acting swept the House into an hysterical frenzy, and the members shouted his vindication. But when the letters were reduced to print they showed he was guilty.

In 1876 and again in 1880 the Republican conventions passed Blaine by because of this scandal. But in 1884 he was nominated for President on the fourth ballot. Millions of Republicans no longer cared about the "Mulligan letters." To them James G. Blaine was innocent and great—the plumed knight of the Grand Old Party.

The "Blaine Legion" cheers at the Republican convention of 1880. But they had to wait four years for his nomination. Maine and the Midwest were Blaine's strongholds.

Maggie Blaine gets the news of her father's nomination at their Augusta, Maine, home. Blaine also had a mansion in Washington, partly paid for by stock-market winnings.

CLEVELAND TELLS THE TRUTH

GILLAM

The Presidential campaign of 1884 was probably the dirti-
est in American history. Here Cleveland (hand in coat)
tells the truth about his private life to a jury of voters
while Blaine (foreground) tries to conceal his sins.

BLAINE, Blaine, James G. Blaine,
The continental liar from the State of Maine!

jeered the Democrats as they marched forth to the
Presidential battle of 1884. Their own candidate
was a bulky meteor in the political skies, a man
whose honesty was almost blinding in its intensity.
In 1881 Stephen Grover Cleveland was a run-of-the-
mill lawyer in Buffalo, New York; in 1882 he was
the "Veto Mayor" of the city, cleaning up a long
accumulation of political graft; in 1883 he was the
reform Governor of the state, fighting the Tammany
tiger tooth and claw. In 1884 the Democratic convention chose him for President. "We love him for
the enemies he has made," cried a Western delegate,
looking straight at the agonized Tammany bosses,
and the fact that machine politicians hated and
feared him was Cleveland's strongest recommendation. The Democrats called him "Grover the Good."

But their smugness was jolted on July 21, when
the Buffalo *Evening Telegraph* exploded the great
bombshell of the campaign. Under the title "A Terrible Tale" the newspaper told how Cleveland had
made love years before to a widow named Maria
Halpin, how a baby had been born and named Oscar
Folsom Cleveland, how Cleveland acknowledged
paternity and offered financial support, and how the
child went to an orphanage and the mother to an
asylum—driven there, according to the *Telegraph*,
by foul and forcible means. The Republicans, of
course, were delighted by this scandal, and turned
it into a naughty little song:

> Ma! Ma. Where's my pa?
> Gone to the White House,
> *Ha! Ha! Ha!*

Cleveland's reaction was typical of his solid common sense. "Whatever you say, tell the truth," he
wired his campaign managers. The truth was soon
publicly told by a leading clergyman and others
who supported the Democratic ticket. They admitted
that their bachelor candidate had formed an "illicit
connection" with Mrs. Halpin in the early 1870's,
and that a child had been born and given his name.
But there was no proof that Cleveland was the father
—other men had been involved. Cleveland had done
a "singularly honorable" thing by assuming responsibility and finding a respectable home for the
orphan. It was *not* true that the mother had been
forced into an asylum: her present whereabouts
were unknown. (Later she settled down with a new
husband in New Rochelle, New York.) Cleveland
had never proposed marriage to her. That was "the
truth," and the Democrats soon regained their optimism. On election night they gathered around the
polling places and sang defiantly:

> Hurrah for Maria,
> Hurrah for the kid;
> We voted for Grover,
> And we're damned glad we did!

"Another Voice for Cleveland" shows Cleveland tor-
mented by the illegitimate child he had acknowledged.

"Rascality's Insult to the Nation" shows James G. Blaine
begging political forgiveness of an enraged Columbia.

RUM, ROMANISM, AND MUGWUMPS

George William Curtis, powerful editor of *Harper's Weekly*, was a Mugwump.

James Russell Lowell, the Republican poet, was one of the leading Boston Mugwumps.

Henry Ward Beecher, Brooklyn pastor and reformer, was a devout Mugwump.

"A Political Poser" *(right)* was a Mugwump appeal to serious-minded voters. The drawing shows a group sitting around a village store and post office in a typical small Republican town. The caption printed with it was a straightforward question: "Should Mr. Blaine be honored with the Presidency when his mere nomination has so shamefully lowered the moral tone of the Republican party?" This appeared on the front page of *Harper's Weekly*, which had been strongly Republican since 1858.

In 1884 many Republican intellectuals and reformers deserted their party and worked for the election of Cleveland. These independents were given the sarcastic name of "Mugwumps," supposedly after a New England Indian word meaning "great captain." Young Theodore Roosevelt and other Republican regulars made savage fun of the Mugwumps, but their revolt seriously hurt Blaine's chances.

During the final week of the campaign, Blaine suffered a really crushing catastrophe. A committee of New York City preachers came to see him at his hotel, and assured him that *they* were not Mugwumps. "We are Republicans," said their spokesman, a Dr. Burchard, "and don't propose to leave our party and identify ourselves with the party whose antecedents have been rum, Romanism, and rebellion." Blaine was so bored and tired that he did not notice Burchard's anti-Catholic slur, which passed off without a contradiction. The newspaper reporters who were there also missed it, but a Democratic shorthand sleuth took down the fatal words, and the Democratic campaign managers made sure that they were widely printed. "RUM, ROMANISM, AND REBELLION" became a headline of doom for the Republicans. Later that same evening Blaine was entertained at dinner by Jay Gould and other unpopular rich men. What Joseph Pulitzer's New York *World* did with that story may be seen below.

Rev. Dr. Samuel Burchard uttered the fatal "Rum, Romanism, and Rebellion."

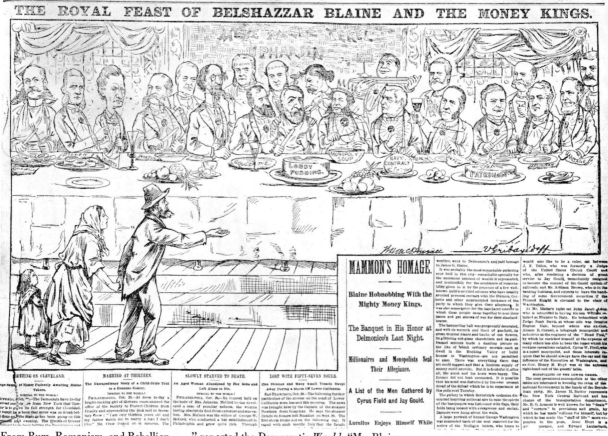

"From Rum, Romanism, and Rebellion . . . ," reported the Democratic *World*, "Mr. Blaine proceeded to a merry banquet of the millionaires at Delmonico's, where champagne frothed and brandy sparkled in glasses that glittered like jewels." To illustrate this scene the *World* published a front-page cartoon by Walt McDougall, showing Blaine between Jay Gould and William H. ("Public Be Damned") Vanderbilt *(wearing crown)*. Others at the table were Andrew Carnegie, Russell Sage, and John Jacob Astor. This banquet and Burchard's blunder cost Blaine the state of New York and the Presidency.

ALONE IN THE WHITE HOUSE

"HENCEFORTH I must have no friends!" exclaimed Grover Cleveland after he was elected President. Grover the Good was big, bull-necked, stubborn, and "ugly-honest" in his attitude toward public office. After he moved into the Presidency he sometimes behaved as though he had never heard of the Democratic party. Instead of dishing out spoils he delivered lectures on good government and reform. But the party bosses kept after him. "The d----d everlasting clatter for office continues . . . and makes me feel like resigning and hell is to pay generally," he wrote after a few months in the White House.

He was irritable because he was lonely. The American public never dreamed, of course, that their 260-pound bachelor President, who gorged himself on steak, ham, fish, and chops for breakfast, and corned beef and cabbage for dinner, was also pining away for love. In the summer of 1885 he proposed to Frances Folsom, a pretty girl just out of college, and was accepted. Then her widowed mother took her off on a European tour. A rumor got around that Cleveland was going to marry the mother, and this made the President cross. "I don't see why the papers keep marrying me to old ladies all the while," he grumbled. In the spring of 1886 Frances returned and the engagement was announced. On June 2 they were married in the Blue Room of the White House.

Frances Folsom was the daughter of Cleveland's law partner. She was 22 and Cleveland 49 when they wed.

The President's wedding was quiet and dignified. But during the honeymoon in Maryland reporters enraged the President by watching him and his bride through spyglasses and peeking into the dishes on their breakfast tray.

Cleveland worked harder than most Presidents. He had
no stenographer, wrote many letters and messages in his
own hand, and answered the White House telephone himself. After his marriage he relaxed by taking carriage rides.

243

"PUBLIC OFFICE IS A PUBLIC TRUST"

THIS FAMOUS SLOGAN was written for Cleveland by a Democratic publicity man, but it described exactly his theory and practice of the Presidency. Night after night he sat up writing vetoes on routine bills —bills to give phony pensions to Civil War veterans, private bills for their widows and dependents, bills to give free seeds to farmers. It was all wrong, said Cleveland, "to indulge a benevolent and charitable sentiment through the appropriation of public funds." In 1887 he vetoed the first big general pension bill, and thus earned the lasting hatred of the Grand Army of the Republic.

Cleveland steps on the log-rolling Congressmen who traded tariff favors at the expense of American consumers.

Cleveland stands guard over the Federal Treasury, while vetoed private pension bills litter the floor of his office.

Cleveland reacts violently to the newspaper gossips who wrote that he drank and beat his wife in the White House.

Cleveland, bothered by a $100-million-a-year surplus piling up in the Treasury, advocates a cut in the tariff.

"The Senatorial Round-House," a *Harper's Weekly* cartoon by Thomas Nast, shows the honorable spokesmen for the American railroads blowing off steam on Capitol Hill. In 1887, after years of complaints against the railroads, Congress reluctantly created the Interstate Commerce Commission, the first government board to regulate private business. The Commission was empowered to prevent rate discrimination, but could not fix new rates. The railroad lawyers and the federal courts hampered its work so effectively that in a few years it ceased to function.

THE LAST DAYS OF GRANT

AT MOUNT MCGREGOR, near Saratoga, New York, General U. S. Grant was slowly dying of cancer of the throat. Yet every day he put on his black silk hat and sat on the veranda of his cottage. Crowds of tourists came and stared silently at him from the road. On June 19, 1885, the members of his family grouped around him while a local photographer took their last picture together.

The closing years of the General's life were full of humiliation and strain. In the 1870's he joined his son *(standing beside his chair)* and a slick Wall Streeter named Ferdinand Ward in starting a brokerage firm. In 1884 Grant & Ward failed for the enormous sum of $16,725,466, and Ward was revealed as a common swindler who had used the great name of Grant to cloak all kinds of frauds. Although Grant was already very sick he tried to recoup his family's fortunes by writing and selling his memoirs. For months he sat in his library and dictated to a stenographer; then, when the cancer had destroyed his voice, he huddled under blankets and shawls, and scribbled on sheets of paper.

This picture of a brave man's race with death touched the nation's heart and won back the popularity Grant had lost while President. After he died, on July 23, an amazing demonstration took place: two former Confederate generals, Joe Johnston and Simon B. Buckner, marched beside Sherman and Sheridan as pallbearers in the funeral procession on Broadway, New York. In his last days Grant had praised the "harmony and good feeling" which were growing between North and South. In his death he brought the two sections closer together than they had been since the war.

THE HAYMARKET BOMB

LABOR'S CRUSADE for an eight-hour day, which started with a rush right after the Civil War, was slowed down to a bitter deadlock 20 years later. On May 1, 1886, there was a nation-wide "eight-hour" work stoppage in which 340,000 union members took part. Two days later the Chicago police fired into a group of "eight-hour" pickets at the McCormick harvester plant, killing one man and wounding many others. The next night, May 4, there was a mass meeting of union members in Haymarket Square to protest the shooting. In the crowd of 3,000 were many socialists and anarchists, who controlled some of the Chicago unions and had helped to elect Mayor Carter Harrison. The Mayor himself was at the meeting, prepared to call it off if there was trouble. About 180 policemen stood at attention near by, listening stolidly to the speeches.

After a while, when nothing much happened, the Mayor went home. Then an English-born teamster named Samuel Fielden climbed on the speakers' wagon and delivered a fiery harangue. "You have nothing more to do with the law . . . ," he shouted. "Throttle it, kill it, stab it, do everything you can to wound it. . . ." This went on for some time, when suddenly the police began to move in. Fielden jumped down from the wagon, exclaiming, "We are peaceable." At that instant someone threw a round, cast-iron, dynamite-filled bomb with a long sputtering fuse. It exploded among the policemen, wounding eight of them fatally and injuring 67 more. This was the first time dynamite was used as a weapon in the United States, and the people in the crowd were as surprised and scared as the policemen. The cops recovered first, however, closed their ranks, drew their revolvers, and charged *(below)*. A great many more workingmen than policemen were killed that night.

When the Haymarket "conspirators" were hanged, November 11, 1887, their last words were reported by Police Captain Schaack. August Spies said, "You may strangle this voice but my silence will be more terrible than speech." Adolph Fischer said, *"Hoch die Anarchie!"* George Engel said, "Hurrah for anarchy!" Albert Richard Parsons said, "O men of America, let the voice of the people be heard . . ." Just then the trap was sprung.

Police Captain Michael J. Schaack wrote a 700-page book about the bombing.

THE FOUR WHO WERE HANGED

for the Haymarket bombing had nothing to do with throwing or making the bomb. They were railroaded to the gallows by Melville E. Stone of the Chicago *Daily News* and other leading citizens because they were labor agitators and outspoken enemies of the capitalist system. Three of them were German-born anarchists. The fourth, Albert Richard Parsons, came from old New England stock and had several ancestors in the American Revolution. He was born in Montgomery, Alabama, fought in the Confederate cavalry at 13, worked as a newspaper reporter and printer in Houston and Galveston, moved to Chicago in 1873, and became active in the printers' union and in socialist politics. He turned anarchist after becoming convinced—through his own experiences with blacklists and union-busting in the newspaper plants—that the American system did not give American workmen a square deal. In his little newspaper, the *Alarm*, he had once urged, "Workingmen of America, learn the manufacture and use of dynamite. It will be your most powerful weapon. . . ." For this he was hanged. The man who really threw the bomb was never identified.

"Between Two Fires" shows a striking worker trying to choose between his employer *(left)* and an anarchist thug.

"Too Heavy a Load for the Trades-Unions" shows a fat foreign agitator wielding his whip over American labor.

THE REACTION AGAINST LABOR

THE HAYMARKET BOMBING was a catastrophe for the labor unions. Newspapers and magazines were filled with antilabor propaganda; through their efforts the eight-hour day became all mixed up in the public mind with dynamite, Karl Marx, free love, and the Russian nihilists. Big employers no longer had any difficulty in smashing the unions in their plants, and the courts, both federal and state, issued numerous injunctions against labor organizations. The once-powerful Knights of Labor disintegrated and almost vanished under this attack.

Meanwhile, in New York City, the conservatives had another scare when Henry George, the "Single Taxer," ran for mayor on a labor ticket. George's scheme for abolishing private ownership of land drew 68,110 votes, but Abram S. Hewitt, a Democratic manufacturer, won with 90,552. Theodore Roosevelt, the Republican candidate, was third.

"Is This the Triumph of Our Republican Form of Government?" shows strikebreaker passing an 1886 picket line.

THE LABOR DESPOT.

THE supreme tyrant of the labor organizations is the walking delegate, the well-fed, well-paid official who performs the functions of a general overseer, and whose fiat is expected to be obeyed without protest or murmur. Not a few of the disastrous strikes of recent years were prolonged, if they were not instigated, by these representatives of the worst elements of discontent. Happily American workingmen seem now to be losing their respect for this class of petty despots, and it is hardly probable that they will be able in future to exercise any such autocratic power as they have so injuriously employed in the past.

It was the peculiarity of the recent great strike in London that it was spontaneous, that it was based upon a real grievance, was entirely free from coercive excesses on the part of would-be bosses, and that it had, from first to last, the genuine sympathy of the great body of the people. The sole obstacle to a settlement was the obstinacy of the dock companies, upon whom the demand for slightly increased compensation was made by the striking laborers. Against these stubborn dock directors were arrayed the merchants, the ship-owners, and all the high officials in church and state, such men as Cardinal Manning, the Lord Mayor, the Bishop of London, and Sir John Lubbock interfering actively in behalf of the strikers, while Lord Randolph Churchill and other men in official life ably championed their cause in public addresses. It was inevitable that, thus sustained, the men on strike should ultimately gain a substantial victory. It will be well if American workingmen shall learn the lesson that, with a just cause, and abstaining from all disorderly and offensive methods, they, too, can depend upon public sympathy, and will be much more likely to win their way than when pursuing an opposite course.

"The Tyranny of the Walking Delegate" was a favorite theme of the antilabor cartoonists. This union official is pictured as a swaggering plutocrat with striped pants and a big cigar, who calls strikes just for the fun of it.

Republican cartoon of 1888 shows Cleveland's friend, Roger Quarles Mills of Texas, opening the tariff floodgate to drown American industry. Mills was one of a colorful group of Southern Congressmen called the "Confederate Brigadiers."

"NO, NO, NO FREE TRADE!"

In 1888 the bloody shirt lay moldering in its grave and the Republicans were looking for a new campaign issue to prevent Cleveland's re-election. They found one when the President suddenly came out for a big cut in the tariff. His position was sound—the so-called "protective" tariff no longer protected most American industries, which could now stand on their own feet and even export at a profit. The protective tariff, in fact, was nothing more than a handy scheme to keep prices high and subsidize big business. It produced mountains of surplus government revenue, taken from the pockets of American consumers.

Cleveland was not a free-trader by any means, but he despised the protective-tariff sham and lashed out against it in his usual blunt style. At his request Congressman Mills of Texas drafted a new tariff lowering duties on manufactured goods, and admitting wool and lumber free. The Mills bill passed the House but died in the Republican Senate.

Cleveland's tariff plans thus came to nothing, but the Republicans cried that he was out to destroy American industry. Their candidate for President was Benjamin Harrison, a frigid little general and Senator, the grandson of President William Henry ("Hard Cider") Harrison. While Harrison stayed quietly at home in Indianapolis the American Iron and Steel Association and other big industrial groups dominated the Republican campaign. Manufacturers who benefited from the tariff were "fried" for more than $4 million in political "fat," which was applied lavishly in crucial states. The Republican national committee treasurer sent the following instructions to his assistant in Indiana: "Divide the floaters into blocks of five and put a trusted man in charge of these five, with the necessary funds, and make him responsible that none get away, and that all vote our ticket."

But the neatest trick of the year was staged by a California Republican named Osgoodby. Pretending to be a former British subject, Osgoodby wrote an innocent-sounding letter to Sir Lionel Sackville-West, the British minister, asking how he should vote. Sir Lionel, who was an unusually stupid diplomat, wrote back that Cleveland was probably the best man from the British point of view. The Republicans published this letter late in the campaign, when it had an effect on Irish voters exactly comparable to the "Rum, Romanism, and Rebellion" blunder of 1884. The election went to Harrison by 65 electoral ballots, though Cleveland was ahead by 95,713 in popular votes.

A Harrison "No Free Trade" parade *(right)* bumps into a Cleveland "Reform" parade on Broadway, New York.

Sir Lionel Sackville-West was dismissed as British minister after he committed the prize political boner of 1888.

THE BILLION DOLLAR CONGRESS

When the Fifty-first Congress convened December 2, 1889, the Republicans in the House had just three votes more than a quorum. Absences and Democratic refusals to answer the roll call blocked all important business until Speaker Tom Reed began counting the House himself. When members failed to answer their names the mountain-shaped Reed listed them as "present and refusing to vote." This ruling produced a storm among the Democrats. "I deny your right, Mr. Speaker," cried one of them, "to count me as present and I desire to read from the parliamentary law on the subject." "The chair is making a statement of fact that the gentleman from Kentucky is present," drawled Reed. "Does he deny it?"

Reed also locked the doors to keep the Democrats in their seats. Congressman "Buck" Kilgore of Texas kicked a door down one day while Reed calmly marked him present. The Democrats charged that Reed was even counting the hats in the cloakroom to get his quorums. But public opinion and common sense were on the Speaker's side, and eventually the Reed-bossed House buckled down and did more work than in any session since Reconstruction.

Its first big job was to get rid of the $97 million Treasury surplus, which it did very easily by voting monthly pensions to a half million Northern veterans. Corporal James Tanner, a professional Boy in Blue who had lost both legs at Bull Run, was appointed Pension Commissioner by President Harrison. In three years the surplus was gone and the Government's pension outlay had jumped to $159 million a year, nearly half the regular budget.

Congress' next step was to pay off big business by raising the tariff. This project was assigned to Congressman William McKinley of Canton, Ohio, who felt the same way toward the protective tariff that a loving husband does toward his wife. The McKinley tariff which was passed in 1890 continued to coddle the old "infant industries," such as iron and steel, and sharply raised the rates on cotton cloth, linen, carpets, thread, tinware, tools, and many foods. Raw sugar was the only article on which the duty was removed, and this profited nobody but the Sugar Trust, which had a monopoly of American refineries. The consumer outcry against the McKinley tariff was immediate and terrific. Prices shot up in country stores, and a nation-wide buyers' strike was organized. The Democrats sent peddlers around the streets with tin cups marked "A 5¢ cup for 25¢ —price raised by the McKinley tariff." Even some Republicans felt that McKinley had gone too far. Secretary of State Blaine went before a Senate committee to argue against the tariff and got so excited that he banged his fist through the top of his high silk hat.

The Fifty-first Congress also passed a new silver act to increase the Treasury's silver purchases, and an antitrust act which prohibited monopolies and combinations "in restraint of trade." Because of Congressional routine, the Antitrust Act carried the name of the grand old Republican from Ohio, Senator John Sherman. But Sherman never understood the law and, according to one of his colleagues, probably never read it. The Republicans did not intend to enforce it anyway, and it soon became a dead letter through adverse court action.

The Fifty-first Congress also achieved considerable notoriety by being the first to spend a billion dollars of the taxpayers' money in peacetime. One day somebody dropped a teasing remark to "Czar" Reed about his "Billion Dollar Congress." His retort became famous. "Yes," he said, "but this is a Billion Dollar Country!"

"God help the Surplus," cried Corporal Tanner, the new Pension Commissioner. Cartoon shows how he scattered it.

THOMAS BRACKETT
REED OF MAINE

(left) was a genial Republican autocrat who established one-man rule in the House of Representatives. Czar Reed had a nasal "down East" drawl and a whiplash wit which contrasted strikingly with his ponderous appearance. His wisecracks were treasured and often repeated. "A statesman," he once said, "is a successful politician who is dead." He squelched the self-righteous Teddy Roosevelt by saying: "Theodore, if there is one thing more than another for which I admire you, it is for your original discovery of the Ten Commandments!"

President Benjamin Harrison *(with grandson)* picked a big-business Cabinet.

Congressman William McKinley said high tariffs encouraged "manly aspirations."

Senator John Sherman was the somewhat unwitting father of the first anti-trust law.

President Harrison *(center)* poses with family and friends at the home of Postmaster General John Wanamaker *(left)* in Philadelphia.

John Painter *(right)*, a leader of the new Populist party, poses with family and friends at his own home in Broken Bow, Nebraska.

Homestead claimants rushing into Oklahoma's Cherokee Strip, September 16, 1893. The American frontier was almost gone by then.

THE 65 BILLION DOLLAR COUNTRY

George Eastman invented the Kodak and made photography boom.

TOM REED was underestimating when he said the United States was a billion dollar country. The national wealth in 1890 was $65,037,091,197. Nearly 40 billion of this was invested in land and buildings, 9 billion in railroads, and 4 billion in manufacturing and mining. This was more than the wealth of Great Britain or of Russia and Germany put together. The United States in 1890 had 63 million people, of whom 17 million lived west of the Mississippi. It led the world in practically all the comforts and necessities of life. Yet, as seen through the lens of George Eastman's new Kodak, it looked dusty and poor more often than it looked comfortable or rich. Perhaps that was because 11 million of its 12 million families lived on an average income of $380 a year.

A news photographer of the 1890's and his handy "detective camera."

257

"A Prayer for Rain" was drawn by the well-known artist, A. B. Frost, who traveled through Kansas in the 1890's.

"Feeding the Pigs" was sketched by Frost in Iowa, where farmers were better off than in the arid plains states.

"The Political Poor Relation," an 1889 cartoon, shows a ragged American farmer intruding on a banquet of tariff-gorged industrialists. McKinley is pouring the whisky and other Congressmen are providing cigars and music.

THE POPULIST REVOLT

"IN GOD WE TRUSTED, in Kansas we busted," said the signs on the covered wagons as they streamed back east in the 1890's. On the Great Plains and also in the South the "farm problem" had become a chronic agony. Whenever the farmers had a bumper year it seemed that the prices of their crops sank to a no-profit level, and whenever they had a drought year or a grasshopper year they went broke anyway. By 1890 a large proportion of the original homesteaders had sold out or quit, and rural America was a billion dollar country in its own special way—a billion dollars in mortgages, which encumbered 28 per cent of its farms.

What was the cause of all this debt and failure? The experts blamed it on a world-wide "overproduction" of food. The farmers did not believe this, and, indeed, it was hard to believe it when one looked at the breadlines and slums of the cities. "The politicians said we suffered from overproduction," cried Mary Elizabeth Lease, a wheat-field orator who was known as the "Kansas Pythoness." "Overproduction when 10,000 little children, so statistics tell us, starve to death every year in the United States. . . . The parties lie to us and the political speakers mislead us. . . . Kansas suffers from two great robbers, the Santa Fe Railroad and the loan companies." And in Georgia the discontented farmers summed up their plight in the slogan, "The makers of clothes are underfed; the makers of food are underclad."

Out of the farmers' distress and doubt came a swirling political tornado: the People's party, whose members were known as Populists. The Populists aimed their crusade directly at organized wealth, which, they believed, was sucking the country dry through monopoly prices, extortionate railroad rates, and tariffs. The Populist platform was the most advanced and thoroughgoing social program yet advocated in the United States: it called for a graduated income tax, popular election of Senators, postal savings banks to compete with private banks, government ownership of railroads, telegraph and telephone companies, a return to the Government of excess land held by railroads and other corporations, laws to protect labor unions, abolition of the Pinkertons' "standing army of mercenaries," and a more elastic money system.

The Populist whirlwind completely wrecked the Billion Dollar Congress. In the 1890 elections the Republicans were swept out of power, Czar Reed was ousted as Speaker, and McKinley himself was beaten for re-election. The new House had 235 Democrats (many of them tinged with Populism) and 88 Republicans. There were also nine Representatives and four Senators who were out-and-out Populists. In 1892 the Populists fused with the Knights of Labor and nominated General James B. Weaver of Iowa for President. He drew more than a million farm and labor votes, but the net result was to bring back to the White House the familiar figure of Grover Cleveland, who had just spent four years in a Wall Street law office, and heartily opposed everything the Populists stood for.

Mrs. Mary Lease, Populist firebrand and mother of four, advised Kansas farmers to "raise less corn and more *Hell*."

The Populists raised hell in the Kansas legislature when Republicans ousted a Populist Speaker and seized control.

Grover Cleveland, a little fatter and more set in his ways, was re-elected President in 1892, despite Populist opposition.

THE GAY
NINETIES

The Chicago world's fair, or Columbian Exposition, opened May 1, 1893. By May 2 the whole country had heard about the "Egyptian Village" and its hootchy-kootchy girls.

Another panic, followed by depression and breadlines, hit the country in 1893.

At Pittsburgh an anarchist shot Henry Clay Frick *(left)*, chairman of the Carnegie Steel Company, after Frick imported 300 Pinkerton gunmen to fight union men at Homestead.

This world's fair sketch was captioned "A Typical American Girl's First Experience In Smoking the Chibouk." Everyone who went to the fair felt like doing something wicked.

THE GREAT FERRIS WHEEL

was invented and built by George Washington Gale Ferris for the Chicago world's fair. The promoters had challenged American engineers to produce something that would rival the Eiffel Tower in Paris. Ferris' Wheel *(below)* rose 250 feet above the Midway and carried 36 cars, each holding 40 passengers, most of whom were scared stiff by the winds that blew in from Lake Michigan. But even the Wheel was not as popular as Sol Bloom's "Egyptian Village" dancers, who were really corn-fed American girls with dark eyes and a little special training. Their "Oriental" dance, wrote an Eastern critic, "is a series of posturings rhythmically performed, in which only the upper part of the body is used. It is a swaying and a movement of the body above the hips to a musical accompaniment . . . which certainly pleases men of simply carnal minds, whether they come from Boston, Oshkosh, or Kalamazoo."

An ad of the Gay Nineties: "There, Miss Wheeler," says the youth, "thanks to Brown's Shoe Dressing, no one would imagine that you had just taken a twenty-mile spin."

A DEBATE ON FREE SILVER

WHILE THE DANCING girls shimmied in Chicago, the country plunged rapidly into another of its periodic depressions. President Cleveland blamed the panic of 1893 largely on the Silver Purchase Act of 1890. The other first-class nations of the world were all on the gold standard, he said, while the United States was frittering away gold to buy silver. In August 1893 he summoned Congress to an emergency session to repeal the Silver Act.

This brought on a fierce debate in his own party, for many Democrats thought the Treasury should coin more silver rather than less. They disagreed flatly with the President and his Wall Street friends about the depression: they said it was caused by too little money, not too much. Their arguments were interesting. In 1865 the circulating money supply of the United States was nearly $2 billion. But in 1890, with twice as many people and three times as much business being done, the money supply was smaller than in 1865. Was it any wonder, asked

Senator Francis Marion Cockrell of Missouri made a highly acrobatic oration for free silver at the special session of 1893. Cockrell was a former Confederate general who snapped his galluses while speaking, smoked a corncob pipe, and wore a long linen duster when off the floor.

Senator William Alfred Peffer, the solemn darling of the Kansas Populists, was strong for free silver. Peffer had been a California gold digger, a Tennessee lawyer, and an editor in Topeka. A magazine writer once said he was "as devoid of personal magnetism as a hitching-post."

the Silver Democrats, that Western wheat-growers and Southern cotton-raisers suffered from lower prices every year, when dollars were getting fewer all the time? The value of money rose under such conditions, and the price of everything else came down. This was good for the people who had money, but it seemed to work out badly for the people who produced food or goods.

The "free silver" solution, which was backed by Western and Southern Democrats and the Populists, was to coin all the silver the Treasury could buy at the standard price of one ounce of gold for 16 of silver. When it was charged that big Western mining interests were in favor of this, Congressman William J. Bryan of Nebraska admitted it. "Is it any more important that you should keep a mercantile house from failing than that you should keep a mine from suspending?" he demanded, thus drawing the lines for a political battle royal between the commercial East and the producing West.

Senator David Bennett Hill of New York provoked great resentment in his home state by voting for free silver. Hill's career, said a New York editor, "has been conspicuously odious for its contempt of law and ... sound morals; there never has been a time when he was not prepared to steal a Legislature, ravage a ballot-box, or perpetrate any infamy promising personal or political advantage."

Senator Daniel Wolsey Voorhees of Indiana, known at Democratic gatherings as the "Tall Sycamore of the Wabash," favored unlimited coinage of silver until President Cleveland bought him off with lavish gifts of patronage. Then Voorhees became a blustering foe of free silver.

Congressman Richard Parks ("Silver Dick") Bland of Missouri, veteran free silverite, swore that "this war shall never cease . . . until the silver dollar shall take its place alongside the gold." He also warned that silver had brought the Democratic party to a "parting of the ways."

A crowd gathers at the Capitol, May 1, 1894, to wait for Coxey's army. The best spots on the stairs are already taken by Congressmen and their secretaries. The sun was very hot that day, and many spectators carried umbrellas.

The Commonweal of Christ Brass Band was in the army.

Coxey's army on the move rarely had more than 500 men.

COXEY'S COMMONWEAL ARMY

AT 11 A.M., Easter Sunday, March 25, 1894, a bugle blew on the outskirts of Massillon, Ohio, and the "Commonweal of Christ"—otherwise known as "Coxey's army"—began its march on Washington, D. C. The army was only a fraction of the four million Americans who had lost their jobs in the depression of 1893. But its methods were new to American politics. At its head a Negro carried the American flag, and close behind came another banner on which the face of Christ was painted, with the words "Peace On Earth, Good Will Toward Men! He Hath Risen!!! But DEATH TO *INTEREST ON BONDS!!*" The "Grand Marshal," mounted on a prancing white stallion, was a California poet named Carl Browne, who wore a broad sombrero, a white lace necktie, and silver-dollar buttons on his buckskin jacket. Behind him in a carriage came "General" Jacob S. Coxey, a mild, round-shouldered man with gold-rimmed spectacles, who owned a profitable sand quarry and horse-breeding farm near Massillon. Coxey was accompanied by members of his family, including an infant son named Legal Tender Coxey.

Among the deputy commanders were an Oklahoma cowboy, a Pennsylvania steel striker, an astrologer in a battered silk hat, a leather-lunged orator who was identified simply as "The Great Unknown," and a half-breed Indian who scouted the road ahead for each day's march. The "army" was a long line of ragged men with sacks of food and blankets on their shoulders. As they

The leaders: Coxey *(right)*, Carl Browne, and Christopher Columbus Jones *(left)*.

hoofed it along the dusty roads they sang, to the tune of "After the Ball":

> After the march is over,
> After the first of May,
> After the bills are passed, child,
> Then we will have fair play.

The bills they wanted had already been written and introduced by the Populist Senator Peffer. One called for government hiring of the unemployed to build macadam roads all over the country. The other would give states, cities, and towns the right to issue noninterest-bearing bonds and deposit them with the Treasury, which would then issue up to $500 million in irredeemable paper money to cover their face value. This was the old Greenbacker plan, brought up to date and considerably enlarged.

For more than a month Coxey's army walked and rode canalboats across Pennsylvania and Maryland, reaching Washington on April 26. President Cleveland and Congress both refused to see them. On May 1 the army started up Pennsylvania Avenue toward the Capitol dome, where a phalanx of policemen and thousands of sightseers were waiting. At the entrance to the Capitol grounds "Grand Marshal" Browne jumped down from his horse and made a dash for the steps. Two policemen knocked him down and dragged him away. Then "General" Coxey kissed his wife, slipped meekly through the crowd, and started to read a petition. The cops arrested him for walking on the grass. That was the end of Coxey's army.

"NOTHING TO

"A MAN WHO WON'T meet his men halfway is a God-damn fool!" growled Mark Hanna, the national boss of the Republican party. His words were aimed particularly at George M. Pullman, one of his large campaign contributors. Late in 1893 the Pullman Palace Car Company in Chicago laid off most of its employees and then began rehiring them at wage cuts of 20 to 25 per cent. The Pullman workers lived in a company town where rents, gas, and water rates were 10 to 25 per cent higher than in the near-by area. The company offered no reduction in these expenses to match its wage cuts, and when a committee tried to discuss the matter with Pullman, three of its members were fired. To suggestions of arbitration Pullman replied: "We have nothing to arbitrate." He also said: "The workers have nothing to do with the amount of wages they shall receive." At this time his company had a $25 million surplus

Union President Eugene Debs, who led the Pullman strike, was a locomotive fireman from Terre Haute, Indiana.

"Giving the Butt"—an on-the-spot sketch by Frederic Remington shows how the Army handled the strikers.

The end of the strike—a trainload of meat leaves the stockyards with a soldier escort July 10, 1894 *(right)*.

ARBITRATE"

and had just paid out $2,520,000 in dividends.

In May 1894 the remaining Pullman workers struck and, a month later, the American Railway Union declared a boycott of all railroads using Pullman cars. There was no serious disorder until July 3, when President Cleveland ordered a regiment of regular army troops into Chicago to enforce a federal court injunction against the strikers. In the rioting which followed 12 men were killed, and the strike was broken. The union leader, Eugene Debs, was sent to jail, where he spent his time reading history and was converted to socialism.

Mayor Hopkins of Chicago and Governor Altgeld of Illinois both protested against the use of federal troops to break the strike. But Cleveland replied: "If it takes the entire army and navy of the United States to deliver a postal card in Chicago, that card will be delivered."

Pullman President George M. Pullman was co-inventor of the upper berth (in 1864) and the lower berth (in 1865).

COMMUNISM AND THE COURT

IN JUNE 1894 the Democrats in Congress enacted a 2 per cent tax on incomes of $4,000 and over. According to Congressman David A. De Armond of Missouri, the income tax was something that ought to cheer up the entire nation. "The passage of the bill," he said on the floor of the House, "will mark the dawn of a brighter day, with more of sunshine, more of the songs of birds, more of that sweetest music, the laughter of children well fed, well clothed, well housed. . . . God hasten the era of equality in taxation and in opportunity!"

Despite Mr. De Armond's enthusiasm, there was nothing new about the income tax. The Republicans had imposed a federal income tax (a higher one, incidentally) during the Civil War, and the Supreme Court had ruled that it was constitutional. But in 1894 the Republican spokesmen went into a virtual panic. The income tax, cried old Senator Sherman, was "socialism, communism, devilism." Joseph H. Choate, the dean of the New York Bar, told the United States Supreme Court that the tax was "a communist march on private property." After much backstage bickering and robe-fluttering the Court reversed itself and voted, five to four, that the Democratic income tax was unconstitutional.

This decision was handed down May 20, 1895, and was denounced the same day by Justice John M. Harlan as a "monstrous, wicked injustice to the many for the benefit of the favored few." The New York *World* called it "another victory of greed over need," and a proof that entrenched wealth would never willingly pay its share toward support of the Government. For more than 25 years, in fact, the federal courts and corporation lawyers, working closely together, had managed to thwart, twist, or kill every new law that limited the privileges of money. The Interstate Commerce Act of 1887 and the Antitrust Act of 1890 were virtually dead, except when used to break strikes through injunctions. The income-tax decision simply threw an uncomfortable spotlight on the fact that the Supreme Court was loaded with big business prejudice.

The Populists were stung to frenzy by the income-tax decision, but their complaints were met with ridicule.

This cartoon from *Puck* is supposed to show what the Supreme Court would look like if the Populists ran it.

Justice Stephen J. Field, 78, the oldest man on the Supreme Court, wrote the most biased opinion against the income tax. It was, he said, an "assault upon capital" and the beginning of "a war of the poor against the rich." Field was a Californian who was appointed to the Court by Lincoln in 1863 and stayed there until his colleagues asked him to resign, in 1897. In 1886 he took part in the famous decision by which the Supreme Court rewrote the 14th Amendment to protect big business from federal and state regulation. The Amendment was originally designed to safeguard the legal rights of "persons" (especially Negro voters), but the Court decided that railroads and other corporations were "persons" too, and therefore entitled to a large number of immunities and privileges.

William Jennings Bryan was the first important political leader from the generation which had grown up since the Civil War. He was born in Salem, Illinois, in 1860, practiced law in Lincoln, Nebraska, served two terms in Congress during the Populist upsurge, and was beaten for the United States Senate in 1894. When he went to the Democratic convention of 1896 he was earning his living as editor-in-chief of the Omaha *World-Herald* and lecturing on silver.

BRYAN AND THE CROSS OF GOLD

ON THE AFTERNOON of July 9, 1896, the Democratic convention at Chicago was a seething mob. Twenty thousand men and women surged back and forth in the Coliseum, cursing and howling down the speakers. The question up for debate was a platform plank calling for the free and unlimited coinage of silver. Most of the delegates were free silverites, but no one had yet appeared on the platform to express to the full their superheated emotions.

At this juncture Delegate William Jennings Bryan of Nebraska was called to the stage. Bryan was already a well-known orator in the free-silver cause: a young man with a large florid face and the manners of a country preacher. As he stood there, with a smile on his lips and his hands clasped in a confident gesture, a strange thrill ran through the mass of delegates. Their shouts died away to a murmur, and then to silence. Bryan's warm, mellow voice penetrated to every corner of the enormous hall.

"Mr. Chairman and Gentlemen of the Convention," he began. "I would be presumptuous, indeed, to present myself against the distinguished gentlemen to whom you have listened if this were a mere measuring of abilities; but this is not a contest between persons. The humblest citizen in all the land, when clad in the armor of a righteous cause, is stronger than all the hosts of error. I come to speak to you in defense of a cause as holy as the cause of liberty—the cause of humanity."

The note of humble righteousness was perfect —his audience sat spellbound while Bryan told how President Cleveland and the Eastern "goldbugs" had been defeated, and the Democratic party captured by the forces of free silver. With a rising challenge in his voice, he continued: "Ah, my friends, we say not one word against those who live upon the Atlantic coast, but the hardy pioneers who have braved all the dangers of the wilderness, who have made the desert to blossom as the rose—the pioneers away out there [*pointing to the West*], who rear their children near to Nature's heart, where they can mingle their voices with the voices of the birds . . . these people, we say, are as deserving of the con-

Uncle Sam and his crown of thorns

sideration of our party as any people in this country. It is for these that we speak. We do not come as aggressors. Our war is not a war of conquest; we are fighting in the defense of our homes, our families, and posterity. We have petitioned, and our petitions have been scorned . . . we have begged, and they have mocked when our calamity came. We beg no longer; we entreat no more; we petition no more. We defy them. . . .

"You come to us and tell us that the great cities are in favor of the gold standard; we reply that the great cities rest upon our broad and fertile prairies. Burn down your cities and leave our farms, and your cities will spring up again as if by magic; but destroy our farms and the grass will grow in the streets of every city in the country. . . .

"If they dare to come out in the open field and defend the gold standard as a good thing, we will fight them to the uttermost. Having behind us the producing masses of this nation and the world, supported by the commercial interests, the laboring interests, and the toilers everywhere, we will answer their demand for a gold standard by saying to them: You shall not press down upon the brow of labor this crown of thorns, you shall not crucify mankind upon a cross of gold."

And with these closing words the 20,000 Democrats let forth one great yell of joy. In Bryan they had found their voice. The next day, still groggy with his eloquence, they handed him their nomination for President.

Somehow, without saying anything new, but with consummate skill and poise, he had spoken for millions of Americans who felt oppressed and baffled by the dominant political and big business regime. For the time being their hopes were concentrated on the dubious scheme to expand the currency by an unlimited coinage of silver. Yet there was a deeper conflict involved: the old enmity of the agrarian for the capitalist, of the Jeffersonian for the Federalist, of the exploited West for the exploiting East. Bryan's free-silver crusade awoke these ancient American forces, and drew them forth to another lusty battle.

The most popular Democratic cartoon of 1896 shows Western and Southern farmers feeding the great American cow, while all the milk goes into Wall Street's pail.

THE BRYAN-HATERS

BRYAN'S NOMINATION scared the nation's conservatives into hysterics. The newspapers screamed that he was a traitor, a faker, a "wretched, rattle-pated boy . . . posing in vapid vanity and mouthing resounding rottenness . . . apt . . . at lies and forgeries and blasphemies." A New York City clergyman burst out from his pulpit that Bryan was "a mouthing, slobbering demagogue whose patriotism is all in his jawbone." The editor of *Harper's Weekly* wrote that the election was a duel to the death between "the dreams and fantasies of Karl Marx" and the "true Americanism" of the Republican party.

Yet if the election had been held in the summer Bryan would probably have won. He made the most energetic personal campaign in history, traveling 18,009 miles, addressing five million people, speaking ten to twenty times a day, rubbing the sweat off his body at night with gin. He attacked the gold standard, big business, and the trusts—"One of the most important duties of government is to put rings in the noses of hogs," he said in one speech. But he started no riots, ignored personal abuse, and kept his sense of humor. When asked to address a crowd of farmers from a manure spreader he cracked: "This is the first time I have ever spoken from a Republican platform."

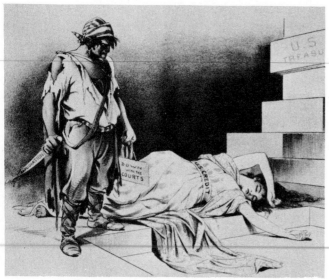

"The Assassin" shows Bryan as the murderer of American credit, through his plan to repudiate the gold standard.

"The Boy on the Burning Deck" shows Bryan sticking to the silver platform, whence many Democrats had fled.

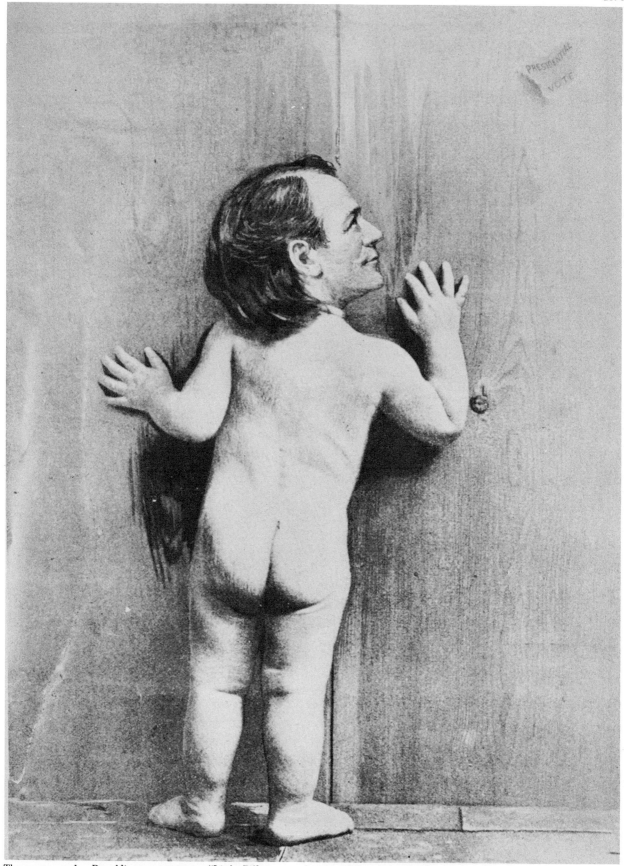

The most popular Republican cartoon was "Little Billy Bryan Chasing Butterflies," which appeared first in *Judge* and was widely reprinted. The cartoonist simply added Bryan's features to a well-known "cabinet photograph."

McKinley on his front porch at Canton, Ohio, addresses members of his old Civil War regiment August 13, 1896.

The Republican "sound money" parade in New York. The silk-hat voters turned out in great numbers to beat Bryan.

"A Man of Mark" shows McKinley in Hanna's palm. This ran in William Randolph Hearst's New York *Journal*.

MARK HANNA AND HIS MAN

THE REPUBLICAN CANDIDATE in 1896 was William McKinley, the Galahad of the protective tariff. McKinley had been beaten for re-election to Congress in 1890, and then bounced back to become the extremely dignified Governor of Ohio in 1891. He could not match Bryan as a whirlwind orator, so the Republican managers kept him home on his front porch, where he wore a long frock coat and made carefully rehearsed speeches to visitors whose railroad fare and expenses were often paid by the Republican national committee.

Meanwhile the real fight against Bryan was waged by Marcus Alonzo Hanna, a Cleveland coal, iron, and newspaper millionaire who had paid $100,000 from his own pocket to secure McKinley's nomination. "Uncle Mark" set up headquarters in New York and shook down insurance companies, railroads, and trusts for the biggest campaign fund ever collected. He opened the books of corporations and assessed the big banks one quarter of 1 per cent of their capital funds to beat Bryan. Standard Oil alone chipped in $250,000; Hanna's total take was between $3 million (as estimated by his friends) and $16 million (as reported by a Congressional clerk). A few rich Wall Streeters tried to get off with $1,000 checks, but Hanna said they were a "lot of God-damn sheep" and it would serve them right if Bryan "kicked them to hell and gone."

To a large extent Hanna's huge fund was collected and spent legitimately. He hired an army of 1,400 Republican campaign speakers who swarmed over Bryan's tracks and wore him down by sheer numbers. He sent out 100 million pieces of campaign literature, miles of boiler-plate publicity, tons of gold elephants, gold bugs, gold hats, and gold sheaves of wheat. On the Saturday before election he staged a "sound money" parade in New York, in which 150,000 businessmen, bankers, lawyers, and clergymen marched up Broadway wearing black hats and coats. Hanna's campaign was based on the idea that American money was in danger, and everybody who had any money should work and vote against Bryan. Strangely enough, McKinley himself did not wholly believe in the gold standard; in his early years in Congress he had voted with the free silverites. But Hanna hushed this up and smothered Bryan with gold. McKinley won by 568,000 popular votes and 95 electoral votes, which was more than most Republicans had hoped for.

Mark Hanna was a square-shooting Republican boss who entertained his associates at enormous breakfasts of corned-beef hash. He believed that the Government existed primarily to help business; after that, business could help the rest of the country. He thought all political speeches were "gas" and idealists who whooped it up for a cause were "hurrah boys." When the Attorney General of Ohio started suit to dissolve the Standard Oil trust Hanna advised him to drop the matter, saying, "You have been in politics long enough to know that no man in public life owes the public anything." Yet Hanna was one of the first big industrialists to sign a union contract, and he cemented a close working agreement between the Republican party and the conservative labor leaders.

Captain Alfred T. Mahan helped promote a world naval race by writing books on the importance of sea power.

Queen Liliuokalani, who tried to rule Hawaii for the Hawaiians, was deposed by American missionaries' sons.

SEA POWER AND SUGAR

"Spaniards Search Women on American Steamers" was a fake atrocity picture, printed by the New York *Journal*.

"BLOOD ON THE roadsides, blood in the fields, blood on the doorsteps, blood, blood, blood," cabled a New York *World* correspondent from Cuba in 1896. "Is there no nation wise enough, brave enough, and strong enough to restore peace in this blood-smitten land?" A revolution against Spanish rule had been raging in Cuba since 1895. American sympathies were strongly with the *insurrectos*, who deliberately wrecked the $30 million sugar industry on the island, hoping in that way to force our armed intervention. Pulitzer's *World* and Hearst's New York *Journal* found that Cuban blood was a great circulation-getter, and they poured it out in every edition.

Meanwhile, in distant Honolulu, American marines and sugar planters had also staged a "revolution" against the native Queen Liliuokalani, and were now asking the President to annex Hawaii.

Both these developments were welcome news to Captain Alfred T. Mahan of the Navy, who for years had been urging the United States to expand beyond its continental borders. To Mahan, whose books on sea power were world-famous, Cuba and Hawaii were only the beginning. Someday, he predicted, the American nation would have to decide the greatest question of all: "whether Eastern or Western civilization is to dominate throughout the earth and to control its future."

Cuban Commander in Chief Máximo Gómez fought an elusive guerrilla war against Spain while awaiting American assistance.

Spanish General Valeriano ("Butcher") Weyler put 400,000 Cubans in concentration camps, where an estimated 210,000 died.

"Cuba Libre!" cried the rebels *(right)*, as they charged a force of loyal volunteers at La Rosa. By 1898 Spain was said to have 140,000 regulars and 50,000 loyal militia in Cuba. But the 50,000 *insurrectos* controlled most of the island outside the big cities.

The *Maine* salutes the Spanish fleet on arrival at Havana. The *Maine* displaced less than 7,000 tons and carried four 10-inch guns.

"REMEMBER THE MAINE,
TO HELL WITH SPAIN!"

On January 25, 1898, the pocket-sized battleship *Maine* appeared in Havana Harbor, in response to a secret request from the American Consul General. Neither the Spanish nor the Cuban rebels were glad to see the *Maine*, but they pretended they were delighted. The Spanish commander sent a case of sherry aboard, and the American officers went ashore to see a bullfight. In Washington the McKinley administration announced the *Maine*'s visit was a "friendly act of courtesy," which everyone knew was a diplomatic lie. The *Maine*'s real assignment was to protect American citizens and salvage American cash and property, if and when the revolution reached Havana.

On the night of February 15, just after its bugler had sounded taps, the *Maine* blew up. No one has ever discovered just what caused the disaster. But 266 American officers and crewmen were killed, and for the rest of the country that was cause enough for war against somebody.

Captain Charles D. Sigsbee was in this comfortable cabin, writing to his wife, when the *Maine* blew up. He was rescued.

After the explosion the *Maine* was a mass of twisted junk, mostly under water. A court of inquiry investigated for a month and decided it was sunk by a submarine mine, externally applied. Later evidence indicated its magazine might have exploded internally.

50,000 REWARD.—WHO DESTROYED THE MAINE?—$50,000 REWARD

NEW YORK JOURNAL
AND ADVERTISER. FIRST EDITION.

NO. 5,572. Copyright, 1896, by W. R. Hearst—NEW YORK, THURSDAY, FEBRUARY 17, 1898.—16 PAGES. PRICE ONE CENT In Greater New York and Jersey City.

DESTRUCTION OF THE WAR SHIP MAINE WAS THE WORK OF AN ENEMY

$50,000!
$50,000 REWARD!
For the Detection of the Perpetrator of the Maine Outrage!

Assistant Secretary Roosevelt Convinced the Explosion of the War Ship Was Not an Accident.

The Journal Offers $50,000 Reward for the Conviction of the Criminals Who Sent 258 American Sailors to Their Death. Naval Officers Unanimous That the Ship Was Destroyed on Purpose.

$50,000!
$50,000 REWARD!
For the Detection of the Perpetrator of the Maine Outrage!

NAVAL OFFICERS THINK THE MAINE WAS DESTROYED BY A SPANISH MINE.

George Eugene Bryson, the Journal's special correspondent at Havana, cables that it is the secret opinion of many Spaniards in the Cuban capital, that the Maine was destroyed and 258 of her men killed by means of a submarine mine, or fixed torpedo. This is the opinion of several American naval authorities. The Spaniards, it is believed, arranged to have the Maine anchored over one of the harbor mines. Wires connected the mine with a powder magazine and it is thought the explosion was caused by sending an electric current through the wire. It can be proven, the brutal nature of the Spaniards will be shown by the fact that they wanted to spring the mine until after all the men had retired for the night. The Maine cross in the picture shows where the mine was exploded.

Hidden Mine or a Sunken Torpedo Believed to Have Been the Weapon Used Against the American Man-of-War---Officers and Men Tell Thrilling Stories of Being Blown Into the Air Amid a Mass of Shattered Steel and Exploding Shells---Survivors Brought to Key West Scout the Idea of Accident---Spanish Officials Protest Too Much---Our Cabinet Orders a Searching Inquiry---Journal Sends Divers to Havana to Report Upon the Condition of the Wreck. Was the Vessel Anchored Over a Mine?

Assistant Secretary of the Navy Theodore Roosevelt says he is convinced that the destruction of the Maine in Havana Harbor was not an accident. The Journal offers a reward of $50,000 for exclusive evidence that will convict the person, persons or Government criminally responsible for the destruction of the American battleship and the death of 258 of its crew.

The suspicion that the Maine was deliberately blown up grows stronger every hour. Not a single fact to the contrary has been produced.

Captain Sigsbee, of the Maine, and Consul-General Lee both urge that public opinion be suspended until they have completed their investigation. They are taking the course of tactful men who are convinced that there has been treachery.

Spanish Government officials are pressing forward all sorts of explanations of how it could have been an accident. The facts show that there was a report before the ship exploded, and that, had her magazine exploded, she would have sunk immediately.

Every naval expert in Washington says that if the Maine's magazine had exploded the whole vessel would have been blown to atoms.

Hearst's New York *Journal* left little doubt that the *Maine* had been sunk by Spaniards. Headlines like these sent the *Journal's* sales above a million a day for the first time. Pulitzer's *World*, which sent its own divers to the wreck, sold 5 million papers a week.

"The Spanish Brute" shows how one American cartoonist reacted to the *Maine* disaster. This was published in bloody colors on the cover of *Judge*. Spanish newspapers retorted with long-winded insults about "Yankee pigs."

President McKinley tries to hush the yellow newspapers, whose war talk is disturbing the goose that laid prosperity.

PRESIDENT MCKINLEY did not want a war. Mark Hanna, Czar Reed, and the other key men of the Republican party did not want a war, even after the *Maine* was sunk. Business was reviving, and a war might be bad for business.

The Spaniards most definitely did not want a war. In Havana Spanish officials went into mourning for the *Maine*'s sailors. From Madrid came all kinds of conciliatory gestures, including an offer to stop fighting the Cubans. Naturally Spain claimed innocence as far as the *Maine* was concerned.

Yet the American war fever rose steadily, whipped up by the "yellow" press and the bellicose followers of Captain Mahan. In Washington the busiest warmonger was Assistant Secretary of the Navy Theodore Roosevelt. "McKinley has no more backbone than a chocolate éclair," he raged, when the President failed to send an immediate ultimatum to Spain. One night a friend met Roosevelt as he was leaving the White House. "Do you know what that white-livered cur up there has done?" cried Teddy. "He has prepared *two* messages, one for war and one for peace, and doesn't know which one to send in!" But on April 11 the reluctant President sent in his war message, "in the name of humanity, in the name of civilization, in behalf of endangered American interests."

"Spanish 'Justice and Honor' Be Darned!" expressed the mood of the whole country after war was finally declared.

THE TEN WEEKS' WAR

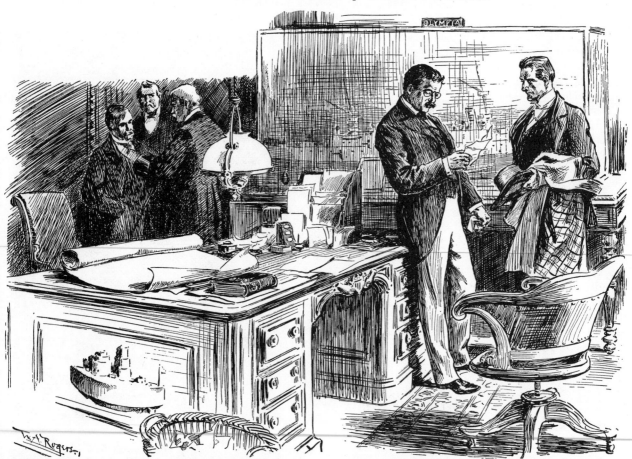

THE WAR WITH SPAIN was surprisingly easy. On May 1 Commodore George Dewey steamed into Manila Bay with the American Navy's Asiatic squadron and sank all the Spanish warships that were there. The American loss was eight men wounded and a chief engineer who died from the heat. On June 20-25 an American army of 15,000 men landed at Daiquirí, Cuba, with a loss of two drowned. On July 1 and 2 the Spanish blockhouses at El Caney and San Juan Hill, near Santiago, were captured in the only severe fighting of the war. On July 3 Admiral Cervera's Spanish fleet tried to escape from Santiago and was destroyed by waiting American warships. "Don't cheer, men, those poor devils are dying!" cried Captain John W. Philip of the *Texas*, as his ship went by the burning *Vizcaya*. Only one American seaman was killed in this encounter.

On July 17, Santiago, the most important Spanish stronghold outside Havana, surrendered to the American invaders. On July 26 the Spanish Government asked for terms, and on August 12 an armistice was signed in Paris. At the last minute came word that American landing forces had taken Manila in the Philippines and Puerto Rico in the Caribbean with no trouble. "HOW DO YOU LIKE THE JOURNAL'S WAR?" gloated the irrepressible New York *Journal*.

It had taken just ten weeks of actual fighting to win an overseas American empire with enough naval bases to satisfy even Captain Mahan for the time being. Except for the toll taken by tropical diseases and the "embalmed beef" which was sold to the Army by American meat-packing firms, our losses were trifling. The Army reported 280 killed in action, the Navy 18. From London American Ambassador John Hay wrote an exulting letter to his friend, Theodore Roosevelt: "It has been a splendid little war," he said.

The band of the battleship *Oregon* plays "A Hot Time in the Old Town Tonight," theme song of the Spanish war, immediately following the Battle of Santiago.

Assistant Navy Secretary Theodore Roosevelt *(leaning against desk)*, a disciple of Captain Mahan, made sure the first battle would be fought 8,000 miles from Cuba. Two months before war was declared he ordered Dewey to get ready to attack Manila.

Naval Constructor Richmond P. Hobson and his crew cling to a raft after a vain attempt to block Santiago Harbor June 3, 1898.

Commodore George Dewey watches from the *Olympia* bridge while his big guns pound the Spanish Asiatic fleet to scrap.

Lieutenant Colonel Roosevelt of the Rough Riders, as depicted by an imaginative artist. When war came Teddy quit his desk in the Navy Department and fought bravely at San Juan Hill. But his cavalrymen had to get off their horses and charge on foot.

Above, an American bayonet rush in the Philippines. Below, reserves of the 20th Kansas volunteers passing through Caloocan February 10, 1899.

Photographs of the Philippine war were less glamorous than the artists' sketches on the opposite page. Above, Minnesota troops outside Manila.

THE THREE YEARS' WAR

To THE DISMAY of most Americans, the real fighting started when the war with Spain was all over. Congress had promised independence to the Cubans, and the promise was kept. But nobody had promised anything to the seven million Filipinos, who had also rebelled against Spain and set up an insurgent government. When their leader, Emilio Aguinaldo, proclaimed their independence, McKinley responded in lofty platitudes: "The presence and success of our arms at Manila imposes upon us obligations which we cannot disregard . . . new duties and responsibilities which we must meet . . . the commercial opportunity to which American statesmanship cannot be indifferent." Aguinaldo got the point—the Americans were in Manila to stay. On February 4, 1899, an American sentry fired on an Aguinaldo insurgent, whose fellow soldiers fired back, and another war was under way.

It took 63,000 American troops, 4,300 American deaths, and three years of dirty fighting to crush the Filipinos. An American general estimated that 600,000 inhabitants were killed or died from the effects of the war on Luzon Island alone. When an American soldier was beheaded by a boloman in a village grocery store, 89 local residents were burned and shot to death in retaliation. And while the statesmen at Washington debated the problem, the blue-shirted American infantry hacked its way through the islands, singing new words to an old song:

> Damn, damn, damn the Filipinos!
> Cross-eyed kakiak ladrones!
>   Underneath the starry flag
>   Civilize 'em with a Krag,
> And return us to our own belovèd homes.

Below, American soldiers and civilians stand on a heap of Filipino bones in the cemetery at Batangas, Luzon.

President McKinley was sorely perplexed by the Philippine "problem." Night after night he walked the floor of the White House and—as he himself said—went down on his knees and "prayed Almighty God for light and guidance." One night the solution came to him—"that there was nothing left for us to do but to take them [the Philippine Islands] all, and to educate the Filipinos, and uplift and civilize and Christianize them, and by God's grace do the very best we could by them, as our fellow men for whom Christ also died." After this inspiration, the President went to bed and slept soundly.

THE IMPERIALISTS

In 1898 the United States acquired its first sizable piece of overseas empire, the Hawaiian Islands, by annexation. Next came the Philippines, Guam, and Puerto Rico—all taken from beaten Spain. In 1899 President McKinley and Kaiser Wilhelm II of Germany divided the Samoa Islands. Once the trend started it was hard to stop, yet there were still many Americans who thought it was wrong. "We are face to face with a strange destiny," wrote the editor of the Washington *Post*. "The taste of Empire is in the mouth of the people even as the taste of blood in the jungle."

On January 9, 1900, while the Senate was still considering the idea of freeing the Philippines, a 37-year-old Senator from Indiana, Albert J. Beveridge, put the new American imperialism into a startling speech. "Mr. President . . . ," he said, "God has not been preparing the English-speaking and Teutonic peoples for a thousand years for nothing but vain and idle self-contemplation and self-admiration. No! He has made us the master-organizers of the world to establish system where chaos reigns. . . . He has made us adepts in government that we may administer government among savage and senile peoples. . . . He has marked the American people as His chosen nation to finally lead in the regeneration of the world. This is the divine mission of America. . . . The Philippines are ours forever. We will not repudiate our duty in the archipelago. We will not abandon our opportunity in the Orient. We will not renounce our part in the mission of our race, trustee, under God, of the civilization of the world."

Albert Jeremiah Beveridge

MANIFEST DESTINY IN KANSAS

Beveridge's words expressed what was stirring in many an American heart. Even before he spoke a Kansas editor named William Allen White had said practically the same thing about Cuba. "Only Anglo-Saxons can govern themselves," wrote White in the Emporia *Gazette* for March 20, 1899. "The Cubans will need a despotic government for many years to restrain anarchy until Cuba is filled with Yankees. . . . It is the Anglo-Saxon's manifest destiny to go forth as a world conqueror. He will take possession of the islands of the sea. . . . This is what fate holds for the chosen people." Bill White was a brash young Republican who thought President McKinley was unbearably stuffy. "He was destined for a statue in the park, and was practicing the pose for it," White wrote of the President. Once while he was interviewing McKinley a photographer arrived to take some pictures. McKinley laid aside his cigar, remarking primly, "We must not let the young men of this country see their President smoking!"

William Allen White

THE OPEN DOOR IN BOSTON

Senator Henry Cabot Lodge of Massachusetts, like Theodore Roosevelt and Captain Mahan, saw the Philippines as steppingstones toward something much bigger. In October 1899, Lodge told an audience in Boston: "Our trade with China has been growing rapidly. We ask no favors; we only ask that we shall be admitted to that great market upon the same terms with the rest of the world. But within a few years we have seen Russia closing in upon the Chinese Empire. . . . If she succeeds we shall not only be excluded from those markets, but we shall stand face to face with a power controlling an extent of territory and a mass of population the like of which the world has never seen. In the presence of such a colossus of despotism and military socialism, the welfare of every free people is in danger." In 1899 Lodge's friend John Hay, who had been promoted to Secretary of State, announced that the United States would henceforth insist on an "open door" of commercial equality in China.

Henry Cabot Lodge

THE DINNER PAIL CAMPAIGN

THE DEMOCRATS made an issue of imperialism in the 1900 election, but they were swamped by a wave of McKinley prosperity. "All we need to do is stand pat," said Mark Hanna, and he was right. The end of the war had touched off a business boom: iron and steel prices were up 100 per cent, raw cotton was up 30 per cent, farm mortgages were being cleared off, factories were sending up smoke, and—as the Republican orators never tired of repeating—the workman's dinner pail was full. The free-silver issue had been destroyed by gold discoveries in Alaska and South Africa, which lowered the price of gold and increased the supply of money.

The Republicans also had a dynamic new campaigner in Theodore Roosevelt, their candidate for Vice President. While McKinley stayed on his front porch again Roosevelt traveled 21,209 miles and made 673 speeches, often accompanied by a body-guard of former Rough Riders. "What about the rotten beef in Cuba?" a Democrat shouted at him in Colorado. And Teddy shouted back: "I ate it, and you'll never get near enough to be hit by a bullet."

In 1900 Bryan was the Democratic candidate again. But his silver-dollar act had turned into a national bore.

This 1900 cartoon shows "Willie" McKinley as the trusts' little boy, with Teddy Roosevelt as his new playmate.

Nurse Mark Hanna sits on Teddy for making too much racket during the campaign. This makes Willie happy.

288

Every Republican parade had a dinner pail. McKinley was re-elected by an 861,459 plurality, the biggest yet polled.

Democratic cartoon shows Mark Hanna as a bellowing dinner pail. But Hanna was a popular campaigner in 1900.

Republican victory cartoon pictures Bryan as a fallen Don Quixote who tried to tilt with the full dinner pail.

*Uncle Sam as a smart little schoolboy shows what
he learned from his war with Spain. "I see be the
pa-apers," said Mr. Dooley, the comic newspaper
philosopher of 1900, "that . . . all we've got to do is
be r-ready f'r to take a punch at Germany or France
or Rooshia or anny counthry on th' face iv th' globe."*

CHAPTER 7

A PORTFOLIO OF CARTOONS IN COLOR

THE UNITED STATES was nearly one hundred years old before it came to know the lanky rube in flag-striped overalls whose picture appears on the opposite page. It is true there was an Uncle Sam in American folklore as early as the War of 1812, and cartoonists drew him in various costumes from 1834 on. But the shaping of Uncle Sam into the nation's permanent symbol was done by a school of cartoonists which flourished in the years from 1870 to 1900. These three decades were the golden age of political cartooning in the United States, when the cartoonists' work was more widely seen and discussed, more vividly drawn and more fearlessly published, and exerted more influence over events than ever before. Many of the best cartoons were published as colored lithographs. A selection of these—in the original colors—appears on the following pages.

Joseph Keppler, who fastened chin whiskers on Uncle Sam, was the greatest of the color cartoonists. Keppler was born in Vienna and followed his family to Missouri in 1867. In St. Louis he was an actor, managed a theatrical company, and started *Die Vehme* ("The Tribunal"), a German-language humorous magazine. It failed and he went to New York, where he became the principal cartoonist for *Leslie's* weekly. In 1876 he started *Puck*, the first successful humorous weekly in the United States. Previous American magazines had been satisfied with one big cartoon in each issue. Keppler published three a week: a full-page front cover, a two-page center spread, and a full-page back cover. His cartoons were exuberant and even gaudy when compared with the cross-hatched products of Thomas Nast. The fact that they were drawn directly on lithographic stones with crayon gave them a freehand air which appealed to many young artists and brought Keppler some able assistants.

Keppler was a Democrat in national politics, but he attacked Tammany Hall and the labor unions as savagely as Nast did. He also caricatured big business, prohibition, Anthony Comstock, and every form of religious intolerance. "The Bosses of the Senate" (pages 300-301) was his masterpiece.

In 1884 *Puck* published the daring "tattooed man" cartoons, showing James G. Blaine stripped down to his skin. Blaine wanted to prosecute Keppler on an obscenity charge, but his friends dissuaded him. The "tattooed man" continued to appear, and played an important part in wrecking Blaine's Presidential hopes. The most famous example (pages 294-295) was drawn by Bernhard Gillam, an English-born artist who was working for Keppler. Gillam happened to be a Republican himself, and voted for Blaine. In 1886 he and his brother-in-law became the owners of *Judge*, which they converted into an effective Republican rival of *Puck*.

Black-and-white cartooning also reached its peak in this period. The New York *Daily Graphic*, beginning in 1873, was the first paper to run cartoons almost every day. In 1884 Walt McDougall began drawing a daily cartoon for Pulitzer's *World*, and when Hearst invaded New York in 1895 he made cartoons an important feature of his paper. Thomas Nast was still the great master of black-and-white cartoonists. But in 1886 he quit *Harper's Weekly* in a dispute over editorial restrictions on his work, and never regained a wide audience.

The colored political cartoons lost their virility around 1900, for two reasons. They had been so powerful that they made bitter enemies for the magazines that used them; Republicans, generally speaking, would not read *Puck*, and Democrats boycotted *Judge*. This did not appeal to the advertisers, who were taking more and more space in the nation's reading matter. Advertising support went to publications which played down their opinions or buried them on an editorial page. Hearst and Pulitzer finished the process by assigning their best cartoonists to draw colored comic strips for the Sunday "funny papers." The great artistic weapon which had been forged by Keppler and his contemporaries dwindled eventually into "Happy Hooligan."

"The Cinderella of the Republican Party and Her Haughty Sisters" is a typical Keppler drawing, crammed with all kinds of symbols which describe the situation in early 1880. President Hayes *(left)* is being snubbed for renomination, while Conkling and Grant *(center)* try for a third term.

WITH APOLOGIES TO J.L. GEROME.

"Phryne Before the Chicago Tribunal," by Gillam, shows James G. Blaine without his white plumes in 1884. Whitelaw Reid of the New York *Tribune* is unveiling the gallant leader before a group of Republican statesmen at the party convention. But all Blaine's old sins are tattooed on his skin.

"Little Roosevelt!!!—The Grand Old Party Must Be Hard-Up!" by Keppler,
is an early jibe at Teddy. Roosevelt refused to join the Mugwumps in 1884.
So here the old party bosses reward him with the armor of leadership. President Chauncey Depew of the New York Central is putting on his helmet.

"A Harmless Explosion," one of Keppler's best, celebrates Roscoe Conkling's resignation from the Senate in 1881, in a fit of anger over patronage. Conkling failed to win re-election, and died from exposure in the blizzard of 1888.

"The Raven" (right) shows President Benjamin Harrison sinking under his grandfather's big hat while Blaine, the raven, croaks "Nevermore" to his hopes for another term. The two Republicans had split over the 1890 tariff.

Keppler's "Bosses of the Senate" is an accurate allegory. By 1889 the upper chamber of Congress was known as a millionaires' club. The presiding officer was a Wall Street banker, and the principal Senators represented oil, lumber, railroad, insurance, silver, gold, utility, and manufacturing interests.

"I'll astonish the nation,
    An' all creation
By my great Presidential Aspiration!
I'll sail over Blaine like a soarin' eagle,
And swoop over Hawley higher 'n a sea-gull,
I'll dance on old Evarts, I'll stand on Depew,
I'll fly clean over the hull low crew—
    Thet's what I'll dew!
I'll light on the libbe'ty-pole, an' crow,
An' I'll say to the gawpin' fools below;
'This ain't no sort of a Flyin' Merman,
Nor Flyin' Dutchman, nor Flyin' German—
    It's ol' John Sherman,
Lightin' out hot fer the nomination,
The liveliest candidate in creation!'"
            *
Slowly, ruefully, some fine day,
We may not hear—or, again, we may—
    It's likely enough—
An aged voice of misery say,
"Wal, I like flyin' well enough,
B'gosh—but the' ain't such a thunderin' sight
O' fun in 't when ye come to light!"

"The Political Darius Green" shows Senator John Sherman trying to take off on his own Presidential boom in 1887, supported by a bloody shirt and a gust of hot air. Down in the corner the tiny symbol of Puck waves him farewell.

"Sour Grapes!" *(right)* pictures Pope Leo XIII as the fox who couldn't get control of the American public schools. Nast and Keppler also published sharp cartoon attacks on Catholic officials who sought to influence the schools.

"The Administration Typewriter," drawn by Gillam for *Judge*, shows Cleveland sweating out a program for his second term in the White House. The President was in constant hot water with his own party for his pro-Wall Street policies. Here he exclaims: "Blame the thing—I can't make it work!"

CROWN OF THORNS USED BY BRYAN IN CAMPAIGN SPEECHES

USED IN BRYAN'S CHICAGO SPEECH CROSS OF GOLD

SPEECH TORN FROM THE BIBLE FROM THE BIBLE

SPEECH PLAGIARIZED FROM THE BIBLE

ANARCHY

BIBLE

HAMILTON

"A Self-Evident Fact," from *Puck*, was an effective satire on Republican tariffs. "Say!" says Uncle Sam, "I want you fellows to distinctly understand that I'm not racing with you!" Even President McKinley eventually changed his mind about high tariffs and advocated reciprocal-trade treaties instead.

"The Modern Bird of American Freedom" shows Mark Hanna as a bloated turkey gobbler, making dollar footprints in the sands of history. This cartoon appeared in *The Verdict,* a weekly started by New York City Democrats for the sole purpose of fighting McKinley and Hanna in the 1900 election.

"No Wonder He Was Ill," by George Luks, also appeared in *The Verdict*.
The President was said to be suffering from heart trouble, caused by over-
smoking, but the Democrats gave him no sympathy. His cigar is labeled with
various Republican "scandals." Hanna is just behind his shoulder, as usual.

In 1900 the industrial edifice of the United States was supported in part by the labor of 1,752,187 children less than 16 years old. In Southern cotton mills like the one below one fourth of the "hands" were children, and 20,000 of them were under 12. Girls of six and seven worked 13 hours a day.

CHAPTER 8

THE BIG STICK REFORMERS

ON SEPTEMBER 6, 1901, President McKinley stood beside a potted palm in the Temple of Music at the Pan-American Exposition in Buffalo, shaking hands with whoever came along. A young man with a pompadour haircut and a dead-pan expression stepped up with his right hand wrapped in a handkerchief, as though it had been injured recently. He put out his left hand to grasp the President's right, and at the same time pressed the "bandage" against the President's broad abdomen. Two sharp reports were heard as he fired a .32-caliber revolver from inside the fatal handkerchief. The President stretched up to the tips of his toes and then slumped down under the palm tree. "Am I shot?" he asked. Then, as he saw the assassin being beaten and kicked on the floor, he gasped, "Let no one hurt him." Eight nights later he died from a bullet wound in his stomach.

On the funeral train from Buffalo to Washington, Senator Mark Hanna was inconsolably bitter, and outspoken as usual. He damned the new President, Theodore Roosevelt, and said, "I told William McKinley it was a mistake to nominate that wild man at Philadelphia. . . . Now look, that damned cowboy is President of the United States!"

The man who killed McKinley was an American-born anarchist named Leon Czolgosz. He explained to the police that he had been "on fire" for months with desire to kill a "great ruler." The state of New York electrocuted him and destroyed his corpse with quicklime and acid. But his crazy act changed the course of American history.

For Theodore Roosevelt, unlike McKinley and Cleveland, and every other President since the Civil War, did not believe in the semidivine rights of big business. As a young assemblyman in New York in the 1880's Roosevelt had blurted out his disgust for the "infernal thieves" and "conscienceless swindlers" who ran certain railroads, and as President he declared open war on the "malefactors of great wealth," which was a phrase he coined himself. Yet Roosevelt was neither a radical nor a born crusader —he was essentially a middle-of-the-road politician with a belligerent disposition and a keen relish for publicity and power. His judgments were always strictly moral: right was right, and wrong was wrong, and it was up to the President to decide which was which, so far as the United States was concerned. Roosevelt never felt the slightest doubt that whatever he decided was right.

The weapon he used on his forays against evil was the celebrated "Big Stick," which became in his hands one of the best-known symbols in American politics. There was nothing new about the Big Stick. Jackson had used it to crush the Bank, and Lincoln had used it against all enemies of the Union. But from about 1868 on it had been tucked away in a closet of the White House, gathering dust and cobwebs. A scholarly definition of the Big Stick would be "the power of the Executive in the Government of the United States."

When Roosevelt dug it out and started waving it around, the other nations of the world instinctively ducked. For they could see—better than most Americans—what a powerful wallop it packed in the twentieth century. Just by waggling it a little Roosevelt scared Latin America into a state of quaking resentment and turned the Caribbean into an American wading pond.

When he swung it at big business he often missed, and he often failed to follow through with specific action. But his bold example inspired a host of reformers who were boring from within the two old parties. These strictly middle-class rebels were called Progressives, or Insurgents, or "New Freedom" Democrats. Their aim was to balance the power of organized money in America by a broader and more vigorous use of the powers of government. Their specific program was about the same as the Populist platform of 1890 and the Bryan platform of 1896. Eventually it became Roosevelt's platform too.

Andrew Carnegie knew little about steelmaking, but he was a genius at driving people who did. After he retired he gave away $350 million and supplied the White House with free Scotch whisky.

John D. Rockefeller made a billion dollars by eliminating competition from the oil industry. "Individualism has gone, never to return," he said. This picture was taken before he wore a wig.

Chauncey Depew was the platitudinous mouthpiece of big business. He did political errands, told jokes at banquets and Republican conventions, and was president of the New York Central.

Andrew Mellon, the Pittsburgh banker, was not a national figure in 1901. But already he had bought up another man's process for making aluminum and was converting it into a rich monopoly.

J. Pierpont Morgan "re-Morganized" railroads, banks, and other major companies, and kept control of them all through voting trusts. "I am not in Wall Street for my health," he growled.

Philip D. Armour and the Chicago "Beef Trust" mechanized the nation's meat. "I like to turn bristles, blood, bones, and the insides and outsides of pigs and bullocks into revenue," he said.

THE MEN WHO OWNED THE COUNTRY

"AMERICA IS GOOD enough for me," said J. P. Morgan, and the response which was made by William Jennings Bryan made even the titans of Wall Street smile. "Whenever he doesn't like it," said Bryan, "he can give it back to us."

At the turn of the century the mighty Morgan was the Jupiter around whom the lesser deities of big business revolved. Through his efforts and those of other trust-builders, competition had been virtually eliminated from the nation's basic industries. Under the "community of interest" system which Morgan sponsored, the heads of big corporations could work together in private while their organizations were supposed to be competing. The Sherman Antitrust Law was no worry: neither Cleveland nor McKinley made any serious effort to enforce it. And the Supreme Court dealt it an almost mortal blow in 1895, when it ruled that the American Sugar Refining Company—which controlled more than 95 per cent of the nation's refined-sugar production—was not a monopoly.

The grand climax of the noncompetitive system came in April 1901, when the United States Steel Corporation was organized by J. P. Morgan & Company. It began with a capitalization of $1,402 million, of which $676 million represented cash investment in plants and property, and $726,846,000 was "water" (promoters' profits, speculation, and "good will"). In order to create this mammoth trust Morgan bought the Mesabi iron mines of Minnesota from John D. Rockefeller and the entire business of Andrew Carnegie, who was the largest single steel producer in the world. In 1899 Carnegie had offered to sell out for $157,950,000. But when Morgan approached him in 1901 he upped his price to $447 million—and got it. To the end of his days Carnegie worried for fear he had asked too little. Once, while breakfasting with Morgan on an ocean liner, he remarked lightly, "I find I made a mistake. I should have asked you for another hundred million." Morgan's reply could not have been crueler. "If you had, I should have paid it," he said.

THE GREAT AMERICAN BOY

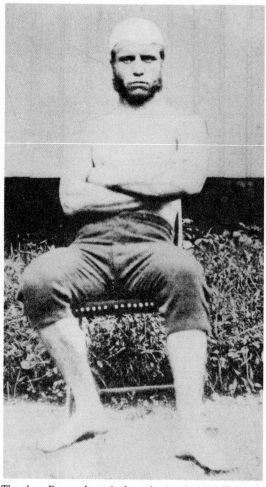

Theodore Roosevelt ready for a boxing bout at Harvard, where he tried for the lightweight championship in 1879.

A gentleman rancher in 1883, Roosevelt brought his cowboy suit east and posed for this photograph in New York.

THEODORE ROOSEVELT, said an acute observer, realized the ultimate dream of every American boy: he fought in a war, killed lions, and became President of the United States. He was 42 when McKinley was shot, and that made him the youngest President in history. He was also the most athletic. He spread a wrestling mat on the White House floor, took jujitsu lessons, and kept up his boxing until a navy officer hit him on the forehead and started a hemorrhage which blinded his left eye.

"You must always remember," said a shrewd British diplomat, "that the President is about six." The greatest moment in Roosevelt's life was at the Battle of San Juan Hill when, as he described it, "I waved my hat and we went up the hill with a rush." After the charge he walked around the field boasting that he had "doubled up a Spanish officer like a jack-rabbit." His predilection for strenuosity and gore originated in his own puny boyhood, when he almost died from asthma, and was teased by other boys for his nearsightedness. His father, a wealthy New York banker, installed a gymnasium in their home, and there young Teddy literally fought his way to physical fitness. He attended Harvard, where he displayed an unfashionable urge to excel in sports and argue with his professors. After

Rough Rider Roosevelt in 1898. He carried 12 extra pairs of glasses to the war, in his pockets and hat lining.

As President, Roosevelt dressed with easy elegance. Earlier in his career reporters called him a New York "dude."

graduation he vacillated between cattle ranching in Dakota, history writing, and Republican politics. He finally concentrated on politics because it offered more fights and a quicker path into the limelight. He became moderately famed as a civil-service advocate and New York City crime-buster, but it was the publicity he got during the Spanish war that made him Governor of New York in 1898, and Vice President in 1901. When an assassin's bullet moved him up to President he announced that he would "continue, absolutely unbroken, the policy of President McKinley." This resolution lasted three or four months.

As police commissioner in 1895-97, Roosevelt made a great deal of noise but failed to abolish sin in New York City.

Edward H. Harriman, despite his mousy look, was a bold Napoleon of finance. Backed by Standard Oil's billions, he hoped to create an American railroad chain around the world.

THE CORNER IN NORTHERN PACIFIC

On May 9, 1901, many a New York stockbroker read the newspaper page at the right and then went down to Wall Street to see the fun. At 10 o'clock the gong sounded in the Stock Exchange and a frantic "short" bid $190 a share for Northern Pacific—a rise of $30 from the day before. In an hour the bidding rose to $1,000 a share, but not a sale was being made and a real panic was under way. For Harriman and Hill, the battling railroad kings, had already "bought" 78,000 more shares of Northern Pacific than there were in the market. And the shorts who had sold them those shares on paper were caught like rats in a trap. At this point the bankers who ran Wall Street stepped in and saved the situation. The shorts were allowed to settle by paying Harriman or Hill $150 for the shares they couldn't deliver. And Harriman and Hill agreed to join hands in a gigantic new railroad trust.

THE RAILROAD KINGS

James J. Hill, the "Empire Builder" of the Northwest, feared that Roosevelt would ruin the country. The President, he complained, never did anything "but pose and draw a salary."

J. P. Morgan *(second from right)* hurried to Washington to plead for a compromise on Northern Securities. Roosevelt refused and the Supreme Court dissolved the company.

EDWARD H. HARRIMAN was the only man in Wall Street who did not fear J. P. Morgan. James J. Hill was Morgan's top railroad expert. In the spring of 1901 these two kings of railroading collided in a race for power which had vast consequences.

Harriman already controlled the Union Pacific and Southern Pacific, which gave him dominance in two thirds of the West. Hill controlled the Northern Pacific and Great Northern, which gave him the other third. The war started when Hill bought the Burlington line, which Harriman coveted. Harriman decided to get even by snatching the Northern Pacific out from under Hill's feet. Buying quietly in the open market, he spent $79,459,000 for Northern Pacific stock and almost had control before Hill realized what was up. Then Morgan plunged into the market and saved Hill in a wild buying spree. At this point the railroad kings quit feuding and pooled their Northwestern interests in the $400 million Northern Securities Company, which was, in effect, a railroad monopoly for one quarter of the United States. Because of the men involved, it could easily be expanded into a national monopoly. Morgan was, of course, its leading sponsor.

In February 1902 President Roosevelt rocked the business world by announcing that Northern Securities would be prosecuted under the Sherman Antitrust Law. Morgan himself rushed to Washington to demand an explanation, but this only made Teddy more determined. It was a question, as he saw it, of which was bigger: the railroad kings and Morgan, or the United States and Roosevelt. To a challenge of that kind he could never back down.

THE CHRISTIAN MEN OF PROPERTY

John Mitchell, president of the union

George F. Baer, the owners' spokesman

On May 12, 1902, the 140,000 anthracite miners of eastern Pennsylvania struck to increase their average pay of $560 a year. Two months later, with the strike still dragging on, a remarkable letter went forth from the Philadelphia office of George F. Baer, chief spokesman for the mine owners. "I beg of you not to be discouraged," wrote Baer to a resident of Wilkes-Barre, a city which had been hard hit by the strike. "The rights and interests of the laboring man will be protected and cared for—not by the labor agitators, but by the Christian men to whom God in His infinite wisdom has given control of the property interests of this country. . . ."

With this pious conviction to strengthen him, Baer steadfastly refused to have any dealings whatever with the United Mine Workers of America or their youthful president, John Mitchell. The miners, whose working conditions had been miserable for years, were equally determined to win some improvement before going back to work.

In the White House President Roosevelt was worried over the effect of the coal shortage on the Congressional elections. To Mark Hanna and others he lamented that he did not have power to bring the two sides together. Then, in a highly characteristic move, he did the very thing he didn't have power to do. On October 3, in response to his telegrams, Baer and Mitchell stood face to face in the President's office.

Roosevelt told them that he could not force a settlement, but pointed out that a winter coal famine would be a catastrophe for millions. "I appeal to your patriotism," he pleaded. Mitchell, who wore a long black coat like a clergyman's, immediately offered to submit to arbitration. But Baer insolently rebuked his host for "negotiating with the fomenters of anarchy," i.e., the union leaders. "We object to being called here to meet a criminal even by the President of the United States," he said after the meeting.

This haughty attitude made Roosevelt furious. He sent word to J. P. Morgan, Baer's banker, that the Army would seize and operate the mines unless the operators agreed to arbitrate. Under pressure from Morgan, Baer sulkily backed down. An arbitration commission was set up, the miners went back to work, and eventually they were awarded a 10 per cent raise. But far more important was the fact that a President of the United States had intervened for the first time to settle—rather than break—a strike.

New Yorkers stand in line for coal during the 1902 strike famine.

This coal miner's union certificate of 1902 gives an idyllic picture of life in the mines. The United Mine Workers was organized in 1890 but almost vanished after losing a big strike in 1894. John Mitchell, who had worked in an Illinois mine at 12, brought it back to vigorous life by uniting the English-speaking and foreign-language miners.

President Roosevelt visited the Culebra Cut and sat in a 95-ton steam shovel in November 1906. "They are eating steadily into the mountain, cutting it down and down," he wrote home to his son Kermit. It took three years to rid the Canal Zone of tropical diseases, and seven more to dig the 50-mile-long Canal. The cost was $275 million.

"I TOOK THE ISTHMUS"

"SOME PEOPLE SAY that I fomented insurrection in Panama," Theodore Roosevelt remarked. "I did not have to foment it; I simply lifted my foot." And in a more formal moment he summarized the Panama Canal episode in a single sentence: "I took the Isthmus, started the Canal, and then left Congress—not to debate the Canal, but to debate me."

The Canal itself had been a prime object of American policy since the Spanish war, when the battleship *Oregon* was forced to make a 71-day voyage around Cape Horn before going into action. When Roosevelt became President, the question had boiled down to a choice of route: Should the Canal be built across 170 miles of comparatively high and dry Nicaragua, using lakes and rivers as connecting links? Or should it cut directly across the narrow, hot, unhealthy Panama Isthmus, which was part of the Republic of Colombia? A Panama canal had been started years before by a private French company, which lost $260 million and the lives of thousands of workmen before it gave up in 1889. Many Americans believed that malaria and yellow fever made the Panama route impossible.

Yet there were important influences in favor of Panama. A picturesque lobbyist named Bunau-Varilla appeared in Washington to sell the French company's "rights." Also very active was William Nelson Cromwell, a New York corporation lawyer who represented the French concern. Through his influence, backed by a $60,000 campaign contribution, the Republican platform of 1900 was rewritten to favor the Panama route, and Senator Mark Hanna made a powerful speech for Panama. Meanwhile the Panama Canal Company of America was quietly organized in New Jersey to exchange stock with the French company. The incorporators were clerks from Cromwell's office, and the capital came from leading Wall Street bankers.

In June 1902 Congress authorized the route across Panama, and agreed to pay $40 million to the "French claimants." No arrangement was made, however, with the Colombian Government, which owned the land.

At this point President Roosevelt leaped in and took charge of everything. Congress had chosen the Panama route; very well, said the President, the Canal shall be built there. To Colombia he made what he called a generous offer: $10 million in cash and an annual rent of $250,000, in return for putting 300 square miles of its territory under perpetual American control. When the Colombian officials hesitated, Roosevelt grew angry; when they rejected his terms, he was outraged. "Those contemptible little creatures in Bogotá," "bandits," "blackmailers," "corruptionists," were a few of the epithets he hurled at them. "We may have to give a lesson to those jack rabbits," he wrote to Secretary of State John Hay.

His first plan was simply to land a sufficient force of American troops to occupy the Isthmus, and go ahead with the Canal. But Bunau-Varilla and some excited Panama secessionists saved him from this. In Bunau-Varilla's room at the Waldorf-Astoria Hotel, on October 14, 1903, the independent Republic of Panama was born. The French agent supplied a $100,000 "liberation fund," a hand-stitched flag, and a copy of a message to be sent to Washington as soon as Panama was free. Three weeks later the Republic was proclaimed in Panama City. The Colombian garrison was bribed into submission, while the new Panama President shouted: "President Roosevelt has made good! . . . Long live President Roosevelt!"

This news reached the White House at 11:31 A.M. on November 6. Seventy-six minutes later the Republic of Panama was officially recognized by Secretary Hay. Seven days later the two countries signed a treaty which gave the United States the Canal Zone, and Panama the $10 million which Colombia had spurned. The $40 million for the "French claimants" was turned over to J. P. Morgan & Company. The names of those who eventually received this money were never made public. But Cromwell's bill for legal services alone was $800,000.

In 1904 the dirt began to fly in Panama. In 1914 the Canal was opened to ships, and in 1921 it was officially declared finished. From the standpoints of engineering, public health, and military security, it was a magnificent achievement. But in our Latin-American relations, it left some painful scars.

Teddy tosses a spadeful of Panama dirt on the capital city of Colombia.

TEDDY EVERYWHERE

THEODORE ROOSEVELT SET a brand-new style in Presidents. Restless, talkative, brimming with physical and mental energy, he put on a one-man show which fascinated the American people and the world. He bounded in and out of the White House, played six sets of tennis in an afternoon, waded icy streams in February, dashed off to the Rocky Mountains to shoot big sheep, slapped visitors on the shoulder, howled "Dee-lighted!" and "Bully!" in his piercing treble voice, and in general set an example of the strenuous life which few voters could emulate, but which many admired. In 1904 it was a cinch for him to be re-elected over a colorless Democrat named Alton B. Parker.

Everything seemed to happen to Teddy. A trolley car struck his carriage one day, bowled him into a ditch, and killed the Secret Service man who was riding beside him. Roosevelt, despite a nasty leg injury, scrambled to his feet and insisted on continuing a long speaking tour. Nature lovers accused him of blood lust because he killed so many wild animals, and Roosevelt published an angry attack on the "nature-fakir" school of literature. San Francisco barred Japanese children from its public schools, in defiance of a long-standing treaty, and Roosevelt was barely restrained from declaring war on California. The New York *World* criticized his Panama Canal activities, and Roosevelt prosecuted the *World* for criminal libel—the first time a President had tried this since 1798. (The Supreme Court ruled unanimously in favor of the *World*.) Unlike McKinley, who hid his cigar from photographers, Roosevelt was a frank exhibitionist and loved to have his picture taken. He was the first President to be photographed frequently in action—partly because of improvements in camera technique, but mostly because he was the world's best camera subject.

"I preach to you, my countrymen, that our country calls not for the life of ease but for the life of strenuous endeavor," said President Roosevelt, shown on the opposite page at a Flag Day rally. "Nothing in this world is worth having or worth doing unless it means effort, pain, difficulty. . . . Let us therefore boldly face the life of strife. . . ." Reporters in straw hats jot down his words.

Roosevelt kept the Navy steaming from one Caribbean port to another to enforce his concept of the Monroe Doctrine.

When the Senate blocked his Santo Domingo "treaty," Teddy snapped, "The Senate is wholly incompetent."

At Portsmouth, New Hampshire, in 1905, Roosevelt ended the Russo-Japanese War, after letting Japan grab Korea.

At Algeciras, in 1906, Roosevelt inserted his Big Stick in a Franco-German squabble over control of Morocco.

SWINGING THE STICK

"I HAVE ALWAYS," said Roosevelt, "been fond of the West African proverb: 'Speak softly and carry a big stick, you will go far.'" At home the President kept the Big Stick handy but did not use it recklessly. In world affairs he swung it hard in several directions.

Especially in the direction of Latin America. The Spanish-speaking nations to the south inspired little respect in Theodore Roosevelt, who never quite got over his personal war with Spain. He once remarked that President Cipriano Castro of Venezuela was an "unspeakably villainous little monkey," and in 1904 he thought he might intervene in Venezuela and collect enough money to pay its debts to various other nations. "It will show these Dagos that they will have to behave decently," he wrote to Secretary of State John Hay, in a decidedly unofficial letter.

Roosevelt did not go into Venezuela, but he did take over the island republic of Santo Domingo in 1904. The Dominican foreign debt totaled $18 million, and Roosevelt decided to pay it off by having the American Navy collect its customs duties. Out of this episode grew the celebrated Roosevelt Corollary to the Monroe Doctrine. According to the Corollary, the United States, in order to avert intervention by a European nation which has just claims against an American nation, may intervene itself and pursue those claims.

Roosevelt was fascinated when Japan attacked Russia in 1904. "Between ourselves—for you must not breathe it to anybody—I was thoroughly well pleased with the Japanese victory, for Japan is playing our game," he wrote to Theodore, Jr. But when Japan kept on winning Roosevelt intervened and asked the two nations to make peace. To the great surprise of the rest of the world, they agreed. For this achievement, Teddy received the Nobel Peace Prize in 1906.

Teddy's antitrust activities were not as strenuous as this cartoon would indicate.

A Democratic campaign display shows Teddy as an American Nero, with various classes of citizens hitched to his Big Stick chariot. Like every strong President, Roosevelt was frequently accused of having a Caesar complex.

A is the Asphalt Trust. This is the way He shakes down the People and makes the thing pay.

"AN ALPHABET OF

ROOSEVELT LIFTED the antitrust law out of its grave but did not try to kill it again with overwork. The Northern Securities case was, in fact, the only important prosecution started during his first term. The President's balanced attitude was admirably summarized by Mr. Dooley, the Irish philosopher in Finley Peter Dunne's newspaper column, who paraphrased a Roosevelt message to Congress as follows: " 'Th' trusts,' says he, 'are heejous monsthers built up be th' inlightened intherprise iv th' men that have done so much to advance progress in our beloved counthry. . . . On wan hand I wud stamp thim undher fut; on th' other hand not so fast.' " Roosevelt did, however, set up the first Department of Commerce, headed by his former private secretary, George B. Cortelyou, and put in it a Bureau of Corporations. The Bureau was assigned to "investigate" the trusts

B is the Beef Trust. This heartless old sinner Makes the People pay double or go without dinner.

C is the Coal Trust, a greedy old bandit, Who squeezes the People. How long will they stand it?

D is the Dough Trust, a wealthy old swell. He looks honest enough;—still, you can't always tell.

E 'S the Electric Trust. Quick as a flash He turns on his current and shocks out your cash!

F is the Fruit Trust, who has a long reach. At robbing the People she's simply a peach.

G is the Glass Trust, a conscienceless villain. To plunder the People he's ready and willin'.

H is the Hydraulic Brick Trust. And say!— You'll be awfully bumped if you get in his way!

I is the Ice Trust; to rob you he'll try, Though this paper once gave him an awful black eye.

J is the Jag Trust (beer, whiskey and sich), While the People get woozey, he merely gets rich!

K is the Kodak Trust;—this is his jest:— "While I press the button, my friends, do the rest!"

L is the Lumber Trust. Take a straight tip:— He'll grab your last cent if you get in his grip.

M is the Match Trust; he won't take a minute Your pocket to pick, if there's anything in it.

JOYOUS TRUSTS"

and find out which were illegal. In 1904 Cortelyou stepped out of his Cabinet job and became chairman of the Republican national committee, where he accepted many large campaign contributions from the same trusts that he had been investigating. This led the Democrats to publish a campaign primer in pictures called "An Alphabet of Joyous Trusts. How They Rob the Common People. Is It Not Time To Stop It *Now*?" which is reproduced on these pages. The cartoons were drawn by Frederick B. Opper of the New York *American*, who attached the following message in verse at the end: "With these alphabet pictures the artist took pains, But he's got to stop now, and with grief nearly busts—'Cause our language but twenty-six letters contains, Though our country contains twenty-six hundred Trusts."

BOODLERS AND

Alderman John Coughlin rose from rubber in a Turkish bath to be lord of Chicago's Levee and the proud owner of a mountain-green dress suit.

OVER CHICAGO there rose a smell. Politically it was the same smell that came from many cities: the smell of tainted money. The people who passed the money from hand to hand called it "boodle." It was boodle when a gas company or a streetcar company or a paving company bribed a city council to pass a swindling franchise or contract. It was boodle also when the madam of a brothel paid off her local ward boss. A splendid example of a full-blown boodler is shown at the left in the photograph of "Bathhouse John" Coughlin, alderman of Chicago's First Ward.

But Chicago had another smell which was distinctly its own—"an elemental odor, raw and crude . . . rich, almost rancid, sensual, and strong." This was the smell of the stockyards, where 25,000 hogs, cattle, and sheep were slaughtered every busy day. The smell did not come from the fresh meat itself, but from the tons of blood, bones, grease, and hooves which were cooked into fertilizer and glue.

In 1906 a 28-year-old Socialist named Upton Sinclair published a novel called *The Jungle*, in which the Chicago stockyards smell was a leading character. The hero of *The Jungle* was Jurgis Rudkus, a Lithuanian laborer who swept up guts in a packing plant for 17½ cents an hour. Unable to realize his dream of a happy home and family because of low wages and filthy working conditions, Jurgis reached the great crisis of his life when his wife was seduced by her boss. He beat up the boss, was jailed and blacklisted, became a tramp, footpad, and strikebreaker, and finally found regeneration in the ranks of the Socialist party. *The Jungle* ended with a Socialist orator shouting from a platform, "Organize! Organize! Organize! . . . Chicago will be ours. *Chicago will be ours!* CHICAGO WILL BE OURS!"

WORKERS IN THE JUNGLE

The author of *The Jungle* presented his readers with gruesome descriptions of the occupational diseases and hazards of "Packingtown": "There were the men in the pickle-rooms, for instance . . . scarce a one of these that had not some spot of horror on his person. Let a man so much as scrape his finger pushing a truck in the pickle-rooms, and . . . all the joints in his fingers might be eaten by the acid, one by one. Of the butchers and floorsmen, the beef-boners and trimmers, and all those who used knives, you could scarcely find a person who had the use of his thumb; time and time again the base of it had been slashed, till it was a mere lump of flesh against which the man pressed the knife to hold it. . . .

There were those who worked in the chilling-rooms, and whose special disease was rheumatism; the time-limit that a man could work in the chilling-rooms was said to be five years. There were the wool-pluckers, whose hands went to pieces even sooner than the hands of the pickle-men; for the pelts of the sheep had to be painted with acid . . . and as for the other men, who worked in tank-rooms full of steam . . . their peculiar trouble was that they fell into the vats; and when they were fished out, there was never enough of them left to be worth exhibiting,—sometimes they would be overlooked for days, till all but the bones of them had gone out to the world as Durham's Pure Leaf Lard!"

Hog trimmers at work in 1906

MUCKRAKERS

The Jungle was the climax of hundreds of magazine articles and dozens of books which had been written since 1900 to protest the corruption in American politics and business. The writers of this school were given the name "muckrakers" by President Roosevelt, who alternately patted them on the back and damned them as "degraded beings." Among the prominent muckrakers of factual material were Ida M. Tarbell, who wrote the natural history of the Standard Oil Company; Lincoln Steffens, who produced the *Shame of the Cities* series for *McClure's* magazine; and Ray Stannard Baker, who exposed corrupt labor leaders. *The Jungle* was the most successful of all the muckraking books. In England it was read with great interest by Winston Churchill, the future Prime Minister, who commented: "This terrible book . . . pierces the thickest skull and most leathery heart. . . . The issue between capital and labor is far more clearly cut today [in America] than in other communities or in any other age."

The effect of *The Jungle*, however, was different from what its author had hoped. The American millions did not rush to join the Socialist party, but they did scream for reform in their meat supply. Sinclair had described how government inspectors in the packing plants were bribed to pass tubercular cattle and hogs dying of cholera; how poisoned rats were shoveled into the meat-grinding machines; and filth scraped from the floor was turned into "potted ham." President Roosevelt read *The Jungle* and hit the White House roof. Before the year was over a stricter meat inspection law was passed by Congress, along with a new Pure Food Act. Sinclair was not happy over this outcome. "I aimed at the public's heart and hit its stomach," he mourned.

Upton Sinclair published *The Jungle* himself after five non-Socialist publishers refused it. For a year it outsold all other American books.

Cleaver men and carcasses

Tending a scalding vat

A battery of sausage makers

HEARST, THE WIZARD OF OOZE

Hearst as a scarecrow rising from a pool of mud appeared in *Harper's Weekly* in 1906, when the yellow publisher ran for Governor of New York. Rival newspapers beat him by exposing his "plundering deals" in Wall Street.

WILLIAM RANDOLPH HEARST wanted desperately to be President of the United States. In his efforts to get there he subsidized petty thieves and gunmen, dragged his newspapers through endless muck, and even preached, at times, for "socialistic" reforms. Yet Hearst was a dismal failure in politics. The reason, perhaps, was his obvious contempt for the American people. Even in his campaign photographs *(below)* he seemed to be staring straight through the average voter toward the White House.

In 1902, through a deal with Tammany Boss Charles F. Murphy, Hearst was elected to Congress from midcity New York. In 1904, as the special pet of union labor, he received 263 votes for the Democratic nomination for President. In 1905 he was actually elected Mayor of New York on an anti-Tammany and antiutility platform, but Tammany thugs destroyed enough Hearst ballots to put their man in City Hall. In 1906 he was narrowly beaten for Governor by Charles Evans Hughes. In 1908, to test his personal power, he set up his own third party and ran a couple of stooges for President and Vice President. They got 83,562 votes out of 15 million. That ended Hearst's chances, but not his hopes.

Hearst's Presidential "boom," which started in his own newspapers, is pictured here as a comic-strip parade.

Hearst married Millicent Willson, a chorus girl, in 1903. They slept in the room where ex-President Arthur died.

Hearst's first son George was born in 1904. This photograph was widely published during Hearst's campaigns.

William H. Taft as Secretary of War. "I think," said Roosevelt one day, "Taft has the most lovable personality I have ever come in contact with. . . . One loves him at first sight."

BIG WILL TAFT

"WE MUST HAVE a candidate," said President Roosevelt to his secretary, as the Presidential election of 1908 drew near. "We had better turn to Taft. . . . See Taft and tell him." Soon his ponderous Secretary of War hurried in to thank the President. "Yes, Will," said Roosevelt. "It's the thing to do."

William Howard Taft was a loyal Roosevelt disciple who tried his best to do everything that Teddy wanted. It was not his fault that he would rather make people happy than mad; that he preferred a big chuckle to the Big Stick. Taft was 326 pounds of solid Republican flesh, wrapped around a kindly heart and a somewhat timid brain. Once when he was asked on a public platform, "What would you advise a man to do who is out of a job and whose family is starving because he can't get work?" he replied, in honest perplexity: "God knows. Such a man has my deepest sympathy."

Taft's weight made him physically lazy, but he could, on important occasions, perform prodigies of work. While Roosevelt was President, Taft was America's No. 1 trouble shooter around the world. He soothed the Filipinos in 1900 by calling them "little brown brothers," and installed a sympathetic American administration in their midst. He negotiated a ticklish deal with the Pope for Catholic-owned Philippine lands, squelched a Japanese-American war scare by making a personal visit to Japan, and stopped a Cuban revolution on another mission in 1906. He supervised the actual construction of the Panama Canal.

Yet despite his services, it was hard for Roosevelt to step aside in his favor. Teddy was only 49, and would have dearly loved to be President the rest of his life. But he had made a public promise never to run again: he gritted his teeth and kept his word. At the Republican convention he deliberately crushed a "Draft Roosevelt" movement and steam-rollered Taft's nomination. The Democrats nominated Bryan again, but Bryan was out of date—Roosevelt had stolen his thunder. During the campaign the restless Teddy worried and fussed and wrote almost daily letters of advice to his candidate. "Hit them hard, old man!" he wrote. "Let the audience see you smile always, because I feel that your nature shines out so transparently when you do smile—you big, generous, high-minded fellow." Taft smiled and smiled, and in November he won by more than a million votes.

Taft aft was an imposing sight. He reminded people of a bison or a battleship.

A publicity man thought up this stunt after Taft beat Bryan. The chorus girl in the barrel is supposed to be paying an election bet in front of the theater where she works.

Grover Cleveland, still gunning for Bryan, died as the 1908 campaign started.

Nelson Wilmarth Aldrich was a cultured millionaire who bossed the United States Senate with iron discipline and ironic wit.

INTO THE troubled waters of tariff revision the new President plunged like a clumsy whale. Roosevelt had scarcely ever wetted his finger in this subject; he left the tariff to such crusty Republican conservatives as Senator Nelson W. Aldrich of Rhode Island and "Uncle Joe" Cannon of Illinois. But in his 1908 campaign, to please his Western supporters, Candidate Taft had committed his party to a lower tariff. In 1909 he called a special session of Congress to carry out his pledge.

By the time the new tariff was finished, however, it was higher than ever. Boss Aldrich of the Senate defied the President and rewrote the bill to suit himself, raising duties on some 600 items. Instead of cracking down as Roosevelt would have done, Taft sweated and begged Aldrich to go easy, and finally swallowed Aldrich's bill.

The Payne-Aldrich tariff was a great victory for the Republican old guard, but it was a severe strain on the Republican party. It led directly to the progressive revolt of 1910 and the Bull Moose split of 1912. The progressives were a fighting group of younger Republicans, mostly from the West and Middle West, who wanted to go further with the reforms that Roosevelt had started. Taft turned his ample back on them and chose a Cabinet which was strongly old guard, and when he also surrendered to Aldrich on the tariff the progressives charged that he was betraying Roosevelt. Teddy himself was not available for comment—he had rushed off to tour Europe and shoot big game in Africa. But when he heard how Taft was behaving he made it clear that he didn't like it.

THE GRAND OLD GUARD WINS A VICTORY

Cartoon of 1909 shows Taft pleading with Aldrich, while the Big Stick gathers dust and Teddy's picture glares.

Speaker Joseph Gurney Cannon was a hard-boiled hayseed who had made himself the autocrat of the House. Cannon first entered Congress in 1873 and won the nickname of "Foul-mouthed Joe" by his barnyard talk. He named the majorities on all committees.

THE RAMPANT

"An insurgent," said Theodore Roosevelt, "is a progressive who is exceeding the speed limit." In 1910 the insurgent progressives got hold of the machinery of Congress and gave the throttle a yank. They drove Nelson Aldrich out of the Senate and teamed up with the Democrats to smash Joe Cannon's power in the House. The insurgent rampage split the Republican vote and produced many Democratic victories in the 1910 elections. In New Jersey a Democratic college president named Woodrow Wilson was elected Governor, and in Ohio a Republican publisher named Warren G. Harding went down to defeat.

"The entire country is insurgent," wrote Franklin K. Lane to Roosevelt, "and insurgency means revolt against taking orders." The insurgents spoke for millions of Americans who believed their Government was still taking too many orders from big business. Between 1908 and 1912 the Hearst newspapers documented this belief with letters stolen from the files of the Standard Oil Company, which showed that a Standard vice president had sent both voting instructions and checks to important members of Congress. Two prominent Senators, an Ohio Republican and a Texas Democrat, resigned in disgrace after these revelations.

Senator Robert M. La Follette of Wisconsin was the insurgents' hard-driving leader. In his home state he had battled the railroads and political bosses to a standstill.

Senator William E. Borah of Idaho was an insurgent when he reached Washington in 1909. But Aldrich didn't know it, and put him on the important Judiciary Committee.

Congressman George W. Norris of Nebraska led the winning fight against Speaker Cannon. Insurgents and Democrats shifted Cannon's powers to the Rules Committee.

INSURGENTS

The progressive insurgents in Congress were not numerous, but they were noisy, shrewd, and determined. Most of them had come up the hard way by fighting in their home states for railroad and utility regulation, workmen's compensation, protection of women and children in industry, and other reforms which were blocked nationally by the Republican old guard and the National Association of Manufacturers. During Taft's regime the progressives accomplished an amazing amount of work in Washington. They provided the country with parcel post and postal savings (despite cries of "socialism"), created a Department of Labor to match the Department of Commerce, and a Bureau of Mines to study and conserve the nation's mineral resources. They pushed through the Mann-Elkins Act, which finally gave the Government some teeth to bite the railroads with in disputes over excessive rates. They passed two important constitutional amendments: the 16th, which authorized a federal income tax, and the 17th, for election of Senators by popular vote instead of by state legislatures. And by snapping constantly at Taft's heels they encouraged him to set a record for antitrust prosecutions: 90 in four years, as compared with Roosevelt's 44 in seven.

Senator Jonathan P. Dolliver of Iowa was the insurgents' best orator. "President Taft," he said, "is an amiable man, completely surrounded by men who know what they want."

Governor Hiram Johnson of California was swept into office in the progressive landslide. He promised to kick the Southern Pacific Railroad out of the state capitol.

Bureaucrat Gifford Pinchot of Pennsylvania accused Taft of wrecking Roosevelt's forest-conservation program. He resigned his post and went to Europe to complain to Teddy.

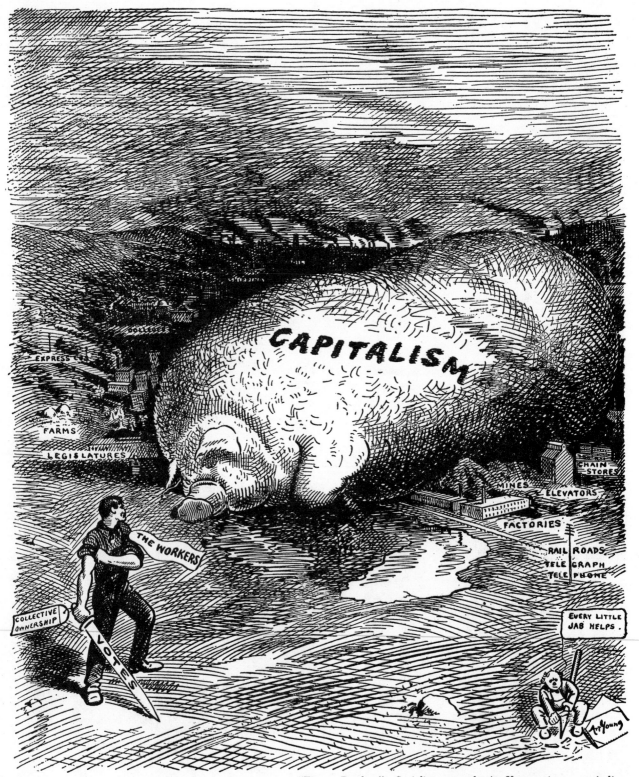

"Time to Butcher," a Socialist cartoon by Art Young, pictures capitalism as a helpless hog. This was published in 1912 by a Kansas weekly.

"Every capitalist is your enemy and every workingman is your friend," Eugene Debs told freight-yard audiences.

SOCIALISTS AND WOBBLIES

IN THE UNITED STATES in 1905, boasted the novelist Jack London, there were one million Socialists who began their letters to each other "Dear Comrade," and ended them "Yours for the Revolution." "Far be it from me," wrote London, "to deny that socialism is a menace. It is its purpose to wipe out, root and branch, all capitalistic institutions of present-day society."

Under President Taft, socialism flourished. Milwaukee sent the first Socialist Congressman, Victor Berger, to Washington. The perennial Socialist candidate for President, Eugene Debs, crisscrossed the country in his "Red Special" train; in 1912 he got 897,011 votes. Out of the Far West came "Big Bill" Haywood and the Industrial Workers of the World, to unfurl their red banners in Lawrence, Massachusetts, and Paterson, New Jersey. The I.W.W. (or "Wobblies," or "I Won't Works") were outright exponents of class warfare who fought their employers with sabotage and violence. All of this was very disturbing to Theodore Roosevelt, who blamed the spread of socialism on "the dull, purblind folly of the very rich."

"Big Bill" Haywood, ex-cowpuncher and miner, led the I.W.W., whose motto was "Good Pay or Bum Work."

Teddy Roosevelt *(center)* returns and is hailed as "the world's first citizen." Young Franklin and Eleanor Roosevelt are at far right.

In Germany Roosevelt met Kaiser Wilhelm II and reviewed the German Army.

In Africa Roosevelt slew 296 lions, elephants, water buffaloes, and other beasts.

THE END OF A BEAUTIFUL FRIENDSHIP

In 1910 President Taft wrote a mournful letter to his predecessor. "It is now a year and three months since I assumed office and I have had a hard time," he wrote. "I have been conscientiously trying to carry out your policies but my method of doing so has not worked smoothly." The letter reached Roosevelt in England, as he was preparing to end his long tour abroad. On June 18 Teddy came home, and received a hero's welcome. But he declined to visit the White House, and spent much time interviewing the anti-Taft insurgents at Oyster Bay. Soon the whole country knew that Roosevelt and Taft were drifting apart.

Taft saw no reason for this, but Roosevelt could find many reasons—all his reforms, he complained, were being undone by Taft and the old guard. The compelling reason, however, was that Teddy was still a strenuous politician and was itching for another big scrap. When the progressives suggested that he oppose Taft for the Republican nomination in 1912, he did everything to encourage them. He charged around the country making speeches, coined a new phrase to describe his program—the "New Nationalism"—and hammered home an old slogan, "I stand for the square deal." He attacked Taft as "disloyal" and guilty of "the grossest and most astounding hypocrisy." At Cleveland, Ohio, he blurted, "My hat is in the ring . . . the fight is on and I am stripped to the buff." Two days later he formally announced his candidacy.

At this Taft turned and struck hard. "I have been a man of straw long enough," the President told the New York *Times*. "Even a rat in a corner will fight!" Using all the tricks of the party machine, Taft's men snatched the 1912 Republican convention from the pro-Roosevelt rank and file. Taft's credentials committee threw out Roosevelt delegates in wholesale lots; Chairman Elihu Root sat behind a barricade of barbed wire and railroaded the nomination to Taft. Roosevelt wanted to grab a pistol and charge. "I wouldn't have wasted a bullet on a policeman," he cried. "I would have got Root and got him quick!" In his rage he ripped his party asunder. Soon the Roosevelt progressives assembled in Chicago and nominated Teddy for a third term.

FOR AULD LANG SYNE.

UNCLE SAM (*philosophically watching the Taft-Roosevelt scrap*). "WAL! I GUESS OLD FRIENDS ARE THE BEST!"

The Roosevelt grin was an important feature of the campaign of 1912. This famous photograph was made by Charles Duprez of Brown Brothers at Oyster Bay, soon after Roosevelt was nominated by the Progressive party.

"The Challenge," drawn by John T. McCutcheon for the Chicago *Tribune*, shows the Progressive Bull Moose chasing the donkey and the elephant into the hills. The *Tribune* and Harold Ickes campaigned for Roosevelt in Chicago.

"I'M FEELING like a bull moose," shrilled Roosevelt to a reporter in 1912, and thereby put antlers on his new Progressive party. For a few glorious months the Progressive Bull Moose cavorted across the political landscape, trampling "special interests" and "moneyed privilege" under its feet. Roosevelt set the keynote for his campaign when he cried to a crowd in Chicago: "We fight in honorable fashion for the good of mankind; fearless of the future; unheeding of our individual fates; with unflinching hearts and undimmed eyes; we stand at Armageddon, and we battle for the Lord."

The Progressive platform called for many reforms: woman suffrage, the direct primary, abolition of child labor, a limit to injunctions against strikes, and the recall of judicial decisions by popular vote. But the Democratic candidate, Dr. Woodrow Wilson, also called for reforms, and so did Taft, for that matter. As the three-cornered campaign wore on, Teddy grew tired and the voters grew distinctly bored. In October there was a flash of drama when an anti-third-term fanatic shot Roosevelt in front of a Milwaukee hotel. The bullet passed through his glasses case and a copy of his speech and lodged in his right lung. But Teddy made the speech on schedule. "There is a bullet in my body," he told his audience. "But it takes more than that to kill a Bull Moose."

In November Roosevelt outran Taft with 4,126,020 votes to 3,483,922. But Wilson got 6,286,214 votes and a huge electoral majority. That fixed the Bull Moose. "There is only one thing to do," said Teddy, "and that is to go back to the Republican party."

Wilson and Taft on the former's Inauguration Day in 1913. Taft was really happy to get out of the White House.

"WE STAND AT ARMAGEDDON"

Riding to battle on his Bull Moose, Roosevelt orders "Barbara Frietchie" Taft to haul down the American flag.

The Bull Moose is Roosevelt's own squalling baby in this cartoon. When Teddy lost interest, the infant languished.

WILSON TAKES THE BIG STICK

OUT OF THE shaded paths of Princeton University, out of a book-lined study, came Thomas Woodrow Wilson, the 27th President. He was a cool and undramatic figure, a "highbrow," a thin-lipped, lantern-jawed scholar with a powerful faith in the American common man. As an historian he could easily document his thesis that the Government had been used too long "for private and selfish purposes." In his pledges for reform he was not far apart from the Bull Moose Roosevelt of 1912. But where Teddy attracted voters by his breast-beating egotism, Wilson won them with sincere and eloquent idealism.

The new Democratic President was a son of the South and of the Presbyterian church. He was born in Virginia in 1856, grew up in Georgia and the two Carolinas, studied and taught at six universities, wrote a Ph.D. dissertation on "Congressional Government," and became the parent of three tall, buck-toothed daughters. As president of Princeton in the early 1900's he embarked on his first reform crusade: to get rid of campus snobbery by abolishing the student clubs. He was defeated, but his efforts attracted much publicity and led to his nomination for Governor on the Democratic ticket in 1910. New Jersey, the mother-state of trusts, was run by a group of business and political bosses who thought they could use Wilson as a respectable front. "How the hell do I know whether he'll make a good governor?" said one of them. "He'll make a good candidate, and that is the only thing that interests me."

But once he was elected and installed at Trenton, Wilson threw off his academic robes and "licked the gang to a frazzle," as one reporter phrased it.

In a little over a year he put through a utility control act, a corrupt political practices act, a workmen's compensation act, and a direct primary act. He appealed for support directly to the voters, and sidetracked the state Democratic machine. His spectacular success made him the leader of the liberal Eastern Democrats. In 1912, with the timely aid of William Jennings Bryan, he won the party's nomination for President, and when Roosevelt split the Republicans he won the election.

A Democratic House and Senate were elected with him, and President Wilson held them rigidly to the hard tasks of reform. In the first 20 months of his administration a Federal Trade Commission was established to stop unfair methods of competition; a stricter antitrust law (the Clayton Act) was passed, which banned interlocking directorates; and the Underwood tariff reduced duties on 958 articles. Specific aid was given to merchant seamen, farmers, and labor unions. Most important of all, from Wilson's viewpoint, was the Federal Reserve Act of December 23, 1913, which took the nation's credit system away from the swollen "Money Trust" and placed it under government control. All these measures were part of what Wilson called the "New Freedom," a moderate reform program which aimed at preserving the free-enterprise system by making it more livable for more people. On only two counts did the New Freedom meet defeat. A law to control the issuance of securities, sponsored by Congressman Sam Rayburn of Texas, was lost in the Senate. And a law to forbid the labor of children under 14 was passed by Congress but was declared unconstitutional by the Supreme Court.

"TO CLEANSE, TO RECONSIDER, TO RESTORE . . ."

"Take my lantern," says old Diogenes to Wilson. "You need it more than I do."

"We have been proud," said Wilson in his Inaugural Address, "of our industrial achievements, but we have not hitherto stopped thoughtfully enough to count the human cost, the cost of lives snuffed out, of energies overtaxed and broken, the fearful physical and spiritual cost to the men and women and children upon whom the dead weight and burden of it all has fallen pitilessly the years through. . . . Our duty is to cleanse, to reconsider, to restore . . . every process of our common life. . . ." But Wilson did not confine himself to words. When his Federal Reserve Act was held up in committee he called in Carter Glass and asked if there were votes enough to win in a showdown. Glass said he thought so. "Then," said the President, "outvote them, damn them, outvote them!"

"Reading the Death Warrant" shows Wilson announcing his bank-control plans.

MEXICO BOILS OVER

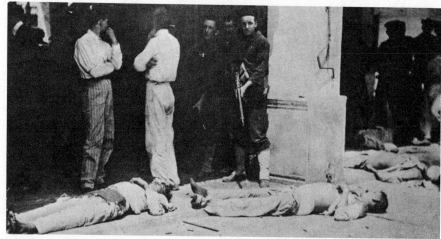

Dead Mexicans litter the pavement in front of the Hotel Diligencias in Vera Cruz, after United States sailors took the city April 21, 1914, and rescued 180 American guests at the hotel.

PRESIDENT Francisco Madero of Mexico was an idealistic middle-class reformer with ideas much like Wilson's. In February 1913 Madero was murdered by the soldiers of General Victoriano Huerta, who set up a reactionary dictatorship in Mexico City. The Huerta regime was welcomed by American businessmen with $1½ billion invested in Mexico. But President Wilson denounced Huerta as a "desperate brute" and refused to recognize his government. "We will never condone iniquity because it is most convenient to do so," he said.

This significant extension of the New Freedom to foreign lands was accompanied by a solid use of the Big Stick. On April 21, 1914, word came to the State Department that a German ship was unloading munitions at Vera Cruz, possibly for anti-American uses. Wilson was roused from sleep at 2:30 A.M. and gave the order to "take Vera Cruz at

Francisco Madero, who wanted the Mexican peons to own the Mexican land, became President through a revolution in 1911. But Madero was not tough enough to hold Mexico.

Victoriano Huerta was the treacherous commander of the Army under Madero. In 1913 he arranged to have Madero assassinated and appointed himself President of Mexico.

Armed Mexicans line up for civil warfare with other Mexicans. After Vera Cruz President Wilson pursued a policy of "watchful waiting" and let Mexico settle its own revolutionary affairs.

once." American warships promptly bombarded the city, and a landing party of sailors and marines captured various buildings. Four Americans and 126 Mexicans were killed, and a new Mexican war seemed inevitable. But when the three leading South American powers—Argentina, Brazil, and Chile—offered to mediate the incident, Wilson accepted and won a partial victory without further fighting. Huerta resigned and went into exile at Forest Hills, Long Island, and a moderate revolutionary named Venustiano Carranza became President of Mexico. Unfortunately, Wilson's tolerance and peaceful intentions could not solve the pent-up land hunger of Mexico's peons. Until 1922 the country was racked by almost continuous revolution and anarchy, in which 400 American citizens were killed, and $200 million worth of American property was destroyed.

"Pancho" Villa kept the revolution going in the North with his army of guerrillas and bandits. In 1916 he raided Columbus, New Mexico, and killed 20 Americans.

Brigadier General John J. ("Black Jack") Pershing was ordered to invade Mexico and get Villa, dead or alive. But Villa was harder to catch than a Mexican *cucaracha*.

AUGUST
1914

On August 21, 1914, the Imperial German Army began its march through Brussels *(above)*. To one American correspondent, the steel-gray German host did not look like anything human—it was "a force of nature like a tidal wave, an avalanche, or a river flooding its banks." And on the 92 million people of the United States, the war in Europe burst as unexpectedly as the Johnstown Flood. In June an Austrian archduke had been shot, and in July Austria had sent an ultimatum to Serbia; but these distant events caused no stir. Then Russia had mobilized. The German Kaiser, fearing the alliance between Russia and France, struck suddenly at France through Belgium. England declared war on Germany. President Wilson called on Americans to be "impartial in thought as well as in action." But the thoughts of most Americans were far from impartial.

American sympathies were strongly pro-Belgian and anti-German. "What Will You Give For Her?" was the name of this cartoon.

"The Coming Bond of Friendship" was a typical American jibe at Wilson's efforts to stay neutral by writing diplomatic notes.

"The Return of the Goth," by Boardman Robinson, showed what many Americans—including Wilson—really thought of Germany.

American opinion was especially outraged when the Germans deliberately destroyed the city of Louvain and shot many civilians.

The *Lusitania*, largest steamer in Atlantic service, leaves New York May 1, 1915.

THE UNTERSEEBOOT 20
SINKS THE LUSITANIA

The *Lusitania* goes down off the Irish coast, sunk by a German torpedo. Among the Americans lost were Alfred Gwynne Vanderbilt, Elbert Hubbard, and Charles Frohman.

SHORTLY AFTER 2 P.M. on May 7, 1915, the German submarine commander *Leutnant-Kapitän* Schwieger made the following notations in his log: "Right ahead appeared four funnels and two masts of a steamer. Clean bow-shot from 700-meter range. Shot hits starboard side right behind bridge. An unusually heavy detonation follows. . . . Life-boats being cleared and lowered to water. Many boats crowded, come down bow first or stern first in the water and immediately fill and sink. The ship blows off. In the front appears the name *Lusitania* in gold letters. . . . I submerge to 24 meters and go to sea." The exploit which he thus described was the torpedoing without warning of the unarmed British luxury liner *Lusitania*, bound from New York to Liverpool with 1,924 passengers and crew, and a cargo which included 4,200 cases of rifle cartridges. Among the 1,198 persons who died were 128 American citizens and 63 small children. Americans grimly braced themselves for a possible declaration of war. But President Wilson was still trying desperately to be neutral. "There is such a thing as a nation being so right that it does not need to convince others by force," he argued. "There is such a thing as a man being *too proud to fight*."

The *Lusitania* sinking was "deliberate murder" and the Germans were "savages drunk with blood," said the newspapers of 1915. But these marchers urged their men to "Keep Cool."

"HE KEPT US OUT OF WAR"

FOR TWO YEARS Wilson kept the United States neutral, but he could not keep it isolated. The war spilled over constantly on American rights and American interests. At first it was the British Navy which caused the most trouble, by blockading Germany and stopping American trade with much of Europe. This was just the kind of violation of our freedom on the seas which had led to the War of 1812. But neither Wilson nor his diplomats could summon up much anger against an England that was battling for her life against the "Huns." "England is fighting our fight," the President said privately, and his words were repeated in strategic places. So a steady stream of protests about the high-handed British Navy flowed from Washington to Whitehall—and were pigeonholed there by mutual consent.

Meanwhile Germany struck back at the blockade by proclaiming and carrying out unrestricted submarine warfare in a wide zone around the British Isles. To Wilson this was a different matter, for it cost American lives as well as American profits. After the *Lusitania* was torpedoed the President sent some really wrathful notes to Berlin, and finally threatened to sever diplomatic relations—a next-to-the-last step toward war. The Germans then made a partial pledge: no more passenger ships would be sunk without warning, provided they did not try to offer resistance. This promise was made in May 1916 and was kept until the 1916 election was over.

Wilson thus went into his campaign for re-election with a diplomatic victory, along with a plump and smiling bride, and a brand-new policy of preparedness. At his request Congress quickly enlarged the Army, Navy, and merchant fleet, and set up a Council of National Defense to co-ordinate American industry. The President himself marched in Preparedness Parades in New York City and Washington, carrying an American flag over his shoulder. But what won him more votes than anything else was the slogan which was coined by an anonymous genius of the Democratic publicity staff—"He kept us out of war."

Wilson and his bride campaign in 1916. After his first wife's death in the White House, the President courted and won Mrs. Edith Bolling Galt.

A Democratic propaganda truck in New York City boasts that Wilson is for peace, prosperity, preparedness, and the extension of the parcel post.

Charles Evans Hughes pointed his finger at many Wilson foibles in 1916 but did not fight very hard. Roosevelt privately called him "the bearded lady."

Theodore Roosevelt campaigned for preparedness and Hughes in 1916. Here Teddy visits the 86th Division in training at Camp Grant, Ill.

"THAT YOU MUST ADMIT"

To THEODORE ROOSEVELT and his red-blooded friends, President Wilson was the spokesman for all the "flubdubs," "mollycoddles," and "flapdoodle pacifists" who were too yellow to fight. If he had been President in 1914, groaned Teddy, he would have stepped in and saved Belgium. By 1915 he had made all his plans to enter the war as commander of an American division in France. But Wilson was too "cowardly" and "ladylike" to declare war and send him there. In 1916 Teddy made his famous "Shadows" speech, based on the fact that Wilson was spending the summer at a New Jersey estate called Shadow Lawn. "There should be shadows enough at Shadow Lawn," Roosevelt said. "The shadows of men, women, and children who have risen from the ooze of the ocean. . . . The shadows of the helpless whom Mr. Wilson did not dare protect lest he might have to face danger; the shadows of babies gasping pitifully as they sank beneath the waves. . . . Those are the shadows proper for Shadow Lawn. . . ."

In 1916, after Roosevelt refused to head another Progressive ticket, the moth-eaten Bull Moose crawled back to the Republican fold and expired. Charles Evans Hughes, former New York Governor and investigator of life-insurance company frauds, had resigned from the Supreme Court to be the Republican candidate. Hughes was honest, dignified, and not very exciting. The Republicans boasted that he had "a record as clean as a hound's tooth, and as straight as a sapling. That you must admit whether you like him or not." Unfortunately, while campaigning in California, Hughes wounded the feelings of Governor Hiram Johnson, the most powerful Progressive in the West.

On election night Hughes had a big lead and went to bed convinced that he had won. A reporter tried to telephone him after midnight, and was informed: "The President cannot be disturbed." "Well, when he wakes up just tell him he isn't President," said the reporter. Twenty-four hours later came the final news from California: Wilson had won the state by 4,000 votes, and with it a bare electoral majority.

"IT IS A FEARFUL THING TO LEAD . . ."

AFTER THE ELECTION Wilson tried to end the war by active mediation. He invited the belligerents to state the "precise objects" for which they were fighting, and offered to help find some common ground between them. But he warned that no nation could win completely, for a peace written "under duress" would not last. This declaration became known as his "peace without victory" speech, and was coldly received by both sides.

Then the German Government decided to resume unrestricted submarine warfare on February 1, 1917, regardless of past pledges. On a memorandum from his admiralty the Kaiser himself wrote in pencil: "Now, once and for all, an *end* to negotiations with America. If Wilson wants war, let him make it, and let him then have it." That finished Wilson's hopes for peace. He promptly severed diplomatic relations, and put guns on American merchant ships. But in March the Germans sank four of them.

On the night of March 31, having called Congress into extraordinary session, President Wilson got up from bed and went out on the south veranda of the White House with his portable typewriter. Mrs. Wilson brought him a bowl of milk and crackers from the kitchen, and then left him. In the hush of early morning the President tapped out the words which he read to Congress *(above)* on April 2: "The present German submarine warfare against commerce is a warfare against mankind. It is a war against all nations. . . . We are accepting this challenge. . . . The world must be made safe for democracy. . . . It is a fearful thing to lead this great peaceful people into war, into the most terrible and disastrous of all wars. . . . But the right is more precious than the peace. . . ."

As he rode through the streets of Washington the crowds along the sidewalks cheered, but the President was pale and silent. "My message today was a message of death for our young men," he said later. "How strange it seems to applaud that."

The United States oil tanker *Illinois* goes down in the English Channel March 18, 1917 *(below)*. This photograph was taken from the German U-boat that sank her.

Congress passed a draft law May 18 and 9,586,508 men registered June 5. Above, draftees parade en route to camp.

Below, the first American troops reach Saint-Nazaire June 26, 1917. In July some of them entered the front lines.

This Signal Corps photograph shows American infantrymen of the Second Division firing a 37-millimeter gun while their buddies crawl and run through a shattered wood. American land forces took their first important part in the war at Montdidier in May 1918. In July, at Château-Thierry, they helped stop the last German drive for Paris. In mid-

September the American Expeditionary Force launched its first offensive in the Saint-Mihiel sector. On September 26 it took over the Meuse-Argonne front and joined in the Allied push that broke the Hindenburg line. This was the biggest battle in U. S. history. It involved 1,200,000 Americans, of whom 10 per cent were killed or wounded.

Millions of women became war workers, farmerettes, trolley conductors, and cops.

Famous illustrators like James Montgomery Flagg drew the Government's war posters.

Tons of sticky peach stones were collected in public barrels to make gas-mask linings.

The Marine Corps enlisted 269 women as stenographers and clerks. These New York "Marinettes" wore men's hats and tunics for their swearing-in.

Hanging the Kaiser was a favorite sport for the cartoonists. This was drawn by Charles Dana Gibson.

FIGHTING THE WAR OVER HERE

IN 19 MONTHS after declaring war the United States built an army of four million men, delivered two million to France, and placed 1,390,000 on the firing line. The Navy licked the submarine menace, losing only one troopship on the route to France. These achievements were remarkable, but the civilian mobilization behind them was even more remarkable. By propaganda, by Presidential decree, and by willing patriotism, the United States became more unanimous than ever before. The brains and hands and even the stomachs of 100 million Americans were made to function as one.

While dollar-a-year men poured into Washington to run the swollen government machine, four-minute men poured out to sell Liberty Bonds, Thrift Stamps, Home Gardens, and the Red Cross. "Do Your Bit," "Food Will Win the War,"

Jack Dempsey, already known as a fighter, toiled in a Seattle shipyard, helping to build the "bridge of ships" to France.

Douglas Fairbanks was a prize salesman of Liberty Bonds for the Treasury. Americans bought more than $18 billion worth of war bonds.

On the eve of the war the eight-hour day was established by Congress for railroad workers and became common in industry. This cartoon from *The Masses* celebrates labor's victory.

"Over There" was a favorite song, over here. The cover shows typical trainees.

and "Swat the Hun" glared from billboards on every side. Overstuffed society ladies said they were "Hooverizing" when they did without wheat on Monday, or meat on Tuesday. A Fuel Administrator in Washington gave an order, and the nation's lights were dimmed; he gave another order, and all the clocks were turned ahead. The War Industries Board under Bernard Baruch converted 28,000 factories into a production "trust" such as even Morgan had never dreamed of. William G. McAdoo, the President's son-in-law, became dictator of the nation's railroads. The German language was banned in schools; German-born musicians and scholars were publicly insulted; Eugene Debs was put in jail, and the New York *Times* printed a rumor that German spies were putting poison in bandages in Philadelphia. It was all part of the home-front war.

Herbert Hoover (right) fed the starving Belgians and became America's food czar.

THE FOURTEEN POINTS

1. Open covenants of peace, openly arrived at, after which there shall be no private international understandings of any kind. . . .

2. Absolute freedom of navigation upon the seas. . . .

3. The removal . . . of all economic barriers and the establishment of an equality of trade conditions among all the nations consenting to the peace. . . .

4. Adequate guarantees . . . that national armaments will be reduced.

5. A free, open-minded, and absolutely impartial adjustment of all colonial claims. . . .

6. The evacuation of all Russian territory, and such a settlement of all questions affecting Russia as will secure . . . for her . . . the independent determination of her own political development and national policy. . . .

7. Belgium . . . must be evacuated and restored. . . .

8. All French territory should be freed . . . and the wrong done to France by Prussia in 1871 in the matter of Alsace-Lorraine . . . should be righted. . . .

9. A readjustment of the frontiers of Italy . . . along clearly recognizable lines of nationality.

10. The peoples of Austria-Hungary . . . should be accorded the freest opportunity of autonomous development.

11. Rumania, Serbia, and Montenegro should be evacuated . . . [and] Serbia accorded free . . . access to the sea. . . .

12. The Turkish portions of the present Ottoman Empire should be assured a secure sovereignty, but the other nationalities which are now under Turkish rule should be assured . . . autonomous development, and the Dardanelles should be permanently opened . . . to . . . all nations. . . .

13. An independent Polish state should be erected . . . which should be assured a free and secure access to the sea . . . .

14. A general association of nations must be formed . . . for the purpose of affording mutual guarantees of political independence and territorial integrity to great and small states alike.

THE WAR OF WORDS

THE LARGEST single factor in the war (said the journalist and historian Mark Sullivan) was the mind of Woodrow Wilson. Wilson's thoughts and words were weapons, and a vast American propaganda machine sowed them around the world. Wilson had said that the United States was fighting not the German people, but the German "ruling class"—and every German was given a chance to ponder this. Wilson had said that there must be no revenge in the peace terms ("peace without victory")—and this was a hope for Germans to grasp at as the German armies began to crumble. The words of Wilson were shot from guns and rockets, scattered from airplanes and balloons, sprayed (for the first time in history) by radio, and smuggled through the enemy lines in many languages. In friendly and allied countries they were circulated in millions of printed copies.

In 1917 the Czar's regime collapsed and the Russian revolutionists made a separate peace with Germany. American agents in Russia were able to pour tons of propaganda into war-weary Germany through its eastern back door. From one of them, a newspaperman named Edgar G. Sisson, came a suggestion that the President boil down his war and peace aims into "placard paragraphs" in American advertising style. "I can get it fed into Germany in great quantities in German translation," promised Sisson, "and can utilize Russian version potently in Army and elsewhere." This proposal was passed on to the White House, where Wilson was writing an outline of his peace terms for Congress. On January 8, 1918, he delivered this speech and included in it a series of short, almost snappy, paragraphs which became universally known as the "Fourteen Points."

The Fourteen Points were more than peace terms: they were terms for a better world. Hammered home by tireless American publicity, they enlisted behind Wilson all the decent desires and emotions which were still alive in every country. Wilson followed them up in February with his famous "self-determination" speech, in which he said: "National aspirations must be respected; people may now be dominated and governed only by their own consent. 'Self-determination' is not a mere phrase; it is an imperative principle of action. . . ." He also promised Germany that "there shall be no annexations, no contributions, no punitive damages." On July 4 he added four more points: (1) "The destruction of every arbitrary power anywhere that can . . . disturb the peace of the world . . ." (this doomed the Kaiser). (2) "The settlement of every question, whether of territory, of sovereignty . . . or of political relationship . . . by the people immediately concerned . . ." on the basis of self-determination. (3) "The consent of all nations to be governed in their conduct toward each other by the same principles of honor and . . . law . . . that govern the individual citizens of all modern States . . ." (an international code of morality). (4) "The establishment of an organization of peace which shall make it certain that the combined power of free nations will check every invasion of right . . ." (a strong League of Nations).

All of these Wilsonian "points" made Theodore Roosevelt snap his teeth in rage. "Sheer nonsense!" he cried. "The American people want Germany smashed." Chairman Will Hays of the Republican national committee sneered that Wilson's real plan was to rebuild the world "in unimpeded conformity with whatever Socialistic doctrines, whatever unlimited government-ownership notions, whatever hazy whims may happen to possess him at the time." But despite Republican sniping, the Fourteen Points constituted the greatest diplomatic victory of the war. And they showed the world that the Big Stick of American ideals could—in the proper hands—be more than a match for the Big Stick of American power.

President Woodrow Wilson, from the painting
by Sir William Orpen

Armistice Day 1918 brought delirious celebrations to New York *(above)* and every American city. After the shouting, the statisticians figured out that the war had cost 130,000 American lives and 42 billion American dollars.

GERMANY GIVES UP

In August 1918 the German generals, blaming "fresh American troops" for their defeats, secretly warned the Berlin Government that the war was lost. The Allied armies of Generalissimo Foch were pushing ahead on the whole French-Flemish front; the Hindenburg line had caved in completely, and the German horde was staggering back, still under discipline, but unable to make a stand. In October, as the Allies neared the Rhine, a "moderate" Chancellor, Prince Max of Baden, was put in charge of the Kaiser's Cabinet and immediately begged Wilson for peace based on the Fourteen Points. The President's reply was sharp: he made several counterdemands, and indicated clearly that the war would go on until Germany got rid of the Kaiser. While Prince Max strove to reassure him, the German retreat became a rout, mutiny started in the submarine fleet, and Red revolutions simmered in Munich, Hamburg, and Berlin. On November 9 the Kaiser abdicated and escaped into Holland. Two days later a delegation of German civilians signed an armistice of total submission in Foch's railroad-car headquarters.

To most Americans the Armistice meant a happy ending to the strain and terror of the war, and that was all they could think about. But to President Wilson it brought the beginning of another grim struggle. Already he had decided that the only way to win a just peace was for him to go to the Peace Conference and fight for it in person. In October he asked the people to back him up by electing a Democratic majority to Congress. This proved to be a blunder—the Republicans raised a cry of "cheap politics" and charged that the President had "practically accused us of treason." "Mr. Wilson wants only rubber stamps, his rubber stamps, in Congress," said Republican Chairman Hays. The result was a Republican majority, small in the Senate, but sizable in the House. Wilson set his jaw and sailed for Europe anyway. In his ears there rang a warning from his old and ailing enemy, Theodore Roosevelt. "Mr. Wilson and his Fourteen Points and his four supplementary points and all his utterances every which way have ceased to have any shadow of right to be accepted as expressive of the will of the American people," Teddy told the world.

German civilians silently watch the American First Division enter Treves December 1, 1918. More than 200,000 American troops joined the Allied Army of Occupation in the Rhineland. A few Americans stayed until 1923.

An American outpost in northern Russia in February 1919. Three American battalions, under British command, fought the Bolsheviki around Archangel and suffered 400 casualties; 9,000 other Americans fought in Siberia.

Woodrow Wilson, the first American President to go to Europe, boards the S.S. *George Washington* December 4, 1918. Seeing him off in a tall silk hat *(center)* is Assistant Secretary of the Navy Franklin D. Roosevelt.

All the Allied kings paid court to Wilson. England's George V *(above)* met him at Charing Cross in London on December 26 and took him home to Buckingham Palace. The Palace was ice-cold for lack of coal. But the King gave Wilson a small electric heater.

Italy's Victor Emmanuel staged a royal banquet for Wilson. But the King's police prevented Wilson from making a speech in Rome.

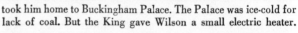

Belgium's Albert escorted Wilson through his war-torn country in June. They lunched in a field of shell holes and red poppies.

"*Vive Vil-son*," cried the French in Paris. One French woman wrote Wilson, "You have saved our fiancés; love blooms again."

"*Viva Voovro Veelson*," screamed mobs in Italy, where peasants worshiped his photograph. Above, Wilson on a balcony in Milan.

ON DECEMBER 13 the President's ship reached Brest, where a crimson carpet was spread through the railroad station to his special train for Paris. The next day Wilson heard what no other American President had ever heard: the voices of millions of Europeans calling and blessing him by name. Miles of glittering bayonets, cascades of roses, and endless, sobbing cheers that seemed to come from the heart of humanity itself—these were part of the welcome that Paris gave Wilson. It was the same in London, which he visited after Christmas. It was the same, and more so, in Milan and Rome, where he went in January. Everywhere the people of the Old World had turned away from their politicians and princes, and looked to the American President for salvation. Wilson was deeply stirred by the ovations, but the official presentations and banquets and champagne-drinking receptions were a heavy drain on his energy. He was nervous, and anxious to get on with the peace treaty.

WILSON
THE
SAVIOR

"Hurrah for Wilson," shouted English crowds who waited in the rain outside Buckingham Palace to see the President's carriage roll by. When he got out of the carriage to make official calls, bevies of British girls scattered white carnations in his path.

On Christmas Day 1918 the President visited the American troops at Humes. Wet snow
was falling, and the French mud was inches deep as Wilson and his party picked their way
across the fields. A little dog wandered out in front and sat down *(above)* as the President
made a rambling, self-conscious speech: "You men probably do not realize with what
anxious attention we have followed every step you have advanced. . . . It has taken a lot of

moral courage to stay at home. But we are proud to back you up everywhere that it was possible. . . . I feel a comradeship with you today which is delightful." But the mud-spattered doughboys found the occasion anything but delightful. They tramped half the day in the snow, and then ate beans for Christmas dinner. And they were frankly bored by Wilson's talk of "peace upon the . . . foundation of right." They wanted to go home.

The Little Four aided Wilson: Baruch (industry), Norman Davis (finance), V. McCormick (trade), Hoover (food).

The Big Four of Paris *(right)* step out for fresh air and a photograph: Lloyd George, Orlando, Clemenceau, Wilson.

The Peace Conference met in the Palais d'Orsay in Paris *(above)*. The finished Treaty was signed June 28 at Versailles.

THE TREATY MAKERS

THE PARIS Peace Conference was called to order on January 18, 1919, with 27 Allied and Associated Powers in attendance. It was an unwieldy body and made a noise (as one Britisher observed) like a "riot in a parrot house." The delegates therefore empowered a Supreme Council of Ten to do the most important work. This also proved too large and gave way in March to the Council of Four, composed of President Wilson, President of the Council Georges Clemenceau of France, Prime Minister David Lloyd George of Great Britain, and Premier Vittorio Orlando of Italy.

Within the Big Four only Wilson stood for a "peace without victory." He argued that the German people must be given a decent national existence, or they would cause another war. His colleagues demanded harsh revenge, vast reparations, a division of the German colonies, and a declaration of German guilt. Clemenceau (the "Tiger") said, "Wilson bores me with his Fourteen Points." Lloyd George blustered about hanging the Kaiser. Orlando quit the Conference when Wilson refused to give Italy the Austrian port of Fiume. The endless inter-Allied bickerings wrecked Wilson's nerves; he caught cold from Clemenceau, who coughed all the time; in April he suffered a physical breakdown. His greatest success was in writing into the Treaty the Covenant of a League of Nations. But to get this he had to compromise on his other thirteen Points.

President Wilson, leaving the Conference, looks at his watch. In his spare time he heard complaints from small nations.

Hiram Johnson *(left)* and William E. Borah led the Senate's isolationists in their successful fight to kill the League of Nations. Wilson had called them "a little group of willful men" in 1917, and they wanted to get even.

THE WILLFUL MEN

WOODROW WILSON was heartsick over the many failures of the Treaty of Versailles. He knew that it was a disappointing document —a travesty on the hopes he had held when he sailed for Europe six months before. But it contained the one thing which promised to bring justice into international relations, and might someday end all wars: the League of Nations. Wilson's conception was that the League would gradually correct the Treaty's shortcomings. "The settlements," he said, "may be temporary, but the processes must be permanent."

Under the United States Constitution, both the Treaty and the League had to be approved by two thirds of the Senate before this country could participate in them. When Wilson came home he found to his horror that the Senate might not approve.

The opposition sprang from many sources. There were the outright isolationists, who had been opposed to the war and were now equally opposed to the entanglements of peace. There were the old-line Manifest Destiny imperialists who did not want the United States hampered in its expansion by any international agreements. ("America first!" cried ex-Senator Beveridge. "Not only America first, but America only!") There were the Irish-Americans and Italian-Americans and German-Americans, who all had their special reasons for disliking the Treaty. But the most important enemies were the Republican party leaders who wanted to cut Wilson's political throat, once and for all. The chief among these was Senator Henry Cabot Lodge, chairman of the Senate Foreign Relations Committee.

Lodge did not attack the Treaty directly, but proposed to "Americanize" it by inserting 14 amendments and reservations. His most important reservation related to Article Ten of the League of Nations Covenant, which stated that League members would act jointly to put down future aggressors. Lodge's reservation was that Congress would have to approve the use of American military forces for any such purpose. This was not much more than a statement of constitutional facts, but Wilson would not agree to it. He hated Lodge as much as Lodge hated him, and he was just as stubborn about it.

On September 3 the President dramatically set out from Washington to carry his case to the people. If the League were beaten or crippled by Senate amendments, he said, "I can predict with absolute certainty that within another generation there will be another world war"; and, "What the Germans used [in this war] were toys as compared with what would be used in the next war." On September 25 Wilson delivered his fortieth speech at Pueblo, Colorado, and was accorded a magnificent ovation. That night on his train he collapsed from nervous and physical exhaustion. One side of his face drooped; his left arm and leg were paralyzed for a time. He was rushed back to Washington, and rumors spread that he was dying or had become insane. From his sickroom in the White House there came one more imperious order to the loyal Democrats in the Senate: not one of the Republican reservations would ever be accepted by the President. It must be the League of Nations as he had planned it, or nothing.

On November 19, 1919, the Senate rejected the Treaty and voted for nothing.

Senator Henry Cabot Lodge of Massachusetts was in favor of a League of Nations until Wilson sponsored it. Then Lodge became the League's worst enemy.

President Wilson is helped through the Washington railroad station after his 1919 collapse. "It would probably have been better if I had died," he said later.

Chicago steelworkers show their strike notices, September 22, 1919.　　By January 8 their union was beaten and the strike was abandoned.

Cartoon of 1919 shows a Red creeping under the flag. He looks like the bearded agitator who appeared in cartoons after the Haymarket bombing.

STRIKERS AND

WITH THE END of the war a long-smoldering industrial conflict burst into flame. During 1919 four million American workers struck for the right to belong to unions which could bargain on equal terms with their employers. The captains of big business—which had grown bigger and richer during the war—fought back savagely to maintain the *status quo*.

The biggest test came when 365,000 steelworkers struck against the United States Steel Corporation and other companies which still maintained a 12-hour day. The Federation of Churches backed the strikers, declaring that their "average week of 68.7 hours . . . and the underpayment of unskilled labor" in the steel industry were "inhuman." But Big Steel, which had made $2 billion in war profits, broke the strike with the aid of military force. In Pennsylvania the coal and iron police went into action: a union organizer was murdered, and strikers were shot or run off the streets in company towns. At Gary, Indiana, federal troops protected strike-

Militia round up suspicious characters during the strike of 1,117 Boston policemen in 1919.   All the strikers were fired and replaced.

RED-BAITERS

breakers. In West Virginia police paid by the Weirton Steel Company forced 118 strikers to kneel and kiss the American flag.

An antiforeign and anti-Red hysteria swept the country along with the strikes. Congress investigated Communist propaganda; the F.B.I. seized hundreds of "radicals" in coast-to-coast raids; and the Justice Department deported 249 "undesirables" to Russia. War veterans smashed up a Socialist newspaper office in New York, and lynched (with gruesome pocketknife emasculation) an I.W.W. member in Centralia, Washington, after a free-for-all gun battle in which four ex-soldiers were killed. Legally elected Socialist legislators were barred from Congress and the New York state legislature. The attacks on old-line Socialists were confusing, because many of them were as anti-Communist as J. P. Morgan himself. But the prevalent American opinion made little distinction—as the Detroit *Journal* said, "Socialism is Bolshevism with a shave."

A. Mitchell Palmer, Wilson's Attorney General, led the Red-hunt of 1919. One supposed Red killed himself bombing Palmer's house in Washington.

At 11:59 A.M., September 16, 1920, a wagon loaded with dynamite and scrap iron exploded at Broad and Wall Streets, New York, which had become during the war the financial capital of the world. Thirty-eight persons were killed and hundreds hurt, but the man who drove the wagon escaped, and police never learned whether he was a "Red" or not. Above, Wall Street just after the blast. Below, the office of J. P. Morgan & Company.

A comradely kiss is exchanged in 1920 between Eugene Debs *(left)*, Socialist candidate for President, and Seymour Stedman, Socialist candidate for Vice President. The bars in the background are those of the federal penitentiary in Atlanta, where Debs was serving a 10-year sentence for wartime sedition when Stedman arrived to notify him of the nominations. As the only man ever to run for President from a prison cell, Debs received 919,799 votes.

WOMEN FINALLY

GET THE VOTE

THESE TWELVE happy ladies were photographed in a San Francisco hotel in November 1919, just after they learned that their state had ratified the woman suffrage amendment to the Constitution. But California was only the 18th state to ratify, and there was still a tough fight before the necessary 36th was won.

For months after this picture was taken the suffragists swarmed from one state capitol to another, pinning yellow jonquils—their campaign flower—to the coats of legislators, and performing prodigies of persuasion. Their foes, both male and female, came close behind with armloads of red roses, the symbol of the opposition.

The final battle was for Tennessee, which yielded to the yellow jonquil legions on August 18, 1920. A few days later the Nineteenth Amendment was formally put in effect, wiping the ancient discrimination of sex from American politics.

In 1920 the Big Stick dwindled to a furled umbrella, in the hands of a blue-nosed tyrant labeled "Prohibition." Alcoholic beverages became illegal on January 16. The nation promptly filled with bootleggers, and an illegal still was found on the farm of the Texas Senator who wrote the 18th Amendment.

CHAPTER 9

NORMALCY AND THE NEW DEAL

"I LIKE to go out into the country and bloviate," said Warren G. Harding, the publisher of the Marion *Star* and Republican Senator from Ohio. What Harding meant by "bloviate" was to make long-winded speeches full of bloated political clichés; he was an expert at wrapping a single idea in several thousand pompous words. On May 14, 1920, he addressed the Home Market Club of Boston, and one of the words he uttered there became the most famous of the year. "America's present need," he said, "is not heroics but healing, not nostrums but normalcy, not revolution but restoration, not agitation but adjustment, not surgery but serenity, not the dramatic but the dispassionate, not experiment but equipoise, not submergence in internationality but sustainment in triumphant nationality."

It was Harding's fondness for alliteration that led him to the lucky choice of "normalcy," which was immediately picked up by the reporters, headline writers, and editorialists of the nation's press, and also by the expert publicists of the Republican national committee, who used it in a phrase that appealed irresistibly to millions of war-weary Americans—"Back to Normalcy!"

It was easy to ascertain what Harding meant by normalcy. He said himself that he loved "the good old times when the Republican protective tariff policy filled the Treasury"—the age of Hayes, and Chester Arthur, and Benjamin Harrison, and McKinley. In one of his typical "bloviations" he tenderly described the American small town where he had grown up in the 1870's and '80's, and concluded as follows: "What is the greatest thing in life, my countrymen? Happiness. And there is more happiness in the American village than in any other place on the face of the earth."

Such nostalgia was wonderfully soothing to a nation which felt it was rushing too swiftly along the highroad of history.

For the United States, in 1920, was in a curiously divided mood. It was proud of its power, and frightened of its pre-eminent position. The little seaboard colonial federation of 1775 had become—in an amazingly short space of historical time—the most conspicuous industrial and financial .giant in the world. Endless demands were made on it to solve the world's biggest worries: the boundaries of Europe, the starving Armenians, the aggressive Japanese in China, the spread of Bolshevism, the disposal of colonies and mandates involving hundreds of millions of people, the settlement of billions of dollars for war debts and reparations, the intricate balancing of world trade and banking, the maintenance of world peace. Out of genuine bewilderment, many Americans turned, with Harding, to recall the blissful picture of the past. For the time being the nation was like a middle-aged man with a prosperous waistline, who had worked hard all week, and, now that Sunday afternoon had come, wanted to lie down and take a nap.

And so, in 1920, the overwhelming majority of Americans voted for Warren G. Harding for President. They voted for the Republican Normalcy of the 1880's, and against the Big Stick, at home or abroad. They voted, it might almost be said, in the spirit of a certain mythical bird which flies through the air backward because it does not want to see where it's going, but likes to look where it's been.

The Sunday afternoon dream of small-town Normalcy lasted through most of a fitful decade, during which the United States became more than ever a land of big cities, big money, and big factories filled with machines. It ended in the economic and social nightmare of the depression, and the lowering clouds of world-wide aggression and fascism. It was superseded in the 1930's by the New Deal of Franklin D. Roosevelt, which brought new reforms and startling political precedents into American life. And it was lost forever in the 1940's, when the United States became the world's foremost military power, and the sponsor of a weapon which was scientifically capable of ending the human race.

The Democrats in 1920 nominated two loyal followers of
Woodrow Wilson and the League of Nations: James M.
Cox of Dayton, Ohio *(right)*, for President, and Franklin
D. Roosevelt of Hyde Park, New York, for Vice President.

"WE DREW TO A PAIR OF DEUCES"

THE KEYNOTE of the Republican convention of 1920 was sounded by Senator Henry Cabot Lodge, who said: "Mr. Wilson and his dynasty, his heirs and assigns, or anybody that is his, anybody who with bent knee has served his purpose, must be driven from all control of the Government and all influence in it. [Prolonged cheers.]" But it was easier for the Republicans to find a common purpose than a candidate. Theodore Roosevelt would have been ideal, perhaps, but he had died the year before. The three strongest contenders were General Leonard Wood of New York, who was backed by Roosevelt's friends and a free-spending section of big business; Governor Frank Lowden of Illinois, the favorite son of the farming states; and Senator Hiram Johnson of California, who commanded the forces of isolation and Progressivism.

In the early balloting Wood and Lowden were almost even, with about 300 votes apiece (493 were needed to win), and Johnson was a steady third with 140. Stringing along behind were Governor Sproul and Senator Knox of Pennsylvania, Senator Harding of Ohio (60 votes), Senator La Follette of Wisconsin, Governor Coolidge of Massachusetts, and Herbert Hoover of California.

That was the situation on the late afternoon of June 11, when Lodge, who was chairman, forced an adjournment. The next day the delegates gathered again and stampeded to Harding, who got 692½ votes on the tenth ballot. This classic deal was arranged during the night in a smoke-filled room in the Blackstone Hotel by a handful of Senators and state bosses who feared a party-splitting deadlock. There were three reasons why they finally decided to give the nod to Harding: (1) he had almost no personal enemies; (2) he had proved over many years that he would do whatever the party leaders wanted him to; and (3) he looked impressive. All these arguments were cleverly exploited at the right time by Harry Daugherty, Harding's campaign manager. Many years before, Daugherty had met Harding on the path to a small-town hotel privy in Ohio and exclaimed, "Gee, what a President he'd make!" Ever since, he had been maneuvering Harding toward the White House.

As for Harding himself, he hardly knew how it happened. He had entered the race—as he thought—to build up his political fences in Ohio, and never had the faintest idea that he could be nominated. About 2 A.M. he was summoned to the Blackstone conference room and told, "Senator, we want to put a question to you. Is there in your life or background any element which might embarrass the Republican party if we nominate you for President?" He went into an adjoining room alone and thought for ten minutes. Then he came out and said "No." The next day, when the shouting was all over, he still seemed bewildered. Reporters crowded around asking for a statement, and the candidate, drawing on his knowledge of poker, gave them one that was modest and accurate. "We drew to a pair of deuces, and filled," he said.

For Vice President the Republicans chose John Calvin Coolidge of Massachusetts, who broke the Boston police strike

Harding campaigned from his front porch in Marion. He carefully took both sides of the League of Nations issue.

THE UNHAPPY

THE NATIONAL ELECTION totals took a great leap forward in 1920. More than 26 million votes were cast, of which Harding and Coolidge received 16 million, Cox and Roosevelt, nine. It was by far the largest plurality ever given to a President.

Yet Harding looked and acted depressed. "I have lost my freedom," he grieved to a home-town friend. He had never wanted to run for President—his wife and Harry Daugherty had pushed him into it. He would much rather have stayed in the Senate, where he could get his cues from more active minds. The truth was that Harding was a good-hearted, hand-shaking politician who was not very bright, and knew it. His own judgment of himself was fair. "I am a man of limited talents from a small town," he said. "I don't seem to grasp that I am President."

Twice a week he sought to banish care by inviting his friends to the White House for poker parties. Liquor flowed freely at these affairs, for the President—like many other Americans—did not take prohibition seriously. The "drys" got after him, however, and he finally confined his drinking to the family bedrooms.

He had other troubles. His wife nagged him, and

Harding in 1921 wore a look of thoughtful earnestness. This photograph was taken soon after he was inaugurated.

Harding was born November 2, 1865, in this Blooming Grove, Ohio, farmhouse.

In 1900 he was the handsome publisher of the Marion *Star*.

In 1920 he posed in the *Star* composing room. He really loved newspaper work.

His wife henpecked him. She was ambitious and jealous.

His Cabinet was a mixture of patriots and rascals. Its members were said to be worth $600 million.

His mistress claimed that Harding fathered this baby girl.

PRESIDENT

made him stop chewing tobacco. He took secret plunges on the stock market, and lost $180,000. His mistress, Nan Britton, slipped into the White House for dangerous trysts. She needed money for her two-year-old baby, and Harding feared the affair might become known.

Worst of all were the rumors of graft and thievery which seeped steadily out of his administration. Harding himself was no crook, but he had not been President long when he learned that some of his friends and appointees were. The revelation shattered his morale, and paralyzed his feeble attempts at statesmanship. In the summer of 1923 he set out from Washington on a vacation and speechmaking tour through the West and Alaska. But his worries rode with him; cryptic messages and mysterious visitors reached his train, and at Seattle he suffered a heart attack. He was taken to San Francisco and put to bed in the Palace Hotel. There, on the evening of August 2, his wife was reading him a magazine article about himself entitled "A Calm View of a Calm Man." "That's good. Go on. Read some more," said the President, and then fell back, dead from a blood clot on the brain.

Harding in 1923 was a sagging, disillusioned old man. This is one of his last pictures, taken in San Francisco.

His manager, Harry Daugherty, became Attorney General.

His friend, Charlie Forbes, got the Veterans' Bureau.

Daugherty's henchman, Jesse Smith, sold Presidential pardons and liquor permits. When things got too hot, Jesse shot himself.

Harding was a capable golfer. He tried to forget his official worries by playing in all kinds of weather.

Steam from the Teapot Dome investigation drove the presidents of three big oil corporations into exile or resignation.

THE SMEAR OF OIL

IT TOOK years of sleuthing to uncover even a partial story of the Harding scandals. Many facts were lost when Attorney General Harry Daugherty burned the ledger sheets of a bank where he and Jesse Smith and other members of the "Ohio gang" had deposited their gains. A Senate committee found Daugherty guilty of selling pardons and permits, and he was ousted from the Cabinet, but he escaped conviction in court twice by hung juries. His lawyer said Daugherty got rid of the records to protect someone else, and most people assumed he meant President Harding.

Harding's crony, Charlie Forbes, whose thieving regime in the Veterans' Bureau cost the taxpayers an estimated $200 million, was sent to a federal penitentiary. So was Thomas W. Miller, the Alien Property Custodian, who—while working under Daugherty's supervision—fraudulently returned nearly $7 million to a German metal firm. Gaston B. Means, a Federal Bureau of Investigation agent who did undercover jobs for "the gang," was imprisoned for bribery. The most sensational case was that of Albert B. Fall, Harding's Secretary of the Interior, who was convicted of receiving a bribe. It was the first time in American history that an officer of cabinet rank had been jailed as a criminal.

Fall was a New Mexico rancher who swaggered around Washington in a broad-brimmed hat, playing the part of a political he-man from the wide open West. Harding first met him in the Senate and was fascinated by his gruff, self-confident manner. He wanted to make him Secretary of State, but Fall preferred the Interior Department. As soon as he was installed there, in 1921, he went to work on the government-owned oil reservations at Teapot Dome, Wyoming, and Elk Hills, California, which had been set aside years before for the Navy. Fall asked Secretary of the Navy Edwin N. Denby to transfer the oil lands to the Interior Department. Denby (a rich Detroit lawyer who honestly didn't know what it was all about) did it. Fall then negotiated secret leases for Elk Hills with Edward L. Doheny of Los Angeles, and for Teapot Dome with Harry F. Sinclair of New York. Doheny gave Fall $105,000 in cash, and Sinclair gave him $304,000 in cash and Liberty Bonds. With this tidy fortune Fall resigned from the Cabinet late in 1922, and retired to his ranch, where he spent so much money on improvements that the neighbors began to talk. After Harding's death he was hauled back to Washington, and perjured himself before a Senate investigating committee. But it was not until October 1929 that he was convicted and sentenced to one year in prison.

Harry F. Sinclair hired detectives to shadow the jurors at his bribery trial. For this he served six months in jail.

Edwin N. Denby, Harding's Secretary of the Navy, was Fall's simple-minded dupe in the oil-lease cases. He stole nothing himself.

Will Hays, Postmaster General and Republican national chairman, took $160,-000 in oil-tainted bonds for his party.

Edward L. Doheny was acquitted of bribing Fall, who was convicted (by another jury) of receiving a bribe from Doheny.

Albert B. Fall was sick and old when justice caught up with him in the oil-lease cases. This photograph shows him being helped into court at his trial in 1929. He admitted taking $100,000 from Doheny, but claimed it was only a "loan." The jury decided it was a bribe.

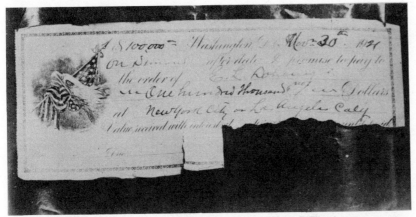

This note from Fall to Doheny was supposed to cover the "loan." The signature was torn off so that Fall need not pay it in case of Doheny's death. As for the $100,000, said Doheny, it was "a bagatelle to me . . . no more than $25 or $50 to the ordinary individual."

Senator Thomas J. Walsh of Montana got the goods on the oil-lease frauds. He began investigating before Harding died.

William Jennings Bryan was an unwelcome ghost with a palm-leaf fan at the 1924 Democratic convention. When the delegates rudely shouted "Louder!" at his once peerless voice, he went back to the Waldorf-Astoria and listened to the proceedings by radio.

Woodrow Wilson *(left, at his Washington home)* lived to attend Harding's funeral. On Armistice Day 1923 he issued a last warning against the "sullen and selfish isolation" of the U. S. On February 3, 1924, he died in his sleep.

DIVIDED DEMOCRATS

THE MORAL COLLAPSE of Republican Normalcy gave the Democrats a promising campaign issue in 1924, but the country didn't want to hear about it. The big city newspapers, in fact, attacked the Senate investigators more savagely than the criminals they exposed. Senators Walsh and Wheeler were called "Montana scandalmongers," "mud-gunners," and "assassins of character" because they persisted in bringing the facts to light. Meanwhile the Democrats were split by quarrels over prohibition and the Ku Klux Klan, which was having a postwar revival. The Northern "wets," led by Governor Alfred E. Smith of New York, wanted to denounce the Klan at their party convention. The Southern and Midwest "drys" rallied behind William G. McAdoo of California, and defeated the anti-Klan resolution by 542-3/20 to 541-3/20. On June 30 balloting for a Democratic Presidential nominee began in Madison Square Garden, New York City. It continued for 102 roll calls and nine sizzling days, during which Smith and McAdoo were hopelessly deadlocked, and their supporters acquired a lasting aversion for each other. On the 103d ballot the exhausted delegates compromised on John W. Davis, a conservative Wall Street lawyer. The Republicans, of course, renominated Harding's successor, "Silent Cal" Coolidge. Insurgents, Socialists, farm and labor groups who could see no choice between the two old parties joined a Progressive coalition which rolled up nearly five million votes for old Bob La Follette of Wisconsin. Davis got eight million, but there were 15 million who preferred to "Keep Cool and Keep Coolidge."

John W. Davis of Long Island and Clarksburg, West Virginia, was the handsome Democratic compromise of 1924.

THE COOLIDGE

"HERE STANDS our country, an example of tranquillity at home, a patron of tranquillity abroad," said President Coolidge on March 4, 1925. "Here stands its government, aware of its might and obedient to its conscience. Here it will continue to stand. . . ." Calvin Coolidge, even with a bundle of Indian feathers perched on top of his wizened face, was a perfect specimen of Normalcy. When he first came to the White House he took a rocking chair out among the pillars of the front porch and sat there in the evenings rocking and smoking a black cheroot. He did less work and made fewer decisions than any other twentieth-century President. "The business of America is business," he said, and he thought the Government should stay out of it.

However, when the stock market needed a shot in the arm, the President knew how to give it. In January 1928 Wall Street itself was scared by an increase in stockbrokers' loans to the "unprecedented" figure of $4,432 million. But Coolidge told a White House press conference that this was only "a natural expan-

Coolidge had a sense of humor. He knew he looked funny in Indian bonnets, but was willing to give people a laugh.

To make the farmers feel better, Coolidge posed as one during vacations in Vermont. Here he wears clean over-alls and polished shoes for a haying picture. A Presidential touring car waits in the background to take him away.

BULL MARKET

sion of business in the securities market," and nothing to worry about. Promptly stocks turned over "in huge volume," and brokers' loans continued to rise.

The Coolidge bull market was a curious tribute to the most frugal of our Presidents. Money was gushing from American factories and pouring from assembly lines: in the 1920's the productive efficiency of American factory workers increased by 30 per cent. But their wages failed to rise proportionately, and more than two million of them were "technologically" unemployed. The other big group of consumers, the farmers, suffered a steady decline in income. The benefits of increased productivity went mostly to the holders of capital, which raised the apparent value of stocks, which speeded up speculation, and fed the big bull market.

Yet even while Americans were gambling billions in Wall Street, they could look at the White House and see their Yankee President paring the public debt. It gave them a feeling that the country was fundamentally thrifty.

Farm prices slumped while industry boomed in the 1920's. "Well, farmers never have made money," said Coolidge.

A stockbroker's office in the 1920's, with a customer's man taking a phone order at left. After Coolidge told the market to go ahead, brokers' loans rose to 8½ billion, which was a good deal more money than there was in circulation.

Charles A. Lindbergh flew from New York to Paris in 34 hours in a Ryan monoplane.

Lucky Lindy, up in the sky—
    Fair or windy, he's flying high—
Peerless, fearless, knows ev'ry cloud,
    The kind of a son makes a mother feel proud. . . .*

THE TEMPO OF THE TWENTIES

So ran the words of a hero-worshiping ballad of 1927. But even the songs about Lindbergh were not as popular as "Yes, We Have No Bananas" and "Barney Google, With His Goo Goo Googly Eyes." Americans of the 1920's sang crazy lyrics, drank bathtub gin, rolled their stockings, and raised their skirts. The age of Cal Coolidge was also the age of flappers, gun molls, tin lizzies, and jazz; of flagpole sitters and debunkers; of Aimee McPherson and Fatty Arbuckle. A large part of the population was engaged in breaking the laws and the Ten Commandments. Under the crust of Normalcy, there was plenty of ferment.

*By L. Wolfe Gilbert and Abel Baer. Copyright 1927 Leo Feist Inc. Used by special copyright permission.

Massachusetts electrocuted two minor anarchists, Nicola Sacco *(right)* and Bartolomeo Vanzetti *(center)*, on a trumped-up murder conviction.

Mr. and Mrs. Sinclair Lewis took a ride on Main Street in a Model T Ford touring car.

The old-time saloon was replaced by speakeasies, where women crowded around the bars with men. College boys carried silver flasks of whisky.

Rudolph Valentino practiced the tango with a Hollywood blonde and a phonograph.

At least 40 million persons saw the movies every week. In *The Big Parade* (above) Renee Adoree took a piece of American gum from John Gilbert.

"Daddy" Browning gave his bride "Peaches" a $160,000 check on her 16th birthday.

TOP HATS
AND RED TAPE

No MATTER how hard it tried, the United States could not resign from the world in the 1920's. Foreign diplomats kept coming to Washington, and signing treaties with ribbons of red tape beside their names. American diplomats traveled to other capitals and signed more treaties, with more red tape. The treaties said that all the nations were opposed to war, and would never go to war again —unless they had to, for some reason or other.

In 1921 President Harding called a disarmament conference in Washington, and Secretary of State Hughes amazed the whole world by declaring that the only way to disarm was to disarm. With complete lack of diplomatic discretion, Hughes listed the capital ships which the American, British, and Japanese Navies ought to sink or stop building—66 of them in all. This idea was so popular with the world's taxpayers that it was promptly written into the Five-Power Naval Treaty.

In 1927 President Coolidge called another conference at Geneva to limit cruisers and smaller warships. But the "big navy" men in the various nations were better organized by then, and they broke up the conference. Coolidge's Secretary of State Frank B. Kellogg had better luck with the Kellogg-Briand Pact to "outlaw" war in 1928. Sixty-two nations signed this treaty and bound themselves to abandon war as "an instrument of national policy." It was understood, of course, that wars for self-defense, or to carry out previous commitments, or to support the League of Nations, or to enforce the Monroe Doctrine, were excepted.

British delegates to the Washington Naval Conference were astounded when the U. S. asked them to stop building four *Hood*-class battle cruisers.

Japanese delegates were glum at getting the short end of the 5-5-3 ratio. But they cheered up when the U. S. agreed not to fortify the Philippines.

German diplomats were correctly cordial in 1928, when Secretary Kellogg *(center)* met Ambassador Count von Prittwitz *(left)* and Counselor Keip.

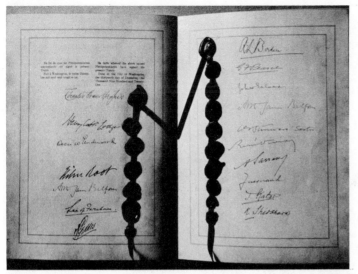

The Four-Power Treaty was a triumph for American diplomats. It untied England from her Japanese alliance and "guaranteed" the Philippines.

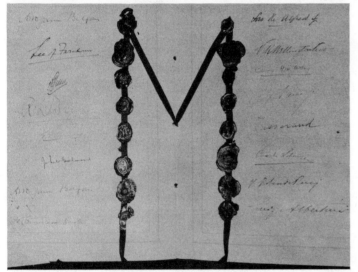

The Nine-Power Treaty guaranteeing China's independence was pushed through by the Americans and British over bitter Japanese opposition.

The Kellogg-Briand Pact to outlaw war was ratified by the U. S. in 1929. On the same day the Senate started action on a bill for 15 new cruisers.

TREATIES OF THE TWENTIES

Among the important treaties which the United States helped negotiate during the 1920's were the following:

The Four-Power Treaty of 1921. This dissolved the Anglo-Japanese military alliance and bound France, Great Britain, Japan, and the United States to "respect" each other's possessions in the Pacific and Far East.

The Five-Power Naval Treaty of 1922. This stopped a navy-building race and froze the Navies of Great Britain, the United States, and Japan at a ratio of 5-5-3 in capital ships.

The Nine-Power Treaty of 1922, by which nine leading nations, including Japan, agreed to respect the independence and territorial integrity of China.

The supplementary agreement between the United States and Japan of February 11, 1922, which gave this country cable rights on the island of Yap.

The debt agreements of 1923 (with Great Britain), 1925 (with Italy), and 1926 (with France), which scaled down their war and peace debts to the U. S. from $10 billion to about $5 billion.

The Dawes Plan of 1924 and the Young Plan of 1929, which reduced the reparations owed the Allies by Germany from $33 billion to $27 billion. The United States was not officially concerned with reparations, but acted as an unofficial, impartial broker.

The Kellogg-Briand treaty of 1928 (Pact of Paris), by which 62 nations, including Germany, Italy, and Japan, renounced war "as an instrument of national policy."

The oil agreements of 1925 (with Great Britain, for an American share of Middle East oil) and 1928 (with Mexico, for the retention of American-owned oil properties secured prior to 1917).

Al Smith demanded a return to states' rights on prohibition—dry states to be dry, wet states to be wet. "The poor, weak, vacillating, broken down Republican machine" had made a mess of liquor-law enforcement, he declared.

Smith's crusade for legal liquor brought him frenzied support in cities like Camden, New Jersey *(above)*. Hoover admitted there were "grave abuses" in prohibition, but insisted it was "a great . . . experiment, noble in motive."

THE HAPPY WARRIOR

THE DEMOCRATS nominated Al Smith for President in 1928, and the nation rocked to the catchy rhythm of his campaign song,

> East side, West side, all around the town,
> The tots sang "ring a rosie," "London Bridge is falling down. . . ." *

The sidewalks of New York had shaped and flavored Al Smith—as a boy he watched the building of the Brooklyn Bridge from a tenement window, and swam from the East River wharves. He became a bicycle coasting champ, and sold fish in the Fulton Market; he frequented a Tammany clubhouse, and got his first political job in the Commissioner of Jurors office. Then he was elected to the Assembly, took a leading role in framing a new state constitution, became sheriff of Manhattan, and Governor of New York. His eight years as chief executive of the nation's most populous state were rich in social progress, conservation of public resources, and educational improvements. He was an able public servant, and a jaunty campaigner who was perfectly named by Franklin D. Roosevelt in his nomination speech at Houston—"We offer one who has the will to win—who not only deserves success but commands it. Victory is his habit—the Happy Warrior—Alfred E. Smith!"

In the campaign of 1928 the Happy Warrior showed no inclination to war against the runaway boom in the stock market. On the contrary, he chose as chairman of the Democratic national committee one of the biggest bulls of Wall Street—John J. Raskob, a millionaire director of General Motors and Du Pont. Smith attacked the Republicans for failing to help the farmers or to develop public water power. But he soon found himself unpleasantly on the defensive. He was an unabashed wet, and the big cities loved him for it. He was also an unashamed Roman Catholic, and the Protestant South and Midwest shunned him. The "Catholic issue" was mostly discussed in whispers, but the Republican national committeewoman from Virginia brought it into the open when she said: "We must save the United States from being Romanized and rum-ridden, and the call is to the women to do so." Herbert Hoover, Smith's Republican opponent, repudiated such intolerance, but benefited from it in the voting. The Solid Democratic South was broken—Hoover carried Virginia, North Carolina, Florida, Tennessee, and Texas. Smith lost New York but carried Massachusetts and Rhode Island, where the Catholic vote was strong. Al's powerful personality brought an unprecedented outpouring of 36 million voters to the polls. Fifteen million voted for him, and 21 million against.

* Copyright 1894, Howley Haviland & Co. Copyright renewed 1921, & assigned to Paull-Pioneer Music Corp. Used by permission.

At 21, Al Smith already owned a brown derby and was active in ward politics.

Smear cartoon of 1928 shows Al inviting Senator Robinson to kiss the Pope's toe.

Republican cartoon shows Smith playing wet with a wet voter, while his running mate, Senator Joseph T. Robinson, talks dry to drys.

Whisperers sneered that Al's plump Irish wife was too dowdy for the White House.

President-elect and Mrs. Hoover visited South America on the U.S.S. *Maryland*, in 1928-29. While there he helped settle a boundary dispute between Peru and Chile.

Hoover was born in 1874 in this farmhouse at West Branch, Iowa. His parents were Quakers.

At 17 he was a hard-working geology student at Stanford.

As Secretary of Commerce he wore earphones at his desk to please the infant radio industry.

A Chicken *for* Every Pot

THE Republican Party isn't a *"Poor Man's Party."* Republican prosperity has erased that degrading phrase from our political vocabulary.

The Republican Party is *equality's* party—*opportunity's* party—*democracy's* party, the party of *national* development, not *sectional* interests—the *impartial* servant of every State and condition in the Union.

Under higher tariff and lower taxation, America has stabilized output, employment and dividend rates.

Republican efficiency has filled the workingman's dinner pail—and his gasoline tank *besides*—made telephone, radio and sanitary plumbing *standard* household equipment. And placed the whole nation in the *silk stocking* class.

During eight years of Republican management, we have built more and better homes, erected more skyscrapers, passed more benefactory laws, and more laws to regulate and purify immigration, inaugurated more conservation measures, more measures to standardize and increase production, expand export markets, and reduce industrial and human junk piles, than in any previous quarter century.

Republican prosperity is written on *fuller* wage envelops, written in factory chimney smoke, written on the walls of new construction, written in savings bank books, written in mercantile balances, and written in the peak value of stocks and bonds.

Republican prosperity has *reduced* hours and *increased* earning capacity, silenced *discontent*, put the proverbial "chicken in every pot." And a car in every backyard, to boot.

It has *raised* living standards and *lowered* living costs.

It has restored financial confidence and enthusiasm, changed *credit* from a *rich* man's privilege to a *common*

utility, *generalized* the use of time-saving devices and released women from the thrall of *domestic drudgery.*

It has provided every county in the country with its concrete road and knitted the highways of the nation into a *unified* traffic system.

Thanks to Republican administration, farmer, dairyman and merchant can make deliveries in *less* time and at *less* expense, can borrow *cheap* money to re-fund exorbitant mortgages, and stock their pastures, ranges and shelves.

Democratic management *impoverished* and *demoralized* the railroads, led packing plants and tire factories into *receivership*, squandered billions on *impractical* programs.

Democratic mal-administration issued *further* billions on mere "scraps of paper," then encouraged foreign debtors to believe that their loans would never be called, and bequeathed to the Republican Party the job of *mopping up the mess.*

Republican administration has *restored* to the railroads solvency, efficiency and par securities.

It has brought the rubber trades through panic and chaos, brought down the prices of crude rubber by smashing *monopolistic rings*, put the tanner's books in the *black* and secured from the European powers formal acknowledgment of their obligations.

The Republican Party rests its case on a record of stewardship and performance.

Its Presidential and Congressional candidates stand for election on a platform of sound practice, Federal vigilance, high tariff, Constitutional integrity, the conservation of natural resources, *honest* and *constructive* measures for agricultural relief, sincere enforcement of the laws, and the right of *all* citizens, regardless of *faith* or *origin*, to share the benefits of opportunity and justice.

Wages, dividends, progress and prosperity say,

"Vote *for* Hoover"

Contributed by a Friend of Mr. Hoover.   Advertisement.

"The slogan of progress is changing from the full dinner pail to the full garage," said Hoover, in a 1928 campaign speech. Above, a famous Republican newspaper ad.

THE GREAT ENGINEER

HERBERT HOOVER might seem cold in manner beside Al Smith, but his vision of the American future was warm and glamorous. "The poorhouse is vanishing from among us," said Hoover in 1928. "Given a chance to go forward with the policies of the last eight years, we shall soon, with the help of God, be in sight of the day when poverty will be banished from this nation." Prosperity and efficiency, and "rugged individualism," were the themes of the victorious Republicans, and Hoover was a sturdy embodiment of these virtues. Born in a small Midwest town, orphaned at the age of ten, he had mastered the techniques of mining and business, made $4 million in foreign enterprises, and returned to the United States during the war to enter public service and politics. Harding named him Secretary of Commerce, and he held the post for eight years, finding many opportunities to aid business in evading the Sherman Antitrust Law. In 1927 he won popularity and publicity by bringing quick relief to the victims of the Mississippi floods. The jealous President Coolidge might sneer at him as "the wonder boy." But in 1928 the nation accepted him as the "Great Engineer" who would organize prosperity on a permanent basis.

NIGHTMARE IN WALL STREET

THURSDAY, OCTOBER 24, 1929, was a cool and cloudy day in the eastern United States, with slight tremors of nervousness in the region of lower Manhattan. At the usual hour of 10 A.M. the gong rang in the New York Stock Exchange, and the tape began its stuttering motion in tickers across the land. The Coolidge bull market had grown bigger under Hoover, despite some feeble efforts by the Federal Reserve Board to restrict it. When the Reserve Board tried to limit loans to brokers, private bankers, led by Charles E. Mitchell of the National City Bank, rushed up and shoveled more money into the market. The Bethlehem Steel Corporation, Standard Oil of New Jersey, General Motors, the Aluminum Company of America, and other big corporations also opened their treasuries to the demand for "call money" —in a short time such "bootleg loans" reached a total of $750 million. While the market fattened on these new offerings Professor Irving Fisher of Yale coined a felicitous phrase: the prices of stocks, he said, had reached "what looks like a permanently high plateau."

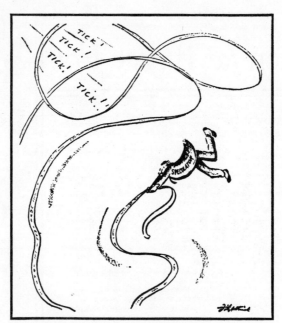

This cartoon version of a speculator's nightmare was drawn in 1929 by D. R. Fitzpatrick of the St. Louis *Post-Dispatch*.

On the morning of October 24, in the first few minutes of trading, some unusually large sales were recorded—20,000 shares of Kennecott Copper at 78, 20,000 shares of General Motors at 56½. Brokers wondered who was selling such large blocks —and why? They talked with their customers, and selling increased. By 11 o'clock a flood of orders to "sell at the market" was pouring in. Prices dropped with each sale: U. S. Steel, which had touched 261¾ in September, fell to 193½. Radio was down from 101 to 44½. The ticker was swamped, and all over the country no owner of stocks could tell what his holdings were worth. The result was a sellers' panic.

Shortly after 12 o'clock five of the city's leading bank presidents met with Thomas W. Lamont of J. P. Morgan & Company and raised a $240 million emergency fund to steady the market. At 1:30 P.M. Richard Whitney, floor man for the Morgan firm, walked up to the trading post for Big Steel and bid 205 for 25,000 shares. Then he strolled around to other posts, buying large blocks of key stocks at the last previous price. In a few minutes he poured between $20 and $30 million on the market's wounds. The effect was encouraging—prices steadied, and some (including Steel) even closed higher for the day. But the strain had been ghastly; the ticker was four hours and eight minutes late, and when it finally stopped chattering it had listed a record 13 million shares sold, and a net loss of $11 billion.

Things looked a little better on Friday and Saturday. Sales were still very heavy, but prices held fairly well. Then on Monday there was another collapse, which the bankers made no effort to stop. On Tuesday, the 29th, the bottom really fell out: leading stocks dropped $40, $50, and even $60 a share; more than 16 million shares were sold. The New York *World* called it "a financial nightmare, comparable to nothing ever before experienced in Wall Street." Yet the very next day the expiring bull market took wistful hope from the voice of an ancient master of capital. John D. Rockefeller, Sr., aged 90, announced: "Believing that fundamental conditions of the country are sound . . . my son and I have for some days been purchasing sound common stocks." Prices improved slightly, and the Stock Exchange governors declared a two-day holiday. But all such palliatives were temporary: prices fell, and fell again, and on the black day of November 13 they fell to the lowest of the year. By that time $50 billion had been eroded from the "permanently high plateau." That was the crash, the death of the big bull market, and the end of Normalcy.

Somber crowds gathered at the Stock Exchange during the crash. Thousands rushed to pawn jewelry or silver to raise "more margin." Some committed suicide. "In Wall Street every wall is wet by tears," reported one newspaper.

These gloomy railroad presidents were photographed on the White House lawn in 1929. They had just promised President Hoover to "spend millions" on a recovery program.

"JUST AROUND THE CORNER"

This jobless veteran maintained his "ragged individualism" by selling apples.

IN OCTOBER 1929 President Hoover declared: "The fundamental business of the country . . . is on a sound and prosperous basis." In January 1930 he said there were "definite signs" that the nation had "turned the corner." In March he predicted that the high point of unemployment would be passed in 60 days. In May he announced: "We have now passed the worst and with continued unity of effort we shall rapidly recover." His words were brave but futile. The crash rolled on, and settled dismally into the depression. The national income dropped from $85 to $37 billion, wages fell off $22 billion, one out of every four farms was sold for taxes. At the end of 1930 there were 3 million unemployed; by 1933 there were 15 million. Five thousand banks closed their doors. Private construction came to an end.

But dividend and interest payments rose to an all-time high of $8 billion in 1931, and never fell lower than the level of 1928. Investors generally continued to collect: wage earners and farmers bore the brunt.

As the economic chasm deepened, the leaders of American business enterprise tiptoed fearfully along its edge. They simply didn't know what to do. President Hoover tried to buck them up by lending them government money, but he declined to give any to the unemployed. "I am opposed," he said, "to any direct or indirect government dole."

The unemployed stood in line for bread and local relief. Depositors stood in line before breaking banks. Farmers stood in line—with shotguns—to stop tax and foreclosure sales.

Andrew W. Mellon, the richest Secretary of the Treasury in American history, didn't think the depression was so bad. His plan for recovery included more wage cuts and less work.

Al Capone was jailed in 1932 for falsifying his income tax. During the 1920's he eliminated his competitors by mur-der, and made Chicago bootlegging a big business. This photograph shows him fishing from his Florida houseboat.

Samuel Insull fled to Greece in 1932, when his utility empire crashed. He was extradited, jailed, and acquitted.

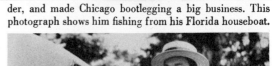

Jimmy Walker, New York's playboy mayor, quit under fire when his shady financial affairs were exposed in 1932.

John Nance Garner of Texas became Speaker of the House after the voters went Democratic in 1930. He attacked Republican tax schemes and jeered Mellon out of the Treasury.

Fiorello La Guardia, New York Republican, was labor's spokesman in Congress.

James A. Farley, New York Democrat, boomed Franklin Roosevelt for President.

FACES OF THE TIMES

THE COLLAPSE of "Republican prosperity" brought gleeful smiles to the faces of veteran Democrats. The House of Representatives rocked with derisive laughter when someone referred to "Uncle Andy" Mellon as the "greatest Secretary of the Treasury since Alexander Hamilton." Mellon had sat in Republican Cabinets since 1921. His policy of reducing and refunding huge blocks of income taxes had added millions to his personal fortune and to the profits of his aluminum, oil, and banking companies. It had also contributed heavily to the bull market, and the crash. Now Mellon suggested that the Government again cut income taxes (which only a few well-to-do people paid) and eliminate estate taxes entirely. The Democrats charged he was trying to make more millions for himself and his family. They pointed to an old law which prohibited a Secretary of the Treasury from engaging in business, and threatened to impeach him "for high crimes and misdemeanors." President Hoover promptly kicked Mellon upstairs to be Ambassador to Great Britain.

As the nation rounded the corner into the 1930's, other familiar faces fell from favor, while new ones rose to fame and fortune.

Japan's seizure of Manchuria ended a decade of treaty-making and relative peace. But Americans were too involved with the depression to care.

THE END OF

On the night of September 18, 1931, a bridge blew up on the South Manchuria Railroad, and with it went a sheaf of treaties. The bridge was in China, but it was owned by Japan and guarded by the Japanese Army. Within 24 hours Japanese troops swarmed out of their barracks in Mukden and took over every key city on 693 miles of the railway. Japanese warships landed soldiers in the Chinese port of Tsingtao, and Japanese planes bombed the fleeing Chinese in Manchuria. There was every indication that the bridge explosion was the signal for a well-arranged plan of conquest.

From Washington, Secretary of State Henry L. Stimson quickly reminded Japan of its obligations under the Nine-Power Treaty and the Kellogg-Briand Pact. Japan replied that it was not breaking any treaties—just keeping order. Stimson asked the League of Nations to act, and the League Council "invoked" the Pact of Paris. But Japan ignored the League. A League commission with an American major general among its members was sent to investigate, but this did not stop the Japanese Army.

Benito Mussolini watched Japan successfully defy the League of Nations, and decided to do it too. The *Duce* had been bossing Italy since 1922.

Adolf Hitler and his Nazis were on the march against the Treaty of Versailles. In 1933 they burned the Reichstag and seized control of Germany.

THE TREATIES

Stimson then declared that the United States "does not intend to recognize any situation, treaty, or agreement" which might be brought about in China by methods contrary to the Kellogg-Briand Pact—*i.e.*, by military force. Japan replied by conquering all Manchuria and transforming it into the puppet state of Manchukuo. A leading Japanese statesman. Viscount Ishii, solemnly warned that if the United States should try to stop Japan's "pacific and natural expansion in this part of the world, then, indeed, a grave situation would be created."

In the face of this, Stimson was stymied. Great Britain and France declined to join his program of nonrecognition—they preferred to string along with the League, where the general helplessness could be shared among many nations. And most of Stimson's fellow citizens were more distressed by the depression than by military lawlessness in the Far East.

"The American people," said the Philadelphia *Record*, "don't give a hoot in a rain barrel who controls North China."

Secretary of State Henry L. Stimson, a onetime protégé of Teddy Roosevelt, tried vainly to revive the Big Stick against Japanese aggression.

The first bonus marchers left Portland, Oregon, in May 1932, and took four weeks to reach Washington. They were organized in military squads.

In June bonus army recruits were pouring in from every part of the country. Above, a New York City contingent.

THE BONUS BOYS

AN ARMY of lean and jobless veterans converged on Washington in the early summer of 1932. Congress had voted them a bonus of about $1,000 apiece, payable in 20 years. But they needed the money now, and they came to get it. One night in July 10,000 of them gathered at the Capitol steps while the Senate voted. Word came out that the vote was No, and a spasm of anger ran through the crowd. If one man had started a rush up the steps there would have been a riot. But someone began to sing "My country, 'tis of thee," and the whole "bonus army" joined in. Then they went back to their tar-paper shacks and greasy soup kitchens and

These bonus marchers arrived from California on the night of July 12, paraded around the Capitol, and then settled down to sleep on the grass, despite police orders to "move on."

On July 28, army tanks rumbled up Pennsylvania Avenue toward the Capitol to join the attack on the bonus veterans.

General Douglas MacArthur *(left)* and Major Dwight Eisenhower watch their troops burn a bonus camp. Below, a bonus army cartoon of Hoover.

hand-dug latrines (which they nicknamed "Hoover Villas") in Anacostia Flats. In the days that followed many of them left Washington, but others stayed on with their families, because they had no particular place to return to. On July 28 President Hoover ordered the United States Army to get rid of these remnants. The Army moved in with tear gas, bayonets, sabers, and torches: an 11-week-old baby died from the gassing, two unarmed veterans were killed, and scores (including women and children) were hurt. It was a sad and bitter climax to the regime of the Great Engineer.

Camp Marks, which had housed 20,000 bonus marchers, burned all night. "Thank God," said President Hoover, "we still have a government . . . that knows how to deal with a mob."

Maryland's Ritchie was a favorite son.

"THE SKIES ABOVE

WHILE THE bonus marchers were still camped in Washington, an army of happy Democrats convened in Chicago. Victory was in the air which blew across Lake Michigan, for the country was deathly sick of Hooverism. "Happy days are here again! The skies above are clear again," warbled the confident supporters of Franklin D. Roosevelt of New York. Governor Roosevelt's plurality of 725,000 in 1930 had set an all-time record in the Empire State, and he was easily the leading contender for the Presidential nomination. But there was also strong support for Al Smith. And Speaker Jack Garner, the favorite of William Randolph Hearst, had Texas and California sewed up.

After three ballots Roosevelt had 682 votes, but he needed 86 more for a two-thirds majority. Smith had 190, Garner 101, and there were 177 scattered. Long

Al Smith was the favorite of the galleries and most New York delegates in 1932. His repeal speech started a wild stampede on the floor. Massachusetts, Rhode Island, New Jersey, and Connecticut stayed by him to the bitter end.

"Reed Is Our Need," yelled backers of Missouri's ex-Senator James A. Reed. Other delegates were not impressed.

Virginia's ex-Governor Harry F. Byrd was another favorite son who waited hopefully for the lightning to strike.

ARE CLEAR AGAIN"

before the convention the redoubtable Al had developed a bitter feeling toward his successor, and now he refused to yield to him. There was a chance for another party-splitting deadlock like that of 1924. At this point a deal was made—Hearst and his floor manager, William G. McAdoo, switched the Garner votes to Roosevelt, and Garner was given second place on the ticket. McAdoo mounted the platform and shouted, "California came here to nominate a President. . . . California, 44 votes for Roosevelt!" That clinched it, and in Albany the nominee was ready. Boarding a chartered plane, he flew to Chicago and accepted at once, in a speech that tingled with challenge: "Let it be from now on the task of our party to break foolish traditions. . . . I pledge you, I pledge myself, to a new deal for the American people."

New York's F. D. Roosevelt favored beer.

"Cactus Jack" Garner had the support of Texas, California, and Hearst, who was grateful because Garner tried to push his national sales tax scheme in Congress. Garner was featured in the Hearst papers as a "Texas Coolidge."

Jimmy Roosevelt telephones the good news from Chicago to Albany. His father had already heard it on the radio.

The candidate's plane arrives in Chicago on July 2. This was the first air trip ever made by a Presidential nominee.

The steel braces which enabled Roosevelt to stand and walk with a cane on his paralyzed legs are visible in this campaign photograph of him and Jack Garner, at Hyde Park in 1932.

Great-grandfather James Roosevelt was a New York sugar refiner and banker.

This Hudson River mansion was Franklin Roosevelt's birthplace, on January 30, 1882.

Grandfather Isaac Roosevelt was a doctor who never practiced his profession.

"FRANKLIN D. ROOSEVELT is an amiable man . . . who, without any important qualifications for the office, would very much like to be President," wrote Walter Lippmann in 1932. Wealth, personal charm, and a name that recalled the great Teddy were Roosevelt's original assets in politics. His first campaign for state senator, in 1910, was more or less a lark in which he drove around Dutchess County in a red touring car, and wore riding pants to party meetings. At Albany he fought Tammany Boss Charles Murphy; in 1912 he became a fervent disciple of Woodrow Wilson. In wartime Washington he was an able Assistant Secretary of the Navy. In 1921 infantile paralysis crippled his legs, but did not cool his natural warmth or lessen his zest for action.

"AN AMIABLE MAN"

Aged 1½, Franklin sat on the shoulder of his father James.

At 18 he was at Groton. The next fall he entered Harvard.

At 23 he married Anna Eleanor Roosevelt, Teddy's niece.

At 35 he was Assistant Navy Secretary, and a practiced shot.

At 38 (right) he campaigned for Vice President and the League of Nations.

At 39 he vacationed in Canada and caught a chill which developed into poliomyelitis.

At 46 he cut short his convalescence to help Al Smith and was elected Governor.

Franklin Roosevelt enjoyed the campaign. This photograph shows him at Topeka, telling American farmers that the New Deal could help them too. "This Nation cannot endure if it is half 'boom' and half 'broke,'" he said.

Assassin Joe Zangara just missed killing Roosevelt at Miami, February 15, 1933.

"FROM THE

THE CAMPAIGN OF 1932 was a contest between hopelessness and hope. For three years the American people had stumbled deeper into the depression, while their President insisted that the Government could do nothing drastic about it. The same private enterprise which had made the crash must cure it, said Hoover, in effect, and all the Government could do was give blood transfusions to business.

Smilingly, almost gaily, Roosevelt disputed this. The Government could help needy people as well as needy corporations, he asserted. "These unhappy times," he said in a famous speech, "call for ... plans ... that build from the bottom up and not from the top down, that put their faith once more in the forgotten man at the bottom of the economic pyramid." The Democratic platform was written for the "forgotten man." It promised federal relief for the

Herbert Hoover looked beaten and tired. If the New Deal won, he predicted, "the grass will grow in the streets of a hundred cities, a thousand towns; the weeds will overrun the fields . . . churches and schoolhouses will decay."

BOTTOM UP"

unemployed, old-age insurance, repeal of prohibition, regulation of stock exchanges, development of public power, special aid to farmers, a balanced budget, and economy.

These pledges were expounded by Roosevelt in a series of speeches which took him before millions of voters and displayed to the full his bubbling good health and infectious optimism. But it all sounded horrible to Herbert Hoover, who had been renominated by the Republicans. His speeches were heavy with doom. "It is a contest between two philosophies of government," he mourned. "Our opponents . . . are proposing changes and so-called new deals which would destroy the very foundations of our American system." In the election 16 million voted for Hoover's voice of despair, 23 million for Roosevelt's voice of hope.

President Hoover seemed glum and President-elect Roosevelt was talkative on Inauguration Day, March 4, 1933.

"ACTION, AND ACTION NOW"

Between November 8, 1932, when Roosevelt was elected, and March 4, 1933, when he was inaugurated, the United States experienced a creeping economic paralysis which was terrifying to watch. An unprecedented series of conferences between the outgoing President and the incoming President-elect failed to help, for neither was willing to compromise. On February 14 the Governor of Michigan proclaimed a "banking holiday"; other states followed suit, and on the morning of March 4 every bank in the country was shut aaginst its depositors.

At 1:08 p.m. that day the voice of the new President was heard from the steps of the Capitol in Washington, and the nation took new courage from his words:

"I am certain [*said Roosevelt*] that my fellow Americans expect that on my induction into the Presidency I will address them with a candor and a decision which the present situation of our Nation impels. . . . Nor need we shrink from honestly facing conditions in our country today. This great Nation will endure as it has endured, will revive and will prosper. So, first of all, let me assert my firm belief that the only thing we have to fear is fear itself—nameless, unreasoning, unjustified terror which paralyzes needed efforts to convert retreat into advance. . . .

"Our distress comes from no failure of substance. . . . Plenty is at our doorstep, but a generous use of it languishes in the very sight of the supply. Primarily this is because rulers of the exchange of mankind's goods have failed through their own stubbornness and their own incompetence, have admitted their failure, and have abdicated. . . . They have no vision, and where there is no vision the people perish. . . . The money changers have fled from their high seats in the temple of our civilization. . . .

"This Nation asks for action, and action now.

"Our greatest primary task is to put people to work. This is no unsolvable problem if we face it wisely and courageously. It can be accomplished in part by direct recruiting by the Government itself, treating the task as we would treat the emergency of a war. . . . We must endeavor to provide a better use of the land for those best fitted for the land. . . . We require . . . safeguards against a return of the evils of the old order. . . . Our Constitution is so simple and practical that it is possible always to meet extraordinary needs. . . .

"I am prepared under my constitutional duty to recommend the measures that a stricken Nation in the midst of a stricken world may require. These measures, or such other measures as the Congress may build out of its experience and wisdom, I shall seek, within my constitutional authority, to bring to speedy adoption. . . ."

"MY FRIENDS..."

On Sunday evening, March 12, Roosevelt reported directly to the people on the banking crisis. He disclosed that many sound banks had been examined and would be reopened Monday under Treasury supervision. Others would be opened later. "I do not promise you that every bank will be reopened or that individual losses will not be suffered," he said, "but . . . there would have been more and greater losses had we continued to drift."

This was the first of the "fireside chats," with the President sitting at a radio "mike" in the White House, and most of the nation listening in at home.

Rex Tugwell had the Brain Trust's boldest brain. He advocated a planned capitalism.

"There is just one thing to do," Tugwell said. "Take incomes from where they are

. . . and place them where we need them." His method was to control production.

Ray Moley, the Brain Trust's chairman, was a moderate reformer and friend of business.

Adolf Berle, conservative Brain Truster, was an expert on corporation behavior.

Harry Hopkins was the New Deal's expert on relief and depression politics. Though not an original Brain Truster, he became Roosevelt's closest friend and White House companion.

THE BRAIN TRUSTERS

"The country is being run by a group of college professors," growled Senator Henry D. Hatfield of West Virginia. "This Brain Trust is endeavoring to force socialism upon the American people." The "Brain Trust" had its origin in early 1932, when Roosevelt invited Professor Raymond Moley of Columbia University to help him prepare his pre-convention statements and speeches. Moley was an expert on criminal law and a clever handler of words—it was he who scraped the old phrase "forgotten man" from his memory and adapted it to a Roosevelt speech. He also introduced the words "new deal" in a memorandum six weeks before Roosevelt was nominated.

Moley brought Rexford G. Tugwell, of the Columbia economics department, and Adolf A. Berle into the early Brain Trust. Later Bernard Baruch contributed a pair of his business protégés—Hugh Johnson and George Peek. These men worked on Roosevelt's campaign speeches and held important government jobs under the New Deal. But there was nothing new about the Brain Trust—it served President Roosevelt in the same way that Alexander Hamilton served President Washington. Its spirit was well expressed in a few lines of free verse written years before by Tugwell:

I have gathered my tools and my charts;
My plans are fashioned and practical;
I shall roll up my sleeves—
make America over!

THE HUNDRED DAYS

Secretary of State Cordell Hull, an old foe of Republican tariffs, ran the New Deal's foreign trade program. In November 1933 he sent the first American Ambassador to Soviet Russia.

IN ITS FIRST 100 days the New Deal moved ahead with swift and vigorous strides. On March 9 Congress met in special session and passed Roosevelt's Emergency Banking Act in four hours. On March 10 the President sent up an economy bill to cut federal salaries and veterans' benefits; Congress passed it March 11. On March 13 Roosevelt asked for legal beer, and Congress quickly complied.

On March 16 Roosevelt proposed the Agricultural Adjustment Act (AAA), to end farm surpluses by paying farmers to produce less. On March 21 he offered his relief program, including the Federal Emergency Relief Administration (FERA), to give $500 million to the states for direct relief; the Civilian Conservation Corps (CCC), to put 250,000 jobless young men to work in the forests at $1 a day;

Secretary of Labor Frances Perkins, first woman Cabinet member, tried vainly to get a minimum wage law in 1933.

General Hugh ("Old Ironpants") Johnson, ex-cavalry officer, was the hard-hitting boss of the New Deal's NRA.

Secretary of Agriculture Henry A. Wallace ran the New Deal's drive for higher farm prices. In 1933 he sentenced 6 million little pigs to death.

and the Public Works Administration (PWA), to lend and spend $3,300 million for building projects. (The New Deal habit of calling everything by initials was catching—soon the President was universally known as "FDR.")

On March 29 he recommended a Securities and Exchange Commission (SEC) to protect investors against dishonest stock flotations. On April 10 he proposed the Tennessee Valley Authority (TVA). On April 13 he called for the Home Owners' Loan Corporation (HOLC) to slow down mortgage foreclosures. On April 20 he took the United States off the gold standard. On May 17 he asked Congress for the biggest New Deal agency of all—the National Recovery Administration (NRA)—to put industry under self-imposed "codes of fair competition." In

June he accepted a Congressional plan for the Federal Deposit Insurance Corporation (FDIC) to insure all bank deposits up to $5,000. On June 16, exactly 100 days after Congress convened, all of these measures (and many more) had been enacted.

This bubbling "alphabet soup" of boards, bureaus, codes, and corporations was the First New Deal. It was thrown together under great stress and strain, and by no means represented a consistent plan or policy. The first banking bill, for instance, was strictly a conservative device to preserve the nation's private bankers under an oxygen tent until they could operate again on their own. The AAA and NRA were chaotic experiments of dubious constitutionality. But the TVA, SEC, and FDIC were permanent reforms of far-reaching significance.

LABOR'S GIANT

ON LABOR DAY, 1937, John L. Lewis sat beside the radio in his home at Alexandria, Virginia, and listened to his own voice being broadcast from a transcription. "Out of the agony and travail of economic America," said the voice of Lewis, "the Committee for Industrial Organization was born. To millions of Americans, exploited without stint by corporate industry and socially debased beyond the understanding of the fortunate, its coming was as welcome as the dawn to the night watcher." While Lewis registered grave approval of Lewis' words, a photographer snapped his picture *(above)*.

The CIO was an outgrowth of Section 7-A of the NRA bill ("Labor's Magna Charta"), which guaranteed the rights of workers to organize unions and bargain collectively. Among the first to benefit from this clause was the Republican president of the United Mine Workers, John L. Lewis, whose impressive eyebrows and picturesque oratory had long helped to disguise the fact that his union was dwindling in numbers and power. Under Section 7-A it bounced back from 150,000 to 450,000 members. Lewis wanted the American Federation of Labor to follow up this success in other mass industries, but the Federation was too snarled up in the craft-union system to do anything effective. At the 1935 AFL convention Lewis brought the issue into the open and attacked the Federation for "a record of 25 years of constant, unbroken failure." The president of the Carpenters' Union called Lewis a "big bastard," and Lewis knocked him down in public. A fortnight later Lewis and seven other union presidents formed the CIO, which began a sensational drive to organize the steel, auto, and other mass production industries. By 1937 the CIO had 3,718,000 members and was making most of the nation's labor news. And its chairman was John L. Lewis.

ON JUNE 1, 1933, J. Pierpont Morgan, Jr., was sitting in a Senate committee room when a Ringling Brothers circus press agent thrust a female midget on his lap. The incident produced a famous photograph *(above)* and a momentary scandal among the Senators, who wanted to question Morgan about the causes of the depression. A little later another group of Senators hauled Morgan on the carpet again to find out what he and other bankers and munitions makers had done to inveigle the United States into war in 1917. Isolationism reached its peak in the mid-1930's with advertisements showing a veteran in a wheel chair under the headline "HELLO, SUCKER." In 1935 Congress passed a law which prohibited the sale of munitions to either side in case of another war.

MORGAN'S MIDGET

"Franklin Double-Cross Roosevelt is a betrayer," shouted Father Coughlin *(right)*. He had his own party in 1936.

THE PERSPIRING PRIEST

THE REVEREND Charles E. Coughlin of Royal Oak, Michigan, was the most popular priest in America in the early 1930's. Five million listeners heard his harsh Irish-Canadian brogue every Sunday, discussing national problems over the Columbia Broadcasting System; tens of thousands sent him dollar bills in the mail. Father Coughlin was regarded as a friend of the New Deal—he had his own "brain trust," and his own pet scheme to save the country. "The restoration of silver to its proper value is of Christian concern," he intoned. "I send you a call for the mobilization of all Christianity against the god of gold." Then the Treasury disclosed that Father Coughlin, through his secretary, was holding 500,000 ounces of silver for a rise in price. His popularity decreased, and he turned against the New Deal. FDR was "anti-God" and a "scab," he rasped. In 1936 Father Coughlin went off the air. But in 1937 he came back, praising Adolf Hitler and denouncing "world Jewry."

Dr. Carl A. Weiss *(left)* put an end to Huey Long's hillbilly dictatorship before it could spread outside Louisiana.

"He's a liar and a faker!" cried Huey Long *(left)* of FDR. "We're just a couple of politicians, him and me," he added.

AND THE DIXIE DICTATOR

ANOTHER DEPRESSION demagogue was Senator Huey P. Long, who also began by supporting the New Deal, and then became Roosevelt's most dangerous enemy in Congress. The red-haired, puffy-faced, cynical "Kingfish" was an amusing political clown to look at and listen to, but he was also the first modern American dictator. "I can buy legislators like sacks of potatoes," he had boasted while Governor of Louisiana, and he fastened his ruthless personal rule on that state by brazen corruption and sheer gall. His "Share the Wealth" scheme was as potent a doctrine in its way as Hitler's National Socialism: it promised every American an income of $5,000 a year, to be paid for by confiscating all fortunes of more than $50 million and all incomes over $1 million. Huey seriously worried FDR and Jim Farley as a third-party threat to Democratic success in 1936. But long before the election Huey was assassinated by a public-spirited Louisiana citizen in the state house at Baton Rouge.

The shooting of Huey Long *(right)* was painted by John McCrady. Huey's guards pumped 61 bullets into young Dr. Weiss.

"The nine old men" of the Supreme Court gave the New Deal its first important defeat. They were *(left to right,* *standing)* Roberts, Butler, Stone, Cardozo, *(seated)* Brandeis, Van Devanter, Hughes, McReynolds, Sutherland.

THE NINE OLD MEN
KILL THE NRA

IN WASHINGTON, in their cozy little chamber in the Capitol basement, the Justices of the Supreme Court pondered the matter of some "unfit chickens" in Brooklyn. When they finished pondering, on May 27, 1935, they dealt the New Deal a savage blow.

The "unfit chickens," according to the National Recovery Administration, had been sold for consumption by the Schechter Poultry Corporation, in

FROM BLUE EAGLE TO DEAD CHICKEN

In the early years of the New Deal the Blue Eagle of the NRA was the omnipresent symbol of "Roosevelt recovery." It was pasted in refrigerators and automobiles, carried in parades, stamped on boxes of breakfast food, and hung in millions of windows. Under the Blue Eagle 700 industries employing 23 million workers imposed codes of fair competition on themselves. The original "blanket code," which served as model for many individual codes, abolished child labor and set a minimum wage of 30 cents an hour. Big business generally liked the NRA, for it permitted certain aspects of monopoly. But consumers, labor, and little business distrusted it, and it expired (as Hugh Johnson had predicted) in a welter of "dead cats" and recriminations.

Blue Eagle window cards were proudly displayed by storekeepers when NRA started.

"That Ought to Jolt Him" shows the Blue Eagle stinging the depression in 1933.

The five young men of the Schechter Poultry Corporation celebrate the demise of NRA in their office in Brooklyn: *(left to right)* Martin Schechter, Aaron Schechter, Joseph Heller (their lawyer), Joseph Schechter, Alex Schechter.

flagrant violation of the Live Poultry Code of Fair Competition. Furthermore, said the NRA, the Schechters paid wages lower than the minimum set by the Code. Therefore the NRA had "cracked down" on the Schechter Poultry Corporation.

To these charges the Corporation replied that (1) it was none of the NRA's business what kind of chickens it sold, for it bought them in New York City and did not engage in interstate commerce; and (2) the NRA was unconstitutional, because it delegated legislative powers to the executive branch of the Government. The Supreme Court agreed unanimously with both these arguments.

President Roosevelt received the news with some heat. "We have been relegated," he said, "to the horse-and-buggy definition of interstate commerce."

"Heat Lightning" shows the Eagle getting stung itself during a Hugh Johnson row.

"The Missing Cog" shows a business chiseler stealing the gear from the Eagle's claw.

Nailed to the wall by the Supreme Court, the Blue Eagle hangs limp and forlorn.

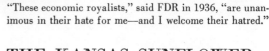

"These economic royalists," said FDR in 1936, "are unanimous in their hate for me—and I welcome their hatred."

THE KANSAS SUNFLOWER

A yellow sunflower with petals of cloth and a friendly businessman's face in the center *(left)* was the symbol of Republican hopes in 1936. The Republican candidate was Governor Alfred M. Landon of Kansas, a wealthy oilman with a personality which evoked such newspaper adjectives as "sound" and "simple." "I think Landon is marvelous," said William Randolph Hearst, and the economic royalists of the East agreed. While they poured millions into his campaign chest, the Republican press built up a picture of "Frugal Alf," "the poor man's Coolidge," and the "Horse and Buggy Governor." Landon coined one clever phrase—"I believe a man can be a liberal without being a spendthrift!"—but most of his speeches were keyed to the "Save-America-from-that-man-in-the-White-House" theme. His running mate, Frank Knox, shouted hysterically to the voters: "Your life insurance and your savings accounts are already in danger!" In November the sunflower withered—Alf Landon was the worst-beaten major-party candidate in American history. He carried Maine and Vermont, and got 17 million votes. But FDR had 28 million votes, and the rest of the 46 states.

FDR AT HIS PEAK

THE END OF THE NRA brought only a brief pause in the onward rush of the Second—and bigger—New Deal. In January 1935 the President gave a foretaste of what was coming in his annual message to Congress. "We find our population suffering from old inequalities," he reported. "In spite of our efforts and in spite of our talk, we have not weeded out the overprivileged and we have not effectively lifted up the underprivileged." New, huge, far-reaching bills were run through the Congressional mill to accomplish these aims. The Social Security Act of 1935 set up old-age and unemployment insurance systems for 26 million employed Americans. The Wagner-Connery Labor Relations Act re-enacted Section 7-A with sharp teeth to bite backward employers. The Strikebreaker Act made interstate transportation of strikebreakers a crime. The Works Progress Administration (WPA) offered semipermanent "made work" relief to the nine million able-bodied Americans who were still unemployed. The National Youth Administration (NYA) assisted in the education and training of 600,000 younger victims of the depression. The Resettlement Administration (RA) aided sharecroppers and submarginal farmers. The Rural Electrification Administration (REA) financed consumer-owned power companies. The Public Utility Act inflicted a "death sentence" on private utility holding companies which did not operate integrated systems. In June the President sent Congress his "Soak the Rich" message, and in August Congress obediently raised taxes on large personal and corporate incomes.

Reform, rather than recovery, was the keynote of the Second New Deal. Labor and the unemployed were its chief beneficiaries, as bankers, businessmen, and farmers had been of the First. It was immediately and continuously attacked, but it was popular with large blocs of voters, and it carried FDR in triumph through the 1936 campaign. In his speech accepting renomination in Philadelphia that year, the President used words which raised the hackles of Republican and Democratic conservatives alike. "The royalists of the economic order," he proclaimed, "have conceded that political freedom was the business of the Government, but they have maintained that economic slavery was nobody's business. . . . These economic royalists complain that we seek to overthrow the institutions of America. What they really complain of is that we seek to take away their power."

With his overwhelming election victory behind him, Roosevelt turned his attention to the only branch of the Government which was still in old guard hands—the Supreme Court. None too gently he urged the "nine old men" to wake up and follow the election returns. On February 5, 1937, he sent to Congress a bill to add as many as six new Justices to the Supreme Court, and 44 new judges to the other federal courts, in all cases where judges had refused to retire at 70. There were, he said, too many "aged or infirm" men on the bench who just didn't understand "the facts of an ever-changing world." But for once he had struck an unpopular issue, and the newspapers and Senators knew it. "COURT-PACKING," shrieked the headlines; "needless, futile, and utterly dangerous," fumed the Senate Judiciary Committee. In the midst of the furor one of the "old men" resigned and the President appointed a New Deal Senator from Alabama, Hugo Black, to succeed him. The Pittsburgh *Post-Gazette* published evidence that Black had once been a member of the Ku Klux Klan, and this heaped more ashes on FDR's head. Black took his seat on the bench, but the Roosevelt plan to enlarge the Court was beaten by the narrow margin of one committee vote. The New Deal never quite recovered from the shock.

Justice Owen J. Roberts pivoted the Supreme Court to a more moderate position.

Justice Hugo Black, first New Dealer on the Court, proved an embarrassing choice.

427

After hauling the New Deal through four feverish years, Congress kicked up its heels in revolt against the "court packing" plan.

THE KICKBACK

Roosevelt's foray against the Supreme Court was stoutly resisted by leading Democratic Senators, and the result was a damaging split in the President's party. Postmaster General Jim Farley tried to strong-arm the opposition by declaring that Senators who had ridden into office "on the President's coattails" should vote for his bill. This infuriated the Senators and insured the defeat of the bill. But while Congress was getting completely out of hand the "nine old men" demurely made peace with the New Deal by suddenly approving the Wagner Act, the Social Security Act, and other key reforms.

428

"What We Need Is Another Pump" is a satire on the New Deal's "pump priming" deficits. While FDR poured $8½ billion into the "emergency," he insisted he was balancing the "regular" budget.

"Just Another Hole" shows FDR tinkering happily with the United States currency. In January 1934 he ended an international exchange war by stabilizing the dollar's gold value at 59.06 cents.

Copyright, 1947, New York Tribune Inc.

"Back Talk from the Dummy" shows Congress refusing to play Charlie McCarthy to FDR's Edgar Bergen. The majority of newspapers, magazines, and cartoonists opposed the Second New Deal.

"His Convenient Other Self" is an attack on the President's role in the 1938 Senatorial primaries, when he endorsed his friends and tried—unsuccessfully—to "purge" some of his prominent foes.

The great drought and dust storms of 1934 ravaged a dozen states and enlarged the New Deal's relief problems. Above, Lamar, Colorado, at the height of "the blow."

Below, auto workers on a sit-down strike in a plant at Flint, Michigan. In 1937 the aggressive CIO signed up General Motors but was still stalemated by Henry Ford.

"I see one third of a nation ill-housed, ill-clad, ill-nourished," said FDR in his second inaugural. Above, two migrant families en route to the California pea fields.

Below, Chicago cops charge CIO pickets at the Republic Steel plant, May 30, 1937. Ten workers were killed, eight shot in the back. But Big Steel signed with the union.

The building of Norris Dam, on the Clinch River near Knoxville, was one of TVA's first big jobs. This photograph was taken at dusk, with the lights going on for the night shift.

TVA—THE YARDSTICK

THE TENNESSEE VALLEY AUTHORITY was a giant undertaking, but its basic idea was simple—to harness the powerful Tennessee River for the benefit of the 4½ million people who lived in its valley.

The power of the Tennessee begins in the Great Smoky Mountains, where the rain falls at the rate of 6,000 tons on an acre of land in a year. Moving, as it must, toward the ocean, this inexhaustible blanket of water drops thousands of feet through the funnels of hundreds of little streams and unites in the Tennessee, which flows 652 miles and falls another 508 feet before entering the Ohio at Paducah, Kentucky. Before TVA almost all this power had been lost in floods and waste, while 98 per cent of the homes along its route were without electricity. TVA ended the floods, opened the river to commerce as far as Knoxville, captured two million kilowatts of electricity, electrified 500,000 homes and businesses, saved millions of acres of eroded lands through improved farming techniques, and made possible the great war plants of Oak Ridge and Muscle Shoals. Its principal tools were 16 big and architecturally beautiful dams which it built on the river and its tributaries. Private utility firms charged that TVA was unfair competition because it paid no taxes. But this was untrue: it was required by Congress to pay sums in lieu of taxes which were as much as or more than its private competitors paid.

As a "yardstick" for computing the fairness of private utility rates, TVA was extremely important. But it was even more important as a yardstick for measuring 100 years of rugged individualism—during which the Tennessee River had run away to waste and destruction—against a decade of intelligent public planning.

Senator George W. Norris of Nebraska, for whom Norris Dam was named, fought many years for TVA. He tried to start it in the 1920's, but Coolidge and Hoover vetoed his bills.

"WAR IS A CONTAGION"

On October 5, 1937, President Roosevelt stood behind a battery of microphones in Chicago and dedicated a new bridge. The occasion called, perhaps, for peaceful platitudes; instead, the President talked of war. "The peace, the freedom and the security of ninety per cent of the population of the world is being jeopardized by the remaining ten per cent," he said. "It seems to be unfortunately true that the epidemic of world lawlessness is spreading. When an epidemic of physical disease starts to spread, the community approves and joins in a quarantine. . . . War is a contagion, whether it be declared or undeclared. . . . We are determined to keep out of war, yet we cannot insure ourselves against the disastrous effects of war and the dangers of involvement."

"I don't believe there will be war just yet," said Republican Senator William E. Borah in July 1939. In September the war began.

The aggressors formed an anti-American alliance in 1940, when Saburo Kurusu conferred with Adolph Hitler *(center pair)*.

THE MARCH OF AGGRESSION

All the major treaties of the twenties were broken before the thirties were half over. Japan started it in 1931. Germany tore up the Treaty of Versailles (1935), took over the Rhineland (1936), seized Austria (1938), partitioned Czechoslovakia with British and French consent (1938-1939), invaded Poland and started World War II (September 1, 1939). Italy conquered Ethiopia (1935-1936), set up a dictatorship in Spain (1936-1939), grabbed Albania (1939), and stabbed France in the back (June 1940). Japan provoked an all-out war with China (1937) and proclaimed a "New Order" (Japanese) for East Asia (1939).

This Spanish Republican soldier was one of the early victims of aggression. He died fighting the Franco Fascist revolt of 1936.

Emperor Haile Selassie of Ethiopia rode out under an umbrella to fight the Italians in 1935. But Fascist planes defeated him.

Japan's Air Force deliberately sank the U.S.S. *Panay* in China in 1937, killing two sailors. Japan's Government apologized.

Chinese civilians were slaughtered by hundreds of thousands by Japanese planes and troops. These are Shanghai bombing victims.

Polish civilians were hanged by the German Army in 1939. But Red Russia made a deal with Hitler and grabbed most of Poland.

French civilians wept as the Nazis swept through their country in 1940, after conquering Denmark, Norway, Belgium, and Holland.

"WE WANT
WILLKIE"

ON A HOT, dusty day in August 1940, Wendell L. Willkie stood up in the back seat of an automobile and charged down Main Street in Elwood, Indiana *(right)*. From a scaffold in Callaway Park that afternoon he looked out over the biggest political rally ever gathered in the United States (200,000 people) and roared defiance at Franklin Roosevelt. "I cannot follow the President in his conduct of foreign affairs in this critical time," cried Willkie. "He has dabbled in inflammatory statements and manufactured panics. . . . He has courted a war for which this country is hopelessly unprepared—and which it emphatically does not want." Then he opened up on the domestic front. "The New Deal has failed," he rumbled. "We must substitute for the philosophy of spending the philosophy of production. . . . Only the strong can be free, and only the productive can be strong."

Willkie was a unique phenomenon in American politics. Six months before the Elwood speech he was known mainly as the president of the billion-dollar Commonwealth and Southern Corporation, and the principal utility foe of TVA. Then he wrote an eloquent article for *Fortune,* asking politicians in general to "abandon this attitude of hate" toward business. In April a little group of New York disciples began organizing Willkie-for-President clubs. In June, when the Republican convention met in Philadelphia, the galleries were packed with irrepressible amateurs shouting, "We want Willkie!" Experienced reporters called it a miracle when Willkie—who had been a Democrat most of his life — snatched the Republican nomination from Vandenberg, Dewey, and Taft.

After Elwood, Willkie barnstormed across the country for 51 days and 18,579 miles in an exhibition of driving personal energy that eclipsed any since the Teddy Roosevelt campaign of 1900. But his appeal was handicapped by two contradictions: (1) he attacked Roosevelt's anti-Hitler policy and also supported it, and (2) he attacked the New Deal and promised to keep its major reforms.

Photographers for the new picture magazine *Life* went behind the scenes in 1940 and made the best photographic record ever compiled of the inner workings of a political convention. The *Life* picture at right was taken in Harry Hopkins' third-term headquarters as "Harry the Hop" *(in shirtsleeves)* and Mayor Kelly of Chicago planned the Roosevelt "draft." On the next page, *Life's* photographer shows a group of influential Roosevelt supporters at dinner: *(right to left, in clockwise order)* Henry Wallace, who was FDR's choice for Vice President; Frances Perkins, Harold Ickes, Attorney General Robert Jackson, Jesse Jones, Mayor Kelly, and Mayor Frank Hague of Jersey City.

"MISTER THIRD TERM CANDIDATE"

"The Suspense Is Terrific" shows everyone waiting for FDR to say yes in 1940.

THE FEAR of war and Wendell Willkie hung over the Democratic convention which met in July. And looming up dangerously ahead was one of the most deeply embedded taboos in American politics—the anti-third-term tradition. FDR had not said whether he would run again or not. But his silence and evasion had already smothered the candidacies of every other Democrat, including Vice President Garner and "Genial Jim" Farley, the party's faithful chairman. Farley arrived at Chicago in a bitter mood; he had a small bloc of votes pledged to him, and he announced that his name would go before the delegates, regardless of what the President did.

The President, apparently, did nothing except stay in Washington and work. But his White House crony, Harry Hopkins, was in Chicago, in a smoke-filled suite of rooms at the Blackstone Hotel, with a direct telephone wire to Roosevelt's desk. To visiting delegates and bosses Hopkins let it be known that FDR would not refuse to be "drafted." Mayor Ed Kelly of Chicago arranged the details, and the "draft" came through on the first ballot. The delegates were resigned rather than enthused—they simply did not want to change Presidents in the middle of a world war. Roosevelt seemed to have the same divided feelings—in an acceptance speech delivered over the loud-speaker at 12:25 A.M. he spoke of his "deep per-

sonal desire for retirement on the one hand," and the "obligation to serve" on the other. "I shall not have the time or the inclination to engage in purely political debate," he added.

But he said nothing about the third-term issue. Wendell Willkie pounded him hard for that. "Just think," thundered Willkie, "here is a candidate that assumes that out of 131 million people he is the sole and only indispensable man." FDR did not reply.

The unofficial rule that no President should serve more than two terms was first stated by Thomas Jefferson, who retired in 1808 while he was still the nation's dominant figure, during a world war which threatened the United States. (Washington's retirement 12 years earlier was for personal reasons—he had no objection to an indefinite number of terms.) Jefferson's example was followed by Madison, Monroe, and Jackson. It was defied by Grant and Theodore Roosevelt, who both tried for third terms, and were beaten. Calvin Coolidge may have been looking for a third-term detour when he made his famous "I do not choose to run for President in 1928" statement—but if so, he outsmarted himself. Under the impact of the new world war, the old tradition gave way. Willkie's 22 million votes set a record for the Republicans. But Roosevelt's 27 million won.

This Republican songsheet made an issue of son Elliott Roosevelt's army rank.

DEMOCRACY'S ARSENAL

Democratic Senator Burton K. Wheeler of Montana said Lend-Lease would "plow under every fourth American boy."

"I CANNOT ASK that every American remain neutral in thought," said President Roosevelt when the Second World War began. And most Americans were not neutral—they hated Hitler, and wanted to see the democracies win. They wanted to stay out of the war, but they fully expected to be drawn in. When France fell and England reeled under the Nazi "blitz," the chances for staying out decreased. Congress voted for a two-ocean Navy, 50,000 airplanes, and peacetime conscription of military manpower. William Allen White organized a nation-wide citizens' Committee to Defend America by Aiding the Allies. President Roosevelt formed a bipartisan Cabinet, with Republicans heading the War and Navy Departments. In September he gave England 50 American destroyers and received in return eight naval bases on British islands or possessions. This bold step was taken at the height of the Presidential campaign, and Willkie called it "the most dictatorial action ever taken by any President." The same month Roosevelt embargoed scrap-iron shipments to Japan, and tried to bolster up China with loans.

After the election, he called for broader measures—"We must be the great arsenal of democracy," he said in December 1940. In January 1941 he disclosed his Lend-Lease plan to send Hitler's foes everything they needed on credit. Despite fierce opposition from the isolationists, Congress approved Lend-Lease, and the flow of American guns, tanks, shells, and planes to the fighting fronts became heavy enough to seriously impair Axis chances for victory.

Bands of isolationist "mothers" roamed Washington during the Lend-Lease debate, praying on the pavements.

Draftees of 1940 take the army oath in Boston. The nation's first peacetime draft registered 16 million men.

U. S. destroyers traded to England in 1940 rest at anchor while American and British gunners exchange information.

American troops land in Iceland July 1941, to guard supply routes from Nazi "rattlesnakes of the Atlantic."

President Roosevelt and Prime Minister Churchill singing hymns on the *Prince of Wales,* Sunday, August 10, 1941.

They sang "O God, Our Help in Ages Past," "Onward, Christian Soldiers," and "Eternal Father, Strong to Save."

THE TWO ATLANTIC CHARTERS

On August 3, 1941, President Roosevelt sailed out of New London, Connecticut, on his yacht, the *Potomac,* for what he called "a fishing trip." He did fish one day off Martha's Vineyard. Then he was transferred secretly to the cruiser *Augusta* and headed for Placentia Bay in Newfoundland, where he arrived August 8. The next morning the new British battleship *Prince of Wales* dropped anchor near by, and semaphores flapped a greeting from the *Augusta.* Would Prime Minister Winston Churchill come to the President's cabin for lunch? The stout, indomitable "Winnie" came aboard promptly, wearing a plain brass-buttoned reefer, and attended by the highest military chiefs of embattled Britain. And so began the momentous Atlantic Conference, in which the United States—though not officially at war—was committed to "the final destruction of the Nazi tyranny."

The formal business of the meeting was the writing of the Atlantic Charter, which Roosevelt hoped to make as important as Wilson's Fourteen Points. As a preliminary, the President had already listed for Congress the "four essential human freedoms"—of speech, of religion, from want, from fear—which he regarded as worthy war aims. The completed Charter declared, on behalf of Churchill and Roosevelt, that "their countries seek no aggrandizement, territorial or other;" that "they respect the right of all peoples to choose the form of government under which they will live;" that "they desire to bring about the fullest collaboration between all nations in the economic field," and "hope to see established a peace which will afford to all nations the means of dwelling in safety. . . ." But overshadowing this diplomatic document was the military charter which the two nations were writing in gunpowder as they guarded their Atlantic lifeline together. For the United States, by occupying Greenland and Iceland in the summer of 1941, and ordering its naval vessels to sink German U-boats at sight, was already fighting at England's side.

Saburo Kurusu, Japanese "peace envoy," arrives to "baby along" America in 1941.

PEARL HARBOR

ACROSS THE WORLD from Newfoundland, the armies of Japan moved south to complete their "Greater East Asia Co-Prosperity Sphere." China was almost finished. Indo-China, with its Vichy French rulers, was an easy prey. At the Atlantic Conference Roosevelt and Churchill agreed the Japanese must be stopped soon. But the United States needed time to arm the Philippines. "Leave that to me," said FDR. "I think I can baby them along for three months."

In November 1941 a smiling Japanese diplomat, Saburo Kurusu, flew to Washington with some "last proposals." While he talked, and while American intelligence officers decoded his messages from home, a Japanese naval force steamed east in the Pacific. On Sunday morning, December 7, Japanese planes swarmed over the island of Oahu. Japanese bombs crashed down on the billion-dollar navy base at Pearl Harbor, on army airfields, and on the city of Honolulu. The "sneak attack" sank or damaged the core of the American Pacific fleet, killed 2,117 sailors, soldiers, and civilians, and united 130 million Americans in a grim desire for vengeance.

American warships go down in crumpled steel and smoke during the Pearl Harbor bombing.

The damage to the Pacific fleet was so serious that the details were not disclosed for a year.

THE MARCH OF DEATH

After the fall of Bataan, approximately 10,000 American and 45,000 Filipino prisoners of war were marched by the Japanese to San Fernando in Pampanga Province, a distance of about 120 miles. The story of their march was officially released by the United States Army and Navy. Following are a few incidents:

The prisoners passed many running streams, but the Japs would not let them drink fresh water. Those who broke out of line to drink were shot and left to die where they fell. But there were filthy carabao wallows beside the road, and the Japs told the prisoners to drink there.

In the village of Lubao, where they were quartered overnight, there was a warehouse of galvanized tin with a sliding door. The Japs pushed in as many men as could stand inside, and placed more men outside the open door. Then they put a steel cable around the building and drew it taut until the men outside the door were squeezed into the building. Then they locked the door. There were no sanitation facilities inside, and no windows. Many prisoners died in the galvanized warehouse.

At the end of each day's march the ones who were too weak to continue were picked out and dispatched in various ways. Some were buried while still alive. American officers were forced at bayonet point to take shovels and aid in this work. Once a man with six inches of dirt over him recovered consciousness and clawed his way to the surface. A Jap ordered an American prisoner to hit him on the head with a shovel. The prisoner did it—to save his own life.

Other sick prisoners who still had some strength were allowed to dig their own graves and crawl in them.

But the death march was only a beginning. In their first two months in Japanese prison camps 2,200 Americans and 27,000 Filipinos died from malnutrition, maltreatment, and deliberate murder.

"I know we've heard of Hitler starving and killing people by the thousands," said a survivor of the death march. "And we've heard of the Japs using living Chinese for bayonet practice. But we're Americans. . . . Those things don't happen to Americans!"

THE LONG ROAD TO VICTORY

THERE WERE TWO MARINES at Pearl Harbor who were firing a machine gun at the low-flying Japanese planes. A bomb burst behind them and a burning fragment embedded itself in one man's back. But he kept on firing while his mate tugged the jagged metal from his flesh.

There was a navy chaplain who grabbed a machine gun and fired away until the attack was over, using his reader's stand as a prop. The story went through the fleet that the chaplain put down his Bible and cried, "Praise the Lord, and pass the ammunition!" Whether the words were exact or not, they became famous and supplied the theme for a jaunty wartime song:

> Yes, the sky pilot said it,
> You've got to give him credit,
> For a sonofagun of a gunner was he. . . .*

Yet despite the courage of Americans under attack, Pearl Harbor was the worst naval defeat in our history. And there was more to come.

On the same December 7 the Japanese bombed American airfields in the Philippines. On December 10 they began an invasion of Luzon with overwhelming superiority in tanks and planes. General Douglas MacArthur's isolated army of 50,000 Americans and Filipinos evacuated Manila and retreated into the Bataan peninsula, where they held out in foxholes until April 9, 1942. The last American stronghold, Corregidor Island, surrendered on May 6. Meanwhile the omnipresent Japs swarmed over Siam, Malaya, the Dutch East Indies, Burma, and the island "steppingstones" of Guam and Wake. Singapore was captured with surprising ease, and the *Prince of Wales* — on which Roosevelt and Churchill had recently sung and prayed—was sunk

* By Frank Loesser. Copyright 1942 by Famous Music Corp.

by a few well-aimed bombs. Racing south toward Australia, the Japs seized New Britain, the northern side of New Guinea, and the Solomon Islands. But when they tried to approach Australia itself, a carrier task force of the American Navy fought them to a standstill in the Coral Sea. In June 1942 came the decisive Battle of Midway, where an all-out Japanese expedition to take the Hawaiian Islands was crushed by our Navy and Army Air Force. In August a few thousand United States marines began a precarious counteroffensive in the Solomons.

But the Pacific was still the secondary theater in the global war. The German armies were the main menace, and in 1941 they were being drawn toward disaster on the steppes of Russia. When Hitler ordered the fatal drive on Stalingrad in 1942, Anglo-American strategy was aimed at giving the Russians all possible support. Round-the-clock bombing raids from Britain struck at German factories and morale. Allied drives from Egypt and French Morocco swept the Axis out of Africa. The Mediterranean campaign of 1943 knocked Italy out of the war, although German armies fought viciously all the way up the Italian boot. Rome was finally taken June 4, 1944. Two days later came D-Day and the Second Front, when the highly trained Allied Expeditionary Force of General "Ike" Eisenhower hit the beaches of Normandy. Anglo-American air power and brilliant armored tactics carved up the Nazis in France and Belgium, and pushed rapidly to the Rhine. In December 1944 came the ghastly Battle of the Bulge, when laughing German SS troops slaughtered unarmed American prisoners and left their bodies piled in the snow. After this last effort the German dragon sank back, convulsed and bleeding, while the mechanized armies from east and west roared in for the kill.

In the Pacific, the turning point came when these marines went ashore on bloody Guadalcanal, August 7, 1942.

In the Mediterranean, Americans and British took the initiative in November 1942 by landing in French Morocco.

Through Tarawa *(above)*, Saipan, Iwo, and Okinawa, the American Pacific offensive rolled northward toward Tokyo. In October 1944 General MacArthur returned to the Philippines and the Navy smashed the last Jap fleet.

Americans entered Paris August 23, 1944, after 11 weeks of fighting in northern France. On September 1 the American First Army crossed into Belgium and nine days later fired the first American shells into Germany itself.

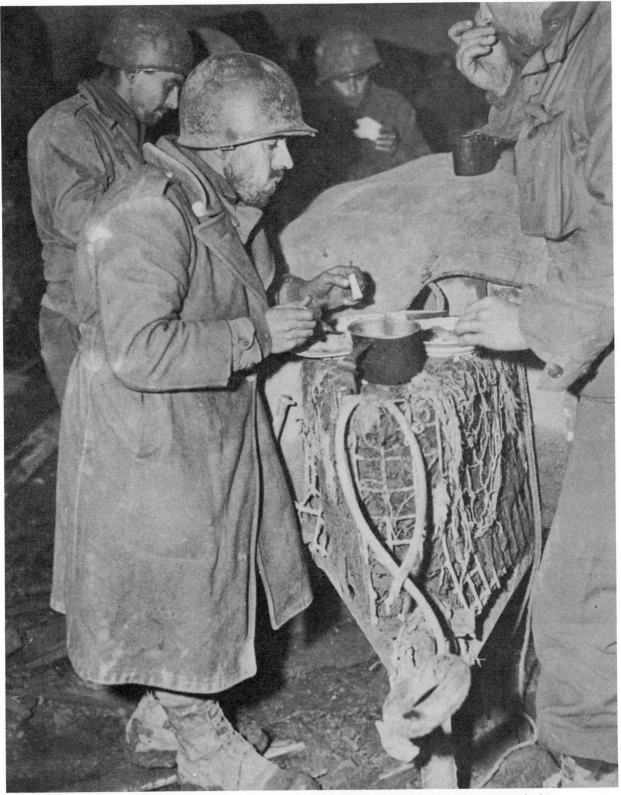

These American GIs are getting their first warm food after 15 days of rugged fighting in the Hürtgen Forest of Germany. The U. S. Army and Navy lost 392,757 dead in the Second World War. The cost in money was $350 billion.

THE ROVING COMMANDER

AN AMERICAN army jeep whirled along a dusty road near Casablanca in January 1943, and the GIs who saw it recognized a familiar figure in the seat beside the driver. "It's the President—no kidding," they told each other. It was true—FDR had flown 4,000 miles from Washington to visit the Allied beachhead and join Winston Churchill in an "unconditional surrender" ultimatum to Hitler. No previous President had ever left the country in wartime, but global strategy called for a globe-trotting Commander in Chief. In 1943 Roosevelt went to Quebec to meet Churchill, to Cairo to meet the rulers of China and Turkey, to Teheran to meet the ruler of Russia. In 1944 he visited his Pacific commanders in Hawaii, and saw Churchill again in Quebec. In 1945 he visited Malta, Egypt, and Russia.

At Teheran, late in 1943, the Allied Big Three got together for the first time. Roosevelt and Churchill agreed to launch a second front in France in May 1944. Stalin agreed to start a new Russian offensive at the same time.

At Casablanca, FDR made the rival French Generals Giraud *(left)* and De Gaulle pose together in photographs.

At Cairo, Roosevelt and Churchill promised the Chiangs that Japan would be stripped of all her Asiatic conquests.

At Quebec, in 1944, the American and British commanders and staffs planned the concluding moves of the war.

Stalin was invited but sent word that he was too busy directing the final drive of the Red armies on Berlin.

Off the coast of Egypt, in 1945, FDR played shipboard host to King Ibn Saud, ruler of a treasure-land of oil.

At Yalta, in 1945, the Big Three agreed to reorganize Poland, dismember Germany, and conquer Japan together.

OLD DOCTOR WIN-THE-WAR

"I WISH REPORTERS wouldn't use that term," grumbled FDR one day in 1943, when a columnist for the Cleveland *Press* mentioned "the New Deal." Later the President explained what he meant. It was like a man who had needed two doctors, he said. Ten years ago, when he first came to the White House, the United States was very sick economically. "Doctor New Deal" was called in, and did the patient a lot of good. But now the nation was not sick the same way—it was suffering from a bad accident called Pearl Harbor. So a different type of specialist— "Doctor Win-the-War"—was in charge of the case. The President thought the newspapers ought to get up to date on this development. (And the newspapers thought both "doctors" looked suspiciously like Franklin D. Roosevelt.)

By the time the 1944 Presidential campaign rolled around, "Doctor Win-the-War" was the main Democratic attraction. Roosevelt was renominated, but he allowed the No. 2 New Dealer, Vice President Henry Wallace, to be dropped from his ticket. And he smothered his Republican opponent, Governor Dewey of New York, more by well-timed jokes, alternated with serious little lectures on the war, than by debating home-front issues. The New Deal played a curious role in the campaign. Dewey attacked it, but endorsed large parts of it. Roosevelt defended it, but preferred not to talk about it. For by 1944 it was apparent that the New Deal was both an accomplished fact and a political liability.

Although some people called him a "tired old man," FDR was still the unbeaten champ of American politics in 1944. "These Republican leaders," he said in one speech, "have not been content with attacks on me, or on my wife, or on my sons—no, not content with that—they now include my little dog Fala." Even Republicans smiled at that.

"It took a war to make jobs under the New Deal," cried the intense young Republican candidate, Thomas E. Dewey.

Sidney Hillman of the CIO rallied remaining New Dealers to FDR. "Clear it with Sidney," jeered the Republicans.

Returning from a 21-day tour to Hawaii and Alaska, the President delivered his first 1944 campaign speech from the deck of a destroyer at the Puget Sound Navy Yard *(above)*. The Pacific war was well in hand, he reported.

Henry Wallace and Harry Truman, who got Wallace's spot on the ticket, did a brother act for the Democrats.

Wendell Willkie, after coining the phrase "One World," was driven out of politics by Middle West Republicans.

"LET US MOVE FORWARD"

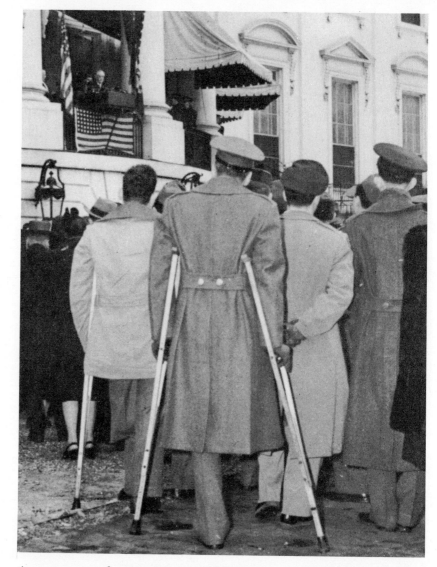

Livadia Palace at Yalta was FDR's home during the last Big Three conference.

He died in this small cottage at Warm Springs, where he recovered from polio.

A DELEGATION of young veterans of World War II attended the fourth-term inauguration at the White House in January 1945 *(above)*. A few days later FDR slipped away for a 6,700-mile trip to the Crimea, and his second conference with Churchill and Stalin. At this meeting the Big Three were more specific than ever: they agreed to support the United Nations, to co-ordinate their military efforts, to share in the future administration of Germany, to let the liberated nations create "democratic institutions of their own choice," to set the eastern frontier of Poland at the Curzon Line of 1919. Russia promised to enter the war against Japan after Germany's surrender, provided her "former rights" (*i.e.,* prior to the Russo-Japanese War) were restored in Manchuria and elsewhere. FDR agreed to arrange this with China.

In March the President was back in Washington, telling Congress part of what had been done. (The Far Eastern agreements were kept secret, for Russia was still officially neutral there.) In April he went to his cottage at Warm Springs, Georgia, for a rest. The annual Democratic Jefferson Day Dinner was due on April 13, and FDR devoted part of his time to composing a brief speech for that occasion, concluding with the typical words: "The only limit to our realization of tomorrow will be our doubts of today. Let us move forward with strong and active faith." That was to be his final message. On April 12, at 1 o'clock, he exclaimed, "I have a terrific headache," and slumped forward on a table that had just been set for lunch. At 3:35 he was dead of a cerebral hemorrhage.

President Roosevelt could walk only with the help of steel braces, a cane, and an aide. This photograph shows him coming out of the White House to greet a group of governors.

Though lacking in leg power Roosevelt could drive his own automobile with the help of special hand controls. Here he chauffers Fala around his estate not long before his death.

The President's coffin in Washington. He was buried in his garden at Hyde Park.

Vice President Harry Truman had just dropped into Speaker Sam Rayburn's office for a bourbon highball when he heard the news from Warm Springs. "I felt like the moon, the stars, and the planets had fallen on me," he said. His family, members of the Cabinet and Congress, and Chief Justice Harlan Fiske Stone gathered around him at

the White House. Harry Truman was so nervous that he could not speak—he took a slip of paper from his pocket with the words of his oath written on it, and held it on top of his Bible. Then his voice began to function, and he read the words firmly. "So help me God!" he concluded, and thus became the 32nd President of the United States.

Victory in Europe came when the remaining German commanders *(left)* surrendered to the Allies at Reims, on May 7, 1945. Hitler and Mussolini had been dead a week.

Victory over Japan came August 14, five days after a second bomb was dropped on Nagasaki. On September 2 the formal surrender was signed on the battleship *Missouri.*

THE MUSHROOM CLOUD

THE SUN was bright over Hiroshima, but when the single bomb was dropped from an American B-29, there was a flash that was brighter than sunlight. Then the city was swallowed in dust, and a mushroom-topped pillar of smoke spurted seven miles into the sky. When the dust and smoke cleared away, and the counting was finished, this was the toll of the bomb: 78,150 Japanese killed, 13,983 missing, 37,425 burned and injured, 176,987 homeless, foodless, or sick. Hiroshima, once an army base and a city of 343,000 people, was 60 per cent destroyed. Proudly, President Truman explained: "It is an atomic bomb. . . . We have spent two billion dollars on the greatest scientific gamble in history—and won." Gravely he added, a few days later: "The atomic bomb is too dangerous to be let loose in a lawless world. That is why Great Britain, Canada, and the United States, who have the secret of its production, do not intend to reveal that secret until means have been found to control the bomb. . . ."

"Oh, what a great day this can be in history," exclaimed President Truman, addressing the delegates who had just written the charter of the United Nations, June 26, 1945.

The President met Josef Stalin behind a wrought iron railing at Potsdam in July. While there he made the final decision on when and where to release the bomb.

"Don't Mind Me—Just Go Right On Talking," a
bored bomb tells world diplomats in the cartoon by
Herblock below. In the 1950's the duel for atomic
supremacy froze into a standoff. Russia shattered
the U.S. bomb monopoly in 1949. By 1954 both
nations had H- (for hydrogen) bombs which were
800 times more deadly than the Hiroshima bomb.

From "Herblock's Here and Now" (Simon and Schuster)

CHAPTER 10

ATOMIC PEACE AND COLD WAR

PRESIDENT TRUMAN was on the cruiser *Augusta*, hurrying home from the Potsdam Conference, when word was flashed that the first atom bomb had been dropped with success on Japan. Chatting with the reporters on shipboard, he told them: "Boys, the real reason I got out of that meeting, and didn't stop [in England], was that I wanted to be away from there before I could be questioned by Uncle Joe or old Attlee about our atomic bomb."

The remark showed how fast the Allied Big Three were splitting apart at the end of the war. Freedom-minded America and regimented Russia had never really trusted each other. After Yalta FDR and Stalin engaged in some angry disputes by radio. Their most serious falling out was over Poland, where Russia was installing a handpicked Communist regime, in violation of her pledge at Yalta to hold "free and unfettered elections."

In April, after Roosevelt died, the Russian foreign minister "Old Ironpants" Molotov stopped at the White House to pay his respects to the new U.S. President. Truman received him formally, and then called him back for a second interview at which he spoke his mind about Poland. Molotov was furious. "I have never been talked to like that in my life!" he exclaimed.

"Carry out your agreements," Truman told him grimly, "and you won't get talked to like that."

At Potsdam the Russians agreed once more to hold elections in Poland. But they were more intent on pressing their claims to the Italian colonies in Africa, and enormous loot in the German Ruhr. They made it clear also that they would continue to treat Eastern Europe as a Communist private preserve.

That was more than Harry Truman was willing to take. "I made up my mind," he wrote in his memoirs, "that I would not allow the Russians any part in the control of Japan. . . . The Russians were after world conquest."

And so, after Potsdam, there were no more Big Three meetings. There was no general peace treaty, and there was no genuine peace. The Russians, without demobilizing their army, set up Red satellite governments in Bulgaria, Rumania, Albania, Yugoslavia, Czechoslovakia, Hungary, Poland, East Germany and North Korea. The Western powers, holding fast to the atom bomb, encircled the Soviets with bases and a remarkable assortment of allies. Both sides used the United Nations to air their grievances and their deadly distrust of each other.

This frustrating state of affairs was something new for the American people. All through their history they had either ignored the world's problems or plunged in to settle them once and for all. Now they were locked in a power struggle which they could neither ignore nor settle—except at the risk of an atomic holocaust. Bernard Baruch, the old-time speculator, gave the right name to the situation. "Let us not deceive ourselves," he said in a 1947 speech. "We are in the midst of a cold war."

In 1957 the cold war was still going on. It had already cost the U.S. more money (nearly $360 billion) than the entire expense of World War II. In Korea, where Communist aggression was met head on, 54,000 American lives were lost and the net result was a truce.

The cold war called for steady nerves and a calm assessment of strength. In most respects, at the end of twelve years, the U.S. was more than holding its own. Its industrial output exceeded that of all the Communist nations combined. In wealth and material well-being it easily led the world. Its diplomacy was rarely a complete success, but Russian failures were more damaging.

At first the cold war was marked by acute attacks of the jitters. Civil rights and minority opinions were trampled on in the stampede for security. But during the 1950's the world's strongest nation regained a reasonably confident mood, with a five-star general in the White House, and missile batteries and roving atomic submarines as accepted features of the global landscape.

The charred base of a steel tower and fused cinders of sand mark the spot in New Mexico where an A-bomb was first tested, July 16, 1945. Director Oppenheimer of the Los Alamos laboratory and General Groves of the Manhattan District stand at the scarred site.

"IT IS NO SECRET..."

INTERNATIONAL TEAMWORK among the scientists gave the United States the atom bomb. The story was one of almost incredible luck. In Italy, in 1934, Enrico Fermi changed the nature of uranium atoms by bombarding them with neutrons. His results were duplicated, with some improvements, by German researchers in 1938. But neither Fermi nor the Germans realized fully what they had done.

Dr. Lise Meitner, who took part in the German experiments and then was exiled by the Nazis, was the first person to grasp the idea that the uranium atoms had actually been *split* into entirely different elements. She suggested this to Niels Bohr of Denmark, in whose laboratory she had taken refuge. It happened that Bohr was just getting ready to come to the U.S. to discuss high problems of physics with his old friend Albert Einstein.

By the time Bohr reached New York an historic cablegram was waiting for him. Meitner had repeated her experiment at Copenhagen and confirmed her daring theory. And just as Einstein himself had predicted back in 1905, the disintegration of matter was accompanied by a colossal release of energy.

This news was announced by Bohr at a conference at George Washington University, on January 27, 1939. It started a race in U.S., British and Canadian laboratories to control the energy of the divided atom and direct it into a chain reaction (which in essence is what an A-bomb is). By this time the Germans had caught on too, and all news of uranium research disappeared from their reports.

On October 11, 1939, President Roosevelt listened to Alexander Sachs, a Russian-born economist and friend of Einstein's, explain what was going on. Sachs handed the President a letter which had been carefully drafted by Einstein and others. FDR appointed a committee and allotted $6,000 from military funds. Out of this grew eventually the "Manhattan Engineer District" of the War Department, a vast atomic monopoly which employed 300,000 scientists and workers and built three hidden cities (Oak Ridge, Los Alamos, Hanford-Richland) to manufacture materials and construct a workable bomb.

The whole project was supersecret so far as the American public was concerned. But as soon as one bomb had been exploded, every capable physicist in the world knew exactly what had been done.

"It [the bomb] is no secret at all to the scientists of other nations," the top U.S. expert, J. Robert Oppenheimer, told Congress in 1946. "It's production by other nations is only a matter of time, and no very long time at that."

Albert Einstein, a German exile, and Hungarian-born Leo Szilard sent the first warning to FDR. This scene and the next two were re-enacted for a motion picture in 1946.

Enrico Fermi *(right)*, who left Fascist Italy in 1939, designed the first "pile" for atomic chain reactions in a squash court at Stagg Field, University of Chicago.

On January 1, 1947, the Army surrendered its control of the atom and five shirt-sleeved civilians took over. Members of the first Atomic Energy Commission *(above, left to right)* were Sumner T. Pike, a seasoned Washington bureaucrat; Robert F. Bacher, a Cornell scientist who had held high rank at Los Alamos; David E. Lilienthal, the chairman, former administrator of the TVA and co-author of the first plan for peaceful development of atomic power; Lewis L. Strauss, a New York banker; and William W. Waymack, a Des Moines newspaper editor.

James B. Conant of Harvard *(left)* and Vannevar Bush of M.I.T. watched the first test shot lying flat on their stomachs, then rolled over and dazedly shook hands.

The first news photos of atomic work at Oak Ridge were released in 1946, while the U.S. made ready to test even bigger bombs at Bikini atoll in the Pacific Ocean.

MISSIONS TO MOSCOW

AFTER the Big Three stopped getting together, the "Little Three" took over. In December 1945 America's Byrnes and Britain's Bevin were in Moscow, trying to deal with Molotov. The agreement they signed gave Russia a toehold in Japan and a full partnership in Korea.

Harry Truman blew up when he heard this news. He called in Byrnes and read him a lecture. "Unless Russia is faced with an iron fist and strong language, another war is in the making," the President told his Secretary of State. "I'm tired of babying the Soviets!"

Slowly an American "get tough" policy took shape. In 1947 came the Truman Doctrine (military aid to Greece and Turkey) and the Marshall Plan (an outpouring of dollars to bolster other nations). Both of these were later merged in the North Atlantic Treaty Organization (NATO), an armed alliance against Communist attack in Europe or North America.

The Russians retaliated in 1949 by closing all roads to Berlin. But Allied planes flew above the blockade, daring the Red Army to open fire.

Secretary of State "Jimmy" Byrnes journeyed to Moscow in 1945 hoping to draft a German peace treaty with Russia. The wily Molotov stalled him off and clinked glasses instead.

Russia's Gromyko and America's Baruch could never agree on atomic controls.

Secretary George Marshall, who followed Byrnes, stands glum and drinkless at a Moscow party in 1947. The U.S. still wanted a German treaty. The Russians still said *nyet*.

While lesser diplomats traveled to Moscow the world's senior statesman went deep into the American Midwest to utter the cold war's most effective propaganda phrase. "From Stettin in the Baltic to Trieste in the Adriatic an iron curtain has descended," Winston Churchill told a 1946 convocation at Westminster College in Missouri. Harry Truman, who sat with Churchill, and Westminster's President McCluer *(left above)* nodded solemn agreement

THE MAN FROM

Every morning Harry Truman was up with the sun, stepping briskly around Washington with his Secret Service guard while most of the government was still in bed. He got more exercise in the late afternoon by paddling dog fashion in the White House pool. In temperament Truman was closer to Teddy Roosevelt than he was to the subtle FDR. He caused a lot of commotion by swinging the Presidential Big Stick. He batted the New Dealers out of his Cabinet, cracked down on striking labor unions, slugged away at the Russians—and missed by a mile in the 1946 elections when the Republicans won control of Congress for the first time since 1930.

Back home in Missouri Truman was known as a late-starting politician who had had some extraordinary luck. As a boy he yearned to attend West Point but was turned down because he wore glasses. He worked as a newspaper wrapper, theater usher and bank clerk, spent ten years as a dirt farmer, and served in World War I as captain of Battery D, 129th Field Artillery, Missouri National Guard.

In the war he got to know Jim Pendergast, whose

Captain Truman wore a Sam Browne belt and baggy pants in France in 1918. His old uniform still fitted in 1945.

Senator Truman in 1942 helped his wife make breakfast in their Washington home.

Vice President Truman was a willing entertainer in 1945.

President Truman on fishing vacations showed a liking for loud sportswear.

Henry Wallace swung hard at Truman's anti-Red policies.

Truman asked Congress to draft railroad strikers in 1946. Just as he did so the strike was called off.

Joe McCarthy dumped smears on the State Department.

MISSOURI

Uncle Tom was boss of the Kansas City Democratic machine. After the war (and after Truman failed dismally in trying to run a haberdashery store) the Pendergasts elected him to a Jackson County administrative job. Truman worked hard and well for the taxpayers, while remaining as helpful as possible to the Pendergast machine. In 1934 the Pendergasts promoted him to the U.S. Senate.

In Washington he fitted snugly into the Capitol's bourbon-and-poker set. He voted the straight New Deal line and won respect by his thorough investigations of military spending. He was picked for Vice President in 1944 because FDR was trying to head off a fight between left-winger Henry Wallace and Southern conservative Jimmy Byrnes.

Then the lightning struck and plain Harry Truman was sitting in the world's most complicated job. His troubles and mistakes were many; his stubborn loyalty to some small-time friends produced some small-time scandals. But he never shirked making a really momentous decision. Before he was through he had plenty of them to make.

"What next " asks Harry Truman in this 1946 cartoon as he holds his aching head and furrowed brow. His worries came in batches.

His close pal Harry Vaughn took seven gift deep freezers.

Vaughn's pal John Maragon was imprisoned for perjury.

Lamar Caudle, a Federal tax prosecutor, was fired by Truman after admitting his wife had received a cut-price mink coat.

Puerto Rican assassins tried to kill Truman in 1950. One was wounded (above). Another and a guard were killed.

Republican Thomas E. Dewey was calmly convinced that he could squash Truman.

State's Righter J. Strom Thurmond got a new Texas hat and 83 electoral votes.

THE WHISTLESTOP CAMPAIGN

"I'M GOING to give 'em hell," promised Harry Truman as he sallied forth from the White House in September 1948. The nation smiled, for it was growing fond of its scrappy President, even though it gave him no chance at all to be re-elected in November. The voters were seething over the runaway cost of living, shortages of meat and housing, and mounting cold-war tensions. The Republican Congress had shown its contempt for Truman by passing over his veto the Taft-Hartley law (which put some shackles on labor unions) and a big tax cut (which favored high-level incomes). The Democrats themselves were splintered into three parties, each with its own Presidential candidate: Henry Wallace for the left-wing Progressives, Strom Thurmond for the right-wing "Dixiecrats," and Truman for what was left in the middle.

The Republican candidate (for the second time) was the model Governor, Tom Dewey, who thought the best idea was to ignore Truman entirely. The public opinion polltakers assured Dewey that his election was in the bag. So he pitched his cultivated baritone voice to painless platitudes—"We are going forward to a new unity. . . . Our future lies before us. . . ."—and scarcely raised a sweat as his 15-car "Victory Special" train coasted around the country.

Truman's strategy was just the opposite: he swung at Dewey and the "do nothing" Congress with language the voters could understand and enjoy *(see opposite page)*. In eight weeks he barnstormed across 22,000 miles, making 271 stinging speeches to Dewey's bland 170. The "Fair Deal" program he presented was simply another New Deal warmed over, but it made an appeal to labor and Middle Western farmers. The Wallace fringe robbed Truman of New York and Thurmond carried four Southern states. But the final result was a stunning political upset: 303 electoral votes for the country boy from Missouri, and 189 for the city slicker with the mustache.

President Truman had the last laugh on the Chicago *Tribune*, November 3, 1948.

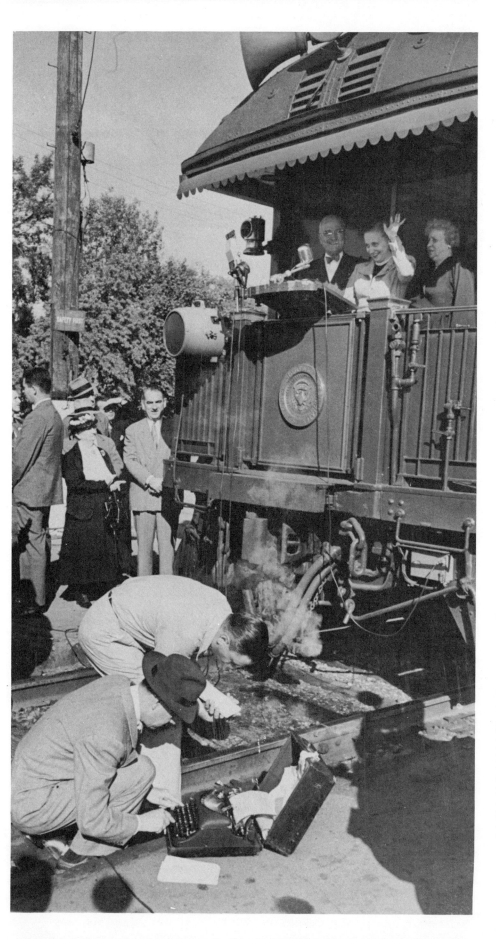

HARRY AND HIS FAMILY

stepped out to greet the voters at every whistlestop in 1948. In speeches Truman "poured it on" as follows:

"That notorious do-nothing Republican Eightieth Congress has stuck a pitchfork in the farmer's back. . . .

"These Republican gluttons of privilege are cold . . . cunning men. They want a return of the Wall Street dictatorship. . . . Your typical Republican reactionary is a very shrewd man with a calculating machine where his heart ought to be. . . .

"The Republicans tell me that they stand for unity. As Al Smith would have said, 'That's a lot of hooey.' And if that rhymes with anything, it's not my fault. . . .

"The unity we have achieved in foreign policy required leadership. It was not achieved by the people who copied the answers down neatly after the teacher had written them on the blackboard. . . .

"I told my doctor that I kept having this feeling that there's somebody following behind me. The White House physician told me not to worry. He said, 'You keep right on your way. There's one place where that fellow's not going to follow you and that's into the White House.' "

All set for an election year Red hunt, four members and the chief counsel of the House Committee on Un-American Activities strike a collective Dick Tracy pose in 1948. Chairman J. Parnell Thomas of New Jersey *(second from left)* was indicted later in the year and served eight months in jail for padding his Congressional payroll.

Eleven top leaders of the Communist Party sit for their portraits outside a New York courtroom in 1949. They were given five-year prison terms for conspiring to "teach and advocate" the overthrow of the government. By 1952 the party's U.S. membership had been hammered down to less than 25,000. In 1954 the party itself was outlawed.

SPIES AND UN-AMERICANS

On march 22, 1947, President Truman issued his Executive Order 9835, which decreed that "there shall be a loyalty investigation" of every Federal employee. During the next four years some three million individuals were examined and cleared, over 3,000 resigned while being investigated, 308 were dismissed as "security risks" and only one— a 27-year-old girl analyst in the Justice Department—was arrested on charges of being a spy.

This gigantic winnowing operation was carried on by secret-police methods which ran counter to the best American traditions. But it was made necessary and even inevitable by the unpleasant facts of the cold war. In 1947 (according to the F.B.I.) there were 80,000 U.S. Communist Party members who received inspiration from Moscow. There was never a chance that this many people could overthrow the American government. But they could spy for Russia, and some of them already had *(see below)*.

The Red menace was a godsend to the House Committee on Un-American Activities, which began its career in 1938 by attempting to prove that the New Deal itself was a Communist plot. Over the years the Committee amassed a million-name file of known or suspected Communists, "fellow travelers," "premature anti-fascists," "dupes," and "bleeding-heart liberals." These categories were now bandied about in headlines while the Committee herded ten Hollywood writers to jail for refusing to answer its questions. In the heat of the 1948 campaign Harry Truman remarked that the Committee's sensational hearings smelled to him like political "red herring."

"Just a Little 'Dirty Business,'" drawn by Fitzpatrick for the St. Louis *Post-Dispatch*, shows a long-nosed Uncle Sam in the uncomfortable role of a wiretapper.

Judith Coplon, who carried F.B.I. reports to a Russian friend in New York, was convicted twice but released by the courts because the F.B.I. tapped her telephone.

Ethel and Julius Rosenberg, devout Communists and deadly spies, were electrocuted in 1953 for their part in a wartime ring that stole A-bomb secrets for Russia.

In the photographs at the right two men are striving to relive their past. Repentant Communist Whittaker Chambers *(left)* rolls his eyes and dredges his mind for details. Alger Hiss *(far right)* looks at an old photo of Chambers and denies he ever knew him by that name. Between them stands Robert Stripling, chief counsel and inquisitor for the Un-American Activities Committee.

THE
PAPERS
IN THE
PUMPKIN

A Truman "red herring" and a Chambers pumpkin report for judgment in a 1948 cartoon. The pumpkin was the winner.

LATE ONE EVENING in December 1948 a pudgy, harassed-looking man drove to his farm in Maryland with two investigators for the Un-American Activities Committee. Switching on the lights in his yard, the man groped around in a patch of pumpkins, found one with a removable top, took out of it some rolls of film, and handed them to the investigators. "I think this is what you are looking for," he said.

He was exactly right. The "pumpkin papers" were the first public documentary evidence of a Communist conspiracy in prewar Washington. When the films were developed and printed they made a stack of enlargements nearly four feet high, consisting of copies of State Department reports, all dated in early 1938. A similar group of documents, which were copied by typewriter but not on film, had been turned over previously to the Justice Department.

The man who produced them was Whittaker Chambers, a senior editor of *Time* magazine, a dairy farmer by avocation, and a self-described "courier" for a Russian spy "apparatus" in the middle 1930s. Chambers swore that he received the bulk of the documents from his "close friend" Alger Hiss, a bright young New Dealer who served ten years in the State Department, traveled to Yalta with FDR, and was secretary-general of the United Nations organizing conference at San Francisco in 1945. "Mr. Hiss," testified Chambers,

"was a devoted, and at that time [1938] a rather romantic Communist." At a public hearing, and before a Federal grand jury, Hiss denied these statements *in toto*. He said he remembered Chambers as a free-lance writer who came to Washington under a different name, used the Hiss apartment for a time, gave the Hiss family a rug, and obtained possession of an old Hiss car. Hiss expressed the belief he was being framed, and demanded vindication.

Which one of the two was lying? For months this nightmarish question obscured every other phase of the cold war. Outwardly Hiss was a model of rectitude and success: an honor graduate of Johns Hopkins and Harvard Law, an ex-secretary of Justice Holmes, the respected president (since 1946) of the Carnegie Endowment for International Peace. Chambers was talented too, but he seeemed to revel in public confessions and accusations; he admitted perjuring himself as late as October 1948. In the end the issue was decided by the damning evidence that Chambers had kept concealed for a decade. Experts proved that most of the typed copies of State Department reports were made on a Woodstock typewriter that had once belonged to Hiss. A 1950 jury found Hiss guilty of perjury and by inference of having been a disloyal official and a spy. Into the prison darkness with him went the remaining political luster of Franklin Roosevelt's New Deal.

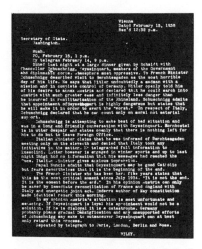

A copied 1938 report on Austria helped convict Hiss. It could also have helped Russia break the U.S. diplomatic code.

The North Koreans captured Seoul and bombed Suwon *(above)* in the opening days of the war. Here South Koreans flee to cover.

President Rhee of South Korea called for American help. General Douglas MacArthur flew in to answer the call.

COMMUNIST PLANES roared across the 38th Parallel on the Asian peninsula of Chosen, on June 25, 1950. They dropped bombs and sprayed bullets on the UN-sponsored and U.S.-supported Republic of [South] Korea. Russian-built late-model tanks opened the way for invasion by the "People's Army" from the North. The sneak attack, just like Pearl Harbor, came at dawn on a Sunday morning.

President Truman got the news at his home in Independence, Missouri. He flew back to Washington and made some fast decisions: he directed General MacArthur in Japan to give air support to the South Koreans, and he rushed the U.S. Seventh Fleet from the Philippines to guard Formosa. But his biggest decision came five days later, when he ordered U.S. ground troops to go into Korea and push the Reds back where they came from.

The United Nations, under U.S. pressure, also acted promptly. The Security Council, on June 27, voted sanctions against North Korea and called on all its members to "repel the armed attack." Russia was away from its seat after staging a walkout six months before, and so could not veto the deci-

AGGRESSION IN THE EAST

The UN's Security Council voted 7 to 1 to punish North Korea. Russia's deliberate absence was a major Communist blunder.

sion *(above, left)*. Red Yugoslavia *(far right)* was on the outs with Stalin, and merely voted "No."

Thus a line was finally drawn in Asia, as it had been in Europe, against further Communist expansion. To many Americans, and especially to the accusing spokesmen of the right-wing "China Lobby," the action seemed too little and too late. Ever since World War II the great land mass of China and its 450 million people had been receding into the Red mists. The U.S. sent money, arms and advice to the Christian generalissimo, Chiang Kaishek. But Chiang's feeble and unpopular regime could not stop the native Communists. In December 1949 Chiang and the remnant of his Nationalist forces fled to exile on Formosa.

Red China was no Russian satellite, but it was working toward the same ends, and it hated and feared the U.S. When MacArthur's counter-offensive rolled into North Korea, the Chinese dragon stirred. And when MacArthur pressed on to the China-Korea border (and rashly sent planes across it) the Chinese poured in 200,000 Red "volunteers," engulfed the UN army, and started an entirely new war.

Dean Acheson, Truman's third Secretary of State, was blamed by Republicans for the Red successes in Asia.

Young U.S. soldiers died in Chinese traps in the bitter retreat from Changjin Reservoir in December 1950. Here their bodies lie beside the road while their comrades trudge to safety.

"OLD SOLDIERS ...FADE AWAY"

OFFICIALLY there was no war in Korea—it was only a United Nations "police action." Yet the fighting and dying went on and on, and the news from the front was agonizing. The Chinese threw in 850,000 men and captured Seoul again. The UN massed 700,000 (mostly Korean "ROKs" and Americans but including contingents from 15 other nations) and pushed back to the 38th parallel. There, where it all began, negotiations were started for a truce that brought victory to nobody.

General MacArthur, who seriously miscalculated the Chinese will to fight, made the same mistake about Harry Truman. After his "home by Christmas" promises backfired, MacArthur drowned out criticism by demanding an all-out war on China. When he wrote a letter to a Republican Congressman, the President "with deep regret" relieved him from command. The old Pacific campaigner came home to America then, for the first time since 1937, and was hailed as the conquering hero he had been in World War II. He drew tears from a solemn session of Congress *(above)* with his farewell oratory: "Like the old soldier of [the] ballad, I now close my military career and just fade away, an old soldier who tried to do his duty as God gave him the light to see that duty." But the final words in the controversy came from another old soldier, General Omar Bradley, who was chairman of the U.S. Chiefs of Staff. MacArthur's war on mainland China, said Bradley, would have been "the wrong war, at the wrong place, at the wrong time, with the wrong enemy."

"I'll be darned!" said "Ike" Eisenhower when he heard that MacArthur was fired.

General Ike received a hero's ovation in Washington after Germany surrendered, in June 1945. "I am neither a Republican nor a Democrat," he said, and that made people like him even more.

THE KIND OF A GUY WE LIKE

"HAD ENOUGH?" demanded the Republican orators in 1952—"Had enough of Korea, corruption and Communism?" The voters had had enough. The contagious grin and victorious record of the Republican candidate for President offered a pleasing antidote for cold-war aches and pains. General Dwight David ("Ike") Eisenhower was one of the most likeable men in the world. His career was a slow-fire success story: the son of humble small-town parents, he had won an appointment to West Point, served ably in the Regular Army through 24 patient years, and was still only a major when World War II began. Six years later he was Supreme Commander of four million men in history's greatest military triumph.

In 1948 the popular Ike could have had the nomination of either major party. He turned them both down with the thoughtful suggestion that "lifelong professional soldiers, in the absence of some obvious or overriding reasons [should] abstain from seeking high political office." Meanwhile he tried being president of Columbia University, and wrote a book, *Crusade in Europe*, that netted him $476,250. In 1949 he went back to France as head of NATO's army. There his office rug was heavily trod by delegations of hungry Republicans. By 1952 he had been persuaded that there were now some overriding reasons why he should run for President.

At 24 he was graduated from West Point with an "A" in football. In studies he ranked 61st in his class.

At 25 he married Mamie Doud, shown with son John.

At 35 (in uniform) he posed with his brothers and parents, at home in Abilene. His father was a mechanic, his mother a devout pacifist.

At 53 he gave a pep talk to his D-Day paratroopers.

At 54, in conquered Berlin, he shared a toast to the Allies' success with Montgomery and Zhukov.

At 57 he looked odd in a college president's garb.

At 61 he won his first political fight, beating Senator Bob Taft *(center)* for the GOP nomination.

"LET'S TALK SENSE..."

"The General," needled candidate Adlai Stevenson, "is worried about my funny-bone. I'm worried about his backbone."

"LET'S FACE IT," said Adlai Stevenson to the worried Democratic convention. "Let's talk sense to the American people. Let's tell them the truth, that there are no gains without pains. . . ." The shortish Adlai with his egg-shaped head and his intellectual slant was facing an almost impossible task in opposing the mighty Ike. He was nominated because of his record as Governor of Illinois, where he had cleaned up a Republican "mess." His grandfather had been Grover Cleveland's Vice President; his father was Woodrow Wilson's friend. Adlai himself had been training for statesmanship since his Ivy League college days. His speeches sparkled with sense and humor, and his political courage won him devotion from liberals everywhere. Addressing the American Legion, he attacked the patrioteers and McCarthyites. In Texas he spurned the offshore oil grab; in Virginia he loud-pedaled civil rights. Both of these normally Democratic states voted against him in November.

Stevenson with a hole in his shoe was snapped while campaigning in Michigan. With him is Governor "Soapy" Williams.

"I SHALL GO TO KOREA"

"Is it amusing," roared candidate Ike, "that we have stumbled into a war [and] have no real plan for stopping it . . . ?"

"BLOOD IN KOREA—POLITICS IN U.N." cried a Republican newspaper headline. Bitterness over the Korean "trap" was a sure Republican vote-getter in 1952. Senator Joe McCarthy, the Republican hatchetman, spoke of "Truman's war" and "twenty years of treason." Ike did his amateurish best, at first, to avoid McCarthy's example. "I do not see how these conditions, having occurred and having been created, how you could stay out of the thing, I don't know," he said. But as the campaign waxed hotter, and fresh writers took hold of his speeches, the general spoke more sharply. On October 24, at Detroit, he promised to "concentrate on the job of ending the Korean war" as soon as the election was over. "That requires a personal visit," he added. "I shall go to Korea." Millions heaved sighs of relief, figuring the fighting was as good as ended. In November Ike breezed into the Presidency, with a popular majority of 6½ million, and an Electoral College sweep of 442 to 39.

Ike *(left)* spent three days in Korea, but refused to permit a big offensive. Final armistice came on July 27, 1953.

"I was born in 1913 in modest circumstances. . . . Most of my early life was spent in a [family grocery] store."

"I should say this—that Pat doesn't have a mink coat. But she does have a respectable Republican cloth coat."

"Remember, folks, Eisenhower is a great man. . . . A vote for Eisenhower is a vote for what's good in America."

Nixon wept 24 hours later when Ike publicly "cleared" him. At right he rests on Senator Knowland's shoulder.

THE DICK NIXON STORY

In September the campaign became, for a night, a soap-opera spectacular. The sponsor was the Republican National Committee, which paid $75,000 for a nation-wide television hookup. The author and hero was young Dick Nixon, Republican candidate for Vice President. The cast included Nixon's wife Pat and a cocker spaniel named Checkers.

To millions of TV addicts the plot seemed familiar. Young Dick was a Navy veteran who came home in 1945 to find the country overrun with Reds and fellow travelers. He fought them by running for Congress, and defeated a California New Dealer. He served on the Un-American Activities Committee, and put the handcuffs on Alger Hiss. In 1950 he ran for the Senate, and another New Dealer bit the dust.

But now in 1952 young Dick was suddenly fighting to save his political life. The left-wingers had him surrounded and were closing in for the kill. They were smearing Dick with stories about an $18,235 fund which had been collected for his benefit by some California oilmen and other patriots. Even General Ike was worried.

Of course (Dick told his audience) there was such a fund. It paid for Dick's and Pat's airline tickets, and luncheons and entertainment and advertising and stamps. But it was all for "necessary political expenses" and "exposing Communism." Not a single dollar ever went into Dick's bank account. In fact he didn't handle the money: the checks were all drawn and signed by a Pasadena lawyer. (So there was no need to mention the fund in Dick's income-tax returns.)

And oh, yes, the Nixons had received another gift from a political admirer—"a little cocker spaniel dog in a crate that [was] sent all the way from Texas. Black and white spotted. And our little girl—Trisha, the six-year-old—named it Checkers. And you know, the kids love the dog, and I just want to say this right now, that regardless of what they say about it, we're gonna [sic] keep it!"

The Nixon performance was pure ham but it rescued his career. Like James G. Blaine in his "Plumed Knight" speech *(page 237)* Nixon confused and captured his audience with a superb job of acting. His success proved that television, which had invaded 21 million homes since 1945, was now an immense force in politics. But expert scripting was needed to obtain the full effect. As Nixon himself remarked later on to an audience of professionals: "No TV performance takes such careful preparation as an off-the-cuff talk."

"You're my boy!" exclaimed Eisenhower, embracing Nixon in their first meeting after the TV speech. Later Ike told a cheering crowd: "He is . . . completely vindicated as a man of honor."

On May 22, 1953, President Eisenhower and members of Congress joined in applauding each other *(above)* over the first legislative fruit of the young administration. "Senate Joint Resolution 13" was speeded to Ike's desk and pen by willing workers in both parties. It surrendered Federal ownership of $80 billion worth of oil and gas in underwater areas adjoining the coastal states—especially Texas, California and Louisiana. The Supreme Court had ruled that this offshore oil was the property of the whole nation. President Truman made it a Navy reserve, and vetoed two bills to give it away. A former U.S. Solicitor-General called the giveaway "the largest wholesale looting of national assets in history." But Texas kept pressing its claim as a matter of sacred states' rights and free enterprise. And Ike had promised during the campaign to sign the bill Texas wanted.

WHAT'S GOOD FOR GENERAL MOTORS

THE END of twenty Democratic years gave American business its happiest thrills since the Calvin Coolidge boom. Prices and profits were soaring already as a vast rearmament program grew out of the Korean war. Business critics were booted out of the government; corporation executives poured in. To run the Defense Department Ike drafted Charles E. Wilson, president of General Motors, which held 60% of all defense contracts. "Engine Charlie" was loath to sell his big block of GM stock—"I thought what was good for the country was good for General Motors, and vice versa," he argued. He sold the stock but his words held true. By 1956 GM had racked up $7 billion in total defense jobs. Its net profits, aided by a timely Republican tax cut, surpassed $1 billion a year. GM's new president Harlow Curtice and board chairman Alfred P. Sloan *(see right)* were understandably pleased.

GM's Curtice, Sloan and Wilson

WAS NOT SO GOOD FOR DIXON-YATES

"For the past twenty years there has been a creeping socialism spreading in the United States," remarked President Eisenhower in 1953. As an example he named the TVA, and hinted he would be willing to sell it. With this encouragement the private-power lobby, which had been barred from the White House since the early New Deal, came back and turned on full steam. In 1954 Ike himself took a hand in pushing through a $107 million contract for two promoters named Dixon and Yates, to build a private generating plant to supply the city of Memphis. The contract was signed by the Atomic Energy Commission as a means of bypassing the TVA. Investigating Senators soon discovered that 1) The AEC itself disapproved the contract until Eisenhower changed the membership; 2) There was no competitive bidding; and 3) A Boston banker whose firm was financial agent for the project helped to draw up the Dixon-Yates contract while employed as government "consultant." All of this added up to a likely scandal and Ike had to cancel the contract, leaving Dixon and Yates to sue for the work they had already done.

Dixon and Yates break ground

AND BAD FOR MULLIGAN & CO.

Under Eisenhower the newspapers found little "corruption" in Washington, but there was plenty of "conflict of interest." A painful case developed around Harold Talbott, Ike's Secretary of the Air Force and occasional bridge-table companion. When Talbott was confirmed he told a Senate committee that he had sold his interests in all companies doing business with the government. But he did not mention a management firm called Paul B. Mulligan & Co., which sold its services to other companies, which *did* do business with the government. Using a Pentagon phone and stationery, Talbott was able to interest defense contractors in taking the Mulligan treatment, and his share of the profits came to $130,000. When he was caught and forced to resign Ike praised his "brilliant" record and Charlie Wilson gave him a Medal of Freedom. But Talbott was still sore. "You haven't done one thing to defend me!" he told his unsmiling boss *(right)*.

Talbott and Wilson break up

General Ike steadfastly refused to fight a real duel with roughneck Joe McCarthy. "Have A Care, Sir!" he warns in this cartoon.

MAN

WITH A

MEAT AX

SENATOR Joseph R. McCarthy of Wisconsin was the terror of the Eisenhower administration during its first two years. He bullied the Secretary of State, savagely tongue-lashed the Secretary of the Army, trampled the President's "Secretary for Peace" (Harold Stassen) and turned his informers loose in every branch of the government. Joe was supposed to be hunting for Reds but he never uncovered a single, courtproof example. Actually he was using the Communist bogy to grab power and publicity.

In 1954 his own arrogance put an end to his effective career. Before that happened a courageous cartoonist, "Herblock" of the Washington *Post*, drew these educational pictures of a political hoodlum at large.

"We Have Documentary Evidence That This Man Is Planning a Trip to Moscow," McCarthy advises the Senate. Ambassador Bohlen was finally confirmed, after Joe smeared him as a "security risk."

"You Wouldn't Criticize Me, Would You, Pal?" shows Joe bearing down on the press, which gave him his start in 1950. He even accused *The Saturday Evening Post* of taking the Communist line.

All cartoons on this spread from "Herblock's Here and Now" (Simon and Schuster) and the "Washington Post"

"I Have Here in My Hand—" has McCarthy offering phony evidence in his televised brawl with the Army. His downfall began when he called a reputable general "not fit to wear that uniform."

McCarthy was censured by his fellow Senators for conduct that "tended to bring the Senate into dishonor or disrepute." He was the fourth Senator in history to receive such a chastisement.

On March 9, 1953, a dozen grim Russians carried Josef Stalin's coffin out of the House of Trade Unions in Moscow to a resting place in Lenin's tomb. During his 73 years the tough old Georgian Bolshevik had done as much as any man to fasten Communist rule on one third of the world. But at his death the tide of Red empire appeared to be close to its high water mark. Stalin's feud with Tito of Yugoslavia had started a chain of events that

led (in 1956) to an all-out revolution in satellite Hungary and semi-autonomy in Poland. In the Far East the U.S. had drawn its line and was on the military alert to defend it. Even in Russia Stalin's successors would soon defame his memory as a "brutal . . . sickly, suspicious" tyrant and bloody-handed killer. Stalin's secret police chief Lavrenti Beria *(far right in black hat, above)* was trapped by his colleagues and shot before 1953 was over.

Dulles at the Geneva Conference meets the new Russian bosses: Party Chief Khrushchev *(right)* and Premier Bulganin. The Russians brimmed over with "co-existence" and vodka at the first big-power meeting since Potsdam.

FOUR TIMES TO THE BRINK

JOHN FOSTER DULLES, said President Eisenhower, is "the greatest Secretary of State I have ever known." He was certainly the most peripatetic. In three years Dulles traveled 226,645 miles, dropped down on 34 nations, and made three trips to the brink of war—in Korea in 1953, in Indochina in 1954, off the China coast in 1955. "The ability to get to the verge without getting into the war is the necessary art," the Secretary explained, in an interview for *Life*. In 1956 he proved his point when America's allies fell off another brink at Suez, where Dulles had escorted them. Dulles (and the U.S.) remained on the verge.

Meanwhile Ike himself seemed to be aiming his foreign policy in quite a different direction. His "atoms for peace" plan (1953) was a real start toward world-wide atomic co-operation, with Russia and the U.S. both chipping in materials and know-how. His "open skies" disarmament scheme, which he announced dramatically at the 1955 "summit" conference in Geneva, was an offer to let Russian planes inspect U.S. military sites—if the Reds would agree to reciprocate. (They didn't.)

From "Herblock's Here and Now" (Simon and Schuster)

"You Sure Everything's All Right, Foster?" inquires Ike, as Dulles hastily stuffs a diplomatic note into a bottle.

Dulles expounds his Suez strategy while Ike ponders at a 1956 White House telecast. Dulles had just moved up to the brink again by withdrawing aid to Egypt for building its Aswan Dam. A nine-days "war" quickly followed.

"Stand Aside, Junior—I Take Over from Here!" the H-bomb tells the A-bomb, in this 1952 cartoon from the New York *Herald Tribune*

THE ULTIMATE HELL-BOMB

In February 1954 President Eisenhower confirmed the news that the world had long known off the record: the U.S. now had a super-weapon whose capacity for dealing death was absolutely unlimited. The new device was variously called the hydrogen, fusion or thermonuclear bomb; it used the heat of an ordinary A-bomb to fuse and transform the nuclei of lightweight elements like hydrogen. In its first secret test in 1952 the prototype of the H-bomb vaporized a small coral island, ripped a hole 175 feet deep in the ocean floor, tossed up a fireball more than three miles in diameter, and released a cloud of radioactive dust 25 miles into the stratosphere. This single pioneer blast was as big as the sum of all the bombs that were dropped on Germany and Japan during World War II—including the two original A-bombs.

But soon much bigger H-bombs were being set off in the Pacific. And in the summer of 1953 it became quite clear that the Russians were making H-bombs too.

This deadlock began a new phase of the cold war which was more chilling than the first. From now on, as the President remarked, there was "no alternative to peace"—at least among nuclear equals. America's industrial superiority meant little if a sneak attack (like the one on Pearl Harbor) could knock out sixty key cities and kill 80 million people. Of course the U.S. Strategic Air Command could swarm out of its hangars and do the same thing to Russia. But "surely [said Ike] no sane member of the human race could discover victory in such desolation."

That was also the view of Dr. J. Robert Oppenheimer, the "father" of the wartime A-bomb, and the eloquent voice of conscience for many American scientists. In 1946 Oppenheimer had been outspoken in demanding civilian control of the atom, along with an international ban on uranium-fission bombs. In 1949 he opposed a "crash" program to manufacture the H-bomb, for practical, political and moral reasons. In 1954, as a belated punishment, he was deprived of his official security clearance by the Atomic Energy Commission.

Physicist Edward Teller pushed the H-bomb to completion after a great debate in 1949. President Truman gave Teller the go-ahead although most scientists voted "No."

Physicist J. Robert Oppenheimer was "walled off" from atomic secrets by order of President Ike. But all the important secrets were already in Oppenheimer's head.

Earl Warren was the popular Republican Governor of California for ten years before Eisenhower appointed him Chief Justice in 1953.

THE

UNANIMOUS

DECREE

THE HUSHED room of the U.S. Supreme Court was filled and expectant. The nine Justices sat in a stately row behind their mahogany bench, their robes deep black against a red velour hanging. In their center the new Chief Justice, Earl Warren, was reading his first important opinion. The date was May 17, 1954.

"We conclude [Warren concluded] that in the field of public education the doctrine of 'separate but equal' has no place. Separate educational facilities are inherently unequal. Therefore, we hold that the plaintiff and others similarly situated . . . are, by reason of the segregation complained of, deprived of the equal protection of the laws guaranteed by the Fourteenth Amendment." From the eight Associate Justices—hailing from Alabama, Indiana, Kentucky, Massachusetts, New York, Ohio, Texas and Washington—there came no word of dissent.

The Court's decision was history-making because it struck down finally the legal basis on which the South had maintained its segregated schools for white and Negro children. It was inspiring because it reaffirmed the great ideals of the Declaration of Independence and applied them to all Americans. It was sensational because it was unanimous.

But it was not effective at once, and no one expected it would be. The Court waited a whole year to let its words sink in. Then it called in attorneys from the protesting Southern states and ordered them to desegregate with "all deliberate speed." Enforcement was left to the lower Federal courts, with the aid of the Justice Department. The President and Congress did nothing to help.

The result, by the end of 1956, was deliberate but not discouraging. More than 320,000 Negro children in nine Southern and border states had been "integrated" into white schools, with a minimum of serious trouble. West Virginia, Missouri and Oklahoma led the way, along with the city of Washington and the town of Clinton, Tennessee. In Louisville *(see opposite page)* there was an especially successful changeover, due to the wisdom and patience of an Alabama-born superintendent, Omer Carmichael. At Little Rock Federal troops, ordered out by President Eisenhower, overrode local prejudice and a rabble-rousing Governor in 1957. But in the deeper South—the hard core of the old Confederacy —two million Negro school children were still without "equal protection."

"WHAT A BELLY-ACHE!"

The President, aged 64, looked radiantly healthy at a press conference on March 30, 1955. He said he was jealous of the White House squirrels who had "a freedom I would personally dearly love."

From "Herblock's Here and Now" (Simon and Schuster)

Ike practiced his putts on the White House lawn. When squirrels interfered they were box-trapped and removed.

At 2:30 p.m., September 23, 1955, President Eisenhower ate a grilled hamburger with two slices of raw onion at the Cherry Hills Country Club near Denver. He had just played 18 holes of golf; after lunch he played nine more. That night he awoke with a heart attack (coronary thrombosis) and was rushed to an Army hospital. For weeks the nation anxiously waited while the heart scar slowly healed.

Ike's dramatic illness clipped $14 billion off Wall Street stock prices and produced some remarkably detailed medical bulletins. It also raised an inevitable question: would (or could) he run in 1956? In February he gave the answer: Yes, "if the Republican Party chooses." "The work that I set out to do four years ago has not yet reached the state of . . . fruition that I then hoped," he added.

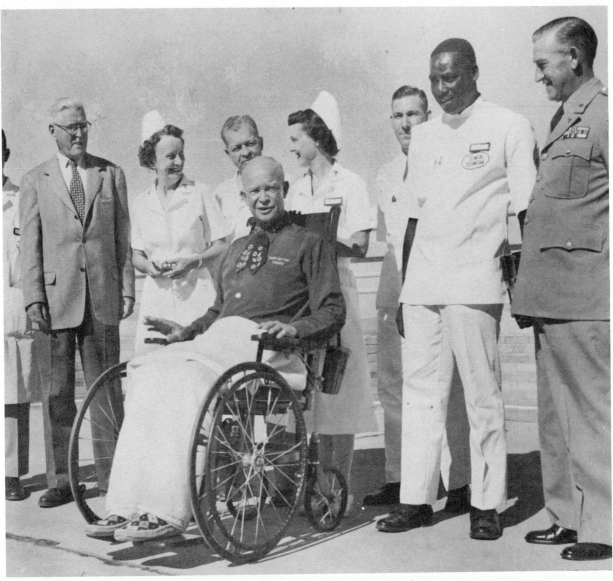

While Ike convalesced in Denver the Eisenhower team under Vice President Nixon carried on "business as usual" in Washington. On October 25 the President posed in his wheelchair. In December he returned to the White House.

In June 1956 Ike was rushed to a hospital again for an operation on a blocked intestine (ileitis), described to the press at a blackboard conference above. "What a bellyache!" murmured the President after he came to.

On election eve in 1956 President Eisenhower stood in front of a White House fireplace and played his part in a nation-wide televised Republican rally. Ike's TV coach, Actor Robert Montgomery, provided cues from a prompting stand at left. Peace and prosperity were the Republican issues, marred somewhat in October by a breath-taking

revolt in Hungary (which was crushed by Russian tanks) and an armed attack on Egypt (which was stopped by the UN). Adlai Stevenson, who also ran again, said it was time to stop testing H-bombs to protect the whole world against radioactive fallout. But without Ike's powerful sponsorship, this suggestion failed to rouse the voters.

Russia's Premier discovered hot dogs in Iowa in 1959. "We make good sausages but yours are better," he said.

Khrushchev's good friend among American capitalists was Cyrus Eaton of Cleveland, shown visiting in Moscow.

THE HUMAN

SPUTNIK

GENERAL IKE's second term had barely begun when the Iron Curtain began to rock and roll under the impact of Nikita S. Khrushchev. "We will bury you!" the Red party chief told Western newsmen in Moscow—but then he explained he only meant that Soviet technology was forging ahead of the capitalist countries. He popped up on U.S. television screens and declared: "Your grandchildren will live under

Beaming Khrushchev met President Eisenhower at Camp David, Maryland, in 1959. They agreed they would try to settle disputes by "peaceful means through negotiation."

Unconvinced Khrushchev, at Moscow exhibit, heard Vice President Nixon explain the wonders of U.S. washers.

Jubilant Khrushchev in 1960 announced capture of a speedy U-2 plane with its photos. "The pilot is quite alive and kicking," he boasted.

Socialism. And please do not be afraid of that." In October 1957 he had something he could really gloat about: the epochal flight of Sputnik I, first man-made satellite to orbit the earth.

Khrushchev became Chairman of the Council of Ministers (equivalent to Premier) in 1959 and from then on was the star of the cold war, emitting threats, insults and goodwill gestures in about equal profusion. Americans generally sympathized with his wrath when he was refused admission to Disneyland in 1959. They were shocked when he sat down in the United Nations Assembly and pounded his desk with his shoe. And they squirmed unhappily when he announced (above) that Russian gunners had downed a U.S. Central Intelligence Agency plane and plucked an American spy from the stratosphere.

A raging Khrushchev resumed the cold-war offensive in 1960, after the U-2 incident. With Marshal Malinovsky looking grim beside him, he called off a Paris summit meeting and told Ike to stay out of Russia. "It might be a good idea," he added, "to take American aggressors by the scruff of the neck and give them a good shake."

CHAPTER 11

THE YEARS
OF KENNEDY
AND JOHNSON

"WE STAND TODAY," said John F. Kennedy, "on the edge of a New Frontier—the frontier of the 1960's, a frontier of unknown opportunities and perils, a frontier of unfulfilled hopes and threats." The day was July 15, 1960, and the junior Senator from Massachusetts stood on the home field of the Los Angeles Dodgers, accepting the nomination for President at the age of 43. Eighty thousand hopeful Democrats roared approval of his words.

The New Frontier was not a new slogan but it suggested adventure and vigorous action, and it dramatized the nation's urge to snap out of its cold-war inertia. President Ike during his second term had concentrated on budget-watching while the eager-beaver rulers of Russia lavished money and scientific brains on building 50-megaton bombs, intercontinental missiles that worked, and the world's biggest rocket boosters. Russia's superiority in space, the exploding birthrate in Red China and elsewhere, the rise of Castroism in Cuba, and the new, impatient, anti-white nations of Africa and Asia were all part of a speedup of history in which—the Democratic platform asserted—American prestige had "steadily declined."

Jack Kennedy hammered hard on this theme in his drive for the Presidency. But his best argument was his public image, which combined a hurry-up appeal to the voters with a not-so-fast coolness in practical politics. Why—he was asked by Adlai Stevenson—did he choose Lyndon B. Johnson of Texas, the head and front of the Senate "Establishment," the master manipulator of Capitol Hill, the symbol of slowdown and compromise to labor lobbyists and civil rights crusaders, to stand beside him in the campaign as candidate for Vice President?

"Because," Kennedy explained, "I want to win."

The ticket was momentarily startling because it merged the New Frontier with the oldest, most conservative power base in American politics—the still fairly solid Democratic South. But the arrangement worked two ways; it also attached Southern party loyalty and the South's most effective politician to the forward pull of the New Frontier. The combination was good for the Democrats, who would have lost in 1960 without the 81 electoral votes they got from Texas and the South. And it was good for the nation three years later, when Kennedy's term was cut short by tragedy, and Lyndon Johnson emerged as a determined, progressive President.

Where and what was the New Frontier, and how could Americans best meet its dangers? Kennedy's advice was pretty abstract but it boiled down to this: don't linger too long around old campfires, and keep your powder dry. During his 1,037 days in office the thoughtful young President with the urgent message grew steadily more proficient in his job. His first Cuban crisis, at the Bay of Pigs, was by his own account a fiasco; his second, a much more serious tussle with Khrushchev over Russian missile sites on the island, developed into a major triumph. The great achievement of his administration—the nuclear test-ban treaty of 1963—was the first real advance in 24 years toward a peaceful end of the atomic arms race.

Lyndon Johnson gave the New Frontier a new name and a set of Texas-sized new dimensions. Yet the Great Society to which he pointed had several familiar features. It included a Coolidge-style business boom, a New Deal as ambitious as FDR's, a formidable use of Teddy Roosevelt's Big Stick, and a program for re-reconstructing the South that would have tickled old Thaddeus Stevens (see page 186.) Johnson's compulsion to do something about everything worked legislative and political wonders during his first two years in the White House. It also involved the U. S. in situations that were agonizing (the stepped-up war in Vietnam) or merely controversial (armed intervention in the Dominican Republic). But Johnson accomplished what Kennedy intended: he provided bold action on all big issues and made the Presidency, once again, the pulpit of American idealism, self-interest, and power.

YOUNG MAN AT THE TOP

Jacqueline Kennedy almost stole the show at her husband's inaugural. Her pillbox hat became a national fad.

JACK KENNEDY LOOKED PLEASED with himself on January 20, 1961, and he had good reasons. He had proved that being a young, telegenic, well-heeled Catholic was no bar to being elected President. His wife was a remarkably fetching First Lady, and waiting to help them brighten up the White House were a three-year-old daughter and a 57-day-old son, John Fitzgerald Kennedy, Jr. The administration was shaping up, in his Cabinet and other appointments, as a talented band of doers and thinkers from big business, labor and politics, the big universities and foundations, and the big Kennedy clan. JFK's euphoria was at its peak as he chatted with a *Time* reporter, a few days before his inauguration. "Sure, it's a big job," he said. "But I don't know anyone who can do it better than I can."

In public Kennedy tried not to sound so brash. His inaugural address stressed world difficulties, and politely urged the Communist nations to engage in coendeavor as well as coexistence. But it was far from humble. In reconnoitering the New Frontier, President John Fitzgerald Francis Kennedy would not be a timid trail boss.

"I DO NOT SHRINK . . . I WELCOME IT . . . LET US BEGIN"

Kennedy was not only the youngest elected President; he was the first whose parents were born after the Civil War. His inaugural address was a proud challenge to his own and oncoming generations. Some memorable passages:

. . . Let the word go forth from this time and place, to friend and foe alike, that the torch has been passed to a new generation of Americans, born in this century, tempered by war, disciplined by a hard and bitter peace, proud of our ancient heritage, and unwilling to witness or permit the slow undoing of those human rights to which this nation has always been committed . . .

Let every nation know, whether it wishes us well or ill, that we will pay any price, bear any burden, meet any hardship, support any friend, oppose any foe to assure the survival and the success of liberty . . . .

To those nations who would make themselves our adversaries, we offer not a pledge but a request: that both sides begin anew the quest for peace, before the dark powers of destruction unleashed by science engulf all humanity in planned or accidental self-destruction.

We dare not tempt them with weakness. For only when our arms are sufficient beyond doubt can we be certain beyond doubt that they will never be employed. But neither can two great and powerful groups of nations take comfort in our present course . . .

So let us begin anew, remembering on both sides that civility is not a proof of weakness, and sincerity is always subject to proof. Let us never negotiate out of fear, but let us never fear to negotiate . . . .

Let both sides, for the first time, formulate serious and precise proposals for the inspection and control of arms . . . Let both sides seek to invoke the wonders of science instead of its terrors. Together let us explore the stars, conquer the deserts, tap the ocean depths and encourage the arts and commerce . . . .

All this will not be finished in the first 100 days. Nor will it be finished in the first 1,000 days, nor in the life of this Administration, nor even perhaps in our lifetime on this planet. But let us begin . . . .

In the long history of the world, only a few generations have been granted the role of defending freedom in its hour of maximum danger. I do not shrink from this responsibility—I welcome it. I do not believe that any of us would exchange places with any other people or any other generation. The energy, the faith, the devotion which we bring to this endeavor will light our country and all who serve it, and the glow from that fire can truly light the world.

And so, my fellow Americans: ask not what your country can do for you—ask what you can do for your country . . . .

For the first White House news conference ever telecast live—on January 25, 1961—Kennedy saved a happy surprise: two U.S. fliers who had been Russian prisoners were free and on their way home. He also announced he was sending more corn meal to the starving Congo, would not resume relations with Castro, wanted Laos to be an uncommitted nation, and had taken steps to "alleviate the distress" among feuding Democrats in New York. [Laughter from the reporters.] The President's professional aplomb on TV, his quiz show exchanges with the press, his quick humor and mastery of detail, were a delight to his audience and a headache to Republicans.

EAST BOSTON...

Grandfather Patrick Joseph Kennedy kept a decent saloon and helped run the Democratic party in Irish East Boston.

"I got Jack into politics. I was the one," the President's father, Joseph P. Kennedy, told an interviewer in 1957. Behind the new man in the White House was an ambitious family clan and an enormous family fortune, estimated during Kennedy's Presidency at over $250 million. Jack's personal share was $15 million, growing from trust funds given him by his father; this made him the richest President ever. His access to all the money he needed was an advantage in all his campaigns. But just as valuable, for political purposes, were the combative spirit, the surplus of masculine sex appeal, and the Irish charm and wit that were part of his birthright.

As a boy Jack was a slow starter: he was underweight, an indifferent student, an earnest but undistinguished athlete. At 19 he entered Harvard but did not show superior talent until his senior year, when his thesis on "Appeasement at Munich" won him a *cum laude*. (The thesis also sold well as a

President Kennedy was born May 29, 1917, in this house in Brookline, Mass.

At 10 he attended a private school and played football.

At 20, a Harvard sophomore, he was on the varsity team, swimming backstroke.

In 1936 Jack *(left center)* vacationed on the French Riviera with all his eight brothers and sisters, his mother Rose *(top right)* and father Joe, who had recently resigned as chairman of the New Deal's SEC. It was Papa Joe who amassed the Kennedy fortune, by killings in Wall Street, movie making, whiskey importing and shrewd investments in real estate.

TO CAPITOL HILL

published book with the title *Why England Slept*.)

Meanwhile his older brother Joe was ringing doorbells and getting elected a delegate to the 1940 Democratic convention. In Jack's words his brother Joe was "the star of our family"—a robust, extroverted type who was already planning to run for Congress in the district their grandfather "Honey Fitz" had represented (East Boston, North Boston and part of Cambridge). Joe talked also of running for Senator and, some day, for President. But after Pearl Harbor Joe Kennedy, Jr., became a Navy pilot and died on a daring mission against German rocket bases in France.

The eyes and hopes of the Kennedys now turned irresistibly toward his skinnier, shyer brother Jack. "I told him Joe was dead and it was his responsibility to run for Congress," Joe, Sr., explained. "He didn't want to. He felt he didn't have the ability . . . . But I told him he had to."

Grandfather John Francis ("Honey Fitz") Fitzgerald was a silver-tongued Boston Mayor and three-term Congressman.

In 1943, in the South Pacific, he lost his PT boat but heroically rescued his crew.

His wartime back injury required surgery in 1954.

While recovering he wrote *Profiles in Courage* at this Palm Beach family home.

Emaciated after his wartime ordeal—and still a bachelor at 29—Jack was showered with votes and sympathy when he won his first Congressional primary in 1946. But one male rival called him "a goddamned carpetbagger" because he had never lived in the Boston–Cambridge (11th) District where his family was famous. He campaigned from a hotel room.

"Why not me?" mused Jack Kennedy, as he pondered the chances of Nixon, Rockefeller, Stevenson, Johnson, Symington, Humphrey and Kefauver in the 1960 Presidential free-for-all. His own prospects looked pretty good. In 1958 he was re-elected Senator with the biggest total vote (1.3 million) ever cast in Massachusetts for any candidate for any office. In 1959 his family equipped him with a private plane to continue his relentless pursuit of delegates. His personal photographer, Jacques Lowe, took this portrait of a political thinker, somewhere over the United States, en route to Nebraska.

THE MAKING OF A CANDIDATE

GETTING ELECTED to the House of Representatives from his grandfather's district was a sure thing for Jack Kennedy. Getting elected to the Senate was harder, but Jack battled through to a startling win in 1952. His opponent was the strong Republican incumbent, Henry Cabot Lodge, Jr., and that year Ike carried Massachusetts by 208,000 votes. (Kennedy won by 70,000.) The whole family pitched in to help: his mother and sisters served tea to the voters, Bobby (aged 27) managed campaign headquarters, and Papa Joe provided plenty of money (including a $500,000 "business loan" to the faltering Boston *Post*, a right-wing Republican newspaper which urged its readers late in the campaign to vote for Kennedy instead of Lodge).

Jack was still unattached when he moved to the Senate, and the *Saturday Evening Post* was ecstatic over "The Senate's Gay Young Bachelor." There was a lot more heart-throb publicity when he married the beauteous Jacqueline Bouvier at Newport in 1953. A year later Jackie was with him when he entered a hospital for surgery to his back, which had been injured in college football, and again more seriously during the war in a fall on his sinking PT boat. The spinal fusion operation was dangerous, and the after-effects were so painful and damaging that they nearly cost him his life. His physical misery kept him out of the Senate during the debate and vote on the motion to censure Senator Joseph McCarthy, a hero to most of the Boston Irish but a

political pain in the neck to Kennedy. He might have paired his vote *in absentia* but he did not arrange to do so, and he offered no apologies later. "What was I supposed to do—commit hara-kiri?" he grumbled to one reporter.

Instead, he wrote a thoughtful book about senators of the past who had risked their careers by taking sides on inflammatory issues. *Profiles in Courage* won a Pulitzer Prize and was on the best-seller lists for years. Less attention was paid by the public to another study which was written in Kennedy's office and distributed to Democratic professionals. This purported to prove that Jack's Catholic affiliation—far from being a handicap in a national campaign—was really an asset. "Catholics consistently turn out to vote in greater proportion than non-Catholics," the report asserted, and there were enough loyal Catholics in "pivotal Catholic states" to provide 261 electoral votes—only five short of a majority. In 1956 the only way Kennedy could test this theory was to try for the Vice Presidential nomination, and it didn't work—he lost. He conceded this defeat so gracefully (on nationwide TV), worked so hard in the next four years to appeal to non-Catholics, and performed so flawlessly in the primaries, that he was way out in front of all other contenders when the 1960 convention began. Even so, it took 15 Midwestern and mountain States, along with 11 urban "Catholic" ones, to give him the nomination for President on the first and only ballot.

Last-minute arrangements for Kennedy's 1960 nomination were checked at his Biltmore Hotel suite by Jack, Bobby, and two aides from Connecticut, State Chairman Bailey *(left)* and Governor Ribicoff. The only hitch in their plans was a loud but futile demonstration for Stevenson.

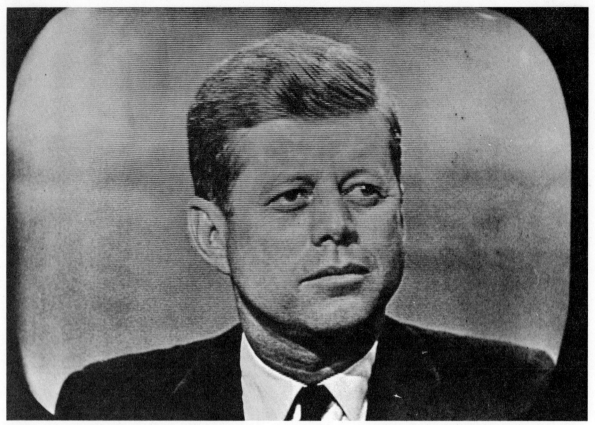

"*Kennedy Or Nixon—Does It Make Any Difference?*" asked historian Arthur Schlesinger, Jr., in the title of his 1960 campaign tract. The difference of opinion among 68.3 million voters was about one-fifth of one percent.

"It's frightening! These hands can change history!" exclaimed the TV makeup man in Bill Mauldin's cartoon.

PROFILES

THE ELECTION itself was the closest since 1888, and it was probably decided within a few seconds when the voters got their first look at the candidates side by side on television. The Republican contender, Vice President Nixon, was the heavy favorite at the start, largely because of his reputation as a TV performer. But in their first "great debate" *(above)* Nixon looked for all the world like a man with shaving and perspiration problems, glumly waiting for the commercial to tell him how not to offend. Kennedy, on the other hand, projected an aura of coolness and confidence, and proved himself before 70 million watchers to be a master of brisk cerebration.

As a nationwide screen test the event was fascinating; as a debate it was disappointingly tame. Spurred on by the complaints of the critics, the candidates in their later appearances disagreed sharply on three specific questions:

Should the U.S. express its formal, diplomatic

"It was an inner music of the soul that separated them," wrote Theodore H. White, the chronicler and bard of the campaign, who reported also that Nixon wore "Lazy Shave" face powder in the first of the great television debates.

IN POLITICS

regrets to Khrushchev over the U-2 spy-plane fiasco? Kennedy, "Yes"; Nixon, "No."

Should the U.S. defend Quemoy and Matsu islands, a few miles from the mainland of China, against all-out Red Chinese attack? Nixon, "Yes"; Kennedy, "No."

Should the U.S. help Cuban refugees to invade Cuba and overthrow Castro? Kennedy, "Yes"; Nixon, "No." But the answers in this case were political camouflage. Nixon already had approved the invasion, which was being arranged in official secrecy by the Central Intelligence Agency. He hoped it might succeed in time to help him win the election. Kennedy didn't know all the details but he was determined not to be beaten by an Administration coup in Cuba. So when Nixon called Kennedy "irresponsible" and Kennedy called Nixon "misinformed" about Cuba, both knew they were not discussing any real difference between them.

"I am not the Catholic candidate ... the church does not speak for me," JFK told Houston Protestant ministers.

THE KENNEDY STYLE

"SHE'S A MARVELOUS DANCER. She's divine," burbled a Senator to a society reporter at the first Presidential reception staged by the incoming Kennedys. Jack was handsome but Jackie in a sleeveless pink sheath was ravishing as they led off with a conservative foxtrot while the Marine Band played "Mr. Wonderful." The New Frontier called for new high levels of sophistication and chic in the White House. Bourbon, canasta and Lawrence Welk were out; daiquiris, *foie gras* and Proust were in. Jackie (according to *Women's Wear Daily*) wore 400 different outfits in public in a little more than a year. Her slender husband advised his staff to lose five pounds apiece, and he let it be known he did not favor button-down shirts, or men who wore clocks on their socks.

Pablo Casals, Princess Grace of Monaco, and all winners of Nobel Prizes were sure bets to turn up at White House parties. The ultimate accolade went to Lieutenant Colonel John H. Glenn, first American to go into orbit (on February 20, 1962). He was invited to Hyannis Port, to water ski with Jackie.

The Kennedys visited Queen Elizabeth, Charles de Gaulle and Nikita Khrushchev (in Vienna) in 1961. Jackie got along very well with Khrushchev. Her husband did not.

The Kennedy kids had fun at the White House. Caroline kept her pony on the lawn and toted dolls in and out of offices. "John-John" crawled under the President's desk in pursuit of telephone wires. Late in 1962 they both invaded his oval office and danced a jig to celebrate their upcoming birthdays (Caroline, 5; John F., Jr., 2).

The U. S. began to catch up in space May 5, 1961, when a Redstone rocket lifted a capsule containing Commander Alan B. Shepard, Jr., to a suborbital height of 116.5 miles. He splashed down in the Atlantic after 35 minutes. Three weeks earlier Russian Major Yuri Gagarin orbited once around the earth—the first such flight in history.

The Peace Corps, a Kennedy brainchild, was delivered at once by Congress and became a worldwide hit. Low-paid volunteers taught and gave practical aid in 48 nations.

At the Bay of Pigs *(below)* beaten rebels were rounded up by Castro's grinning *milicianos*. The U.S. supplied the spotted uniforms for jungle fighting that never occurred.

EDUCATION OF A PRESIDENT

WHILE PRESIDENT KENNEDY was dancing to the music of "Mr. Wonderful" bad news from Cuba's Bahía de Cochinos was pouring into his office. The long-planned liberation attempt by anti-Castro refugees bogged down on the very night—April 18, 1961 —of the Kennedys' gala reception for Congress and the Cabinet. The President left the party at 11:45 P.M. and went directly, in white tie and tails, to a grim meeting with his advisers. At 1:00 A.M. he approved an order to the Navy aircraft carrier *Essex*: Provide unmarked jet cover for one hour only, beginning at 6:30 that morning, for the rebel invaders' supply boats and the tiny rebel air force of slow-moving B-26's. Because of a time-zone mixup (or some other snafu) this order was not carried out. At the end of the day (April 19) the invasion attempt was finished. Some 1,500 free Cubans were killed or captured by Castro's swarms of militia. Four U.S. citizen volunteers who piloted rebel B-26's were never heard from again.

It was not a big miltary disaster and—because Kennedy had insisted on it—no U.S. forces took part in the fighting. But the rebels were organized, armed, trained and transported by the U.S. Central Intelligence Agency, and their invasion plan was approved by the Joint Chiefs of Staff. In the thinking of the world's power politicians that made the Bay of Pigs the most damaging blow to American prestige since Russia exploded its first atomic bomb.

Who was to blame? "I am..." said the President, who took his medicine manfully in public. In private he sounded willing to share the responsibility with unnamed "experts." "How could I have been so far off base?" he exclaimed to his special counsel and confidant, Ted Sorensen. "How could I have been so stupid, to let them go ahead?"

After the Bay of Pigs he made all the big moves on his own initiative. In Laos, the Congo, on the University of Mississippi campus, and in his confrontation with U.S. Steel over price-raising, he achieved considerable if sometimes painful success. But at the Berlin Wall, in South Vietnam, and even on Capitol Hill, the New Frontier looked like the old standoff.

A Kennedy project that was soon forgotten was his 1961 letter in *Life*, with do-it-yourself drawings, urging every U.S. family to build its own backyard "fallout shelter."

East German Communists wired the Brandenburg Gate and split Berlin with a thick stone wall in 1961. Kennedy hurried in a crack battle unit to reinforce the U.S. garrison and called up 82,000 reserves.

Neutralist Buddhists, opposing dictator Ngo Dinh Diem, cremated themselves in Saigon. Kennedy sent "advisers" (U.S. troops) to Diem, but did not regret his 1963 fall.

Khrushchev in 1961 treated Kennedy like a schoolboy and told him Soviet policy in Berlin was "absolutely irrevocable."

U-2 photo above revealed Russian base. Below, U.S. destroyer and plane checked Soviet ship taking missiles back home.

EYEBALL TO EYEBALL

On October 18, 1962, President Kennedy received Soviet Foreign Minister Andrei Gromyko in his White House office. Kennedy sat in the padded rocking chair he used to ease his 23-year-old backache. Gromyko perched on a slip-covered sofa and tried to ease Kennedy's mind about the Russian military buildup in Cuba. Soviet weapons and installations in Cuba—said Gromyko—"pursued solely the purpose of contributing to [Castro's] defense," and were not designed to strike offensive blows beyond the borders of Cuba. These statements, the President told the American people four nights later, were "false."

This time Kennedy had the goods on the Russians. Aerial photos showed that Soviet technicians had equipped a series of sites to launch medium (1,000-mile) and intermediate (up to 2,500-mile) ballistic missiles which could carry nuclear warheads. Their range covered most of the U.S., industrial Canada and Central and South America as far as Lima, Peru. Speaking directly to Nikita Khrushchev, in a White House telecast, Kennedy warned that a nuclear missile fired from Cuba against any Western Hemisphere nation would be considered "an attack by the Soviet Union upon the United States, requiring full retaliatory action." He also imposed a Navy blockade against Russian (or other) ships carrying "offensive" weapons to Cuba. This was a serious action, and the Russians took it seriously. Within a week they began dismantling their bases and loading salvaged missiles on ships for the long voyage home. Khrushchev made angry countercharges, but he cut his losses in Cuba. He had learned how far he could go.

Kennedy in 1962 told Khrushchev to take his missiles out of Cuba or risk nuclear war. Khrushchev removed the missiles.

"A STEP TOWARD REASON . . ."

The end of the Cuban missile crisis cleared the cold-war air for a while. Moscow agreed to a U.S. scheme to link the Kremlin and White House with "hot line" teletypewriters, so there could be instant communication in times of immediate danger. President Kennedy broke a precedent and let the Russians buy American wheat. In August 1963 British, Soviet and U.S. diplomats crowded around a table in Moscow and watched the signing of a treaty that few of them had expected to see. By it the Big Three nuclear powers agreed to heed the fallout menace and end bomb tests in the atmosphere, in space and under water—everywhere except in underground caves. The Senate approved the treaty by a surprising 80-19 vote. President Kennedy signed it in Washington *(left)* on October 7, calling it "not the millennium [but] a step toward peace—a step toward reason—a step away from war . . ."

NONVIOLENCE ON THE MARCH

In Birmingham, Alabama, thousands of Negroes and a handful of whites signed "commitment cards," which read: "I HEREBY PLEDGE MYSELF—MY PERSON AND MY BODY—TO THE NONVIOLENT MOVEMENT. THEREFORE I WILL ... REFRAIN from the violence of fist, tongue, or heart." The persons and bodies of civil-rights marchers were roughly handled by the Birmingham police. But dogs, hoses, billy clubs and bombs could no longer stop Southern Negroes. Nor could state and local segregation laws, or the magnolia-flavored, slavery-based "traditions" that had served to nullify their citizenship since the end of the first Reconstruction *(see page 223).*

On June 12, 1963, an upholder of the Southern way of life hid in some bushes behind a home in Jackson, Mississippi. From there he fired a fatal rifle bullet into the back of Medgar W. Evers, college graduate, father of three, and field secretary in Mississippi of the 54-year-old National Association for the Advancement of Colored People. This cowardly murder, and the televised news pictures from Birmingham and elsewhere, shocked the nation and President Kennedy. On June 19 Kennedy asked Congress to rush a drastic new civil rights bill, designed to give the Federal government the power and means to reconstruct the South, again.

On Good Friday morning, April 12, 1963, the Reverend Martin

Birmingham marchers were knocked down with fire hoses but won local desegregation of lunch counters, rest rooms and drinking fountains.

Freedom riders from North and South defied segregation in bus stations in 1961. In Alabama their bus was bombed.

Luther King, Jr., *(in front)* changed into his jail-going clothes and led a Birmingham march that defied an Alabama injunction.

"Segregation now ... segregation forever!" vowed Governor George C. Wallace of Alabama at his 1963 inaugural.

The U.S. charged a Mississippi sheriff *(right)* with conspiracy in the murders of three civil rights workers. Insufficient evidence freed him.

West Berliners put up a platform so the President could look over the hated wall. East Berliners took his picture.

TIME TO LOOK AROUND

THREE DAYS AFTER his civil rights plea to Congress President Kennedy took off for Europe, on a trip that combined business, blarney and barnstorming. At Bonn he drew bigger crowds than Ike or De Gaulle and restored, according to *The New York Times*, "the intimate relationship between [the U.S. and West Germany] that has been lacking for the last two years." In Berlin he was hailed as a conquering hero, although the wall was still there. In Eire he addressed the Dail and Seanad in joint session and attended a wonderful family reunion. At Naples, speaking to the commanders of NATO, he got in some tough digs at the opposition: "Communism has

In Rome he had a private talk with the new Pope Paul VI. Then he introduced his sister Jean (Mrs. Stephen Smith).

At Dunganstown in County Wexford he posed with his Irish cousins and enjoyed a picnic in an ancestral barnyard.

sometimes succeeded as a scavenger, but never as a leader. It has never come to power in any country that was not disrupted by war or internal repression, or both. It is clear that this system is outmoded and doomed to failure . . ."

Back home after ten hectic days, the President seemed reassured and refreshed. America's "steadfast role" in the cold war had earned "the abiding trust and respect" of the West Europeans, he told White House reporters.

During the fall he made other trips, with next year's election and U.S. voters in mind. A September swing dropped him down for speeches in Penn-sylvania, Minnesota and Nevada (which voted for him in 1960) and Wisconsin, North Dakota, Montana, Wyoming, California, Oregon and Washington (which didn't). In November he flew to Texas, where the Democrats were in a mess. Senator Ralph Yarborough suspected Lyndon Johnson and Governor John Connally of scheming to put someone else in his seat, and he refused to appear with them. On the morning of November 22 Jack Kennedy left his Fort Worth hotel and found Yarborough on the sidewalk. "Ralph, you get in the car with Lyndon. Now get in," he ordered. Then he got in his own car, with Connally, and headed for Dallas.

On a sunny September afternoon in Montana, at the fair grounds in Billings, it was just like 1960 all over again.

"Mr. President, you can't say Dallas doesn't love you," said Mrs. Connally (center) during the last motorcade.

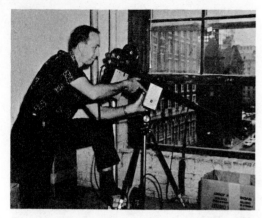

Re-enacting the crime, an FBI photographer aims the killer's rifle and four-power telescopic sight from the sixth-floor window of the schoolbook warehouse.

Photo taken through rifle sight shows an open car like the President's about to enter triple underpass leading to Stemmons Freeway in Dallas.

THE UNBELIEVABLE EVENT

DALLAS WAS HOSTILE political territory but the midtown crowds that greeted the 12-car Kennedy motorcade were friendly and lavish with their cheers. When Mrs. Connally turned and remarked to the President, "You can't say Dallas doesn't love you," Jackie beamed and her husband replied: "That is very obvious."

Just at that moment the President's limousine was leaving downtown Dallas and approaching the big square warehouse of the Texas School Book Depository. On the sixth floor, facing on Elm Street, a window was open. A man crouching there with a mail-order rifle looked down into the open car as it moved along at about 11 miles an hour. Then he focused on the President, from behind, and fired three bullets in less than eight seconds. One pierced Kennedy's neck and went on to inflict three wounds on Governor Connally. Another, instantly mortal, tore through the President's skull. Still another missed. Those were among the accepted facts of a tragedy that immersed the nation in shock and grief as nothing since Lincoln's death had done. The assassin never confessed or explained. He was never adjudged insane, or shown to have a specific motive. But an investigation by a Presidential commission, headed by Chief Justice Earl Warren, found him guilty without any doubt—and without any accomplices.

Real-life photo made November 22 shows Kennedy's foot (white arrow). Secret Service man bends over him. Black arrow points to the wounded Governor.

VIOLENCE IN DALLAS—
THE VERDICT OF
THE WARREN COMMISSION:

Enlargement shows a man's head pinpointed in the position where Kennedy sat. These three photos were exhibits prepared for the Warren Commission.

THE DALLAS TIMES HERALD
FINAL EDITION

CONTINUOUSLY PUBLISHED FOR 87 YEARS · THE TIMES 1876 · THE HERALD 1888 · CONSOLIDATED 1888

67th Year—No. 205 · ★ · DALLAS, TEXAS, MONDAY EVENING, NOVEMBER 25, 1963 · Telephones— · 3 Parts · Price Five Cents

Mourning Nation Bids Chief Farewell
Tip to FBI Warned of Oswald Death

Photographer Bob Jackson of the Dallas *Times-Herald* caught the moment of death for Lee Harvey Oswald. Millions saw this killing on national television.

The man who killed President Kennedy was Lee Harvey Oswald, 24, who learned to shoot in the U.S. Marine Corps and met his wife Marina at a dance in the Palace of Culture in Minsk in March 1961. At that time Oswald was a self-proclaimed defector to Russia and had tried to renounce his American citizenship. In 1962 he claimed it back, borrowed $435.71 for travel expenses from the Embassy in Moscow, and returned with Marina to Texas. His political opinions, which he took very seriously, were a jumble of juvenile Marxism and defective spelling (he was a ninth-grade dropout). Between Soviet Communism and American capitalism, he wrote, "There is no choice, one offers opprestion the other poverty. Both offer imperilistic injustice, tinted with two brands of slavery." In October 1963 Oswald was hired at $1.25 an hour to fill orders on the upper floors of the Texas School Book Depository.

His domestic life, which had never been tranquil, was by then a failure. Marina declined to live with him and complained in front of others about his marital "inadequacy." After one of their separations Oswald carried his rifle along a Dallas street and shot through a window at Edwin A. Walker, retired Major General and frequent speaker at right-wing rallies. On November 16 Marina told her husband she wished to forgo their usual weekend reunion. On November 21 he appeared without notice at the house where she lived, offered to buy her a washing machine, and did not speak when she came to bed. Next morning he left his wedding ring on the dresser, a wallet with $170 (almost all the money he had) in a drawer, and went to the garage where he kept his rifle. About 8 A.M. on November 22 he smuggled the weapon into the warehouse.

He was soon arrested, and might have confessed, except for a second, needless killing in the basement of Dallas police headquarters. On Sunday morning November 24, a man known as Jack Ruby, who managed two sleazy night clubs, and had closed them to mourn for the President, pushed through reporters and cameramen and shot the handcuffed prisoner in the stomach.

"I couldn't stop crying," Ruby explained. "I never felt so bad in my life, even when Ma or Pa died."

"I WILL DO MY BEST"

LYNDON JOHNSON was in the second car behind Kennedy's when the first shot was heard. A Secret Service agent, Rufus Youngblood, whirled around from the front seat, hit the Vice President on the shoulder and yelled, "Get down!" He jumped over and literally sat on Johnson while their car raced after the President's to Parkland Memorial Hospital. A thought raced through Johnson's mind: "They're trying to kill us all."

President Kennedy was pronounced dead at 1 P.M. (CST). At 1:16 Dallas police radio reported that Patrolman J. D. Tippit had just been shot dead in the street by a "suspect"—actually by Lee Harvey Oswald. Kenneth O'Donnell of the White House staff urged Johnson to get out of Dallas at once. "What about Mrs. Kennedy?" he asked, and learned she was near her husband's body, and would not leave without it. "Neither will we," he said.

At 2:38 P.M. at heavily guarded Love Field in Dallas, he stood in the cabin of *Air Force One* and took the oath which made him the 36th President. At 6 P.M. (EST) the plane touched down at Andrews Air Force Base in Maryland. Kennedy's coffin was transferred to a waiting ambulance; his successor walked to a microphone and spoke briefly to the nation:

"This is a sad time for all people ... For me it is a deep personal tragedy ... I will do my best ...."A helicopter ferried him to the White House lawn and he spent a few minutes alone in the Oval Room. Then he went across the street, to the offices he had used as Vice President, and got down to work. First he wrote two letters, in longhand, to Caroline and John F. Kennedy, Jr. After that the meetings, staff discussions and phone calls (to Harry Truman, General Ike, Herbert Hoover, among many others) went on for hours, and continued after he reached home, bringing three assistants to spend the night. It was 3:30 A.M. on November 23—exactly 16 hours after a Secret Service agent pushed him down and sat on him—before Lyndon Johnson called it a day.

The new President took the oath with his hand on Kennedy's

Catholic Bible. Afterward Johnson turned and kissed Mrs. Kennedy on the forehead. "You're so brave to do this," he whispered.

At 13 and in long pants, Lyndon towered over his brother and sisters: Lucia, Josefa, Rebekah and Sam Houston.

At 26, a rising New Dealer, he visited Mexico on his honeymoon.

At 33, after Pearl Harbor, he did a hitch in the Navy.

LBJ, THE WRANGLER

"THIS ADMINISTRATION," announced President Johnson, "here and now, declares unconditional war on poverty in America." That was in January 1964, after he was in charge six weeks. Johnson's feeling toward poverty was based on experience. His childhood home lacked running water; his father, a farmer and Texas legislator, went broke three times. ("In Republican administrations," LBJ always hastened to add.) Lyndon shined shoes in Johnson City (named for his pioneer family) and sold socks to other students to help pay his way through Southwest Texas State Teachers' College.

In 1931, aged 23, he arrived in Washington as secretary to Richard M. Kleberg, the ranch king and Congressman. From then on the wheelings and dealings on Capitol Hill, the back-scratching, arm-twisting and occasional mayhem that were much of the political and legislative process, were Johnson's life and his passion. He took a lower-paid job as assistant doorkeeper to find out all he could about the House of Representatives. Speaker Sam Rayburn

helped push him along; so did Franklin and Eleanor Roosevelt. The biggest push came from Claudia Alta ("Lady Bird") Taylor, a Texas girl who married him in 1934. It was her father who loaned Johnson $10,000 to run and get elected to Congress the first time, in 1938.

In 1963, when fate made him President, Johnson was as well trained for the job as a genuine, lifelong professional could be. He looked as strong as a steer, despite a 1955 heart attack. His personal poverty was long since behind him: he and his wife had accumulated property worth four million dollars or maybe fourteen million, depending on which accounting you believed. Having made it big in private enterprise and politics, he now set for himself an even higher goal in Presidential achievement. "We must make sure," he said in 1965, "that every family in America lives in a home of dignity, in a neighborhood of pride, a community of opportunity, and a city of promise and hope." That was quite an order to fill, even for Lyndon Baines Johnson.

In 1948 *(right)* he went after a Texas seat in the Senate in a style that later became widely known. His tiny 87-vote majority in the Democratic primary all came out of one box in Jim Wells County that his opponent charged was stuffed. But it put LBJ in the Senate. In 1951 he was party whip, in 1953 the minority leader, and by 1955 he was the youngest Senate Majority Leader any party ever had. In 1960 he battled Kennedy hard for the nomination for President. When he lost he took second place for the same reason that Kennedy offered it: the Democrats needed his talents to win.

The Johnsons entertained often and well at their LBJ Ranch in central Texas where the President obliged photographers by pretending to round up a Hereford. He was born a few miles away, August 27, 1908, at Stonewall, Gillespie County, on the Pedernales River.

HIGH NOON
AT
THE COW
PALACE

Rockefeller was eloquent in defeat. "There is no place in this Republican party for those who would infiltrate its ranks, distort its aims, and convert it into a cloak of apparent respectability for a dangerous extremism," he said.

"JUST A MINUTE—just a minute, please," begged Governor Nelson A. Rockefeller of New York at the Republican Convention of 1964. His audience answered with angry howls that showed they cared nothing for moderate Republicans who often sounded like consensus Democrats. The delegates wanted a voice, not an echo, and they already had it in Barry Goldwater, the cactus-tongued Arizona Senator who was nominated for President by a huge, first-ballot majority.

In spite of the panic among Republican losers it was a little hard to see Goldwater as a national menace. He stumbled through his prepared speeches, took

The moderates made it easy for Barry. Rockefeller's divorce and 1963 marriage to "Happy" Murphy (above) probably cost him the nomination.

Henry Cabot Lodge, a moderate, beat Rocky in the New Hampshire primary. Then Rocky beat Lodge in Oregon.

Goldwater was bitter in his acceptance speech. "I would remind you that extremism in the defense of liberty is no vice," he told the delegates. "Those who do not care for our cause, we don't expect to enter our ranks in any case."

color photographs as a hobby, and referred to his electioneering activity as "pooping around." But he preached an old-fashioned, agin-the-government conservatism that won him a frenzied following among the new rich of the West and Southwest, segregationists of the South and North, haters of the Eastern "establishment," and stalwarts of the John Birch Society, whose members were instructed to believe that even General Ike was a Communist agent. When Rockefeller asked the convention to repudiate the extremists, he knew he didn't have a chance—the San Francisco Cow Palace was full of them.

Michigan's Governor Romney, a moderate moderate, slid out of contention early.

Pennsylvania's Governor Scranton, in life-sized cardboard, simply got carried away.

"I don't think I ought to get involved," said General Ike in a Herblock cartoon.

Johnson got 42.6 million votes, an all-time high, and won big majorities in Congress. He also helped the Los An-geles police catch a pickpocket. The man reached out for a wallet, and came up with the President's hand instead.

In Texas the President proudly presented his pick for Vice President: Senator Hubert Humphrey of Minnesota.

"Ouch!" said the President, and winced in pain when his bandaged right hand was wrung by still another voter.

THE PERSONAL TOUCH

"ALL THE WAY with LBJ!" bellowed the President of the United States, using a bullhorn to lead cheers for himself in a campaign parade in Peoria. Lyndon Johnson could have won re-election without leaving the White House Rose Garden; instead he stormed around the country, handshaking his way through clutching mobs and suffering bumps and blisters. It was less than a year since the Dallas shooting and his Secret Service guard was frantic. But the Johnson campaign strategy—which already embraced poverty, prosperity, civil rights, war, peace and "responsibility"—reached its peak in an uproarious display of Presidential empathy.

Goldwater never had a chance. Many influential Republicans disowned him, or stayed clear of his "death wish" campaign. When he gained support among Southern Democrats he lost the Negro vote en masse. When he tried personal abuse of the President—"faker," "phony," "Whitewash House"—Johnson asked the Lord to forgive him. And when he earnestly tried to expound his conservatism he put large numbers of voters to sleep.

On one likely issue of the year he was outmaneuvered by a master. "Make no bones of this," he said in his acceptance speech. "We are at war in Vietnam." And he denounced Johnson, Kennedy and Eisenhower for failing to make the war more extensive by bombing Communist North Vietnam.

Johnson managed this one with ease. While other Democrats called Goldwater a trigger-happy warmonger, the President pulled the trigger and began bombing military bases and routes in North Vietnam.

Johnson's habit of pulling beagles' ears to hear them yip may have cost him a few votes. He said the dogs liked it.

Goldwater touched a famous nose "for luck" at Lincoln's tomb in Springfield, Illinois. Even Abe did not help him.

In New York, Uncle Robert Kennedy, en route to the U.S. Senate, showed up for campaign pictures with John F., Jr.

President Johnson stands in front of a reconstruction of his 1908 birthplace, now located on his LBJ Ranch.

In 1958 Senator Lyndon B. Johnson wrote a short essay, "My Political Philosophy," for the scholarly Texas Quarterly. In the 1960's it could still stand as the credo of a strong-minded President:

"I am a free man, an American, a United States Senator, and a Democrat, in that order.

"I am also a liberal, a conservative, a Texan, a taxpayer, a rancher, a businessman, a consumer, a parent, a voter, and not as young as I used to be nor as old as I expect to be—and I am all of these things in no fixed order.

"I am unaware of any descriptive word in the second paragraph which qualifies, modifies, amends, or is related by hyphenation to the terms listed in the first paragraph. In consequence, I am not able—nor even in the least interested in trying—to define my political philosophy by the choice of a one-word or two-word label . . . .

"At the heart of my own beliefs is a rebellion against this very process of classifying, labeling, and filing Americans under headings . . . Knowing the folks at Johnson City and Blanco and Stonewall and Hye as I do, I know that it would be much more difficult for me to secure a unanimous agreement among them than among the Senators in Washington. Yet in this . . . my neighbors . . . or all of the constituency of Texas are not different from Americans everywhere. There is likely to be merit in the views of a minority, quite as much as there is wisdom in the views of a majority . . .

"This leads to a listing of the tenets of my own beliefs . . . I would set them down this way:

"First, I believe every American has something to say and, under our system, a right to an audience.

"Second, I believe there is always a national answer to a national problem, and, believing this, I do not believe there are necessarily two sides to every question.

"Third, I regard achievement of the full potential of our resources—physical, human and otherwise—to be the highest purpose of government policies next to the protection of those rights we regard as inalienable.

"Fourth, I regard waste as the continuing enemy of our society, and the prevention of waste—waste of resources, waste of lives, or waste of opportunity—to be the most dynamic of the responsibilities of our government.

"These tenets, I concede, are simple. They are certainly personal. For these are not tenets I have embraced or adopted, but, rather, beliefs I have—over fifty years—developed and come to follow from my own experience."

Acknowledgments

I am particularly grateful to Charles Tudor for his creative work in designing the original (1947) edition of this book. The style he conceived and carried out so effectively has been followed—as well as I and others could do it—in the sections added in 1957 and 1965 (pages 458-531).

For assistance in locating pictures I am indebted to D. Jay Culver of Culver Pictures Inc.; to Henry B. Collins, Jr., and the late Arthur Brown of Brown Brothers; John J. Fletcher and Joseph Luppino of United Press International; Meyer Goldberg and Henry Grund of Wide World Photos, Inc.; Doris O'Neil and Joan Norton-Taylor of the *Life* picture collection at Time Inc.; Arthur B. Carlson of the New-York Historical Society; and many other picture specialists and librarians. Frederick H. Meserve, George T. Bagoe, H. Armour Smith and Mrs. M. Handy Evans were generous in allowing me to reproduce photographs from their private collections. Herbert L. Block of the Washington *Post* has been especially kind in permitting me to use a number of his wonderful cartoons. K. Chester, the photographer, helped me through some tight spots with his camera.

Mrs. Charles Steinheimer gave the book its name and researched and checked the first edition. Peter Schwed, M. Lincoln Schuster, and my first editor, the late Jack Goodman, have all taken an interest in this book above and beyond the call of business. I am deeply grateful to them and to my other good friends who are now or were formerly with Simon and Schuster. To Harold Matson, my literary agent, I want to say in public: "Thanks, Hal, for your many good deeds in my behalf."

—R.B.

Picture Credits

6—NOTE: Pictures omitted from the list below have been reproduced from originals in the possession of the author. However, he is not able to supply prints or further information. Those who wish to obtain prints of pictures published in this book should contact one of the agencies listed below, or a library or historical society which has a large picture collection. The following abbreviations are used in this list:
BROWN—Brown Brothers, New York City
CULVER—Culver Pictures, Inc., New York City
EUROPEAN—European Picture Service, New York City
GRANGER—The Granger Collection, New York City
HANDY—L. C. Handy Studios, Washington, D.C. (now part of Library of Congress collection)
KEYSTONE—Keystone View Co., Inc., New York City
UNDERWOOD—Underwood & Underwood, New York City (NOTE—Most of the pictures credited here to Underwood are currently available from other agencies, or from the Library of Congress and other public sources.)
UNITED PRESS—United Press International, New York City
WIDE WORLD—Wide World Photos, Inc., New York City

Page   Owner
ii—UPPER, HARVARD UNIVERSITY, FOGG MUSEUM OF ART—LOWER, HISTORICAL SOCIETY OF PENNSYLVANIA
xi—LIBRARY OF CONGRESS
xii—CULVER
2-3—CULVER
4—CENTER, LEFT, BROWN—CENTER RIGHT, CULVER—LOWER LEFT, CULVER—LOWER RIGHT, BROWN
5—THE PENNSYLVANIA ACADEMY OF THE FINE ARTS, PHILADELPHIA
6—CENTER AND LOWER RIGHT, CULVER
7—LOWER LEFT, BROWN
8—HUNTINGTON LIBRARY, SAN MARINO, CALIF.

9—UPPER RIGHT, BETTMANN ARCHIVE
10—CENTER, CULVER
11—CULVER
12—CULVER
13—NEW-YORK HISTORICAL SOCIETY
14—NEW YORK PUBLIC LIBRARY (BOTH)
15—RIGHT-HAND ROW, THIRD AND FOURTH FROM TOP, OLD PRINT SHOP, NEW YORK—LOWER LEFT, CULVER
16—MR. CHARLES FRANCIS ADAMS, BOSTON, MASS., *courtesy of* FRICK ART REFERENCE LIBRARY
17—UPPER LEFT, YALE UNIVERSITY ART GALLERY—LOWER LEFT, STATE CAPITOL, RICHMOND, VA., *photographic reproduction by* A. L. DEMENTI STUDIO, RICHMOND—LOWER CENTER, CULVER—LOWER RIGHT, HARVARD UNIVERSITY, FOGG MUSEUM OF ART
18—CULVER
19—UPPER LEFT, NEW YORK PUBLIC LIBRARY—CENTER, CULVER
20—UPPER, NEW-YORK HISTORICAL SOCIETY
21—UPPER, FREE LIBRARY OF PHILADELPHIA—LOWER RIGHT, NEW YORK PUBLIC LIBRARY
22—UPPER, BROOKLYN MUSEUM
24—LEFT, PORTRAIT OF JOHN QUINCY ADAMS *from* MUSEUM OF FINE ARTS, BOSTON—LEFT, VIEW OF WASHINGTON, D. C., *from* BETTMANN ARCHIVE
26—UPPER, HUNTINGTON LIBRARY, SAN MARINO, CALIF.—LOWER LEFT, ST. ANDREW'S SOCIETY, CHARLESTON, S. C., *courtesy of* FRICK ART REFERENCE LIBRARY
27—OLD PRINT SHOP, NEW YORK (BOTH)
28—DEPARTMENT OF JUSTICE, WASHINGTON, D. C.
29—UPPER RIGHT, NEW-YORK HISTORICAL SOCIETY
32—HUNTINGTON LIBRARY, SAN MARINO, CALIF.
33—NEW-YORK HISTORICAL SOCIETY (BOTH)
36—CULVER
37—TOP RIGHT, NEW-YORK HISTORICAL SOCIETY—SECOND FROM TOP, CULVER

38-39—WASHINGTON UNIVERSITY, ST. LOUIS
39—RIGHT-HAND COLUMN, CULVER (BOTH)
40—LOWER LEFT, BETTMANN ARCHIVE
41—UPPER, NEW YORK PUBLIC LIBRARY—LOWER RIGHT, BETTMANN ARCHIVE
42—FROM "THE INTIMATE LIFE OF ALEXANDER HAMILTON," BY A. M. HAMILTON, *courtesy of* CHARLES SCRIBNER'S SONS, PUBLISHERS
43—UPPER, FROM THE PAINTING LENT BY MEMBERS OF THE HAMILTON FAMILY TO THE MUSEUM OF THE CITY OF NEW YORK
44—CULVER
45—KEYSTONE
47—UPPER, NEW-YORK HISTORICAL SOCIETY—LOWER, HUNTINGTON LIBRARY, SAN MARINO, CALIF.
49—THE GROLIER CLUB, NEW YORK
50—LOWER, BROWN
51—LOWER RIGHT, NEW YORK PUBLIC LIBRARY
52—UPPER LEFT, MRS. EDWARD R. C. HASKELL, CHARLESTON, S.C., *courtesy of* FRICK ART REFERENCE LIBRARY—UPPER CENTER, TENNESSEE HISTORICAL SOCIETY—UPPER RIGHT, NEW-YORK HISTORICAL SOCIETY
53—UPPER LEFT, MISS KATHERINE TURNER, LEXINGTON, KY., *courtesy of* FRICK ART REFERENCE LIBRARY—UPPER CENTER, BUFFALO HISTORICAL SOCIETY—UPPER RIGHT, YALE UNIVERSITY ART GALLERY—LOWER RIGHT—NEW-YORK HISTORICAL SOCIETY
54—UPPER LEFT, CULVER
56—UPPER, NEW-YORK HISTORICAL SOCIETY—LOWER LEFT, NEW YORK PUBLIC LIBRARY
57—UPPER, NEW-YORK HISTORICAL SOCIETY—LOWER RIGHT, HANDY *from* CULVER
58—UPPER, NEW YORK PUBLIC LIBRARY—LOWER, NEW-YORK HISTORICAL SOCIETY
59—HUNTINGTON LIBRARY, SAN MARINO, CALIF.
60-61—NEW-YORK HISTORICAL SOCIETY

BRARY OF CONGRESS—LOWER, UNITED PRESS

431—UPPER, FARM SECURITY ADMINISTRATION PHOTO BY DOROTHEA LANGE *from* LIBRARY OF CONGRESS—LOWER, UNITED PRESS

432—BROWN

433—LIFE PHOTO BY THOMAS D. McAVOY, *copyright by* TIME INC.

434—UPPER, WIDE WORLD—LOWER LEFT, LIFE PHOTO BY THOMAS D. McAVOY, *copyright by* TIME INC.—LOWER RIGHT, UNITED PRESS

435—UPPER LEFT, ROBERT CAPA-PIX—UPPER RIGHT, KEYSTONE—CENTER LEFT, UNITED PRESS—CENTER RIGHT, PICTURES INC.—LOWER LEFT, ACME—LOWER RIGHT, MOVIETONE NEWS

436-437—WIDE WORLD

438—UPPER, LIFE PHOTO BY JOHN PHILLIPS, *copyright by* TIME INC.—LOWER LEFT, CARL SOMDAL, CHICAGO TRIBUNE

439—UPPER, LIFE PHOTO BY JOHN PHILLIPS, *copyright by* TIME INC.

440—CENTER LEFT, WIDE WORLD—OTHER PICTURES, UNITED PRESS (ALL FOUR)

441—UNITED PRESS

442-443—UNITED PRESS (BOTH)

444—UNITED PRESS

445—LOWER LEFT, UNITED PRESS—LOWER RIGHT, WIDE WORLD

446—UPPER, U. S. MARINE CORPS—LOWER, LIFE PHOTO BY BOB LANDRY, *copyright by* TIME INC.

447—UNITED PRESS

448—CENTER, U. S. ARMY SIGNAL CORPS—LOWER LEFT, PATHE NEWS—LOWER RIGHT, WIDE WORLD

449—UPPER, LIFE PHOTO BY GEORGE SKADDING, *copyright by* TIME INC.—LOWER, WIDE WORLD (BOTH)

450—UPPER LEFT AND LOWER RIGHT, UNITED PRESS (BOTH)—LOWER LEFT, LIFE PHOTO BY THOMAS D. McAVOY, *copyright by* TIME INC.

451—UPPER, LIFE PHOTO BY GEORGE SKADDING, *copyright by* TIME INC.—LOWER LEFT AND RIGHT, UNITED PRESS (BOTH)

452—WIDE WORLD (UPPER RIGHT AND LOWER LEFT)—UNITED PRESS (UPPER LEFT)

453—UPPER, LIFE PHOTO BY THOMAS D. McAVOY, *copyright by* TIME INC.—LOWER LEFT, LIFE PHOTO BY GEORGE SKADDING, *copyright by* TIME INC.—LOWER RIGHT, UNITED PRESS

454-455—WIDE WORLD

456—UPPER LEFT, LIFE PHOTO BY RALPH MORSE, *copyright by* TIME INC.—UPPER RIGHT, PHOTO BY LARRY KEIGHLEY, REPRINTED BY SPECIAL PERMISSION OF THE SATURDAY EVENING POST; *copyright 1946 by* CURTIS PUBLISHING COMPANY, INDEPENDENCE SQUARE, PHILADELPHIA, PA.—LOWER LEFT, LIFE PHOTO BY THOMAS D. McAVOY, *copyright by* TIME INC.—LOWER RIGHT, PICTURES, INC.

457—WIDE WORLD

458—FROM "HERBLOCK'S HERE AND NOW," *courtesy of* SIMON AND SCHUSTER

460—UPPER, UNITED PRESS—LOWER, MARCH OF TIME, FROM THE MOVIE "ATOMIC POWER" (BOTH)

461—UPPER, TIME PHOTO BY BOB WHEELER, *copyright by* TIME INC.—LOWER LEFT, MARCH OF TIME, FROM THE MOVIE "ATOMIC POWER"—LOWER RIGHT,

UNITED PRESS

462—UPPER, PICTURES, INC.—LOWER LEFT, LEO ROSENTHAL, PIX INCORPORATED—LOWER RIGHT, UNITED PRESS

463—KANSAS CITY STAR

464—UPPER LEFT, J. L. WILLIAMS, KANSAS CITY STAR—CENTER LEFT AND CENTER, UNITED PRESS—CENTER RIGHT, UNITED PRESS—LOWER LEFT AND CENTER, WIDE WORLD (ALL THREE)—LOWER RIGHT, D. R. FITZPATRICK, ST. LOUIS POST-DISPATCH

465—UPPER RIGHT, JACK LAMBERT, CHICAGO SUN-TIMES—CENTER LEFT, UNITED PRESS—CENTER RIGHT, WIDE WORLD—LOWER LEFT, LIFE PHOTO BY HANK WALKER *copyright by* TIME INC.—LOWER RIGHT, TIME PHOTO BY J. G. ZIMMERMAN *copyright by* TIME INC.

466—LEFT, WIDE WORLD (BOTH)—LOWER RIGHT, LIFE PHOTO BY W. EUGENE SMITH *copyright by* TIME INC.

467—LIFE PHOTO BY THOMAS D. McAVOY *copyright by* TIME INC.

468—UNITED PRESS (BOTH)

469—UPPER, D. R. FITZPATRICK, ST. LOUIS POST-DISPATCH—LOWER RIGHT, HARRIS & EWING—LOWER LEFT, UNITED PRESS

470-471—UPPER, LIFE PHOTOS BY THOMAS D. McAVOY *copyright by* TIME INC. (BOTH)—LOWER LEFT, D. R. FITZPATRICK, ST. LOUIS POST-DISPATCH—LOWER RIGHT, LIFE PHOTO BY CHARLES STEINHEIMER *copyright by* TIME INC.

472—UPPER, LIFE PHOTO BY DAVID D. DUNCAN *copyright by* TIME INC.—LOWER, WIDE WORLD

473—UPPER, LIFE PHOTO BY RALPH MORSE *copyright by* TIME INC.—LOWER, LIFE PHOTO BY HANK WALKER *copyright by* TIME INC.

474—LIFE PHOTO BY DAVID D. DUNCAN *copyright by* TIME INC.

475—UPPER, LIFE PHOTO BY MARK KAUFFMAN *copyright by* TIME INC.—LOWER, WIDE WORLD

476—HARRIS & EWING

477—UPPER RIGHT, HARRIS & EWING—CENTER LEFT, JEFFCOAT STUDIO, ABILENE, KANSAS—CENTER, LIFE PHOTO BY EDWARD CLARK *copyright by* TIME INC.—CENTER RIGHT, U. S. ARMY SIGNAL CORPS—LOWER LEFT, UNITED PRESS—LOWER CENTER, LIFE PHOTO BY JERRY COOKE *copyright by* TIME INC.—LOWER RIGHT, LIFE PHOTO BY MARK KAUFFMAN *copyright by* TIME INC.

478-479—UPPER, LIFE PHOTOS BY MARK KAUFFMAN *copyright by* TIME INC. (BOTH)—LOWER LEFT, WIDE WORLD—LOWER RIGHT, UNITED PRESS

480—LEFT (TOP THREE) LIFE PHOTOS BY GEORGE SILK *copyright by* TIME INC.—LOWER LEFT, UNITED PRESS—LOWER RIGHT, WIDE WORLD

481—LIFE PHOTO BY JOE SCHERSCHEL *copyright by* TIME INC.

482—WIDE WORLD

483—UPPER AND CENTER, UNITED PRESS (BOTH)—LOWER, WIDE WORLD

484-485—ALL CARTOONS BY HERBLOCK FROM THE WASHINGTON POST AND "HERBLOCK'S HERE AND NOW" *courtesy of* SIMON AND SCHUSTER

486-487—SOVPHOTO

488—LIFE PHOTO BY CARL MYDANS *copyright by* TIME INC.

489—UPPER, FROM "HERBLOCK'S HERE AND NOW" *courtesy of* SIMON AND SCHUSTER—LOWER, WIDE WORLD

490—CARTOON BY ARLT, NEW YORK HERALD TRIBUNE

491—UPPER, LIFE PHOTO BY N. R. FARBMAN *copyright by* TIME INC.—LOWER, LIFE PHOTO BY ALFRED EISENSTAEDT *copyright by* TIME INC.

492—HARRIS & EWING

493—LIFE PHOTO BY JAMES BURKE *copyright by* TIME INC.

494—UPPER, LIFE PHOTO BY GEORGE SKADDING *copyright by* TIME INC.—LOWER, FROM "HERBLOCK'S HERE AND NOW" *courtesy of* SIMON AND SCHUSTER

495—UPPER, UNITED PRESS—LOWER, LIFE PHOTO BY EDWARD CLARK *copyright by* TIME INC.

496-497—LIFE PHOTO BY EDWARD CLARK *copyright by* TIME INC.

498—UPPER LEFT AND LOWER RIGHT, WIDE WORLD (BOTH)—UPPER RIGHT, UNITED PRESS

499—UPPER, UNITED PRESS (BOTH)—LOWER, WIDE WORLD

500—LIFE PHOTO BY BILL BRIDGES, *copyright by* TIME INC.

502—UNITED PRESS

503—WIDE WORLD

504—WIDE WORLD (ALL FIVE)

505—UPPER RIGHT, CENTER LEFT AND LOWER, WIDE WORLD (THREE)—OTHER PHOTOS, UNITED PRESS (TWO)

506—JACQUES LOWE, *from* "THE KENNEDY YEARS" BY EDITORS OF THE NEW YORK TIMES AND VIKING PRESS, *copyright by* THE VIKING PRESS, INC.

507—WIDE WORLD

508-509—UPPER, WIDE WORLD (BOTH)—LOWER LEFT, ST. LOUIS POST-DISPATCH CARTOON BY BILL MAULDIN—LOWER RIGHT, UNITED PRESS

510—UNITED PRESS

511—WIDE WORLD

512—UPPER, UNITED PRESS—LOWER, WIDE WORLD

513—UPPER RIGHT, LIFE DRAWING BY WEXLER *copyright by* TIME INC.—LOWER LEFT, WIDE WORLD—LOWER RIGHT, UNITED PRESS

514-515—LEFT CENTER, UNITED PRESS—OTHER PHOTOS, WIDE WORLD (ALL FOUR)

516-517—BOTTOM ROW, SECOND FROM LEFT, WIDE WORLD—OTHER PHOTOS, UNITED PRESS (ALL FOUR)

518—UNITED PRESS (BOTH)

519—UPPER AND LOWER RIGHT, WIDE WORLD—LOWER LEFT, UNITED PRESS

520-521—ALL PHOTOS, WIDE WORLD—FRONT PAGE OF DALLAS TIMES HERALD *courtesy of* THE DALLAS TIMES HERALD, *photo copy by* GRANGER

522-523—WIDE WORLD

524—UNITED PRESS (ALL FOUR)

525—WIDE WORLD

526-527—ALL PHOTOS UNITED PRESS (FIVE) EXCEPT BOTTOM LEFT, WIDE WORLD—CARTOON FROM "STRAIGHT HERBLOCK" *courtesy of* SIMON AND SCHUSTER

528—UNITED PRESS (ALL THREE)

529—UPPER RIGHT, UNITED PRESS—LOWER, WIDE WORLD (BOTH)

530—UNITED PRESS

Index

Abilene, Kans., 477
Abolitionists, 96, 97, 111, 133, 135, 137, 141, 143, 146, 154, 172
Acheson, Dean, 473
Adams, Abigail, 24
Adams, John, 17, 20, 24-26, 28, 29, 31, 33, 37
Adams, John Quincy, 24, 69, 72, 74, 75, 77, 78, 83, 84, 116
Adams' Express, 137
Adoree, Renee, 393
Advertising, 127, 211, 261, 291, 362
Agricultural Adjustment Act, 418, 419
Aguinaldo, Emilio, 285
Aiken, William, 143
Air-conditioning, 125
Air Force One (Presidential plane), 522, 523
Alabama, 160, 161, 516, 517
Alamo, 98, 99
Alarm, The, 249
Alaska, 192, 193, 288, 451
Albania, 435, 459
Albany, N. Y., 95, 203
Albert of Belgium, 366
Aldrich, Nelson W., 336, 338
Alexander I of Russia, 72
Alexander II of Russia, 192
Algeciras, 326
Algerian War, 65
Alien Acts, 28, 29
Allegheny River, 4
Allen, William (Lieutenant), 48
Allen, William (Senator), 111
"Alphabet of Joyous Trusts, An," 328, 329
"Alphabet soup," 419
Altgeld, John Peter, 267
Alton, Ill., 97, 153
Alton Observer, 97
Aluminum Company of America, 400
Alsace-Lorraine, 362
"America First!" 373
American Federation of Labor, 228, 420
American Fire Company, 207
"American Hogarth, The," 62
American Iron and Steel Association, 253
American Legion, 478
American Railway Union, 267
American Revolution, 1, 4, 6-10, 18
American Sugar Refining Company, 213, 315
"American System," 69, 415
"American Talleyrand," 100
Ames, Fisher, 19
Ames, Oakes, 204
Anacostia Flats, 409
Anarchists, 117, 248, 249, 260, 313
Anderson, Robert, 161, 165
Andersonville Prison, 191, 237
Annapolis, Md., 11
Anthony, Susan B., 214, 215
Anti-Federalist party, 13, 20, 21
Anti-foreign issue in American politics, 28, 127, 375. See also Chinese in U.S.
Anti-Masonic Almanac, 94
Anti-Masonic party, 94, 103
Anti-Nebraska men, 145
Antitrust Law. See Sherman Antitrust Act

Apple-seller, 402
Appomattox, 179
Arbuckle, Fatty, 392
Arbuthnot (munitions trader), 64
Archangel, 365
Argentina, 72, 349
Arkansas, 29, 166
Armenia, 381
Armistice Day, 364
Armour, Philip D., 315
Army of Northern Virginia, 168
Army of the Potomac, 169, 177
Arnold, Benedict, 9
"Arsenal of Democracy," 440
Arthur, Chester A., 232, 233, 333, 381
Arthur, Timothy Shay, 128
Articles of Confederation, 11
Ashburton, Lord, 108
Assassinations, 180, 230, 231, 313, 422, 423, 520-522
Assassinations, attempted, 147, 182, 260, 345, 414, 465
Assumption bill, 18
Astor, John Jacob (1763-1848), 56
Astor, John Jacob (1822-1890), 241
Atchison, David, 146
Atlanta, the, 233
Atlanta Penitentiary, 377
Atlantic Charter, 441
Atlantic Conference (World War II), 441, 442
Atomic bomb, 456, 457, 458-460, 469, 490, 491. See also Fallout, Hydrogen bomb, Test ban treaty.
Atomic Energy Commission, 461, 483, 491
Atomic Peace, 459
"Atoms-for-Peace" plan, 489
Attlee, Clement, 459
Atzerodt, George, 182, 183
Augusta, Me., 237
Augusta, the, 441, 459
Australia, 445
Austria, 435
Austria-Hungary, 72, 350, 362

Babcock, Orville, 205
Baby-kissing, 221
Bacher, Robert F., 461
Badger, George E., 145
Baer, George F., 320
Bailey, John, 507
Baker, Ray Stannard, 331
Baltimore, Md., 15, 56, 57, 77, 94, 163, 226, 227
Baltimore and Ohio Railroad, 77, 226
Baltimore Republican, 104
Bank of the United States (first), 19
Bank of the United States (second), 67, 81, 90-92, 100, 126, 313
"Banking holiday," 416
Banks, Nathaniel P., 143
Barnum, P. T., 124
Barron, James, 48
Baruch, Bernard, 361, 370, 417, 459, 462
Batavia, N. Y., 94
Battles:
    Bunker Hill, 6

Concord, 6
Trenton, 6
Monmouth, 6
New York, 6
Yorktown, 7
Tippecanoe, 52-54
Lake Erie, 54
Thames River, 54
Chippewa, 54
Lundy's Lane, 54
Lake Champlain, 54
Bladensburg, 56
New Orleans, 60, 61
San Jacinto, 99
Resaca de la Palma, 112
Churubusco, 112
Buena Vista, 112, 113, 122
Monterey, 113
Bull Run, 168, 169
Gettysburg, 168-170
Shiloh, 169
Vicksburg, 169
Fredericksburg, 169, 178
Chancellorsville, 170
Antietam, 171
Petersburg, 171
Shenandoah Valley, 177
Atlanta, 177
Wilderness, 178
Manila Bay, 282
El Caney, 282
San Juan Hill, 282, 283, 316
San Diego, 282, 283
Montdidier, 358
Château-Thierry, 358
Saint-Mihiel, 359
Meuse-Argonne, 359
Bataan, 444, 445
Corregidor, 445
Coral Sea, 445
Midway, 445
Stalingrad, 445
Rome, 445
The Bulge, 445
Guadalcanal, 445
Tarawa, 446
Saipan, 446
Iwo, 446
Okinawa, 446
Hürtgen Forest, 447
Changjin Reservoir, 474
Bay of Pigs, 501, 512, 513
Bayard, James, 33
"Bearded Lady," 355
Beecher, Henry Ward, 240
Belgium, 350, 355, 361, 435, 445, 446
Belknap, William, 204
Bell, Alexander Graham, 214
Belle Isle Prison, 191
Belmont, August, 149
Bennett, James Gordon, 126
Benton, Thomas Hart, 88, 89, 93, 107, 133, 149
"Benton's Mint Drops," 93
Berger, Victor, 341
Beria, Lavrenti, 487
Berle, Adolf A., 417
Berlin, 477, 513, 518
Berlin airlift, 462
Berlin Wall, 513, 518
Bethlehem Steel Corporation, 400
Beveridge, Albert J., 287, 373
Bevin, Ernest, 462
Bicycles, 261, 317, 397. See also Velocipede

Biddle, Nicholas, 90, 91, 100, 103, 126
"Big business," 213, 313-315, 374, 381, 402. See also "Money power"
Big Parade, The, 393
Big Stick, 313, 326, 327, 336, 347, 348, 362, 380, 381, 407, 501
"Big Three," 448, 449, 452, 459, 462
Bikini atoll, 461
Bill of Rights, 13
Billings, Mont., 519
"Billion Dollar Congress," 254, 259
Bingham, George Caleb, 118-121
Birch, John, Society, 527
Birmingham, Ala., 516, 517
Birney, James G., 111
Black, Hugo, 427
"Black Dan," 66
"Black Friday," 202
Black Hills, 215
"Black Laws," 187, 188
"Black Republicans," 149, 153
"Black Tom," 117
Blackstone Hotel, Chicago, 383, 438
Blaine, James G., 223, 231, 236-241, 254, 291, 294, 295, 298, 299, 480
Blaine, Maggie, 237
Bland, Richard Parks, 263
Bland-Allison Act, 225
"Bleeding Kansas," 146, 147, 149
Blizzard of 1888, 298
Block, Herbert. See Herblock
"Bloody shirt," 223, 237, 253, 302
Bloom, Sol, 261
Bloomer, Amelia, 125
Blooming Grove, Ohio, 384
Blow, Henry T., 150
"Blue Bellies," 167
Blue Eagle, 424, 425
"Blue Elliptical Saloon," 103
Blue laws, 20
"Blue Lights," 59, 108
"Bluebeard of New Orleans," 224
Bohlen, Charles E., 485
Bohr, Niels, 460
Bolivar, Simón de, 72
Bolivia, 72
Bolshevism, 375, 381
Bonus Army, 408-410
"Boodle," 330
Boone, Daniel, 38, 39, 70
Boonesborough, Ky., 39
Booth, John Wilkes, 180-183
Borah, William E., 338, 372, 434
"Border Ruffians," 146
Boston, Mass., 6, 8, 15, 77, 96, 97, 216, 240, 287, 504, 505
Boston, the, 233
Boston Centinel, 63
Boston Massacre, 24
Boston Police Strike, 375, 383
Boston Post, 507
Boston Weekly Messenger, 51
"Bottle and the Pledge, The," 128, 129
"Bourbon Democrats," 223
Bovay, Alvan, 143, 145
Bowie, James, 99
"Boys in Blue," 194, 208, 209, 223
Braddock, Edward, 4
Bradley, Omar, 475

Brady, Mathew, 170
"Brain Trust," 417
Braintree, Mass., 24
Brandeis, Louis D., 424
Brazil, 204, 349
Breadlines, 211, 260, 402
Breckinridge, John
  (1760-1806), 28
Breckinridge, John (1821-1875),
  159
Britton, Nan, 384, 385
Broken Bow, Neb., 256
Brokers' loans, 390, 391, 400
Brookline, Mass., 504
Brooklyn, 240
Brooklyn *Eagle*, 126
Brooks, James, 205
Brooks, Preston, 147
Brooks Brothers, 175
Brother Jonathan, 111, 176
Browere, John, 80
Brown, Henry, 137
Brown, John, 146, 154, 155
Brown Brothers, 344
Browne, Carl, 265
Browning, "Daddy," 393
Browning, "Peaches," 393
Bryan, William Jennings, 263,
  270-274, 288, 289, 306, 307,
  313, 315, 335, 347, 388
Buchanan, James, 148-150, 161
Buckner, Simon B., 247
Buddhists, 513
Buffalo, N. Y., 239, 313
Buffalo *Evening Telegraph*, 239
Bulganin, Nikolai, 488
Bulgaria, 459
Bull market, 390, 391, 397, 400,
  405
Bull Moose, 344, 345. *See also*
  Progressive Party
"Bully Brooks," 147
Bunau-Varilla, P. J., 323
Burchard, Samuel, 241
Bureau of Corporations, 328, 329
Bureau of Mines, 339
Burlington Railroad, 319
Burma, 445
Burr, Aaron, 20, 33, 42, 45, 50
Burr, Theodosia, 45
Bush, Vannevar, 461
Business, government aid to, 16-19,
  37, 199, 402, 414, 419. *See also*
  Tariff
Butler, Andrew Pickens, 147
Butler, Benjamin F., 172, 187, 224
Butler, Pierce, 424
Buyers' strike, 254
Byrd, Harry F., 410
Byrnes, James F., 462, 465

Cabinet:
  Washington's, 16, 17, 21
  Adams', 24
  Jefferson's, 37
  Jackson's, 84, 85
  Tyler's, 106
  Lincoln's, 180
  Johnson's, 187
  Grant's, 196, 204
  B. Harrison's, 255
  Taft's, 336
  Harding's, 384, 386
  F. D. Roosevelt's, 418, 440
  Kennedy's, 502
Cairo Conference (World War II),
  448
Calhoun, John C., 53, 67, 84-89, 91,
  92, 133-135, 160
Calhoun, Mrs. John C., 84, 85

California, 111-113, 131, 133, 135,
  148, 355, 378, 410, 411, 480,
  482, 492
California Compromise, 133, 135
Cambridge, Mass., 6
Camden, N. J., 396
Camp David, Md., 498
Camp Grant, Ill., 355
Campaign funds, 90, 149, 208, 253,
  274
Canada, 54, 108, 154, 456, 460
Canning, George, 72
Cannon, Joseph G., 336-338
Canton, Ohio, 274
Capitol, 56, 57, 118, 163, 264, 265,
  408, 409, 416
Capone, Al, 404
Cardozo, Benjamin, 424
Carmichael, Omer, 492
Carnegie, Andrew, 241, 314, 315
Carnegie Endowment for
  International Peace, 471
Carnegie Steel Company, 211, 213,
  260
Caroline (private plane), 506
Carpetbaggers, 188, 222, 223, 505
Carranza, Venustiano, 349
Carson, Kit, 107
Cartoons in American history, ii,
  xii, 21, 59, 90, 206, 207, 218,
  219, 291
Casablanca Conference (World
  War II), 448
Casals, Pablo, 510
Cass, Lewis, 122
"Cast-Iron Man, The," 92
Castle Garden, 288
Castle Pinckney, 160,161
Castro, Cipriano, 327
Castro, Fidel, 501, 503, 509,
  512-514
Catholic issue in American politics,
  127, 149, 241, 302, 303, 397,
  500-502, 507, 509
Caucus, 62, 63, 75
Caudle, Lamar, 465
Censure Resolution, 93
Centennial Exposition, 214, 215
Central Pacific Railroad, 204
Centralia, Wash., 375
Cervera, Admiral, 282
Chambers, Whittaker, 470, 471
Changjin Reservoir, 474
Chappaqua, N. Y., 208
Charles, William, 59
Charleston, S. C., 15, 77, 87, 161,
  164, 165
Chase, Salmon, 145, 187
Chase, Samuel, 28, 37
Chattanooga, 179
Checkers, 480
Cherokee Strip, 257
Chesapeake, the, 48
Chesapeake Bay, 56
Cheves, Langdon, 52, 53
Chiang Kai-shek, 448, 473
Chicago, 145, 153, 194, 248, 249,
  266, 267, 271, 330, 345, 404,
  410, 411, 438
Chicago, the, 233
Chicago *Daily News*, 249
Chicago Massacre, 54
Chicago *Tribune*, 187, 234, 344, 466
Chicago World's Fair. *See*
  Columbian Exposition
"Chicken for every pot," 399
Child labor, 45, 312, 345, 347, 424
Chile, 72, 349, 398
China, 212, 287, 381, 395, 406, 407,
  435, 440, 442, 448, 452, 473,
  475, 489, 501, 509

"China Lobby," 473
Chinese in U.S., 130, 131, 228, 229
Choate, Joseph H., 268
Chosen Peninsula, 472
Christiana, Pa., 137
Churchill, Winston, 331, 441, 442,
  445, 448, 449, 452, 463
Cincinnati, Society of the, 23
Cisco, Calif., 198
"Civil Disobedience," 117
Civil rights, 501, 516, 517, 529
Civil Service, 221, 223, 232
Civil War, 164-179, 191, 196, 211,
  213, 224, 268
Civilian Conservation Corps, 418
Clark, William, 41
Clay, Henry, 52, 53, 55, 68-70, 75,
  78, 81, 87, 90-93, 96, 102, 103,
  111, 132, 133, 135, 140, 237
Clay, Mrs. Henry, 140
Clayton Antitrust Act, 347
"Clear it with Sidney," 450
Clemenceau, Georges, 370, 371
Cleveland, Grover, 235, 238, 239,
  241-244, 252, 253, 259, 263,
  265, 267, 305, 313, 315, 335,
  478
Cleveland, Mrs. Grover, 242
Cleveland, Oscar Folsom, 239
Cleveland, Ohio, 163, 342
Cleveland *Press*, 450
Clinton, De Witt, 42, 76, 77
Clinton, George, 20, 21
Clinton, Tenn., 492
"Clinton's Ditch," 77
Coal, 320, 321
Cobb, Howell, 70
Cobbett, William, 20
"Cock of Kentucky," 52
Cockburn, George, 57
Cockrell, Francis M., 262
"Co-existence," 488
Coffin Handbills, 78, 79
Cold War, 459, 469, 470, 477, 491,
  498, 499, 501, 515, 519
"Cold Water Army," 129
"Cold Water Mayor," 129
Colfax, Schuyler, 205
Colombia, 72, 323
Colt revolving pistols, 113
Columbia, S. C., 223
Columbia River, 41
Columbia University, 417, 477
Columbian Exposition, 260, 261
Columbus, N. M., 349
Comic strips, 291, 333
Commerce Department, 328
Committee for Industrial
  Organization, 420, 430, 431,
  450
Committee to Defend America by
  Aiding the Allies, 440
Common Sense, 37
Commonweal of Christ. *See*
  Coxey's Army
Commonwealth and Southern
  Corporation, 436
Communistic societies, 126
Communists, 374, 375, 459, 460,
  462, 468-473, 477, 480, 484-487,
  519
"Community of Interest," 315
Compromise of 1850. *See*
  California Compromise
Comstock, Anthony, 291
Comstock Lode, 200
Conant, James B., 461
Concord, Mass., 6, 117
Confederate Army, 166-169, 178,
  179
"Confederate Brigadiers," 252

Confederate States of America,
  160, 161, 163, 165, 166, 169,
  172, 184
Congo, The, 503, 513
Congress (including House of
  Representatives and Senate):
  Caucus system, 62, 63, 75
  Corruption in, 18, 19, 204, 205,
    236, 294
  Deadlock over Speaker, 142, 143
  Declares war, 53, 65, 113, 281,
    356
  Elects President, 33, 75, 220
  Famous leaders, debates and
    speeches in, 19, 31, 36, 37, 52,
    53, 66-71, 81, 86-93, 103, 116,
    117, 131-135, 140, 141, 144,
    145, 147, 161, 185-187, 223,
    224, 236, 254, 255, 259, 262,
    263, 287, 298, 300-302, 336-339,
    372, 373, 405, 428, 429, 433,
    454, 455, 480, 524
  Important laws passed by, 18, 19,
    28, 29, 37, 48, 69, 70, 93, 113,
    145, 187, 188, 223-225, 228,
    245, 254, 268, 285, 323, 331,
    336, 338, 347, 354, 357, 380,
    395, 408, 418-420, 427, 432,
    440, 482, 483, 512, 524. *See
    also* Tariff.
  Investigations and hearings, 100,
    101, 191, 217, 218, 375, 386,
    387, 389, 421, 465, 468-471,
    483-485
  Marches on, 265, 408, 409
  Meeting place burned, 56, 57
  Member banished from U.S.,
    174, 175
  Original organization, 11
  Partiality for own members, 4
  Personal encounters on the floor
    of, 29, 147
  Rejects petitions, 97, 116
  Suppresses nude pictures in
    report, 138
Congress of Industrial
  Organization. *See* Committee
  for Industrial Organization
"Congressman is a hog, A," 204
Conkling, Roscoe, 223, 230,
  232, 293, 298
Connally, John B., 519-521
Connally, Mrs. John B., 519, 520
Connecticut, 9, 59, 410
Connecticut Compromise, 11
Conscience Whigs, 117, 126,
  133, 141, 143
Constellation, the, 27
Constitution, 1, 11-13, 19,
  31, 37, 45, 92, 96, 135, 150,
  373, 416
Constitution, amendments:
  First Ten, 13
  Twelfth, 33, 75
  Thirteenth, 188
  Fourteenth, 188, 269, 492
  Fifteenth, 188, 233
  Sixteenth, 339
  Seventeenth, 339
  Eighteenth, 380
  Nineteenth, 378, 379
Constitution, the, 55
"Continental, not worth a," 10
Continental Army, 4, 6, 7, 9, 10
Continental certificates, 18
Continental Congress, x, 4, 6, 9-11,
  18, 70
"Contraband," 172
Conventions:
  1831, Anti-Masonic, 94
  1840, Whig, 103

1852, Whig, 140
1868, Republican and Democratic, 194, 195
1880, Republican, 230
1884, Republican, 294, 295
1896, Democratic, 270, 271
1908, Republican, 335
1912, Republican, 342
1912, Progressive, 345
1920, Republican, 383
1924, Democratic, 388, 389
1932, Democratic, 410, 411
1940, Republican, 436
1940, Democratic, 438, 439
1960, Democratic, 500, 501
1964, Republican, 526, 527
Cooke, Jay, 211
Coolidge, Calvin, 383, 384, 389-392, 394, 399, 433, 439, 483
Cooper, Peter, 225
Copenhagen, 460
Coplon, Judith, 469
"Copperheads," 174, 175, 177
Corliss, George H., 215
Cornwallis, Charles, 7
Cortelyou, George B., 328, 329
Corwin, Thomas, 117
Cotton Whigs, 117
Coughlin, Charles E., 422
Coughlin, John, 330
Council Bluffs, Iowa, 145
Council of National Defense, 354
"Court packing," 427-429
Cow Palace, 527
Cox, James M., 382, 384
Coxey, Jacob S., 265
Coxey's Army, 264, 265
Crawford, William H., 75
Crédit Mobilier, 204, 205
"Creeping socialism," 483
"Crime Against Kansas, The," 146, 147
Crisis, The, 37
Crockett, Davy, 99
Cromwell, William N., 323
Croquet, 221
"Cross of Gold," 271, 306
Crusade in Europe, 477
Cuba, 149, 276-278, 281-283, 285, 287, 335, 501, 509, 512-515
Cumberland Gap, 38
Cumberland Road, 69, 77
Curtice, Harlow, 483
Curtis, George William, 240
Curzon Line, 452
Custer, George A., 215
Custer, Tom, 215
Czechoslovakia, 435, 459
Czolgosz, Leon, 313

"D-Day," 445, 477
Daguerre, Louis J. M., 114
Daguerreotype, 114
Dallas, Texas, 519-523
Dallas Times Herald, 521
Dardanelles, 362
"Dark horse," 110, 230
Dartmouth College vs. Woodward, 37
Daugherty, Harry, 383-386
Davis, Jefferson, 135, 145, 160, 161, 163, 165, 172, 184, 185, 188, 237
Davis, Mrs. Jefferson, 135
Davis, John W., 389
Davis, Norman, 370
Dawes Plan, 395
Dayton, Jonathan, 29
Dayton, William L., 149
Dayton, Ohio, 174, 175

Dearborn, Henry, 54
De Armond, David A., 268
"Death sentence." See Public Utility Act
Debs, Eugene, 266, 267, 341, 361, 377
Decatur, Stephen, 46, 47, 59, 65
Declaration of Independence, x, xi, 16, 24, 31, 45, 97, 134, 150, 163, 492
De Gaulle, Charles, 448, 510
Delaware, 13, 81, 127
Delaware River, 6
Delmonico's, 241
Democracy (discussions and definitions), 12, 16, 24, 31, 35, 37, 45, 81, 356
Democratic party:
Origins, 31, 81. See also Anti-Federalist party, Republican party (Jeffersonian), Working Men's party
Leaders and bosses, 20, 21, 33, 84, 92, 93, 100, 110, 134, 205-207, 220, 230, 242, 262, 263, 270, 332, 333, 346, 347, 382, 396, 397, 412, 413, 423, 438, 439, 464, 465, 478, 500, 501, 504, 505, 524, 525, 530, 531
Splits, 100, 117, 143, 152, 159, 262, 263, 388, 389, 428, 429, 466
Anti-slavery members help organize Republican party, 143
Merges with Liberal Republicans (1872), 208
Comeback after Civil War, 195, 220, 238, 239
See also Conventions, Elections, "Copperheads," "Dixiecrat" party, Doughfaces, Locofocos, Tammany
Democratic societies, 21
Dempsey, Jack, 361
Denby, Edwin M., 386
Denmark, 435, 460
Denver, 229, 494, 495
Depew, Chauncey, 296, 297, 314
Depressions:
1819, 70
1837, 40, 100
1873, 210, 211, 227
1893, 260, 265
1930's, 381, 402, 403, 406, 407, 414-417, 424, 427. See also Panics
de Stoeckel, Baron, 192
Detroit, Mich., 54, 479
Detroit Journal, 375
Dewey, George, 282, 283
Dewey, Thomas E., 436, 450, 466
Dictatorship issue in American politics, 6, 7, 92, 327, 423
Die Vehme, 291
Diem, Ngo Dinh, 513
Disneyland, 499
District of Columbia, 18, 133, 204
"Dixiecrat" Party (1948), 466
Dixon, Edgar, 483
"Doctor Win-the-War," 450
Doheny, Edward L., 386, 387
Dolliver, Jonathan P., 339
Dom Pedro of Brazil, 214
Dominican Republic, 501
Donelson, Emily, 84
Donkey (Democratic symbol), 218, 230, 344
"Do-nothing 80th Congress," 466, 467

"Don't swap horses crossing a stream," 176, 177
Dooley, Mr., 139, 290, 328
Doud, Mamie. See Mrs. Dwight D. Eisenhower
Doughfaces, 122, 126, 135, 143, 149
Douglas, Stephen A., 144, 145, 147, 152, 153, 158, 159
Douglas, Frederick, 153
Dover, N. H., 157
Dow, Neal, 129
Downing, Major Jack, 90, 91
Draft Law (1917), 357
Draft Law (1940), 440
Draft Riots (1863), 174, 175
Dred Scott decision, 149, 150, 152, 153
Drew, Daniel, 202
Drexel, Morgan & Co., 210, 211
Duels, 36, 42, 43, 83, 121
"Duke of Braintree," 31
Dulles, John Foster, 488, 489
Dunne, Finley Peter. See Mr. Dooley
Duprez, Charles, 344
Dust storms, 430
Dutch East Indies, 445
Dwight, Timothy, 31

Earl, Ralph, 82
Eastman, George, 257
Eaton, Cyrus, 498
Eaton, John H., 84
Eaton, Peggy, 84, 85
Eaton, William, 47
Eccaleobion, 125
"Economic royalists," 426, 427
Egypt, 445, 448, 449, 489, 497
"Egyptian Village," 260, 261
Eight hour day, 201, 248, 250, 361
Einstein, Albert, 460
Eisenhower, Dwight D., 409, 445, 475-484, 489, 491, 492, 494-499, 501, 507, 522, 527, 529
Eisenhower, Mrs. Dwight D., 477, 498
Eisenhower, John, 477
Elberon, N. J., 231
Elections:
1792, 20, 21
1796, 24
1800, 31, 33, 78
1808, 50
1816, 63
1820, 73
1824, 75, 81
1828, 78, 81
1832, 90
1840, 103-105
1844, 110, 111
1848, 122
1852, 140
1856, 148, 149
1860, 158-160
1864, 176, 177
1866, 187
1867, 189
1868, 194, 195
1871 (N.Y.C.), 207
1872, 208, 209, 213
1876, 220, 221, 225
1878, 225
1880, 230
1882 (N. Y. State), 235
1884, 217, 238-241
1888, 253
1890, 259
1892, 259
1896, 271-274
1900, 288, 289, 306, 310

1904, 324, 327
1908, 333, 335
1910, 338
1912, 344, 345
1916, 354, 355
1920, 377, 381-384
1924, 389
1928, 396, 397
1932, 414, 415
1936, 422, 426, 427
1940, 439
1944, 450, 451
1946, 464
1948, 466
1952, 478, 479
1956, 496, 497
1960, 500, 501, 508, 509
1964, 528, 529
Electoral College, 33, 220, 479
Elephant (Republican symbol), 218, 219, 344
Elizabeth II of England, 510
Elk Hills, Calif., 386
Elliptical steel spring, 77
Elwood, Ind., 436, 437
Emancipation, 96
Emancipation Proclamation, 172, 188
"Embalmed beef," 282, 288, 311
Embargo of 1807, 48
Embargo of 1811, 51, 52
Emergency Banking Act of 1933, 418
Emerson, John, 150
Emerson, Ralph Waldo, 117, 137
Emporia Gazette, 287
Engel, George, 249
England. See Great Britain
"Entangling alliances," 34
Envelopes, 124
Equal Rights party, 217
Era of Good Feelings, 62, 63, 66, 75
Erie Canal, 76, 77
Erie Railroad, 202, 203, 205
"Erie War," 202
Essex, the, 513
Essex County, Mass., 51, 59
Essex Junto, 59
Ether anesthesia, 124
Ethiopia, 435
Evers, Medgar W., 516
Extremists, 526, 527

"Fair Deal," 466
Fairbanks, Douglas, 361
Fairview Inn, Baltimore, 69
Fala, 450, 453
Fall, Albert B., 386, 387
Fall River Line, 203
Fallout, 497, 513, 515
Farewell Address, 23, 26
Farley, James A., 405, 423, 428, 438
Farm mortgages, 259, 288
Farm prices, 225, 263, 391, 419
"Farm problem," 258, 259. See also Populist party
Farmers, 15, 31, 34, 213, 214, 225, 235, 390, 391, 402, 466. See also Homesteaders, Agricultural Adjustment Act, Dust storms
Farnsworth, Elon John, 168
Fascism, 381, 435
Federal Bureau of Investigation, 375, 386, 469
Federal Convention, 11
Federal Deposit Insurance Corporation, 419

Federal Emergency Relief Administration, 418
Federal Reserve Act, 347
Federal Reserve Board, 400
Federal Trade Commission, 347
Federal Union (discussions and definitions), 11, 12, 86, 87, 135, 143
Federalist, The, 12
Federalist cockade, 1, 23
Federalist party, 1, 2, 9-13, 16, 17, 19-21, 24, 26, 28-34, 37, 45, 48, 51, 52, 58, 59, 62, 81, 103, 149
Federation of Churches, 374
"Fellow travelers," 469
Fermi, Enrico, 460
Ferris, George Washington Gale, 261
Ferris wheel, 261
Field, Stephen J., 269
Fielden, Samuel, 248
"Fifty-four Forty or Fight!," 111
Fillmore, Millard, 127, 135, 139, 149
"Fire-bell in the night, A," 70
"Fire-eaters," 152
"Fireside chats," 416
Fischer, Adolph, 249
Fisher, Irving, 400
Fisk, Jim, 202, 203, 205
Fitzgerald, John F., 505
Fitzpatrick, D. R., 400, 469
Fiume, 371
Five-Power Naval Treaty, 394
Flagg, James Montgomery, 360
Flint, Mich., 430
Florida, 29, 64, 65, 160, 161, 220, 397
Floyd, John B., 161
"Flying Dutchman," 100
Flying machine, 77
Foch, Ferdinand, 364
Forbes, Charles, 385, 386
Ford, Henry, 430
Ford, "Model T," 393
Ford's Theatre, 180, 184
Forest Hills, L. I., 349
"Forgotten man," 414, 417
Formosa, 472, 473
Fort Johnson, 164, 165
Fort McHenry, 56
Fort Snelling, 150
Fort Sumter, 161, 164, 165
Fort Yukon, 192
Fortress Monroe, 184
Fortune Magazine, 436
Foster, Stephen, 177
"Foul-Mouthed Joe," 337
"Four Freedoms," 441
Four-Power Treaty, 395
Fourteen Points, 362, 365, 371, 441
France, 7, 19, 26, 29, 40, 41, 48, 72, 192, 350, 355, 360, 362, 371, 395, 407, 435, 440, 442, 445, 446, 448, 464, 477
Francis I of Austria, 72
Franco, Francisco, 435
Franklin, Benjamin, ii
Franklin Evans; or, The Inebriate, 128
Frazier, Daniel, 46
Free silver. *See* Silver issue
"Free Soil, Free Speech, Free Labor, and Free Men," 143
Free Soil party, 122, 143
Free Soilers, 133, 142, 143, 146, 149
Free State Hotel, 146

"Free Trade and Seamen's Rights," 55
Freedmen's Bureau, 188
Freedom Riders, 516
Freeport, Ill., 153
Freeport Doctrine, 152, 153, 159
Frémont, Jessie Benton, 107, 148, 149
Frémont, John Charles, 107, 113, 148, 149
Frick, Henry Clay, 260
Frohman, Charles, 352
Front porch campaigns, 274, 288, 383
Frontier, 38-41, 69, 107, 108, 130, 131, 198, 199, 215, 257
Frost, A. B., 258
"Frying the fat," 253
Fugitive Slave Act, 133, 135-137, 141
"Full dinner pail," 288, 289, 399
Fulton, Robert, 40

"Gag rule," 116
Gagarin, Yuri, 511
Gallatin, Albert, 37
Gardner, Alexander, 170
Garfield, James A., 230-232
Garner, John Nance, 405, 410-412, 438
Garrison, William Lloyd, 96, 97
Gary, Ind., 375
Gem Saloon, N. Y. C., 128
General Motors Corporation, 397, 400, 430, 483
Genêt, Edmond Charles, 19, 21
Geneva Conference (1927), 394, (1955), 488, 489
George, Henry, 250
George III of England, 24, 59
George V of England, 366
George Washington, the, 365
George Washington University, 460
Georgia, 81, 160, 178, 184, 259
Germany, 342, 350, 351, 353, 354, 356, 362, 365, 394, 395, 407, 435, 441, 445-447, 449, 452, 456, 459, 460, 462, 476, 491, 518
Gerry, Elbridge, 51
Gerrymander, 51
Gettysburg Address, 172, 173
Gibson, Charles Dana, 360
Gilbert, John, 393
Giles, William B., 37
Gillam, Bernhard, 291, 295, 305
Girard, Stephen, 56
Giraud, Henri Honoré, 448
Glass, Carter, 347
Glenn, John H., 510
"Go Ahead" Americans, 144
Gold, 130, 131, 288
"Gold-bugs," 271, 274
Gold corner, 202, 203
Gold standard, 225, 262, 272, 274, 419
Goldwater, Barry M., 526, 527, 529
Golf, 385, 494
Gómez, Máximo, 277
Gould, Jay, 202, 203, 205, 228, 241
Graft, 100, 101, 204, 205, 384-387. *See also* Speculators
Grand Army of the Republic, 244. *See also* "Boys in Blue"
Grand River, 107
Grange, 225, 235
Grant, Nellie, 196, 231
Grant, Ulysses S., 113, 114, 178,

179, 187, 191, 194, 196, 197, 203, 204, 208, 209, 211, 215, 218, 219, 230, 237, 246, 247, 293, 439
Grant & Ward, 247
"Grass will grow in the streets," 271, 415
Great Britain, 1, 19, 26, 48, 52-57, 59-61, 64, 72, 108, 109, 111, 172, 253, 350, 354, 371, 394, 395, 407, 435, 440, 441, 445, 449, 456, 460
"Great Debates," 508, 509
"Great Engineer," 399
Great Northern Railroad, 319
"Great Pacificator," 68, 87
Great Society, 501
Greece, 462
Greeley, Horace, 104, 107, 126, 128, 143, 158, 159, 172, 208, 209, 219
Greenback party, 224, 225
Greenbacks, 195, 224, 225, 265
Greenland, 441
Griswold, Roger, 28, 29
Gromyko, Andrei, 462, 514
Groton, 413
"Grover the Good," 239
Groves, Leslie R., 460
Grundy, Felix, 52, 53
Guam, 287, 445
Guerrière, the, 55
Guiteau, Charles J., 231

Hague, Frank, 438, 439
Haile Selassie of Ethiopia, 435
Halpin, Maria, 239
Hamilton, Alexander, 11-13, 16-18, 20, 21, 23, 24, 29, 31, 33, 42-45, 403, 405, 417
Hamilton, Mrs. Alexander, 43
Hamilton, Philip, 42
Hamlet, James, 137
Hampton, Wade, 223
Hancock, Winfield Scott, 230
Hanford-Richland, Wash., 460
Hanna, Mark, 266, 274, 275, 281, 288, 289, 310, 311, 313, 320, 323
"Happy Hooligan," 291
"Happy Warrior," 397
Hard cider campaign. *See* Log Cabin campaign
Hard Shell Democrats, 158, 159
Harding, Warren G., 338, 381, 383-386, 389, 394, 399
Harding, Mrs. Warren G., 384
Harlan, John M., 268
Harper, James, 127
Harper, Robert G., 29
Harpers Ferry, 154, 155
Harper's Weekly, 165, 168, 169, 176, 189, 206, 207, 218, 240, 245, 272, 291, 332
Harriman, Edward H., 318, 319
Harrisburg, Pa., 163
Harrison, Benjamin, 253-256, 298, 299, 381
Harrison, Carter, 248
Harrison, William Henry, 54, 103-106
Hartford Convention, 59, 62, 87
Harvard University, 316, 413, 461, 471, 504
"Hat in the ring," 342
Hatfield, Henry D., 417
Havana, 278, 281
Hawaii, 212, 276, 287, 442, 445, 448, 451
Hay, John, 282, 287, 323, 327

Hayes, Lucy, 220, 221
Hayes, Rutherford B., 220, 221, 223, 227, 230, 292, 293, 381
Haymarket bombing, 248-250
Hayne, Robert Y., 86-89
Hays, Will, 362, 365, 386
Haywood, Bill, 341
"He kept us out of war," 354
Healy, George P. A., 88
Hearst, George, 333
Hearst, William Randolph, 274, 276, 279, 291, 332, 333, 338, 410, 411, 426
Hearst, Mrs. William Randolph, 333
"Hell-bomb," 491
"Hello, Sucker," 421
Herblock, 458, 484, 527
Hermitage, The, 83, 93
Herold, David, 182, 183
Hewitt, Abram S., 250
Hill, David B., 263
Hill, James J., 318, 319
Hillman, Sidney, 450
Hindenburg Line, 359, 365
Hiroshima, 456, 457, 458
"His Fraudulency," 221
Hiss, Alger, 470, 471, 480
Hitler, Adolf, 407, 422, 434, 435, 436, 440, 444, 445, 448, 456
Hobson, Richmond P., 282
Hoe cylindrical press, 127
Holland, 24, 365, 435
"Hollywood ten," 469
Holmes, Oliver Wendell, 471
Holy Alliance, 72
Home Owners' Loan Corporation, 419
Homer, Winslow, 201
Homestead, Pa., 260
Homesteaders, 199, 257, 259
"Honest Abe," 158
Honolulu, 276, 442
Hootchy-kootchy girls, 260, 261
Hoover, Herbert, 361, 370, 383, 396-400, 402, 405, 409, 414-416, 498, 522
Hoover, Mrs. Herbert, 398
"Hoover Villas," 408, 409
"Hooverizing," 361
Hopkins, Harry, 417, 438
Hopkins, J. P., 267
"Horse-and-buggy," 425
"Hot Line," 515
"House Divided," 152, 153, 158
House of Representatives, *see* Congress
Houston, Sam, 99
Houston, Tex., 509
Hubbard, Elbert, 352
Hudson's Bay Company, 107
Huerta, Victoriano, 348, 349
Hughes, Charles Evans, 333, 355, 394, 424
Hull, Cordell, 418
Hull, Williams, 54
Humphrey, Hubert H., 506, 528
Humphreys, David, 21
Humphreys, S. P., 48
Hungary, 459, 487, 497
"Huns," 350, 351, 354
Huntington, Collis P., 204
Hyannis Port, Mass., 510
Hyde Park, N. Y., 412, 413, 453
Hydrogen bomb, 458, 490, 491, 497

"I had rather be right than be President," 102
"I took the Isthmus," 323
Ibn Saud of Arabia, 449
Iceland, 440, 441

Ickes, Harold, 344, 438, 439
Illinois, 39, 152, 153, 478
Illinois, the, 356
Immigration, 228
Impeachments, 37, 187
Imperialism, 276, 286-288.
　　See also "Manifest Destiny"
Impressment, 48
Inaugurations and inaugural
　　addresses:
　　Washington's, 2, 3
　　Jefferson's, 34
　　Madison's, 50
　　Jackson's, 83
　　Buchanan's, 149
　　Jefferson Davis's, 160
　　Lincoln's first, 163
　　Wilson's, 345
　　FDR's first, 415, 416
　　FDR's fourth, 452
　　Truman's first, 454, 455
　　Kennedy's, 502
　　Johnson's, 522, 523
Income tax, 259, 268, 339, 405,
　　427, 480
Independence Hall, 62.
　　See also State House,
　　Philadelphia
Independence, Mo., 472
Indiana, 39
Indianapolis, 163, 253
Indians, 15, 19, 38, 39, 52, 54,
　　64, 199, 215
"Indispensable man," 439
Indo-China, 442, 489
Industrial Workers of the World,
　　341, 375
Industry, 3, 15, 16, 18, 66, 70, 213,
　　252, 253, 257, 300, 312, 314,
　　315, 347, 354, 360, 361, 391,
　　424. See also "Big business,"
　　Business, Trusts, Wall Street,
　　and names of individual cor-
　　porations and railroads
Ingersoll, Robert G., 236
Injunctions in labor disputes,
　　250, 266-268, 345, 405
Insull, Samuel, 404
Insurgents. See Progressive
　　Republicans
"Integration" of schools, 492
Interstate Commerce Act of 1887,
　　268
Interstate Commerce Commission,
　　245
Iowa, 258, 506
Ireland, 518, 519
"Iron Curtain," 463
"Irrepressible conflict," 145
Ishii, Kikujiro, 407
Isolationists, 372, 373, 383, 421,
　　440
Italy, 362, 367, 371, 395, 406, 435,
　　445, 460

Jackson, Andrew, 19, 60, 64, 65,
　　75, 78, 79, 81-87, 89-95, 100,
　　102, 103, 111, 114, 115, 313,
　　439
Jackson County, Mo., 464, 465
Jackson, Rachel, 78, 83
Jackson, Robert, 438, 439
Jackson, Thomas Jonathan, 169
Jackson, Mich., 143
James, Reuben, 46
Japan, 138, 139, 326, 327, 335,
　　381, 394, 395, 406, 407, 435,
　　440, 442, 444-446, 448-449,
　　452, 456, 459, 462, 472, 491
Jay, John, 1, 12, 19, 33

Jay Treaty, 19
Jazz, 392
Jefferson, Thomas, 11, 16, 18-21,
　　23, 24, 28, 29, 31-35, 37, 40,
　　41, 45-50, 53, 62, 67, 69, 70,
　　80, 81, 96, 439
Jeffersonian Republicans. See
　　Republican party (Jeffersonian)
Job-hunters, 106, 230, 242.
　　See Civil Service
John Bull, 111, 176
"Johnny Rebs," 166
Johns Hopkins University, 471
Johnson, Andrew, 182, 185, 187
Johnson, Hiram, 339, 355, 372, 383
Johnson, Hugh, 417, 419, 424, 425
Johnson, Lyndon B., 500, 501, 506,
　　519, 522-525, 528-531
Johnson, Mrs. Lyndon B., 522-524
Johnson, Richard M., 53
Johnston, Joseph, 247
Jones, Christopher Columbus, 265
Jones, Jesse, 438, 439
Jonesboro, Ill., 153
Judge magazine, 273, 280, 291,
　　305, 306
Judiciary Act of 1801, 37
Jumel, Betsy Bowen, 45
Jungle, The, 330, 331

Kansas, 145-147, 154, 188, 199,
　　258, 259, 287, 340, 426
Kansas City, 465
"Kansas Pythoness," 259
"Kansas War," 146, 147
"Keep Cool and Keep Coolidge,"
　　389
Kellogg, Frank B., 394
Kellogg-Briand Pact, 394, 395,
　　406, 407
Kelly, Ed, 438, 439
Kendall, Amos, 84
Kennebec Journal, 237
Kennecott Copper, 400
Kennedy, Caroline, 502, 510, 522
Kennedy, John F., 500-510, 512-
　　516, 518, 524, 529
Kennedy, John F., Jr., 502, 510,
　　522, 529
Kennedy, Mrs. John F., 502, 507,
　　510, 519-523
Kennedy, Joseph P., 504, 505, 507
Kennedy, Mrs. Joseph P., 504, 507
Kennedy, Joseph P., Jr., 504, 505
Kennedy, Patrick Joseph, 504
Kennedy, Robert F., 507, 529
Kentucky, 29, 38, 127, 167
Kentucky Resolves, 28
Keppler, Joseph, 291, 293, 296,
　　298, 300, 302
Key, Francis Scott, 56
Khrushchev, Nikita, 488, 498, 499,
　　501, 509, 510, 514, 515
Kilgore, "Buck," 254
"King Andrew the First," 92, 93
King, Rev. Martin Luther, Jr.,
　　516, 517
"Kingfish," 423
"Kitchen Cabinet," 984
Kleberg, Richard M., 524
Knights of Labor, 228, 250, 259
Knights of the White Camellia, 190
Knowland, William, 480, 498
Know-Nothing party, 127, 149
Knox, Frank, 426
Knox, Henry, 11, 17
Knox, Philander C., 383
Kodak, 341
"Koon-Skinners," 111
Korea, 326, 459, 462, 472, 473,

475, 477, 479, 489
Korean War, 459, 472-475, 479,
　　483
Krimmel, John Lewis, 62
Ku Klux Klan, 190, 191, 195,
　　389, 427
Kurusu, Saburo, 434, 442

Labor Department, 339
Labor (including labor unions),
　　34, 95, 126, 143, 156, 157, 159,
　　200, 201, 208, 213, 219, 225-
　　228, 248-251, 259, 260, 266,
　　267, 275, 291, 320, 321, 330,
　　331, 333, 341, 347, 374, 375,
　　390, 391, 402, 420, 427, 464,
　　466. See also Injunctions in
　　labor disputes, Strikes
"Labor's Magna Charta," 420
La Follette, Robert M., 338,
　　383, 389
La Guardia, Fiorello, 405
Lamar, Colo., 430
"Lame ducks," 33, 161
Lamont, Thomas W., 400
Landon, Alfred M., 426
Lane, Franklin K., 338
Lane, Harriet, 149
Laos, 503, 513
La Plata. See Argentina
Lawrence, Kans., 146
Lawrence, Mass., 201, 341
"Lazy Shave," 509
League of Nations, 362, 371-373,
　　382, 383, 394, 406, 407, 413
Lease, Mary E., 259
Lee, Robert E., 113, 154, 166,
　　168, 169, 178, 179
Legree, Simon, 136
"Lemonade Lucy," 221
Lend-Lease, 440
Lenin, Nikolai, 486
Leopard, the, 48
Leslie's Weekly, 155, 156, 180,
　　193, 201, 291
"Let us begin," 502
"Let us have peace," 196
Lewis, John L., 420
Lewis, Meriwether, 41
Lewis, Sinclair, 393
Liberal Republicans, 204, 208
Liberator, The, 96, 97
Liberty Bonds, 360, 361, 386
Liberty party, 111
Liberty poles, 1, 9
Life magazine, 438, 489, 513
"Life-saving station," 221
Lilienthal, David E., 461
Liliuokalani of Hawaii, 276
Lincoln, Abraham, 39, 117, 128,
　　143, 152, 153, 158-160, 162,
　　163, 165, 166, 172-174, 176-
　　178, 180, 181, 197, 224, 232,
　　269, 313, 529
Lincoln, Benjamin, 10
Lincoln, Mary Todd, 180
Lincoln-Douglas debates, 152, 153
Lindbergh, Charles A., 392
L'Insurgente, 27
Lippmann, Walter, 413
"Little brown brothers," 335
Little Eva, 136
"Little Giant," 145, 152
"Little Mac," 176, 177
"Little Magician," 100
"Little rebellion now and then,
　　A," 35
Little Rock and Fort Smith Rail-
　　road, 237

"Little Three," 462
"Little Van," 85, 100
"Little Wizard," 160
Livingston, Brockholst, 42
Livingston, Edward, 37
Livingston, Robert R., 40, 41
Lloyd George, David, 370, 371
Lockport, N.Y., 76
Lockwood, Belva, 217
Locofocos, 100, 103, 106
Lodge, Henry Cabot, 287, 373, 383
Lodge, Henry Cabot, Jr., 507, 526
Log cabin campaign, 103-105
Log cabins, 39, 158, 230
"Log rolling," 244
Logan, John A., 194
London, Jack, 341
Long Branch, N. J., 203
Long, Huey, 422, 423
Longstreet, James, 178
Los Alamos, N. M., 460
Louisiana, 81, 160, 172, 220, 222,
　　422, 423, 482
Louisiana Purchase, 40, 41, 45
Louisville, Ky., 492, 493
Lovejoy, Elijah P., 97
Lowden, Frank, 383
Lowe, Jacques, 506
Lowell, James Russell, 240
Lowell, Mass., 157
Loyalty investigations, 468-471
Luks, George, 311
Lusitania, 352-354
Lynn, Mass., 156, 157
Lyon, Matthew, 28, 29

McAdoo, William G., 361, 389, 411
"Macarony," 8
MacArthur, Douglas, 409, 445,
　　446, 472, 473, 475
McCarthy, Joseph R., 464, 479,
　　484, 485, 507
McCarthyites, 478
McClellan, George B., 176, 177
McCluer, Franc, 463
McClure's Magazine, 331
McConnell, Felix G., 129
McCormick, Vance, 370
McCormick Harvester Company,
　　248
McCrady, John, 423
McCulloch vs. Maryland, 37
McCutcheon, John T., 344
Macdonough, Thomas, 54
McDougall, Walt, 241, 291
McKinley, William, 254, 255, 258,
　　259, 274, 278, 280, 281, 285-
　　289, 308, 310, 311, 313, 315,
　　316, 324, 381
McKinley tariff, 254
Macon, Ga., 188
McPherson, Aimee, 392
McReynolds, James Clark, 424
Madero, Francisco, 348
Madison, Dolly, 50, 57
Madison, James, 11, 12, 20, 37, 50,
　　52-54, 56, 57, 63, 81, 439
Mahan, Alfred T., 276, 281, 282,
　　287
Maine, 70, 108, 109, 129, 237, 426
Maine, the, 278-281
Maine prohibition law, 129
Malaya, 445
Malcomb, John, 8
"Malefactors of great wealth," 313
Malinovsky, Rodion, 499
Malta, 448
Manchukuo, 407
Manchuria, 406, 407, 452
"Manhattan Engineering

District," 460
"Manifest Destiny," 111, 126, 192, 212, 287, 373
Manila, 282, 285, 445
Mann-Elkins Act, 339
Mansfield, Josie, 203
Maragon, John, 465
Marblehead, Mass., 51
Marbury vs. Madison, 37
March of Death, 444
Marcy, William L., 84
Marion, Ohio, 383
Marion *Star*, 381, 384
Marmaduke, Meredith Miles, 120, 121
Marshall, George Catlett, 462
Marshall, Jim, 131
Marshall, John, 1, 33, 37, 45, 83, 92
Marshall Plan, 462
Marshfield, Mass., 108
Martinsburg, W. Va., 226
Marx, Karl, 126, 272
Maryland, 56, 127, 167, 242, 410, 470
Maryland, the, 398
Mason, James Murray, 135
Masons, 94
Massachusetts, 4, 10, 13, 51, 59, 94, 157, 167, 224, 392, 397, 410, 506, 507
Massachusetts *Centinel*, 13
Massachusetts Institute of Technology, 461
Masses, The, 361
Massillon, Ohio, 265
Mauldin, Bill, 508
Max of Baden, 365
Maximillian of Mexico, 192, 193
May, Captain, 112
Means, Gaston B., 386
Meat inspection law, 331
Meitner, Lise, 460
Mellon, Andrew, 314, 403, 405
Memorial Day, 194
Memphis, Tenn., 145, 168, 483
Mercer, Sarah, 126
"Merchants of Death," 421
Mesabi iron mines, 315
Mexican War, 111-114, 117, 122, 140
Mexico, 72, 98, 99, 111-113, 117, 148, 192, 193, 348, 349, 395
Mexico City, 112, 113
Miami, 414
Michigan, 39, 188, 416, 478
"Midnight Judges," 37
Militia, 6, 7, 10, 23, 56, 60, 64, 127, 147, 154, 160, 167, 226
"Mill-Boy of the Slashes," 69
Miller, Thomas W., 386
"Millions for defense, but not one cent for tribute!" 26
Mills, Roger Q., 252, 253
Milwaukee, 341, 345
Minimum wage, 418, 424, 425
Minority Presidents, 75, 149, 159, 221, 253, 345
Mint juleps, 106
Mint (U.S.), 19
Minutemen, 6, 7
Missile crisis, 514, 515
Mississippi, 160, 187, 222, 516, 517
Mississippi River, 23
Missouri, 70, 118-121, 146, 147, 149, 150, 153, 154, 167, 410, 464, 466, 492
Missouri, the, 456
Missouri Compromise, 70, 71, 133, 145, 150
Mitchell, Charles E., 400
Mitchell, John, 320, 321

Moley, Raymond, 417
Molotov, Vyacheslav, 459, 462
"Money changers," 416
"Money power," 90, 300, 301, 347
Money problems, 9, 10, 16, 70, 93, 224, 259, 262, 263, 274, 288, 347, 391, 429. *See also* Greenbacks, Silver issue, Gold standard
Monopoly, 81. *See also* Bank of the United States, "Big business," Trusts
Monroe, James, 63, 65, 67, 69, 72, 73, 439
Monroe Doctrine, 72, 326, 327, 394
Montana, 215
Montenegro, 362
Montgomery, Ala., 160, 161
Montgomery, Robert, 496, 497
Monticello, 34, 50
Montreal, 54
Moore, Thomas, 35
Morgan, J. P., 210, 211, 315, 319, 320
Morgan, J. P., Jr., 421
Morgan, J. P., & Co., 276, 315, 323, 400. *See also* Drexel, Morgan & Co.
Morgan, William, 94
Mormons, 124
Morocco, 326, 445
Morris, Gouverneur, 23
Morris, Robert, 18
Morristown, N. J., 9
Morrisey, Joseph B., 386
Moscow, 462, 463, 469, 485, 486, 498, 499, 515
Mount McGregor, N.Y., 247
Mount Vernon, 7, 15
Movies, 393
Muckrakers, 331
Mugwumps, 240, 241, 296
Mulligan letters, 237
Murphy, Charles F., 333, 413
Muscle Shoals, 432
Mussolini, Benito, 406, 456

Nagasaki, 456
Napoleon Bonaparte, 29, 40, 41, 45, 48, 49, 53
Nast, Thomas, 169, 206-209, 218, 219, 245, 291, 302
National Association of Manufacturers, 339
National City Bank, 400
National Era, 136
National Recovery Administration, 419, 420, 424, 425
National Republican party, 81, 103
National Union party, 177, 185
National Women's Suffrage Association, 216
National Youth Administration, 427
Native American party, 127
Nazis, 407, 440, 441, 460
Nebraska, 145
Nebraska Bill, 145, 152
Negro suffrage, 180, 187-189, 194, 208, 223
Negro troops, 172, 187
Neutrality Act of 1935, 421
Nevada, 200
New Britain, 445
New Deal, 381, 411, 414, 415, 417-419, 422-424, 427-430, 436, 450, 464, 465, 466, 469, 471, 480, 483, 501
New England, 15, 31, 45, 59, 63, 66, 108, 127, 141, 228
New Freedom, 313, 347, 348

New Frontier, 501, 502, 513
New Guinea, 445
New Hampshire, 13, 219
New Jersey, 338, 347, 410, 468
New Jersey Plan, 11
New London, Conn., 95
New Mexico, 133
New Nationalism, 342
New Orleans, 96, 168, 214, 223
New Rochelle, N. Y., 239
New York *American*, 329
New York Central Railroad, 202, 213, 234, 296, 314
New York City, 2, 6, 14, 15, 21, 77, 95, 127, 128, 174, 175, 195, 201, 202, 205-207, 241, 247, 250, 253, 274, 310, 317, 333, 364, 376, 397, 404, 408, 468
New York *Commercial Advertiser*, 95
New York *Daily Graphic*, 210, 212, 234, 291
New York *Daily News*, 174
New York *Herald*, 126, 155, 218, 318
New York *Herald Tribune*, 490
New York *Journal*, 274, 276, 279, 282
New York *Morning News*, 111
New York State, 9, 11, 33, 77, 78, 81, 111, 167, 220, 223, 232, 239, 241, 263, 313, 317, 332, 333, 355, 375, 397, 410, 413
New York Stock Exchange, 202, 318, 400, 401. *See also* Bull market
New York *Sun*, 230
New York *Times*, 163, 206, 218, 342, 361
New York *Tribune*, 107, 126, 208, 209, 295
New York *World*, 216, 241, 268, 276, 279, 291, 324, 400
Newfoundland, 441
Newport, R. I., 233, 507
Newspapers, 1, 10, 12, 13, 15, 20, 23, 26, 28, 58, 81, 90, 113, 126, 234, 244, 281, 291, 332, 333, 389, 429. *See also* names of individual newspapers and editors
Niagara River, 54
Nicaragua canal route, 323
Nickel Plate Railroad, 234
"Nine old men," 424, 428
Nine-Power Treaty, 395, 406
Nixon, Richard M., 468, 480, 481, 495, 499, 506, 508, 509
Nixon, Mrs. Richard M., 480
"No; no; not a sixpence!," 26
Normalcy, 381, 389, 390, 392, 400
Norris, George W., 338, 433
Norris Dam, 432
North Adams, Mass., 228
North Atlantic Treaty Organization, 462, 477, 518, 579
North Bend, Ohio, 103
North Carolina, 13, 166, 397
Northern Pacific Railroad, 211, 318, 319
Northern Securities Company, 319, 328
Northwest Territory, 39
Northwest Territory Ordinance, 70, 150
Norway, 435
Nullification, 28, 86, 87, 92

Oak Ridge, Tenn., 432, 460, 461
O'Brien, James, 206

O'Donnell, Kenneth, 522
Ogle, Charles, 103
"Ograbme," 51
Ohio, 39, 188, 274, 338, 381, 383
"Ohio Gang," 386
"Ohio Gong, The," 111
Ohio River, 70, 136
Oil issue in politics, 386, 387, 395, 449, 478, 482
Oklahoma, 257, 492
"Old Abe," 163
"Old black mammy," 145
"Old Bruin," 139
"Old Buck," 149
"Old Bullion," 93
"Old Fuss and Feathers," 113, 140
Old Guard, 336
"Old Hickory," 75, 78, 83
"Old Ironpants," 419, 459
"Old Ironsides," 55
"Old Rough and Ready," 113, 122
"Old Soldiers...Fade Away," 475
"Old Tippecanoe," 103
"Old Zack," 122
Olympia, the, 283
Omaha *World-Herald*, 270
"On to Canada!," 53, 54, 55
"One third of a nation," 431
"One World," 451
"Open door," 287
"Open skies," 489
Oppenheimer, J. Robert, 460, 491
Opper, Frederick B., 328, 329
Order of the White Rose, 190
Oregon, the, 282, 323
Oregon boundary, 108, 111
Oregon Territory, 72, 107
Oregon Trail, 107
Orlando, Vittorio, 370, 371
Orpen, William, 363
O'Sullivan, John L., 111
O'Sullivan, T. H., 170
Oswald, Lee Harvey, 521, 522
Oswald, Mrs. Lee Harvey, 521
Ottawa, Ill., 153
Our American Cousin, 180
"Our Country...may she always be in the *right*," 64, 65
"Our Union—It must be preserved!," 86
Oyster Bay, 342, 344

Pacific Railroad, 198, 199
Pact of Paris. *See* Kellogg-Briand Pact
Paine, Lewis, 182, 183
Paine, Thomas, 37
Painter, John, 256
Pakenham, Edward, 61
Palais d'Orsay, 370, 371
Palm Beach, Fla., 505
Palmer, A. Mitchell, 375
Panama, Republic of, 323
Panama Canal, 322-324, 335
Pan-American Exposition, 313
Panay, the, 435
Panics:
    1819, 70
    1837, 100
    1873, 210, 211, 213, 218
    1893, 260, 262
    1929, 400, 401
    See also Depressions
Paris Peace Conference (World War I), 365, 370, 371
Parker, Alton B., 324
Parsons, Albert R., 249
Pasadena, Calif., 480

Patapsco River, 56
Paterson, N. J., 341
Patronage, 223, 263, 298. *See also* Job-hunters, Spoils system
Patrons of Husbandry. *See* Grange
Paul B. Mulligan & Co., 483
Payne-Aldrich tariff, 336
Peace Corps, 512
"Peace without victory," 356, 362
Peaceable coercion," 48, 53
Peale, Charles Willson, 4
Pearl Harbor, 232, 442, 443, 445, 472, 491
Peek, George, 417
Peel, Robert, 111
Peffer, William A., 262, 265
Pendergast, Jim, 464
Pendergast, Tom, 464
Pennsylvania, 4, 9, 13, 23, 77, 78, 374
Pennsylvania Railroad, 226, 234
Pensacola, Fla., 64
Pensions, 224, 254
Pentagon, 483
"People's Army," 472
People's party. *See* Populist party
Periscopic spectacles, 125
Perkins, Frances, 418, 438, 439
Perry, Matthew Calbraith, 138, 139
Perry, Oliver H., 54
Pershing, John J., 349
Peru, 72, 398
"Peter Porcupine," 20
Petersham, Mass., 10
Philadelphia, 9, 11, 13, 14, 15, 18, 19, 23, 62, 77, 95, 105, 127, 163, 194, 256, 361, 436
Philadelphia, the, 47
Philadelphia *Public Ledger*, 104
Philadelphia *Record*, 407
Philadelphia *Spirit of the Times*, 126
Philip, John W., 282
Philippine Islands, 282, 284-287, 335, 394, 395, 442, 444-446, 472
Philippine War, 284, 285
Photography, 114, 170, 257, 324
Pickering, John, 37
Pickering, Timothy, 59
Pierce, Franklin, 135, 145, 196
Pike, Summer T., 461
Pinchot, Gifford, 339
Pinckney, Charles Cotesworth, 26, 33
Pinckney, Thomas, 24
Pinkerton detective agency, 259, 260
Pittsburgh, Pa., 4, 15, 23, 226, 260, 314
Pittsburgh *Post-Gazette*, 427
"Plumed Knight," 236, 480
Pocahontas, 37
Poker, 383, 384
Poland, 362, 435, 449, 452, 459, 487
Politics (discussions and definitions), v, vi, 1, 12, 23, 118, 255
Polk, James K., 110, 111, 113, 117
Polka, 124
Pope Paul VI, 518
"Popular sovereignty," 145, 146
Populist party, 256, 259, 263, 265, 268, 306, 313
Porter, Peter B., 53
Portland, Me., 129
Portland, Ore., 408
Portsmouth, Treaty of, 326
Potomac, the, 441

Potomac River, 18, 75, 168
Potsdam Conference (World War II), 456, 459, 488
Pottawatomie Massacre, 146, 154
Powhatan, the, 139
"Prayer of Twenty Millions," 172
Preparedness, 290, 354, 355, 436, 440
Presidency (definitions, discussion and examples of Presidential action), 21-23, 34, 35, 73, 81, 84, 85, 87, 90-93, 102, 106, 110, 122, 135, 149, 172, 180, 185, 187, 196, 220, 232, 242-244, 286, 299, 304, 305, 311, 313, 316, 317, 322-327, 334-336, 346, 347, 356, 362-373, 383-385, 390, 391, 399, 402, 414-417, 426-429, 434, 440, 441, 448-451, 464-467, 482-484, 494-497, 501-503, 512-515, 524, 525, 528, 529
President, the, 55
President's Oath, 2, 455
Press. *See* Newspapers
Preston, Thomas, 24
Prince of Wales, the, 441, 445
Princess Grace (of Monaco), 510
Princeton, N.J., 9, 15
Princeton explosion, 106
Princeton University, 33, 347
Profiles in Courage, 505, 507
Progressive party (1912), 344, 345, 355
Progressive party (1924), 389
Progressive party (1948), 466
Progressive Republicans, 313, 336, 338, 339, 342, 383
Prohibition, 129, 149, 208, 291, 380, 384, 389, 396, 397, 410, 415, 418. *See also* Temperance
Promontory Point, Utah, 198
Proust, Marcel, 510
"Public be damned, The," 234, 235
"Public office in a public trust," 244
Public Utility Act, 427
Public Works Administration, 419
Puck, 268, 291, 302, 308
Pueblo, Colo., 373
Puerto Rico, 282, 287
Pulaski, Tenn., 190
Pulitzer, Joseph, 241, 276, 279, 291
Pullman, George M., 266, 267
Pullman Palace Car Company, 266, 267
"Pump priming," 429
"Pumpkin Papers," 470, 471
Pure Food Act, 331
"Purge," 429

"Quarantine Speech," 440
Quebec Conference (World War II), 448, 449
Quemoy and Matsu islands, 509
Quincy, Ill., 153
Quincy, Mass., 116

Racial issues in American politics, 149, 153, 158, 160, 422. *See also* Ku Klux Klan, Reconstruction, White supremacy, Civil rights
Radical Republicans, 185, 187, 188, 191, 208
Radio, 362, 388, 399, 411, 414, 415,

420, 422, 423, 434, 438, 440, 450. *See also* "Fireside chats"
Radio Corporation of America, 400
Rahway, N. J., 217
"Rail Splitter," 152, 158, 159
Railroads, 77, 125, 145, 198, 199, 225-227, 234, 235, 245, 259, 269, 274, 313, 315, 318, 319, 338, 339, 361, 402. *See also* names of individual railroads
Rain-in-the-Face, 215
Rainey, Joseph Hayne, 222
Randolph, Edmund, 17
Randolph, John, 36, 37, 53, 71, 96, 100, 135
Raskob, John J., 397
Rathbone, Henry R., 180
Rayburn, Sam, 347, 454, 524
Rebel yell, 169
Recall, 345
Reciprocal trade, 308
Reconstruction, 186-191, 208, 220, 222, 223, 516
Reconstruction Acts, 187
Red Army, 462
Red baiting, 374, 375
Red Cross, 360
"Red Fox of Kinderhook," 100
"Red herring," 469
"Red Special," 341
Reed, James A., 410
Reed, Thomas B., 254-256, 259, 281
Reid, Whitelaw, 294, 295
Religious issue in American politics, 31, 37, 306. *See also* Catholic issue in American politics
"Remember the *Maine*," 278
Remington, Frederic, 266
Reparations, 381, 395
Republic (definition and discussion of), 12
Republic Steel Massacre, 431
Republican party:
  Origins, 143, 145, 148-150, 152, 158, 159. *See also* Abolitionists, Conscience Whigs, Free Soil party, Liberty party, Native American party, Whig party
  Leaders and bosses, 145, 152, 186, 187, 196, 197, 204, 205, 213, 221, 223, 230, 236, 237, 254, 255, 274, 275, 286, 287, 292-299, 302, 310, 311, 316, 317, 324-327, 334-339, 355, 372, 373, 383-386, 390, 398, 399, 403, 436, 437, 450, 466, 476, 477, 479-481, 526, 527
  Splits, 240, 241, 342, 343, 526, 527
  Merges into National Union party (1864), 177. *See also* Progressive Republicans, Radical Republicans, Boys in Blue
Republican party (Jeffersonian) 20, 21, 23, 28, 29, 31, 33-35, 37, 42, 45, 48, 50, 51, 59, 62, 63, 67, 75, 81, 84, 106
Resettlement Administration, 427
Revels, Hiram Rhoades, 222
Revolution, right of, xix, 10, 31, 35
Revolutionary War. *See* American Revolution

Reynolds, Mrs. James, 31
Rhee, Syngman, 472
Rhode Island, 11, 13, 59, 167, 397, 410
Ribicoff, Abraham, 507
"Rich and well born," 16
Richland, Wash. *See* Hanford-Richland, Wash.
Richmond, Va., 167, 169, 179
Riker, Richard, 42
Rio Grande, 99, 111, 113
Riots, 9, 10, 19, 22, 24, 29, 97, 127, 137, 175, 202, 226, 227, 229, 248, 266, 267, 408, 409, 431
Ripon, Wis., 143, 145
Ritchie, Albert C., 410
Rittenhouse, David, 21
"Roanoke," 71
Roberts, Owen J., 424, 427
Robinson, Boardman, 351
Robinson, Joseph T., 397
Rock Island, Ill., 150
Rockefeller, John D., 314, 315, 400
Rockefeller, John D., Jr., 213
Rockefeller, Nelson A., 506, 526, 527
Rockefeller, Mrs. Nelson A., 526
"Roks," 473
Romney, George W., 527
Roosevelt, Eleanor, 342, 413, 524
Roosevelt, Elliott, 439
Roosevelt, Franklin Delano, 342, 365, 381, 382, 384, 397, 405, 410-418, 422-429, 431, 434, 436, 438-442, 445, 448-453, 459, 460, 464, 465, 470, 471, 524
Roosevelt, Isaac, 413
Roosevelt, James (Franklin's great-grandfather), 413
Roosevelt, James (Franklin's father), 413
Roosevelt, James (Franklin's son), 411
Roosevelt, Kermit, 322
Roosevelt, Theodore, 241, 250, 255, 281-283, 287, 288, 296, 313, 316, 317, 319, 320, 322-328, 331, 334-336, 338, 339, 341-344, 347, 355, 362, 365, 383, 407, 413, 436, 439, 464
Roosevelt, Theodore, Jr., 327
Roosevelt Corollary, 327
Root, Elihu, 342
Rosenberg, Ethel and Julius, 469
Ross, Robert, 57
Rothermel, Peter Frederick, 133
Rough Riders, 283, 288
Rowland's Steel Works, 66
Royalist issue in American politics, 23, 28
Ruby, Jack, 521
"Rugged individualism," 314, 399, 432
"Rum, Romanism, and Rebellion," 241
Rumania, 362, 459
Rural Electrification Administration, 427
Rush, Benjamin, 11
Russia, 72, 172, 192, 212, 287, 327, 350, 362, 365, 418, 435, 445, 448, 449, 452, 458, 459, 462, 469, 471-473, 477, 486-489, 491, 497, 498, 499, 501, 503, 514, 575, 579
Russo-Japanese War, 326, 327, 452

Sacajawea, 41
Sacco, Nicola, 392
Sachs, Alexander, 460
Sackville-West, Lionel, 253
Sacramento, Calif., 131
Sage, Russell, 241
Saigon, Vietnam, 513
St. Clare, Augustine, 136
St. Louis, Mo., 150, 151, 196
St. Louis *Post-Dispatch*, 400, 469
Salem, Mass., 15
"Salt River," 122
Saltillo, Mexico, 114
Samoa, 287
Sampson, Charles T., 228
San Antonio, Texas, 114
San Francisco, 130, 131, 324, 385, 470, 526, 527
San Martín, José de, 72
Santa Ana, Antonio Lopez de, 98, 99
Sante Fe, 107, 113, 145
Santa Fe Railroad, 259
Santiago, Cuba, 282
Santo Domingo, 326, 327
Saratoga Springs, N. Y., 143
Saturday Evening Post, The, 485, 507
"Scalawags," 188
Schaack, Michael J., 249
Schechter Poultry Corporation, 424, 425
Schlesinger, Arthur, Jr., 508
Schurz, Carl, 204
Schuyler, Philip, 43
Scott, Dred, 150, 151. *See also* Dred Scott decision
Scott, Winfield, 112, 113, 140
Scranton, William W., 527
Scribner's Magazine, 228
Seattle, 385
Secession, 28, 45, 71, 149, 160, 161, 163
Securities and Exchange Commission, 419, 504
"Security risks." *See* Loyalty investigations
Sedition Act, 28, 29, 31
"Self-determination," 362
Senate. *See* Congress
"Senate is wholly incompetent, The," 326
Seneca Chief, 76, 77
Seneca Falls, N. Y., 125
Seoul, Republic of Korea, 472, 475
Serbia, 350, 362
Seward, William H., 136, 143, 145, 182, 192, 193
Seymour, Horatio, 194, 195
Shadow Lawn, 355
Shakers, 125
Shame of the Cities, The, 331
"Share the Wealth," 423
Sharp's rifles, 146
Shaw, Lemuel, 157
Shays, Daniel, 10
Shays' Rebellion, 10, 11, 13
Shepard, Alan B., Jr., 511
Sheridan, Philip, 177, 247
Sherman, John, 254, 255, 268, 302
Sherman, William, T., 177-179, 247
Sherman Antitrust Act, 254, 255, 268, 315, 319, 328, 399
Sherman's march, 179
"Sherwood Forest," 106
Siam, 445
Siberia, 365
"Sick chickens." *See* Schechter Poultry Corporation

Sigsbee, Charles D., 278
Silver, 200
"Silver Dick," 263
Silver issue, 225, 254, 262, 263, 271, 272, 274, 288, 306, 422
Silver Purchase Act of 1890, 262
Sinclair, Harry F., 386
Sinclair, Upton, 330, 331
Singapore, 445
Sisson, Edgar G., 362
Slavery, 70, 71, 83, 96, 97, 103, 116-118, 131, 133-137, 142-147, 149, 150, 152-155, 159-161, 172
Slaves, 11, 15, 64, 83, 96, 97, 114, 137, 150, 151, 172. *See also* Emancipation Proclamation
Sloan, Alfred P., 483
Sloat, John Drake, 112
Smith, Alfred E., 389, 396, 397, 399, 410, 411, 413, 467
Smith, Mrs. Alfred E., 397
Smith, Jesse, 385, 386
Smith, Joseph, 94
Smith, Mrs. Stephen, 518, 519
Smyth, Alexander, 54
"Soak the rich," 427
Social Security Act, 427, 428
Socialism, 208, 267, 341, 417
Socialists, 143, 228, 248, 249, 330, 340, 341, 375, 377, 389
Soft Shell Democrats, 158, 159
Solid South, 223, 397, 501
Solomon Islands, 445
Songs *(mentioned or quoted):*
  "Jefferson and Liberty," 34, 35
  "The Drum," 43
  "The Star-Spangled Banner," 56
  "Anacreon in Heaven," 56
  "Mechanics, Carters, Laborers," 95
  "Let Van from His Coolers of Silver Drink Wine," 104
  "Tippecanoe and Tyler Too," 104
  "General Harrison's Log Cabin March," 104
  "As Rolls the Ball Van's Reign Doth Fall," 105
  "Blow the Trumpets," 111
  "Oh! California, That's the Land for Me," 131
  "The Black Ship," 139
  "Buchanan and Fremont," 148
  "Brave Little Jessie Forever," 149
  "Fremont and Victory," 149
  "Rogue's March," 157
  "Little Mac," 177
  "Dixie," 180
  "Ma! Ma! Where's My Pa?," 239
  "Hurrah for Maria," 239
  "After the March Is Over," 265
  "A Hot Time in the Old Town Tonight," 282
  "Damn the Filipinos," 285
  "Over There," 361
  "Lucky Lindy," 392
  "Yes, We Have No Bananas," 392
  "Barney Google," 392
  "Sidewalks of New York," 397
  "America," 408
  "Happy Days Are Here Again," 410, 411
  "I Wanna Be a Cap'n, Too," 439
  "O God, Our Help in Ages Past," 441
  "Onward, Christian Soldiers,"
441
  "Eternal Father, Strong to Save," 441
  "Praise the Lord and Pass the Ammunition," 445
  "Mr. Wonderful," 510, 513
Sons of Liberty, 8
Sons of Saint George, 20
Sons of Saint Tammany. *See* Tammany
Sorensen, Theodore C., 513
"Sound money," 274
South Africa, 288
South Carolina, 67, 81, 87, 147, 160, 161, 188, 222, 223
Southern Pacific Railroad, 319, 339
Southwest Texas State Teachers College, 524
Spain, 23, 40, 64, 65, 72, 206, 276-282, 285, 287, 435
Spanish-American War, 282, 283, 390, 317, 323
Speakeasies, 393
Speaker of the House, 29, 53, 69, 116, 142, 143, 237, 254, 255, 337, 338, 405
Specie payment, 224
Speculators, 17-19, 38
Spies, August, 249
Spiritualism, 124, 208
Spoils system, 84, 100, 230
Spot Resolutions, 117
Springfield, Ill., 153, 162
Springfield, Mass., 10
Sproul, William Cameron, 383
Sputnik I, 499
"Square Deal," 342
Squatter law, 145
Squirrels, 494
Stagecoaches, 35, 69, 77, 83, 131
Stagg Field, University of Chicago, 460
Stalin, Joseph, 448, 449, 452, 456, 459, 473, 486, 487
Stalwarts, 230
Standard Oil Company, 211, 213, 274, 275, 318, 331, 338, 400
Stanford University, 399
Stanton, Edwin M., 184, 187, 218
Star of the West, 161
Star Route frauds, 232
Stassen, Harold, 484
State House, Philadelphia, 9
Staten Island, 234
States' rights, 28, 37, 53, 118, 396
Steamboats, 40, 77
Stedman, Seymour, 377
Steffens, Lincoln, 331
Stephens, Alexander H., 160, 161
Steubenville, Ohio, 221
Stevens, Thaddeus, 94, 186-188, 237, 501
Stevenson, Adlai E., 478, 497, 501, 506, 507
Stimson, Henry L., 406, 407
Stock tickers, 211, 400
Stokes, Edward, 203
Stone, Harlan Fiske, 424, 454, 455
Stone, Melville E., 249
Stowe, Harriet Beecher, 136
Strauss, Lewis L., 461
"Strenuous life," 324
Strikebreaker Act, 427
Strikes, 156, 157, 159, 201, 226-228, 248, 266, 267, 320, 374, 375, 430, 431, 464
Stripling, Robert, 468, 470, 471
Suez Canal, 489
Suffrage, 11, 13, 81. *See also* Negro suffrage, Woman

suffrage
Sullivan, Mark, 362
"Summit" conference, 488, 489, 499
Sumner, Charles, 145-147
Sunflower, 426
Supreme Court of the United States, 28, 37, 92, 149, 150, 268, 315, 319, 324, 347, 355, 424, 425, 427, 428, 482, 492
Surplus (Treasury) 253, 254
Surratt, Mary, 182, 183
"Survival of the fittest," 213
Sutherland, George, 424
Sutter, John, 131
Sutter's Fort, 131
Suwon, Republic of Korea, 472
Swartwout, Samuel, 100
Szilard, Leo, 460

Taft, Robert A., 436, 477
Taft, William Howard, 334, 335, 339, 341-343, 345
Taft-Hartley law, 466
Talbott, Harold, 483
"Tall Sycamore of the Wabash," 263
Tammany, 20, 21, 31, 33, 100, 195, 205-207, 209, 239, 291, 333, 397
Taney, Roger B., 150
Tango, 393
Tanner, James, 254
Tarbell, Ida M., 331
Tariff, 1, 18, 66, 67, 69, 87, 108, 208, 230, 244, 252-254, 258, 259, 274, 298, 308, 336, 346, 347, 381, 418
"Tariff of abominations," 87
"Tattooed Man," 291, 294, 295
Taylor, Zachary, 111, 113, 122, 123, 128, 135
Tea tax, 8
Teapot Dome scandal, 386, 387
Teheran Conference (World War II), 448
Telegraph, 110, 113, 124, 127, 139, 149, 163, 198
Telephone, 214, 243
Television, 480, 489, 496, 503, 507-509, 514, 516, 521
"Tell the truth," 238, 239
Teller, Edward, 491
Temperance, 128, 129, 220, 221
Ten-hour day, 95, 100
Ten Nights in a Bar-Room, 128
Ten per cent plan (for reconstruction), 180, 185, 187
Tennessee, 38, 129, 166, 172, 187, 379, 397
Tennessee River, 432
Tennessee Valley Authority, 419, 432, 433, 436, 461, 483
Tenskwatawa, 52
Test-ban treaty, 501, 505
Texas, 98, 99, 111, 160, 161, 397, 410, 411, 478, 480, 482, 500, 501, 519, 524, 525
Texas, the, 282
Texas Quarterly, 531
Texas Rangers, 111
Third term issue, 218, 219, 230, 293, 438, 439
Thomas, J. Parnell, 468
Thoreau, Henry, 117
Thrift Stamps, 360
Thurmond J. Strom, 466
Tidelands oil giveaway. *See* Oil issue in politics
Tiger (Tammany symbol), 206, 207
Tilden, Samuel J., 220, 224

Time magazine, 470, 502
Tippit, J. D., 522
"Tired old man," 450
Tisdale, Elkanah, 51
Tito, Marshal (Josip Broz), 486
"To the victor belongs the spoils," 84, 85
"Too proud to fight," 353
Toombs, Robert, 147
Topeka, 414
Tories, 8, 9
Treaty of Ghent, 57, 59, 61. *See also* names of treaties
Trenton, N. J., 77
Tripoli, 65
Tripoli War, 46, 47
Truman Doctrine, 462
Truman, Harry, 451, 454-456, 459, 462-470, 472, 475, 479, 482, 491, 522
Truman, Mrs. Harry, 464, 467
Truman, Margaret, 467
Trusts, 213, 235, 254, 259, 272, 274, 288, 300, 301, 314, 315, 327-329, 339, 347
Tugwell, Rexford G., 417
Tunis, 65
Turkey, 362, 448, 462
"Turn the rascals out," 208
Turner, Nat, 97
Tuscaloosa *Independent Monitor*, 190
Tweed, William M., 205-207
Tweed Ring, 205-207, 209
Tyler, John, 106-108, 111
Tyler, Mrs. John, 106

U-2 intelligence planes, 499, 509, 514
Un-American Activities Committee, House of Representatives, 468-470, 480
"Uncle Andy," 405
"Uncle Billy," 192, 193
"Uncle Mark," 274
Uncle Sam, xii, 111, 281, 290, 291, 308, 309, 360, 469
Uncle Tom's Cabin, 136
Underground Railroad, 137
Unemployment, 100, 211, 265, 335, 391, 402, 427. *See also* Relief, federal
Union. *See* Federal Union
Union League, 194
Union Pacific Railroad, 202, 319
United Mine Workers of America, 320, 321, 420
United Nations, 452, 456, 459, 470, 472, 473, 475, 497, 499
United States (description):
in 1790, 14, 15
in the 1840's, 124, 125
in 1876, 214, 215
in 1890's, 256, 257, 260, 261
in 1920's, 381, 392, 393
See also Frontier
United States, the, 55
United States Army, 37, 54, 64, 107, 111-114, 131, 160, 161, 166-169, 172, 173, 177-179, 184, 187, 188, 215, 266, 267, 282-284, 285, 320, 354, 357-360, 368, 369, 375, 409, 442, 444-447, 472-474, 477, 485. *See also* Militia
United States Central Intelligence Agency, 499, 509, 513

United States Joint Chiefs of Staff, 513
United States Marines, 47, 154, 155, 276, 349, 360, 445, 521
United States Navy, 27, 46, 48, 54-56, 64, 65, 112, 113, 139, 168, 232, 233, 276, 278, 279, 282, 283, 326, 327, 348, 349, 354, 360, 394, 395, 440, 442, 444-447, 472, 482, 514. *See also* names of individual ships
United States Steel Corporation, 315, 374, 400, 431, 513
United States Strategic Air Command, 491
University of Mississippi, 513
Uranium research, 460
Utah, 124, 133, 217

Valentino, Rudolph, 393
Vallandigham, Clement L., 174, 175, 177
Valley Forge, 6
Van Buren, Martin, 81, 84, 92, 100, 101, 103, 122
Vandenburg, Arthur H., 436
Vanderbilt, Alfred Gwynne, 352
Vanderbilt, Cornelius, 202, 203, 213
Vanderbilt, William H., 234, 235, 241
Van Devanter, Willis, 424
Vanity Fair, 162
Vanzetti, Bartolomeo, 390
Vaughn, Harry, 465
Velocipede, 77
Venezuela, 72, 327
Vera Cruz, 113, 348, 349
Verdict, The, 310, 311
Vergennes, Vt., 29
Vermont, 20, 29, 81, 94, 426
Versailles Treaty, 371, 373, 407, 435
Veterans' Bureau, 385, 386
"Veto Mayor," 239
Vetoes, Presidential, 81, 90, 92, 187, 244, 433, 466
Vice Presidency, 24, 33, 42, 86, 89, 92, 106, 127, 185, 205, 232, 288, 313, 317, 382, 383, 411, 439, 451, 454, 465, 480
Victor Emmanuel of Italy, 366
Vietnam, 501, 513, 529
Villa, "Pancho," 349
Virginia, 4, 9, 11, 33, 34, 81, 97, 155, 163, 166, 167, 172, 397, 410, 478
"Virginia Dynasty," 63, 73
Virginia Plan, 11
Virginia Resolves, 28
Vizcaya, the, 282
Volck, Adalbert, 162
Von Prittwitz, Count, 394
Voorhees, Daniel W., 263

Wade, Ben, 143, 145
Wagner-Connery Labor Relations Act, 427, 428
Waiilatpu, Ore., 107
Wake Island, 445
Walden Pond, 117
Waldorf-Astoria Hotel, 323, 388
Walker, Edwin H., 521
Walker, James J., 404
Wall Street, 2, 14, 100, 149, 196, 202, 203, 210, 211, 213, 259,

272, 274, 300, 305, 315, 318, 319, 323, 332, 376, 389, 390, 391, 397, 400, 401, 467, 494
Wallace, George C., 517
Wallace, Henry A., 419, 438, 439, 450, 451, 464-466
Walsh, Thomas J., 387, 389
Wanamaker, John, 256
War (discussions and definitions of), 52, 178, 179, 282, 434
War debts, 381, 395
War democrats, 177, 185
"War Hawks," 52-55
War Industries Board, 361
"War ... is all hell," 179
War of 1812, 53-61, 66, 67, 291, 354
Ward, Ferdinand, 247
Warm Springs, Ga., 452, 453
Warren Commission, 520, 521
Warren, Earl, 492, 498, 520
Washington, George, 1-7, 11, 13, 15, 16, 19-24, 26, 30, 31, 96, 417, 439
Washington, Martha, 4, 22, 23
Washington, D.C., 18, 24, 35, 149, 167, 169, 230, 265, 408, 409, 492
Washington, D.C., burning of, 56, 57
Washington Monument, 135
Washington Naval Conference, 394
Washington Post, 287, 484
"Watchful waiting," 349
Waterville College, 97
Waymack, William W., 461
Wayne, Anthony, 9
"We stand at Armageddon," 345
"We the People," 11-13
Weaver, James B., 259
Webster, Daniel, 45, 66, 67, 81, 87-89, 91, 107-109, 132, 133, 140, 141
Webster, Mrs. Daniel, 88
Webster-Ashburton Treaty, 108
"Wedding of the Waters, The," 76
Weehawken, N. J., 42
Weirton Steel Company, 375
Weiss, Carl A., 422, 423
Welk, Lawrence, 510
West Branch, Iowa, 399
West Point, 215, 464, 477
West Virginia, 167, 375, 492
Western powers, 459
Western Union, 202
Westminster College, Mo., 463
Weyler, Valeriano, 277
"What a Belly-ache!" 494
Wheeler, Burton K., 389, 440
Wheeling, W. Va., 69
Whig coon, 105, 111
Whig party, 103-106, 108, 111, 116-118, 122, 140, 143
Whisky Rebellion, 22, 23
Whisky Ring, 205, 208
Whisky tax, 19, 22, 23
"Whistlestop Campaign," 466
White, Theodore H., 509
White, William Allen, 287, 440
White House, 24, 34, 57, 75, 83, 84, 102, 103, 196, 221, 232, 314, 384, 390, 453, 464, 488, 496, 502, 510
White House news conference, 503
"White supremacy," 152, 185, 190, 223
"Whitewash," 101
"Whitewash House," 529
Whitman, Marcus, 107

Whitman, Walt, vi, 126, 128, 213
Whitney, Richard, 400
Whittier, John Greenleaf, 53
Why England Slept, 505
Wide Awake Clubs, 158, 159
"Widows and orphans," 19, 92
Wigfall, Louis, 161
Wilhelm II of Germany, 287, 342, 356, 365
Wilkes-Barre, Pa., 320
Williams College, 231
Williams, E. Mennen, 478
Willkie, Wendell, 436-440, 451
Wilmot, David, 117
Wilmot Proviso, 117, 131, 133
Wilson, Charles E., 483
Wilson, Edith Bolling Galt, 354, 356
Wilson, James, 13
Wilson, Woodrow, 338, 345-351, 353-356, 362, 363, 365-373, 375, 382, 383, 389, 413, 441, 478
Wiltz, L. A., 222
Wire tapping, 469
Wirt, William, 94
Wisconsin, 484
"Wobblies." *See* Industrial Workers of the World
Woman suffrage, 216, 217, 345, 378, 379
Women in politics, 104, 148, 149, 216, 217, 335
Women's Wear Daily, 510
"Wonder Boy," 399
Wood, Fernando, 128, 174
Wood, Leonard, 383
Woodhull, Victoria, 217
Wool, John E., 114
"Workies," 95
Working Men's party, 95
Workmen's compensation, 339, 347
Works Progress Administration, 427
World War I, 350-362, 364, 365, 421, 464
World War II, 434, 435, 439-452, 456, 457, 459, 473, 475, 477, 491
Wright, Jonathan Jasper, 222
Wyoming, 216, 217

XYZ Affair, 26

Yale University, 400
Yalta Conference (World War II), 449, 452, 459, 470
"Yankeedoodledom," 126
Yap, 395
Yarborough, Ralph, 519
Yates, Eugene, 483
Yokohama, 139
Yorktown, 7
Young, Art, 340
"Young Hickory," 110
Young Plan, 395
Youngblood, Rufus, 522
Yugoslavia, 459, 473, 486

Zangara, Joseph, 414
Zhukov, Gregori, 477